EVERY REVOLUTION
Was First a Thought

EVERY REVOLUTION
Was First a Thought

THE CIVIL WAR AND
TRANSCENDENTALISM IN
TRANSATLANTIC
CONTEXT

AREN LERNER CRAIG

University of Massachusetts Press
AMHERST AND BOSTON

Copyright © 2025 by University of Massachusetts Press
All rights reserved

ISBN 978-1-62534-889-0 (paper); 890-6 (hardcover)

Designed by Jen Jackowitz
Set in Minion Pro
Printed and bound by Books International, Inc.

Cover design by adam b. bohannon
Cover art by William Bauly, *Our Heaven Born Banner*, lithograph, ca. 1861.
Courtesy Library of Congress.

Library of Congress Cataloging-in-Publication Data
A catalog record for this book is available from the Library of Congress.

British Library Cataloguing-in-Publication Data
A catalog record for this book is available from the British Library.

A portion of this research was previously published as "Precedence over the Pentateuch: The Social Impact of Transcendentalism," *New England Journal of History* 77, no. 1 (Fall 2020): 51–77, and is reprinted here with permission from the *New England Journal of History*.

This work has been supported by the
University of Massachusetts Press's Authors' Fund for Scholarship.
For more information, visit
https://www.umasspress.com/authors-fund-for-scholarship/.

The authorized representative in the EU for product safety and
compliance is Mare-Nostrum Group.
Email: gpsr@mare-nostrum.co.uk
Physical address: Mare-Nostrum Group B.V.,
Mauritskade 21D, 1091 GC Amsterdam, The Netherlands

Dedicated to Michael Kots
His years were short but his example of
commitment to his ideals still shines brightly.
In gratitude for his "pure purpose and noble endeavor,
humblest service and costliest sacrifice."
—Joshua Chamberlain

Contents

A Note on Language ix
Acknowledgments xi

INTRODUCTION
1

CHAPTER ONE
Scottish Philosophy of Character
19

CHAPTER TWO
German Philosophy of Character
40

CHAPTER THREE
American Transcendentalist Philosophies of Character
59

CHAPTER FOUR
Philosophies of Gender and Femininity
83

CHAPTER FIVE
Masculinity and Bildung in the Civil War
106

CHAPTER SIX
The European Inheritance on Race and Character
132

CHAPTER SEVEN
Race and Character in America
154

CHAPTER EIGHT
The Political Character of the Nation
193

CHAPTER NINE
The Nation's Geographic Character
223

CONCLUSION
242

Appendix 251

Notes 255

Index 289

A Note on Language

I have retained the traditional use of "man" or "mankind" employed by the historical writers this work studies in the sense that they used it, as an inclusive term to indicate humanity in general. Where the phraseology is my own and it does not confuse the commentary on the original texts, I generally use humanity or humankind. Period sources quoted within the book also employ such terms as "slave," "master," "Negro," "colored," "savage," and "Indian." These are retained within citations to demonstrate the social and intellectual contexts of the period under study. I recognize the offensive and sensitive nature of such terms in today's landscape. They are not in any way intended to excuse or countenance disrespect toward the racial and ethnic groups discussed.

In designating racial and ethnic identities outside of citations, I have followed current social preferences and industry standards for terminology and capitalization. I use "Black" most frequently for those of African ancestry, as the topic, time period, and philosophies under study span the Atlantic world. For those specifically in the United States, I also use "African American." Likewise, I employ "white," "European," or "European American" for those of European ancestry living on either side of the Atlantic or specify by country of origin, such as "German" or "Irish." "Indigenous" or "Native American" is used to designate the first inhabitants of the North American continent. I am aware that these designations and capitalization practices are not the preferred language of all individuals within any of these cohorts and that the accepted practices may change at any time. No language used here is intended to convey favoritism, offense, or exclusion.

All italics and emphases within the quoted materials throughout the book are original to the sources.

Acknowledgments

This research was supported by librarians and archivists at the University of Aberdeen, Harvard University, the Massachusetts Historical Society, and the Wisconsin Historical Society, as well as the digitalization efforts of the staff at the numerous digital archive holdings researched for this book. To them I extend my gratitude.

From my time as a student, I wish to thank the professors who have assisted and refined my thinking on the topics examined in this book. Most especially, my gratitude goes to my advisers at the University of Aberdeen, Dr. Michael Brown in history and Dr. Beth Lord in philosophy, for all their support and expertise in shaping this research in its dissertation form. Special thanks goes to Dr. Vernon Volpe of the University of Nebraska at Kearney History Department, for supervising portions of my research completed at the master's level. Various initial stages of my work were assisted by the expertise of Dr. Roy Koepp, Dr. David Vail, and Dr. Mark Ellis at the University of Nebraska and Dr. Kenneth Howell and Dr. Stewart Bennett at the American Military University. I extend my gratitude to Dr. Bradford Bow (University of Aberdeen, history) and Dr. Ralph Jessop (University of Glasgow, literature and philosophy) for the time, thought, and interest they invested in this research and their suggestions for improvement. I am indebted to Dr. Peter Wirzbicki (Princeton University) for the thorough reading, detailed discussion, and encouragement he lent to the final stages of writing this book.

I am grateful for the expertise and assistance that Brian Halley and all the staff at the University of Massachusetts Press extended in the process of bringing the work to publication.

Finally, I acknowledge the support and encouragement of my family, most particularly the suggestions, editing assistance, and hours spent proofreading my writing put in by my mother, Mary Lerner, over the years. I could not have reached this point without her. My sister, Hannah, contributed with stacks of Civil War books from the library, singing Civil War duets with me, and her constant friendship. My husband Auston and daughters Mary Rose and Cecilia joined the family while the work was in progress. They didn't have much choice in sharing me with my book but deserve acknowledgment for their forbearance nonetheless. They have provided me with the necessary joy and grounding in the present to ensure that the past wouldn't consume me entirely.

EVERY REVOLUTION
Was First a Thought

INTRODUCTION

On May 24, 1856, a young, obscure German immigrant, who was working as a mechanic in Missouri, penned in his diary, "To realize this possibility, to elaborate my individuality into true ideality, into universality, into harmony with that . . . upon which nature depends, this is the problem of life before me."[1] In this phrase, Henry Conrad Brokmeyer summarized not only the problem of his own life but that before the life of the United States in this period as well. There was a revolution facing the nation, the second American Revolution, as the Civil War was sometimes called. It was a national upheaval grounded in the moral questions of slavery and states' rights, driven by economic, political, racial, social, and religious concerns. But it took place within a transatlantic philosophical revolution as well. "Every revolution was first a thought in one man's mind," noted Ralph Waldo Emerson in 1836, "and when the same thought occurs to another man, it is the key to that era."[2] What thought prompted this philosophical revolution? It was, at its heart, the idea that each human being was a self-actualizing agent, whose inner reality and personal development could shape his or her own destiny. This thought is indeed an indispensable key to understanding the era, as it was an essential element in the intellectual movement culturally defined as Romanticism and philosophically defined as Idealism. This transatlantic philosophical movement became known, in the United States, as American Transcendentalism. Members of this movement preached an overarching conviction that all people were participants in the divine mind and had a duty to develop their character accordingly. These philosophical norms around character spilled out of the private sphere and became a political force during the Civil War, driving the social reforms of the era and becoming the internalized worldview of Northern soldiers in their commitment to the Union and their readiness to accept the ordeal of war as an opportunity for personal growth and self-mastery.

Philosophical misunderstandings of the era have frequently surfaced in historical monographs. These are often demonstrated by treatment of the culture of the period as a secondary, even paradoxical aspect to the war itself or as the perceived need to apologize on behalf of historical figures for holding beliefs that seem to be questionable, embarrassing, emotional, and even childish folly. Many scholars have recognized to a greater or lesser degree that "Romanticism," as it is usually termed in works of history, played a role in the culture of the era, but even when recognized, historians have often been uncomfortable with it and concluded that it had little to do with the realities of warfare, being merely employed as a coping mechanism rather than shaping a worldview. Few of these works serve as a thorough history of ideas, and their portrayal of the beliefs that constituted Romanticism remains ambiguous. Civil War historians have critiqued, excused, and puzzled over the intellectual and cultural threads apparent in the historical literature from the period, frequently unable to reconcile what appears on the surface to be contradictory aspects of the Civil War experience. Unable to place these intellectual threads into a meaningful philosophical context, the verdict has often been one of dismissal, leading to the conclusion that the Civil War generation had no valid or cohesive philosophical framework from which to approach the crisis.[3]

However, when situated into its transatlantic intellectual context and when the interpretation of character, the self, and an individual's role in the world is examined in depth, the culture of the Civil War does become one that is consistent, sophisticated, and intelligible. My intention in this book is to provide an in-depth study of the European precedents of Transcendentalist thought that will display the cohesiveness of the movement's philosophical outlook, actions, and impact on the culture at large. Transcendentalism was, in my interpretation, largely an American amalgamation of Scottish Common Sense and German Idealist philosophical ideas, weaving together an understanding of the world that was both grounded in the experience of the senses but that interpreted those perceptions as manifesting a spiritual reality that existed within and beyond them and depended on the individual's morally developed character to correctly understand and implement in the world of human interaction. When these Scottish and German philosophical frameworks are applied politically and socially to the life of the nation and the political concerns that drove its populace toward the Civil War, Brokmeyer's individuality, universality, and harmony emerge as philosophical questions surrounding character, gender, race, and nationhood.

The Transcendentalists' imprecise interpretation of the German philosophy in particular has at times been stressed as a way to indicate that their reading of German philosophy "could not have been of decisive importance" to their intellectual growth.[4] The focus on the correctness of the American adoption and understanding of European philosophy, rather than in the Transcendentalists' assimilation of its ideas to their own uses and application to American contexts, significantly obscured the depth of the Transcendentalists' thinking on societal and political issues. Many terms and phrases they employed cannot be properly understood without the background of their philosophical usage, in both the Scottish Common Sense and the German Idealist traditions. Without a recognition of the German influence, the Transcendentalists can also appear to have a shallower grasp of Scottish Realism than was the case, as their employment of Realist terms, without the alteration or reinterpretation they received in light of Idealism, would be incorrect. Overlooking these influences risks both crediting the Transcendentalists with undue originality as well as failing to recognize the philosophical depth in their statements.

The meaning and scope of Idealism and Romanticism, when these terms are employed by historians, are often loosely defined. For instance, in Ethan J. Kytle's collective biography of five 1850s abolitionists, he employs Romanticism as a catchall phrase with little explanation as to what "romantic racialism," "romantic nationalism," "romantic intuition," and "romantic affectation" had in common with one another or what made them "romantic." Also unclear is what they shared with an affinity for nature, perfectionism, immediatism, self-culture, martial heroism, Manifest Destiny, or sentimentalism, the other cultural elements he singles out as romantic.[5] There are even scholars who argue that the philosophy of Idealism should not be confused or equated with Romanticism. According to this view, Romanticism was a form of ontological realism, and not Idealism, for it did not seek the absolute and held that "beliefs cannot be ultimately justified."[6] The opposing interpretation, which I share, sees Romanticism as a current existing within Idealist philosophy, informed by the philosophy and manifesting in poetic and artistic forms of, at heart, the same interests and convictions. In this second vein, Frederick Beiser argues that it can be understood as *objective* idealism, a "middle path between a complete materialism on the one hand and a total subjective idealism on the other hand.... It alone could interpret the world as a manifestation of the ideal—and so avoid materialism—but it could also allow the world to exist independent of the subject—and so escape subjective idealism."[7] Beiser's definition, I believe, captures the essence of Transcendentalism as the American merging point of Romanticism and Idealism. In the United States, the cultural and literary currents identified as Romanticism rely so heavily on the introduction of Idealist philosophy that to separate them leaves too significant an aspect of the American experience a matter of mere poetry alone, which too many historians have done. But when viewed in light of a cohesive, objective Idealism, the driving sources for the political and social action that also define this "Romantic" era of American history are illuminated. The locus of both can be found in Transcendentalism.

I hope that this recognition will help the modern reader avoid the predisposition to reject Romanticism as something too simplistically sentimental and quaint to be given serious consideration. Charles Taylor noted how, instead of understanding Romanticism as a variety of self-formation by autonomous agents, many moderns view it as a lapse back into a pre–Scientific Revolution belief in an anthropocentric universe ordered for the good of man, in which he is a passive recipient of preordained identity. However, as Taylor demonstrated, this was far from the case. It was not a "failure of nerve, a nostalgic return to earlier, comfortable illusions" of man's place in a meaningful cosmos.[8] If anything, the Romantic framework of the Idealists portrayed mankind as the creator of his own destiny more strongly than the mechanistic theories of such Scientific Revolution philosophers as John Locke, Francis Bacon, and Isaac Newton, in which man was portrayed as a passive cog in the wheel of the universe and whose mind was a tabula rasa awaiting sensory input. The Idealists' vision, rather, emphasized man as a self-actualizing agent who, to reach full self-realization, required freedom from outer constraints to find harmony with the larger role of nature, since "nature knows no fixed boundaries at the limits of the body," and to thus unite his feeling with the larger flow of life.[9] This ideal of feeling was not mere maudlin sentimentality, but in the understanding of the era, it was an expressive activity, an active power of the mind associated with the will. As an expressive faculty, it was a power that was imperative to develop if man should realize the goal of self-actualization as a rational, autonomous being. This understanding suggests that the too-frequent habit among historians of excusing the Civil War era's culture as a faulty lapse of manliness, opposing and inexplicable to the war itself, fails to harness an essential element in American conceptions of the war as a process of individual and national spiritual growth, development, and self-actualization. In turn, this view fails to recognize the role of the European philosophies of the era, the importance of the American Transcendentalists, and the impact of their views on the social and political reforms that motivated the Civil War.

The role of the ideal character in intellectual history provides an important lens for interpreting the actions and viewpoints of history's participants. Ideals of character should not be seen as an external imposition placed on a person but an integral, perhaps *the* integral, part of what a person believes and wishes themselves to be and thus a person's purpose within history itself. As Charles Taylor observed, to suppose that humans could function in the world or have any sense of themselves as a *self* free of these frameworks is "utterly impossible." The individual's interpretation of the world and understanding of their orientation within the moral framework are what makes an individual an individual self and shapes one's understanding of the world. This means, Taylor goes on to state, that the significance of the self is not limited to the sphere of philosophers but is also "the great unsaid that underlies widespread attitudes in our civilization" and becomes cultural mentalities. Taylor identifies a few key points of the Romantic-era mentality. In the Neo-Stoic movement of the late sixteenth and early seventeenth centuries, he sees "the growing ideal of a human agent who is able to remake himself by methodical and disciplined action." This led to the Cambridge Platonists' insistence that nature tended toward the good rather than moral goodness being imposed from without. Thus, in Romanticism, "a central part of the good life must consist in being open to the impulse of nature" and "having certain sentiments as well as of aiming at or doing certain things."[10] Gerald N. Izenberg further identifies a major tenet of Romanticism as the expansion of the idea of individuality and individualism from a utilitarian Enlightenment view that "all men are created equal" and largely the same to an emphasis on the uniqueness of each person. He writes, "A new, complex, and radical conception of individuality lay at the heart of basic ideas and tropes about aesthetics, nature, love, religion, and politics in English and French Romanticism."[11] This conception was also true of American Romanticism, and individuality of the archetypal character undergirded the approach to seemingly unrelated elements of political life. In this book, I aim to identify what the archetypical character was in the Civil War North, what sentiments and ways of doing things informed the mentality of the Civil War era, and thus what framework of ideal character permeated even unconsciously the assumptions about the self and the self's orientation within the moral space. These assumptions provide the key to what the Civil War meant to its participants—why they participated in it, how they oriented themselves within it, and how their ideals of individuality and the self guided their beliefs, behaviors, and interpretations of the era's political events.

Every Revolution Was First a Thought joins a small body of more recent works that call attention to the philosophical components of the Civil War era. Peter Wirzbicki has masterfully examined the intellectual and social intersections between Black and white Transcendentalists in the fight for abolition. His work demonstrates that Transcendentalism was both shaped by and shaped the language and impetus for abolition of Black and white thinkers alike and that their Black counterparts helped drive the white Transcendentalists out of isolation and into activism.[12] Matthew Stewart has provided an exploration of the influence of German thought, particularly that of Ludwig Feuerbach and G. W. F. Hegel, on the religious-intellectual journey and abolitionism of Theodore Parker, Frederick Douglass, and Abraham Lincoln, though his construal of this as an indication of a return to atheism and the Enlightenment differs considerably from what I present here.[13] Ethan J. Kytle's collective biography, as discussed above, also recognizes the role of Romanticism in the new activist abolitionism of the 1850s. He views this as a positive role, in contrast with Philip F. Gura's similar collective biography that carries forward a long-standing interpretation of Transcendentalism and Romanticism as hindering effective reform.[14] These works together present a welcome trend toward greater recognition of the intellectual climate of the era and the importance of philosophy in creating its distinctive currents. While they contain some cursory discussion, however, none of these books delve in depth into what the philosophical ideas themselves were, which is where my work enters the conversation.

Other books with which I engage include that of Harry S. Stout, who argued that the Civil War populace demonstrated grievous moral failures in their prosecution of the war, valuing bigotry and political loyalties above human life, and he denounced the wartime literature as completely failing to address the "issues of war [or] the mystery of death," claiming that it instead glorified the carnage through false portrayals of gallantry, heroism, and romanticism.[15] The political climate of the twenty-first century has clearly left its mark on historians' treatment of the Transcendentalists and their place in the Civil War, whether seen as purveyors of "extremism" and "terrorism" and to be blamed for the Civil War, as Randall Fuller has posited or, like John Buehrens, praised as examples of the commitment to science, human rights, and global unity that our society ought to imitate.[16] Robert Gross's 2021 tome on the social world of Concord, Massachusetts, emphasized the individualism of Concord Transcendentalists, whereas their transatlantic context emphasizes their cosmopolitan and activist convictions.[17]

Prior to these books, several scholars addressed the religious elements of Civil War culture, questions of soldier motivation, the process of philosophical transfer, and the reformist activities of the Transcendentalists. Without philosophical influences being considered, the accounts of religiosity fall short of identifying why these currents impacted the Civil War era differently from the Revolutionary era, when ministers were instructed by political elites to preach politics from the pulpit, or even during World War II when church attendance and membership were actually higher than during the Civil War. Studies of soldier motivation have largely remained social histories, with little involvement in intellectual history methods. Accounts of philosophical transfer inquire only minimally into the details of what the philosophies taught or how Americans applied the ideas in daily life, whereas the earlier works on Transcendentalism's reforming impulse typically confine their examination to the 1830s and 1840s, consequently leaving out the Civil War itself.[18] Despite the encouraging recent developments in the historiography of the period, a cohesive philosophical examination remains wanting. I strive to bring together these disparate "Romantic," religious, and cultural threads into a singular account that will present a unified look at the intellectual history of the era as a story of philosophy in action.

To begin this account, we look back across the Atlantic to a watershed moment in philosophical history, the skepticism of David Hume, and the subsequent answers that the Scots and Germans attempted to offer. Chapters one and two address the aspects of these intellectual foundations that are of special importance to the formation of Transcendentalist philosophy. These philosophers' writings traveled to America, Americans traveled to Europe to explore the emerging currents of thought more deeply, and a transatlantic dialogue began that shifted the worldview of both regions. In the United States, the Transcendentalists were an integral link in the chain of dissemination and cultural adaptation, and from their efforts, a vision of the ideal character percolated throughout Northern culture. In chapter three, we dive into how the Transcendentalists married the Scotch and German philosophies and created their vision of character and the journey of self-improvement. The remainder of the book will examine the ways in which individuals ranging from the US president and members of Congress to common soldiers and frontier women—sometimes directly, oftentimes unawares—attained a conviction of themselves as autonomous agents who framed the philosophical conception of the Civil War as a crucible of moral character, individually, racially, and nationally.

To dissect these philosophical currents in detail, I focus primarily on the writings of Thomas Reid, Thomas Brown, and Dugald Stewart from the Scots; Immanuel Kant, Johann Gottfried von Herder, and Georg Wilhelm Friedrich Hegel, of the Germans; and the impact of these European philosophers on the intellectual growth of Ralph Waldo Emerson, Henry David Thoreau, and Margaret Fuller, as well as Walt Whitman on occasion. I selected these philosophers from among the Common Sense school for their primacy in the movement, in the case of Reid, and for demonstrating a movement toward Idealism which made it easier for the Transcendentalists to retain and reconcile Scottish writings with the Germans. The German authors I chose to focus on represent three gradations within Idealism that enable for broad examination of philosophical options available within the philosophy. There are many other German writers who were also highly popular with and influential on the Transcendentalists, such as Johann Fichte, Friedrich Schelling, Friedrich Schiller, August and Friedrich Schlegel, Friedrich Schleiermacher, Wilhelm and Alexander Humboldt, as well as the philosopher, mystic, and writer Emanuel Swedenborg. Including all these writers and influences would be beyond the scope of a single work, and thus I selected Immanuel Kant as the starting point of Idealism, Johann Herder as the representative of the middle ground, and Georg Hegel as the post-Kantian. I selected the Transcendentalists based on their status as the individuals who are the most famous and as those within the movement often seen as the least political or activist. Doing so will, I hope, demonstrate that "orthodox" Transcendentalist thought itself provided the foundation and key to all its adherents' reformist actions and that these activities did not constitute a departure from the philosophy.

My approach is primarily that of an intellectual history, tracing the lines of thinking present, the intellectual development of the historical actors, and the mental frameworks applied to the historical events they experienced. To demonstrate the broader impact for the era, however, I expand into some cultural history methodology as well, including personal diaries of Civil War soldiers, newspaper editorials, and the era's songs and poetry, as well as the formal intellectual accounts of the philosophers and the Transcendentalists themselves. Through this approach, I demonstrate that rather than a phenomenon distinct from and secondary to the war experience, this Transcendentalist paradigm was a cohesive philosophical approach to the world, the self, and the human experience that profoundly shaped the period.

The St. Louis Hegelians of which Brokmeyer, whose meditations opened this chapter, was a member were an offshoot of the New England Transcendentalists, and both groups grappled with many of the same questions. The answers they reached drove them to specific political responses to the events of the Civil War era, and in turn, these answers impacted the general public's interpretation of these events. Despite much focused modern scholarship, both biographical and historical, that has effectively demonstrated otherwise, the place of the American Transcendentalists in the broader narrative remains on the sidelines. The early American reception of European philosophy is a well-studied and widely acknowledged area of historical inquiry, with works by scholars such as Bernard Bailyn, Gordon Wood, and more recently C. Bradley Thompson, addressing in detail the sources, interpretations, and applications in the United States of the philosophical thinking that was circulating in the transatlantic world.[19] In contrast, apart from specialized monographs on philosophy itself or biographies of specific American philosophers, attention to the everyday impact of philosophy on the country's culture after the turn of the nineteenth century has been lacking in the general histories. With the growth of the nation in size, industrialization, ethnic diversity, and Christianization following the Second Great Awakening, however, these older sources of philosophy no longer proved satisfactory to many Americans, and an important shift in philosophical frameworks began.

Early nineteenth-century Americans like the Transcendentalists were heir to the writings produced by the philosophical school of Scottish Realism, or the Common Sense School. These perspectives shaped the questions that the

Transcendentalists formed regarding the interaction of the self with the world, the structure of the human mind, and the role of emotion, intuition, and the reforming possibilities latent therein. This Scottish philosophy established itself in the United States when John Witherspoon, a Scottish immigrant, was elected as president of Princeton University in 1768. He presented the Scottish Enlightenment to the American public "as a way to strengthen the union of piety and reason," and his interpretation encouraged the American reception of other Common Sense philosophers, including Thomas Reid and James Beattie, creating "an Evangelical and American politicised version of the Scottish Enlightenment at Princeton."[20] Scottish Enlightenment thinkers addressed different political concerns throughout the transatlantic Age of Revolution and continued to resonate with the political culture in the early American republic. Because the Scottish Enlightenment addressed political questions brought before the Western mind by the American and French Revolutions and popular unrest within the United Kingdom, including Scotland itself, the philosophy was well-suited to a revolutionary and postrevolution America. The Scots examined these political developments less for specific issues than for broadly applied principles in the interest of discovering patterns of modernity, nationhood, and the progression of humanity under various historical conditions. Furthermore, it shaped both their ability to voice radical views and impacted their ideas on how to avoid a repetition of the excesses and horrors accompanying the French Revolution while still maintaining its positive principles. Dugald Stewart, for instance, faced political pressure to conceal or retract his support for more radical policies but also moderated his views of revolutionary figures and movements as excesses increased.[21] His solution to the competing influences was to offer a vision for what Charles Bradford Bow has termed a "didactic Enlightenment" that strove to mitigate reactionary anti-Enlightenment tendencies by "properly educating the public how to perfect the mind" so as to avoid irrational influences and create a moral society.[22]

As manifested by the Scottish writers, curiosity into conditions of human social development, nationhood, and the emphasis on an educated common people who possessed intellectual faculties shared by all was imperative to the fledgling United States, and employment of these beliefs easily supported a democratic route to a virtuous nation. The Transcendentalists were steeped in this philosophical background and never challenged many of its tenets. But new questions were surfacing in American political and social life that were not met with complete satisfaction by the Scottish thinkers. To fill the gaps they perceived, the Transcendentalists began incorporating more diverse works into their philosophical canon.

One of the principal sources for new intellectual, spiritual, and political frameworks to which Americans turned in the first decades of the nineteenth century was the burgeoning philosophy and attendant cultural currents issuing from Germany. These German theories also proved particularly relevant to the young American nation as events in Germany during the last decades of the eighteenth century and the beginning of the nineteenth had been a time of upheaval, change, and reassessment for the Germans as well. Germany was not yet a single unified nation as it would become in 1871, and an ongoing struggle for hegemony existed between the Prussian kingdom and Austria, the seat of the Holy Roman Empire. In addition to these internal struggles, in 1792 various areas of the German states came under attack by revolutionary France, followed by the invasion of Napoleon and annexation into the First French Empire. Many of the German philosophers welcomed Napoleon's invasion and celebrated the revolutionary ideas of France, but following his conquest, their position as a conquered nation also presented questions of what constituted nationalities when governments were in flux.[23]

Concurrent with these political upheavals, growth of fields such as natural history and natural and moral philosophy during this period challenged traditional assumptions about the age of the earth, origins of the human race, biblical literalism, and the authority of Scripture. Already grappling with the French threat to their identity as a people, Germans during this time were also faced with fundamental questions about the world, their place within it, and the basis of their cultural character. They questioned the source of government, the purpose of life, and the substance of the world itself. The philosophers of this period, a transition between the German Enlightenment, the Aufklärung, and the Romantic Sturm und Drang movement, wrestled with these questions in an intense dialogue of philosophical works, which carried defining intellectual, sociopolitical, and religious significance for the populace of the United States over the following decades as well as for the Germans.

The American Transcendentalists were instrumental in bringing these German philosophies into US circulation. Much like the German Idealists themselves, the Transcendentalists formed a cohesive philosophical movement based on close acquaintanceship and engagement in philosophical discussion with one another. They were informed by the same body of European philosophical works and interested in the same philosophical questions. While their individual conclusions and interpretations of these works and one another's writings often varied, they were rarely in conflict with one another's reflections but worked together to refine, interpret, and implement the philosophical issues in which they were interested. Broadly painted, the Transcendentalists' beliefs held that God was a divine spirit, present within but also beyond creation, who was accessible to all without mediation. They rejected the divinity of Jesus and the authenticity of miracles and elevated nature as a second scripture of equal or higher importance than the written Scripture, which they viewed as an inspired but largely historical work. Transcendentalism reached beyond the confines of any specific group, as it was a nondenominational and unstructured religious impulse that could be adopted by members of other congregations and religious persuasions as well. Thus, its numbers vary based on whether one categorizes only the leaders of the group as belonging to the movement or includes those who expressed interest in reading and discussing the ideas, attending lectures or churches led by the Transcendentalists, as well as those who applied the ideas in various reform activities. I have taken the latter approach to create a more thorough picture of Transcendentalism's cultural influence. The core group of Transcendentalists include Ralph Waldo Emerson, Henry David Thoreau, the Alcott family, and Margaret Fuller. But many others were also heavily involved with the Transcendentalist movement, such as the educational reformers Elizabeth, Mary, and Sophia Peabody and Horace Mann; George and Sophia Ripley and their supporters at their utopian socialist community of Brook Farm; Dorothea Dix, and Samuel Gridley Howe and Julia Ward Howe, advocates for mental health and disability reform; and ministers William Ellery Channing, Theodore Parker, Parker Pillsbury, Moncure Conway, and James Freeman Clarke. Moreover, the contemporaneous view of two other famous Northern ministers, Henry Ward Beecher and Horace Bushnell, classed them as generally Transcendentalist as well. The Massachusetts senator Charles Sumner was close with many of the circle, and William Herndon, Lincoln's law partner at their practice in Illinois, was an enthusiastic reader of Theodore Parker's printed sermons, as well as other Transcendentalist writings. A full list of significant figures I have identified as associated with Transcendentalism is provided in the appendix.

The Unitarian church, with which all of the major, and many of the lesser, Transcendentalist figures were associated at some point, played a role in the origin and dissemination of Transcendentalism. The Unitarians were completing their separation from the Congregationalists in 1825, and when Massachusetts ended the practice of government support for the Congregational Church as the established church of the state in 1833, the Unitarians replaced the Congregationalists as the most influential denomination in Boston and gained authority over Harvard University and a number of the city's other significant cultural establishments. The high social standing of many of the Unitarians lent them a cultural impact surpassing their actual numbers, which still ranked below that of Methodists, Baptists, and Congregationalists in Massachusetts. In the 1850 census, the value of Unitarian church property in Massachusetts far outstripped any other denomination. The wealth and social status of the Unitarian membership is demonstrated by their ability to establish a private soldier aid organization, the Sanitary Commission, during the Civil War. Despite some disputes between the Unitarian hierarchy and individual Transcendentalists, such as Emerson, many Transcendentalist beliefs still spread through means of the Unitarian church. Though not a conclusive measurement of Transcendentalism's reach, the incidence of Unitarianism is useful for establishing a rough estimation. Only one Unitarian church was recorded in the South in the 1860 census, whereas 276 Unitarian churches were recorded in the North. The majority of these were in New England, 158 in Massachusetts, and the westernmost churches noted were in Illinois, Missouri, and California. The Unitarian church sustained an especially strong cultural influence in the North during the war because it remained united for abolition while all the other major religious denominations splintered along a regional divide over the question of slavery or avoided any statements on or involvement in political issues to prevent regional separation. This, combined with the wealth and social standing of many members, helped the Unitarian church retain a more influential presence than those denominations weakened by regional divisions. And although the church was not unanimously in support of abolition, much of its leadership was in favor, as evidenced by an 1845 pamphlet titled *American Slavery: A Protest against American Slavery*, authored and signed by 173 Unitarian ministers, which, assuming one minister per church, equaled almost two-thirds of the total number of Unitarian churches counted in the 1860 census.[24]

The majority of noteworthy Northern poets, writers, and newspaper reporters from this period were also involved or at least familiar with Transcendentalism. These writers drew inspiration from Transcendentalism in their treatment of nature as a living force, their emphasis on the educational role of emotion and individual experience, and their interest in growth in character. The theories of art informing the Hudson River School of painting also manifested the Idealist understanding of the world and strove to portray the philosophical framework in visual form. The Transcendentalist writings themselves reached a larger readership than has often been recognized. For instance, the *Dial*, the literary magazine produced by the Concord Transcendentalists, was long portrayed as a failure. However, Susan Belasco's research revealed that its subscription list of three hundred was actually a "highly respectable" figure at the time for such a publication. Its four-year lifespan was in fact twice as long as most periodicals of the era.[25] Other largely Transcendentalist publications included *The Western Messenger* (1835–41), *Boston Quarterly Review* (1838–42), *The Present* (1843–44), *The Harbinger* (1845–49), *Massachusetts Quarterly Review* (1847–50), *Aesthetic Papers* (1849), *Spirit of the Age* (1849–50), *Una* (1853–55), *Atlantic Monthly* (1857–present), *The Radical* (1865–72), and *Index* (1870–86). The printed edition of William Ellery Channing's 1819 sermon, "Unitarian Christianity," ranked as the most extensively purchased pamphlet since Thomas Paine's 1776 *Common Sense*, and in addition to his church membership of 2,500 parishioners, Theodore Parker's printed sermons sold over 50,000 copies between the United States and England.[26]

In conjunction with Transcendentalist publications, the reach of their spoken word was also significant. Emerson's lecture circuit reached as far west as California, and he delivered an estimated 1,500 or more lectures in his lifetime. Based on an average of the numbers in attendance that Emerson recorded in his journals from 1835 to 1862, we can estimate that 622,000 Americans heard Emerson lecture in person. For context, this number is nearly equivalent to the population of Maine, twice that of Vermont or New Hampshire, and half the population of Massachusetts during this period. This estimate may be higher than accurate, as almost certainly some of the same individuals attended more than one of his lectures. However, including the years in which Emerson did not record his audience sizes and considered alongside the estimate that 400,000 Americans attended a lecture every week, with at least 4,000 community organizations dedicated to sponsoring public lectures, it may still be relatively accurate. During the winter of 1837–38 alone, 13,000 people attended Boston's winter lecture series, in which the majority of speakers were Transcendentalists.[27] Although they cannot definitively assert the extent of Americans' exposure to the ideas of the European philosophers of concern here, these figures help suggest a general outline by which their influence penetrated American cultural thought during the period leading up to the Civil War.

The numerous women who were present within the Transcendentalist circle prove that Americans even outside higher education were also becoming fully acquainted with German thought. Elizabeth Peabody authored an essay titled "*On the Spirit of the Hebrew Scriptures*" (1834), clearly inspired by Herder's work of a nearly identical title, and her successful bookshop in Boston carried the German writings, as well as works of the American Transcendentalists; European Romanticists such as Samuel Taylor Coleridge and Thomas Carlyle; and Victor Cousin and Theodore Simon Jouffroy, writers in the French school of Common Sense philosophy. Another Transcendentalist, Eliza Buckminster Lee, translated several German works, including such novels as *Walt and Vult* (1804) by the popular German author Jean Paul Richter, as well as authoring a biography of Richter and publishing several of her own novels. Margaret Fuller was deeply influenced by the German novelist and poet Johann Wolfgang von Goethe, whom she researched for a biography that never materialized. In her published book *Woman in the Nineteenth Century* (1845), which sold 1,000 copies in one week, Fuller extolled the status of women in Germany as the cause of their cultural success, referencing writers such as Friedrich Schiller and Richter, as well as Goethe and Anne Louise Germaine de Staël-Holstein, typically known as Madame de Staël, whose work first introduced many Americans to the German cultural revival. Likewise, Walt Whitman never received a higher education yet reviewed over two hundred books for the newspapers, ranging from Goethe to William Cullen Bryant, Carlyle, and Coleridge. He noted that his poem "Roaming in Thought" was inspired by reading Hegel, and he included Kant, Johann Gottlieb Fichte, Wilhelm Schelling, and Hegel in the poem "The Base of All Metaphysics."

Similarly, Brokmeyer and William Torrey Harris, the founders of the Hegelian club that formed in St. Louis, Missouri, in 1858, both first learned of Hegel's system through the Transcendentalists rather than direct university study or, in Brokmeyer's case, through exposure in Germany itself from which he had emigrated in 1844. St. Louis proved a prime location for the formation of this group, as it contained a large contingent of the politically exiled Forty-Eighters from Germany. During the 1850s, Brokmeyer worked on translations into English of Hegel's *Phenomenology of Spirit* (1807), *Logic* (1812), and eventually the texts of *The Philosophy of Right* (1820) and *The Philosophy of History* (1837), which became the foundational works referenced by the Transcendentalist movement. In addition to viewing the Hegelian dialectic as the only method that could solve the sectional tensions of the country, the St. Louis Hegelians emphasized Hegel's importance for improving educational methods and guiding labor and social reform.[28]

Preceding them, a lesser-known group in Ohio, centered in Cincinnati, has more recently been recognized as a significant Hegelian presence as well. This group included John Bernard Stallo, Peter Kaufmann, August Willich, and Moncure Conway. All of these but Conway were German immigrants. In 1848, Stallo, as professor of mathematics and German at St. Xavier's College in Cincinnati, published a philosophical work under the cumbersome title of *General Principles of the Philosophy of Nature[:]With an Outline of Some of Its Recent Developments among the Germans, Embracing the Philosophical Systems of Schelling and Hegel and Oken's System of Nature* that devoted some 200 pages to Hegel's thought, a copy of which was owned by both Emerson and Bronson Alcott. In this work, in addition to treating the subject of the natural world, Stallo engaged with Hegel's philosophy on government in *The Philosophy of Right* (1820). Kaufmann's *The Temple of Truth, or the Science of Ever-Progressing Knowledge* (1858) followed Hegel's dialectic system in its discussion on the process and form of knowledge and the ideal of perfecting mankind in socialist utopian reform. Emerson also owned and read this book. Conway believed Hegel had created "an epoch in the history of the human mind."[29] Willich, a participant in the 1848 revolutions and a sometime collaborator with Karl Marx and Friedrich Engels, understood Hegelian ideas mainly as a philosophy of communistic labor reform, but his egalitarian principles influenced his conduct during the Civil War as well, which helped him rise through the ranks from a private in the 9th Ohio Volunteer Infantry to major general by the end of the war, revered for treating his soldiers with dignity and thereby helping them retain their primary identity as free citizens rather than professional soldiers. Each of these Ohio Hegelians represented Hegel's philosophy to their fellow Americans as one of liberalism, perfectly compatible with democratic institutions, and a system of thought that furthered the development of liberty, both in thought and in social action.

All three of the Transcendentalists I primarily focus on in this book—Ralph Waldo Emerson, Margaret Fuller, and Henry David Thoreau—were thoroughly familiar with the Scottish Common Sense School of philosophy and personally read the works of Thomas Reid, Dugald Stewart, and Thomas Brown. Emerson and Thoreau gained this knowledge from their study at Harvard, at which the Common Sense works made up an important part of the curriculum. Fuller pursued this knowledge through private study and extensive reading from the Harvard library, which, as a woman, was the only access to the university that she was able to secure. All were acquainted with Kant's philosophy as well, either through direct sources such as those translated and excerpted in Transcendentalist Frederic Henry Hedge's 1847 *Prose Writers of Germany* or through the secondary works of Victor Cousin, Samuel Taylor Coleridge, and Madame de Staël. Likewise, all three were well read in Goethe, a literary disciple of Herder, whose poems, plays, and fictional work *Wilhelm Meister* (1795–96), one of the first novels of the bildungsroman, or character development, genre, were mainstays of Transcendentalist thought and which they all referenced frequently in their own writings. Emerson quoted from the writings of Arnold H. L. Heeren, a German historian steeped in Herderian philosophy, which Emerson must therefore have been exposed to from some source. Both Emerson and Thoreau also read Stallo. Emerson read Hegel's *Introduction to the Philosophy of History*, included in *Prose Writers of Germany*, and a second work, which is unclear as to whether it was the *Philosophy of Right* or *Logic*. Emerson was further instructed in Hegelian thought by his German friend Emmanuel Vitalis Scherb in 1849 and 1851 and grew increasingly familiar with Hegelian thought during the 1860s. Robert Richardson, in his biography of Emerson, credits his introduction to Hegel for the "fresh energy" that drove Emerson to delve deeper into three important themes that surface in his journals at this period: the approach to history as a typological system of the World-Soul's development, his interest in the Hegelian concept of freedom, and the conflict between freedom and determinism.[30] Excerpts from Herder's writings were likewise included in *Prose Writers of Germany*, and Fuller recorded reading and translating Herder with William Ellery Channing. She demonstrated at least a cursory knowledge of Hegel as well, writing of "Hegelianism" in somewhat loose terms. All three were also familiar with their contemporary American historian George Bancroft's *History of the United States* (1834), which he wrote on the platform of Herder's philosophy of nationalism and historical development and in which he described the formation of the United States as the culmination of "the idea of freedom."[31]

Thus, there exists substantial evidence that these Scottish and German philosophers were known, read, and disseminated by the Transcendentalists.

When repeatedly encountered in various works and spoken of among the Transcendentalists, these philosophies of the Scottish Realist and the German Idealist Schools could hardly have avoided becoming an influence on the individual intellectual formation of the Transcendentalists, their conception of the world and national events, and the adaptation of a specific vision of the ideal political character that would impact the larger populace in the ways illustrated above. Recognizing the Transcendentalists as influential actors in the crisis elucidates the broader intellectual climate in which the Civil War took place. Rather than reflecting mere sentimentalism, shrouding the true war with poetic imagery, or striving to conceal reality under false romantic forms, as historians and literary scholars have too frequently done, an examination of the Transcendentalists' thoughts on key issues of the Civil War experience, here identified as character, gender, race, and nationhood, illustrates the distinctive philosophical framework they used to understand and shape the Civil War crisis. Rather than entering the continuing debate as to whether it was a war over a single main cause, such as the Union, states' rights, slavery, labor systems, gender ideals, or Victorian standards of home and family, approaching the wartime ideals of the American North as a cohesive reflection of a philosophical paradigm demonstrates that each of these causes can be integrated into one interconnected worldview, traceable to the frameworks provided by the fusion of Scottish and German philosophies from which the Transcendentalists molded an influential American system of thought. The foundational paradigm of universal moral character, and its particular application to questions of gender, race, and nationality, build a detailed picture of the philosophical context in which the Civil War took place. It was a revolution of ideas that defined the era, and the cultural context of the war cannot be adequately understood without a thorough comprehension of the nuanced depths of philosophical thought that informed it.

Chapter One
SCOTTISH PHILOSOPHY OF CHARACTER

On July 25, 1865, Brevet Major General Orlando B. Willcox delivered a farewell address to his division: "You will carry about you in civil life a sense of your own worth," he informed his soldiers, "and self-respect will characterize those who have done so well . . . by their Country. Keep high the standard of your honor; preserve your honesty and integrity, and the worthy returned Soldier will purify the atmosphere of home, State and Country, by his own simple and steadfast purity of Character."[1]

Such statements would have been no surprise to his listeners. References to ideals of character and warfare as a test of this character appear in many writings from the Civil War and provide an essential psychological framework. Many scholars such as James McPherson and Thomas Rodgers have concluded that Civil War soldiers demonstrated a vastly higher level of personal dedication and investment in the causes of the war than in other American conflicts.[2] Rather than a cause of social dissociation, psychological trauma, or moral degeneration, a majority of Civil War participants wrote of the war as an opportunity for personal growth, character development, and an elevating influence in their private lives and the life of the country. There are few instances of soldiers complaining of loss of identity, abuse, or personal unimportance compared with the frequency of such instances in the literature from other wars, becoming markedly apparent with World War II and increasing through the Vietnam War era.[3] There have been many causes proposed to explain these tendencies, ranging from sociopolitical and economic to religious, but some aspects not yet fully explored are the theories of mind and the model of character development provided by the European philosophies of the period and disseminated to the American public through the Transcendentalists.

The American Transcendentalists inherited a bifurcated philosophical tradition on theories of character, the mind, and the process of acquiring knowledge. The most significant models were provided by the Scottish Common Sense writers and by the German Idealists, both of which as schools of thought were attempting to offer a solution to the philosophical problems concerning the validity of knowledge and experience that David Hume, most significantly, had posed in the mid-eighteenth century in his *Treatise of Human Nature*.[4] Hume's speculations formed a watershed moment in philosophy, causing European philosophy to diverge down two paths, broadly categorized as Realism and Idealism, or, in Emerson's classification, materialists versus idealists. These two standpoints were closer together at the time of their divergence than they would later become, and there was much overlap and agreement originally even between what became the opposing arguments. But by the nineteenth century they had grown further apart, and thinkers in Britain such as Samuel Taylor Coleridge and Thomas Carlyle were attempting to reunite the two threads. In the United States, the American Transcendentalists took up the same challenge. They did not reject Common Sense or substitute it with Idealism, as has sometimes been portrayed.[5] Rather, the Transcendentalists retained many foundational elements of the Scottish philosophy, expanding on it and tweaking it at times to reconcile with the new propositions of the Idealists. There are five critical areas in particular in which the Transcendentalists continued to ground themselves in Common Sense philosophy: its rebuttal of Humean skepticism; its introduction of the imagination as a vital component of knowledge; its portrayal of the human mind as an active agent rather than a passive recipient of external sensations; the distinction between the role and function of reason and understanding in the mind; and the suggestion that observation and perception themselves could become moral actions. These convictions retained a hold on the Transcendentalists' understanding of the self and gained a new vibrancy under their hand.

The first of these continuing influences on Transcendentalist thinking is Reid's response to Hume. When Hume is read, as both the Scots and Germans generally did, as a Pyrrhonian skeptic of knowledge itself rather than an academic skeptic of the proposed systems for explaining knowledge, his controversial argument addressed a core epistemological issue. In his treatment of impressions and ideas, he touched on the question of how, or if, the mind encounters the real world or whether perception consists of mental representations and if either the senses or representations can be trusted as imparting absolute knowledge. Hume contended that the empiricism derived from Locke could not explain experience; instead, actual experience, the perceiving of objects and the discerning of cause and effect, was a matter of habitual expectation. This implied a mental process that allowed one to make sense of the world while assuming it was consistent, unchanging, and predictable. If the mind only experienced sensory inputs, as Locke's empirical tabula rasa argument portrayed, experience could never form a coherent or continuous experience and a man could never learn anything, for there was nothing in the moment of sensation by which to deduce cause and effect. According to Hume, then, causal connections were no more than habitual expectations: "From causes, which appear *similar*, we expect similar effects. This is the sum of all our experimental conclusions."[6] He was, in fact, arguing for a form of representationalism in that he believed a coherent and connected experience consisted of the mind's expectations regarding the world. In this way, he anticipated the understanding of knowledge as representation that the Idealists would later reach, but Hume contended there was no way to prove that this mental representation had anything to do with the real world and thus to claim certain knowledge of anything was fallacious.

Unlike the Idealists, Hume argued that if reality were contained within representations, there was no rational explanation as to why even the mythical creations we could imagine were only the combination of things already experienced by the senses. A gold mountain did not empirically exist but combined two concepts that did: that of gold and that of mountain. He wrote, "All this creative power of the mind amounts to no more than the faculty of compounding, transposing, augmenting, or diminishing the materials afforded us by the senses and experience." It did not itself create a single concept of experience. Furthermore, Hume argued that the representations in the mind never constituted as concrete an experience as sensory perception did. There was, he pointed out, "a considerable difference between . . . when a man feels the pain of excessive heat . . . and when he afterwards recalls to his memory this sensation, or anticipates it by his imagination." Meanwhile, principles of causality, morality and justice—which cannot be traced to any sense impressions—can only be based on our habitual associations of ideas. He concluded, "Custom, then, is the great guide of human life" for forming coherent experience, and personal taste and desire for a certain outcome alone drove moral decisions, because absolute knowledge of either the temporal or moral realm was questionable.[7] Read as a skeptic in this way, Hume thus threw into question both the rationalist and empiricist concepts of knowledge and the validity of the philosophical conclusions reached by his contemporaries and forebears regarding the relationship between perception and reality.

The Scottish Common Sense philosophers' response strove "to contain both realism (empiricism) and intuition (idealism) into one system."[8] This was something that in many ways the Transcendentalists, too, tried to maintain. However, this attempt was not always satisfactory. Thomas Reid's rejoinder to the epistemological question of empiricism versus representationalism was largely to deny that it was an issue that needed to be addressed. He argued that mental representation was not the basis of experience and that humanity's common sense suggested that we are in direct, nonrepresentational contact with an actual external world. In other words, Reid argued that the objects of our knowledge—what we think about, compare, and remember—were not representations of the world but elements of the world itself. In answer to Hume's thesis that such pure empirical knowledge was not possible, Reid posited that some features of human belief originated in the mind itself simply because God placed them there. Such beliefs included the concept of the self, "not because it is a self whose conscious thoughts are to be justified by God's veracity, nor because it is an agent constituting evidence," but because we simply must believe these principles as themselves "the basis of all justification and explanation."[9] Thus he admitted that such issues as Hume raised were inexplicable but believed that they must be assumed, and because they lie beyond human capacity to understand, it must be supposed that God authored them.

Reid dismissed it as pointless to question whether one could theoretically experience the world in the way that everyone plainly did experience it. These were intuitive judgments, Reid believed, and as such were first principles, meaning that they were a point from which reasoning began and that reasoning could not be carried any further backward from them. These "*first principles, principles of common sense, . . . self-evident truths,*" could be identified as such from consistent traits: denial of them was false and absurd, whereas belief in them was "necessary to all men for their being and preservation."[10]

Reid was "not concerned to answer questions of justification" for these convictions. They were self-evident truths that needed no argument, for "what is evident forces assent," he believed.[11]

Furthermore, Reid took issue with the concept of representationalism, which he classified as "the Way of Ideas" that had lurked in Western philosophy since Plato and continued to influence the writings of those such as Hume. Reid did not subscribe to the belief that ideas or images mediated experience of the world. He argued that this suggestion was not consistent with faculty psychology—a common philosophical conception of the mind as constituted of distinct mental and emotional functions—for it reduced all the mental powers to a single action, that of conception. It allowed for no differentiation between faculties such as judgment or perception, for instance.

Accordingly, Reid challenged the concept of universals, which described a metaphysical concept of general, repeatable, and recurrent qualities demonstrated in various individual objects, or particulars. "Life," for instance, was a universal, whereas "Napoleon's life" was a particular. Universals were not actually perceivable, Reid argued. In fact, they were "impossible" for it was not self-evident "that any being should exist which is not an individual being."[12] This idea of universals strayed too far into abstraction and metaphysics. However, he admitted the possibility for the conception of nonexistent objects such as centaurs. But this also was not a form or a universal in a Platonic sense because it was created in the human mind directly through a social process, not through perception of nature. How this reconciled with his overall thesis of direct sensory perception of real objects or of first principles infused into the human mind directly from God is a problematic question.

One key to understanding Reid's stance lies in his discussion of the relationship between a mental function and a sensation. "Sensations are, for Reid, 'in us,' be they tactile, visual, olfactory, auditory or gustatory. . . . From these subjective sensations arise our experiences of non-subjective objects, i.e., trees, rocks, buildings."[13] This translation of sensations to mental conceptions was done by the same process, and with the same lack of intrinsic connection, that words signal to our minds the thing spoken of. These, too, were learned socially, rather than inherent in nature. "The word and what it means are totally different and . . . the connection is arbitrary," yet the "transition from one to the other seems inexorable."[14] Just as it mattered little why a word came to denote a particular object, it mattered little why sensations led to experience of a particular object. The important fact, to Reid, was that they did so.

The second element that the Transcendentalists gained and retained from Common Sense—the emphasis on the imagination—can be credited to Dugald Stewart. Stewart was a student of Reid's, a younger philosopher contemporary with the childhoods of many Transcendentalists, who began teaching at the University of Edinburgh at the age of nineteen. His writings were central to Common Sense in the United States. Although he remained close friends with Reid, Stewart's philosophy contained a few notable differences. He emphasized that a conviction of material existence even when an object was removed from the senses was necessary to make meaningful experience out of sense perception, and he preferred the phrase "fundamental laws of human belief" over Reid's "principles of common sense," believing it better avoided misinterpretation by immaterialists, since intuitive senses were not principles from which any absolute truth could be formed with certainty.[15] But most important to the Transcendentalists was Stewart's treatment of the imagination. Reid had categorized imagination as a separate faculty from conception but did not develop his discussion of it in any great depth. Stewart, however, believed that imagination, imaginative literature and poetry, were essential to the formation of moral character. He did not hold that imagination was a faculty but that it grew out of intentional and habitual education, study, and experience. Therefore, it was an intellectual attribute that required cultivation and was essential to strengthening the faculties of the moral sense, the ability to discern right and wrong, and thus to produce public virtue. Imaginative literature, Stewart maintained, played an important role "as a way to exercise the faculties of mind" and elevate "the intellectual and moral welfare of society."[16] Not only did Stewart stress the importance of the imagination in the moral life but he also voiced the conviction that imagination, literature, and poetry, in having a positive impact on personal character, would from there extend to shape the political life of a nation. As with the Transcendentalists, these pursuits were not viewed as solitary, antisocial, or apolitical undertakings but as essential building blocks of a moral society.

◇◇◇

In the early American Republic, these Scottish conceptions of character formation were widely accepted. John Witherspoon, a Scottish immigrant who assumed the presidency of Princeton University in 1768, was largely responsible for first disseminating Scottish Common Sense philosophy in the

United States. From there it quickly gained acceptance until by the time of Witherspoon's death in 1794 it had "attained the status almost of academic orthodoxy in American philosophy" and informed the logic of such critical documents as the Declaration of Independence, of which he was a signatory.[17] Witherspoon could count among his students a president and vice president of the United States—James Madison and Aaron Burr—as well as twenty-one senators, thirty-nine congressmen, nine cabinet officers, twelve state governors, and three justices of the Supreme Court. This percentage of government officials is impressive, given the small area and population that the United States could boast at the time.

By the end of the eighteenth century, the primacy of Scottish Common Sense was also well established at Harvard, the Transcendentalists' alma mater, introduced through David Tappan and continued by a steady presence of Common Sense–adhering professors up to the time of the Civil War. Douglas Sloan points out that the religious acceptability of this philosophy in Scotland did much to give it this status in the United States, as it "carried neither the stigma of atheism, frequently associated with the French materialists, nor even the stain of religious heterodoxy" present among English philosophers and polemicists such as Joseph Priestley or Thomas Paine. "This," Sloan writes, "was especially important in the American colleges where churches were strongly represented if not in complete control."[18] Moreover, it was a philosophy that proved acceptable to diverse denominations, ranging from the Transcendentalists and the Unitarians to Episcopalians, Calvinists, and Presbyterians. Thomas Reid's *Inquiry into the Human Mind* was the book borrowed most frequently from the Harvard library between 1795 and 1820. It was ousted from top place only by Dugald Stewart's *Elements on the Philosophy of the Human Mind*, which held top rank from 1820 until 1845.[19]

Levi Hedge, professor of natural religion, moral philosophy, and civil politics at Harvard and father of the Transcendentalist Frederic Henry Hedge, authored a highly influential textbook titled *Elements of Logick; or a Summary of the General Principles and Different Modes of Reasoning*. The sources he used to formulate this work included Locke's *Essay on the Understanding*, Reid's *Essays on the Intellectual Powers*, Stewart's *Elements of the Philosophy of the Mind*, and another major work from the Scottish Common Sense School, James Beattie's *Essay on Truth*, among others. Hedge's book briefly covered the "affections and operations of the mind," such as perception, attention, comparison, and analysis; "terms and propositions"; "judgment and reasoning," including moral versus demonstrative; induction, syllogisms, and sophisms; and finally, guidelines for method, disputation, and interpretation. In the first section, outlining the operations of the mind, Hedge's citations came almost exclusively from Reid and Stewart.[20] Hedge's work remained a prominent philosophical text into the 1870s.

Emerson was a student of Hedge and studied from this textbook, even writing his final senior paper in college as an ode to the wisdom of Scottish Common Sense, "the school in which Reid and Stewart" labored, on ethics and the moral sense.[21] Reid, Emerson stated, attempted to right the "outrage upon the feelings of human nature" that Hume had committed. Reid was the "chief champion" of the Common Sense School and strove to establish "a code of propositions as axioms which no rational being will dispute." However, Reid's argument was, Emerson concluded, not "made with such complete success as to remove the terror which attached to the name of Hume" entirely.[22]

Another influential author and Harvard professor of moral philosophy, Francis Bowen, presents a similar journey of intellectual development to that of the Transcendentalists, which is somewhat surprising considering that he launched a series of written rebuttals to Emerson's essays when they first appeared. At Bowen's appointment to Harvard in 1853, he taught the standard Common Sense philosophy of Reid. By the 1860s, he had modified his teaching to reflect the slant given the philosophy by Sir William Hamilton, who incorporated influences from the German philosophers, notably in his collected edition of the works of Dugald Stewart. By the 1870s, Bowen had converted fully to the philosophical system of German Idealism, particularly that of Hegel. James Walker, who filled Hedge's professorship in 1839, also published annotated editions of Reid and Stewart that contained extensive citations on the concepts they presented taken from other philosophical writers, including Cousin, Jouffroy, Hamilton, and Kant. As the editor of the *Christian Examiner*, Walker also published numerous pieces on Scottish Realism, as well as German Idealism and the American Transcendentalists' writings. He thus provided several venues for philosophical comparison and discussion.

Hamilton and other Scottish writers following in the tradition of Reid were important in shaping Americans' understanding of Scottish Common Sense. Noah Porter, professor of moral philosophy at Yale from 1846 until his inauguration as university president in 1871, held that Hamilton was "the greatest writer and teacher among living Englishmen," although he disagreed with some of Hamilton's views.[23] The Transcendentalists actually made more specific references to these later Scottish writers than to Reid himself. Emerson made several direct references to Hamilton, and the Transcendentalists almost certainly would have read Hamilton's essays in the *Edinburgh Review*, which was the source of much of their philosophical reading. In his journal, Emerson, for instance, listed having read writings by Thomas Brown and Dugald Stewart in the *Review*, in addition to books containing larger collections of their works, such as Brown's *Lectures on the Philosophy of the Human Mind* from the Boston library.[24] Margaret Fuller also made specific mention of reading Brown's essays and of "dipping into Brown, Stewart, and that class of books." She would eventually describe the impact of Common Sense philosophy in her life as "that coarse, but wearable stuff woven by the ages,—Common Sense," which, she claimed, under the severe tutelage of her father, acted as "a thick curtain of available intellect" that "secluded and veiled" her "true life."[25] Yet a repudiation of this variety was the exception among the Transcendentalists and probably stemmed from Fuller viewing it, before the meliorating influence of the German philosophers, as valuing only masculine traits and leaving her feminine qualities undeveloped. The male Transcendentalists such as Emerson and Thoreau, educated in the Common Sense system throughout their university time, continued to reflect the outlines of this philosophy in their thinking, often without specific acknowledgment of its source. Rather than a lack of Common Sense influence, however, they took this model for granted, for its framework appears with some regularity in their writings and was important in shaping their conceptions of the delineation of mental faculties, the moral sense, and intuition, particularly.

This delineation of the mental faculties outlined the third essential piece of Common Sense frameworks that the Transcendentalists retained. In Reid's employment of the term, Common Sense did not mean good judgment but rather "common" as a faculty that every individual human being alike possessed; hence knowledge was not a sphere for the learned alone but was accessible to all. These universal powers of the mind Reid identified as the faculties, to be differentiated from habits that were those powers acquired through personal effort. He further classified the faculties as active and passive, granting the process of passive reception of stimuli to the physical senses but retaining the activity of the receiver as an essential element in the act of perception. Again, these powers were subdivided into those of the will, or reason, embracing active impulses such as "appetites, passions, affections," and those of understanding, which included "our contemplative powers; by which we perceive objects; by which we conceive or remember them; by which we analyze or compound them; and by which we judge and reason concerning them."[26] Reid understood these faculties as being the end point of analytic reasoning about the mind, for they were "phenomena which we cannot resolve into any other." It was traced back as far as could be, uncovering the "ultimate phenomena" that proved it to be part of "the Constitution of the System, or a Law of Nature," the "operation of him that made the System."[27] It was in this light that Emerson could state that "God is . . . the ideal of Character," for the end point of all mental phenomena, as Reid had stated, was, to Emerson, summed up as God.[28] The Transcendentalists believed that bringing one's faculties into harmony with first principles and thus their original constitution as patterned by God would bring one into harmony with God, and an individual human character would then reflect God's character.

Reid's classification of understanding as the powers possessed "by means of our external senses," and reason as the active power that interpreted what the senses perceived is one of his frameworks most consistently reflected by the Transcendentalists.[29] Unlike Reid, however, they established a hierarchical preference for the internal over the external as is indicated in Emerson's statement, "There is no doctrine of the Reason which will bear to be taught by the Understanding," from his groundbreaking Divinity School Address.[30] In his essay on nature, Emerson also discussed this separation of mental powers. "Every property of matter is a school for the understanding,—its solidity or resistance, its inertia, its extension, its figure, its divisibility. . . . Meantime, Reason transfers all these lessons into its own world of thought, by perceiving the analogy that marries Matter and Mind," he wrote. "Nature is a discipline of the understanding in intellectual truths. . . . The exercise of the Will or the lesson of power is taught in every event. . . . Sensible objects conform to the premonitions of Reason and reflect the conscience. All things are moral."[31] And once moral, they bore an applicability to human life: "A grand will, which, when legitimate and abiding, we call *character*, the height of manhood," stated Emerson.[32] In writing his letter proposing marriage to his second wife, Emerson also used this delineation as a way to state that his intention was balanced between the practical and the spiritual, driven by rationality and by affection. He was, he stated, "rejoiced in my Reason as well as in my Understanding by finding an earnest and noble mind."[33] These statements of Emerson's are some of the more explicit assertions that reflect the paradigm of faculty psychology and describe what Emerson envisioned as constituting character.

Thomas Reid's work in this area was essential to the final merged ideal of character development that the Transcendentalists promoted, for their education in the Common Sense School preceded their acquaintance with German thought and continued to provide a foundational understanding of the human mind. Reid supplied the initial outlines of what constituted a balanced character based on the model of faculty psychology. This model was not particular to Common Sense but entered the American educational system largely through the writings of this school and was reencountered by the Transcendentalists in the work of Samuel Taylor Coleridge. Reid's system advocated achieving harmony of all the faculties, the lesser faculties, such as passions and appetites, being properly subordinated to the higher ones, such as logic and memory, for if these were not well-balanced, "the divinely intended harmony of the system" was destroyed and a person failed to reach his or her potential. A good character was achieved when the instinctual impulses were controlled by the reasoning faculties, and thus everything remained under the control of the will rather than the whims of the passions.[34] Reid was in no way an Idealist and approached the question of character from a standpoint that was diametrically opposed to the German writers that the Transcendentalists later grafted onto their conception of character. However, the Transcendentalists were little concerned with philosophical formalism and borrowed what suited them from many diverse systems.

Reid also introduced a conception of ideas that helps explain how the Transcendentalists managed to marry his philosophy with the disparate stance of the German authors. Reid took issue with Hume's assertion that sensory perception only comprehended a representation of the actual thing, not the thing-in-itself. Daniel Walker Howe has summarized Reid's position as follows: "An idea was not a representation, but an activity. Things in themselves were the objects of the activity."[35] Although Reid kept this proposition firmly within the bounds of individual human minds, the Transcendentalists expanded the possibilities of this suggestion into a structure of the divine mind as thinker and the objects perceived as visible activity of that mind. Things-in-themselves could then be understood as the creative activity of the divine mind, which, holding objects in thought, also held them in reality. In his essay "The Over-Soul," Emerson wrote, "The act of seeing and the thing seen, the seer and the spectacle, the subject and the object, are one."[36] Tangible objects were an idea and a representation of an activity at the same time, he posited, but it was the divine mind rather than human minds to which this categorization related. Emerson thus suggested that it was only by accessing and harmonizing one's individual mind with the divine mind that the idea behind a representation could be perceived and understood in its spiritual reality. Through perception of this activity of the divine mind, the divine mind itself could be understood and reliable knowledge attained.

Reid's writings supported this argument, given his discussion that in matter itself there existed nothing grand, powerful, wise, good, or beautiful. These were attributes not of matter but of mind, Reid wrote. For, as he discussed in relation to a written work, the text could portray these qualities but they did not originate there. "They are ascribed to the work figuratively, but are really inherent in the author," Reid stated. In attributing these qualities to a book itself or other material substance, he concluded, we are in fact recognizing an intellectual quality, of which the material is "the effect, or sign, or instrument, or to which bears some analogy" to the quality of mind it represented.[37] And because there can be no effect without having a first cause, the physical world made the qualities of God, as first cause, knowable. "Given that the cosmos contains creatures with life, power, intelligence, and moral virtue, the first cause must have those features as well."[38] Reid observed that "the more accurately we search into the Human Mind, the stronger traces we every where find of his Wisdom who made it." And investigating these faculties and attributes became, according to Reid, "a Hymn to the Creator," for the use of the mind led one to be admitted "into the Counsels of the Almighty," and even the passions "cannot be barren of praise to him, nor unproductive to ourselves," when used for a noble purpose.[39]

It was in this kind of recognition of material effects as the demonstration of immaterial causes that the Transcendentalists consistently grounded their interpretation of the natural world and in which Common Sense remained a foundational element in their worldview. Emerson's essay "Nature," one of his earlier writings, shows a noticeable continuity with Reid. As Reid had described the attributes of nature as signaling the attributes of its Creator, Emerson believed that the beauty of the world was more than sensory enjoyment. Good and beautiful attributes were found in mind, and not in matter, as Reid had stated. Thus, Emerson reaffirmed, nature became an "object of the intellect," or the objectively visible activity of the divine mind. Perceiving this divine activity related the personal experience of beauty to a call to virtue and hence to virtuous action, which caused it to become an "active power" of the mind, Emerson wrote. Thus "the beauty of nature reforms itself in the mind, and not for barren contemplation, but for new creation," Emerson reasoned, therefore beauty was a participation in the divine thoughts demonstrated in the observable objects of nature.[40] His discussion of nature, then, was not one of passive and abstract appreciation. Rather, he was arguing for a type of character formation in which nature assisted as an idea, or activity, and an intellectual attribute of the divine mind, from which human minds garnered all they could become. The understanding of faculty psychology such as Reid's that Emerson learned at Harvard and the ideals of self-developing these faculties in accordance with the divine hierarchy of attributes displayed by nature became a bedrock in the Transcendentalist conception of character and informed the bulk of their reform and political actions.

Emerson went on to consider the universe as the demonstration of the faculties of the divine mind, delineated as the faculties of reason and understanding. Although inconsistent with the standard Common Sense categorization for human faculties and now blended with Hegel's classifications, Emerson demonstrated his original debt to Reid's concept. Hegel had made a unique distinction between reason (*Vernunft*) and understanding (*Verstand*). In Hegel's treatment, which Coleridge also followed, understanding was the faculty used to make sense of the material world, but reason was the intellectual and imaginative process used to make sense of it and thus the phenomenon with which philosophy should be interested. Reason, to Hegel, was virtually synonymous with idea, the absolute spiritualized consciousness of reality. This was, in turn, the final infinite form and substance, power and consciousness, namely, God. Hence, in Hegel's philosophy, reason was not a human capacity but the immanence of God within the individual. Following this, Emerson suggested that reason was that divine faculty which manifested as the visible world. Divine reason displayed itself as "types," or representations of itself, visible as the blue sky, the earth, space and planets, men and animals, Emerson wrote. Divine understanding contained the causes, meanings, and universal essences existing behind and beyond the visible appearances. Human understanding revealed these "ultimates"—or *universals*, in Hegel's language—and when this understanding stimulated reason "to more earnest vision, outlines and surfaces become transparent, and are no longer seen; causes and spirits are seen through them," Emerson concluded.[41] This model of the mind can, therefore, shed significant insight into the Transcendentalists' understanding of both the human mind and of God, explaining why they gravitated toward designations such as divine mind, as well as elucidating what they meant by humanity's participation in that mind, and the ways in which they saw this model as leading toward activity rather than simple personal contemplation. For through this model of the mind, sensory perception and the observable world contributed to the identification of the divine, which revealed the ideal hierarchy for the mind's faculties and thus established virtue, which developed the ideal personal character.

Reid's discussion of the moral sense was also important to the Transcendentalists in utilizing his philosophy in their conception of character. Reid categorized the moral sense as an active faculty and one that, like "the external senses, is the testimony of nature."[42] This placed the moral sense into human nature itself rather than viewing it as an imposition of God upon an initially depraved character. It suggested that the world contained moral elements, that morality could be learned from nature, and that morality was natural to humanity. This was a step away from orthodox Calvinism and ideas of predestination. Instead, it made way for the predominance of free will in religious thinking and supported ideals of self-sanctification through the suggestion that "the perfection of the divinely inspired 'moral faculty' provided the primary source for moral behavior" and "that the cultivation of these innate powers better served God and benevolent affections between people than the philosophical concept of necessity," or determinism.[43] Reid viewed his take on the moral sense as completing a deficiency remaining from Francis Hutcheson's treatment of the question, found in *An Inquiry into the Original of Our Ideas of Beauty and Virtue*. Hutcheson, a professor of moral philosophy in Glasgow from 1729 to 1746, had left the moral sense as a feeling of love, pleasure, or approbation, without indicating whether a judgment was involved in the sensation, thereby leaving it to appear as a passive power.[44] Reid, in contrast, stressed that the moral sense was an active power, aligned with the will and reason, a power that perceived and judged moral truths with as much certainty as the physical senses perceived and judged material surroundings.

This was part of a larger dispute between two lines of philosophical thinking to which Reid was heir, the one described as "ethical sentimentalism" and the other as "moral realism" or "rational intuitionism."[45] Francis Hutcheson had played an important role in forming this distinction. Kenneth Winkler has asserted that Hutcheson cannot be included in the school of moral realism, for following Hutcheson's line of reasoning based on a Lockean model of sense realism, the only category of *idea* that Hutcheson's treatment can fall under is what Winkler delineates as Locke's third classification: an idea that arises apart from any accompanying sensation, a conception of the *quality as it is in itself*, something that Locke believed impossible for a human mind. This concept of "*idea*" does not rely on an external sense and hence cannot be considered a realist theory of idea. Thus Hutcheson, in using this third theory of *idea* when he speaks of a moral sense, cannot be a moral realist, for, states Winkler, there is nothing empirical in his portrayal of how the moral sense discerns what is moral.[46]

David Norton has argued the opposite case, believing that Hutcheson was not following Locke's classification of the senses and pointing out that Hutcheson specifically disagreed with Locke in limiting the senses to only the five external functions. Norton posits that Hutcheson was describing another, internal sense that he believed perceived situations and actions. This sense did still rely on external stimulation, but not a material quality contained within a physical body. Perception was the action of receiving a sensible idea, or a sensory input. A second-order idea arose in response to this input, what Hutcheson termed a "concomitant idea." Morals were concomitant ideas, sensations stimulated by external input but interpreted by an internal sense. Thus, Norton's concept of Hutcheson's moral philosophy falls within a framework of moral realism. He notes that this thought distinguishes Hutcheson from "emotivism or subjectivism," as Winkler contended, and shows that he believed "the moral sense to be that principle of human nature which can and does enable us to apprehend and distinguish particular, objectively real features . . . of the world about us." This moral sense resulted in objective knowledge of vice and virtue and the ability to "make moral judgments that are correct or incorrect, true or false."[47]

Although Reid perceived Hutcheson's argument on the moral sense to be deficient in lacking the inclusion of judgment, his reading of Hutcheson was closer to that which Norton renders, with a connection apparent between Hutcheson's concomitant ideas and Reid's intellectual attributes of material bodies. Reid suggested that the object perceived and the sensation it elicited have nothing in common with each other, for "the former are not of kin to the latter, nor resemble them in any one feature," he wrote. They were "as certainly and manifestly unlike" as the point of a sword and the pain it caused. Therefore, Reid concluded that either human conceptions "are ideas of sensation, or they are not. If any one of them can be shown to be an idea of sensation, or to have the least resemblance to any sensation," he would concede the argument but did not believe that this could be proven.[48] George Berkeley was an Irish scholar and Anglican bishop who had argued for reality only as existing in consciousness, and Reid believed that he had proven beyond argument that reason could not infer the existence of matter from sensation and that Hume had proven that reason could not infer our own existence by our sensations. Therefore, Reid saw only one solution: We believe in our minds, our sensations, and our conceptions of secondary qualities like extension, motion, or mass because they are first principles. We believe in them because "by the constitution of our nature, we are under necessity of assenting to them. Such principles are parts of our constitution" and if deceived in this, "we are deceived by Him that made us."[49]

Similarly, Reid's theory of moral perception held that the moral sense, like the physical senses, perceived the external world, but not through direct relation between the externality observed and the sensation produced. It was not sight of a hand reaching into the water to save a drowning man that caused a moral perception but the secondary qualities, or relational properties, like Hutcheson's concomitant ideas—in this case the objective and the motivation that caused the hand to act to save the drowning man.[50] The moral property of the hand's motion was not immediately perceivable to the sense of sight. Likewise, sight alone could not discern the lack of moral intent in an equally redeeming action, that of mice chewing a rope binding a captive man.[51] But through the first principles imprinted in the moral faculty of the mind, the morality of the first action could be perceived, whereas the merely consequential nature of the second was likewise discerned. However, the primary qualities received by the physical senses were essential to the perception of this morality, for the moral properties were contained in the "behavior and countenance of agents" and not in the observer's sentiments.[52] Just as it is evident that "nonmoral qualities such as being intelligent, frightened, stingy, cheeky, determined, etc., are qualities of persons and their intentions, beliefs, etc.," we can be certain that "moral qualities are also qualities of persons and things in the mind that are expressed in behavior" and can be reliably perceived and judged.[53] Thus Reid does not strictly fall into either a moral realist or an ethical sentimentalist camp, holding that physical sensation had to be perceived first but also interpreted by the first principles known in the moral sense. He classified a sentiment as a feeling regarding which we make a judgment. Therefore, morality is grounded in sentiment but also requires the initial feeling to be received through the senses and the judgment reached from those feelings to be based on a first principle. This understanding of sentiment and moral feeling was essential to the Transcendentalists and to the culture of the Civil War.

Margaret Fuller, in particular, referenced theories of the moral sense also obtained from Thomas Brown, another philosopher of the Scottish School, who on several points differed significantly from Reid and Stewart. He added an additional layer of interpretation onto the issue of the moral sense through his theory of association. Brown believed that all Reid had described was sensation and not perception at all. Returning to Reid's analogy of the sword, the problem as Brown saw it lay in the fact that Reid ended with a description of the sensation of pain and the properties of the sword's material, which singly, as Reid himself saw, had nothing to do with each other. But, Brown concluded, the actual act of perception "is a sensation suggesting, by association, the notion of some extended and resisting substance" that one of the five senses alone "never could have afforded; but which, when once received from any other source, may be suggested by these as readily as any other associated feeling that has frequently co-existed with them."[54] The material point of a sword and the sensation of pain were thus perceived together through the common association with death.

Three powers of the mind acted in any instance: the sensation, the association, and, from the coexistence of these two, perception. Accordingly, Brown painted a theory of both physical senses and emotions acting together as a codependent unit jointly producing the experience of the world. "Though there may never have been in the mind any proximity of the very images compared," he wrote, "there may have been a proximity of each to an emotion of some sort, which, as common to both, might render each capable indirectly of suggesting the other." He likened the perception of unmarred snow with innocence and a cheery youth with a spring morning. No external resemblance suggested the comparison but rather association, the "common emotion excited" by each.[55] Dugald Stewart repeated this theory, suggesting that although beauty in a literal sense "denotes what is presented to the organ of Sight," the perception was "afterwards transferred to moral qualities by an associating process."[56] Hence the perception of pain could be elicited by the point of a sword through the emotional association with danger or death. And the morality of saving a drowning man versus the amorality of mice chewing a rope was discerned through the associations present in each instance. Brown and Stewart consequently made sense perception and emotion essential aspects of perception, giving perception a moral component.

Margaret Fuller made a statement suggestive of the influence of Brown's association theory in her thinking when she remarked on experiencing a colorful field of wildflowers. "Whether sensuously by the optic nerve, unused to so much gold and crimson with such tender green, or symbolically through some meaning dimly seen in the flowers, I enjoyed a sort of fairyland exultation," she wrote.[57] In other instances, her reflections on the interplay of nature with emotion also suggest this interpretation. She wrote about settlers of the West drawing from the landscape some dim conception of "its moral and its meaning" and of striving herself to "woo the mighty meaning of the scene." Its moral lesson could not "be seen by being stared at," she maintained, but had to be learned through "daily and careless familiarity" with nature, indicating that she believed true perception consisted of more than visual stimulation alone.[58]

Thoreau also wrote in ways which suggest the Transcendentalists' utilization of Brown's theory to discern moral lessons in nature. He contrasted the immoral actions of humanity in the case of slavery with the moral goodness of nature, who "has been partner to no Missouri Compromise." In seeing and smelling the beauty of a water lily, "the emblem of purity," for instance, the moral lesson was taught to "so behave . . . that when we behold or scent a flower, we may not be reminded how inconsistent your deeds are with it; for all odor is but one form of advertisement of a moral quality, and if fair actions had not been performed, the lily would not smell sweet," that is, the improper emotional association with the physical sensation would prevent true perception. "The foul slime stands for the sloth and vice of man, the decay of humanity; the fragrant flower that springs from it, for the purity and courage which are immortal," Thoreau concluded.[59]

Emerson also occasionally expressed an understanding that reveals his acquaintance with Brown's views. For instance, he mentioned how the objects of the senses conformed to the "premonitions," or one could say the concomitant ideas or associations, of reason, leading to one of Emerson's favorite phrases, "All things are moral."[60] This conclusion becomes possible in a Common Sense framework only if a sensory perception, an emotion, and a judgment are all present at the same time. Merely seeing a landscape with the physical eyes is not moral. Feeling an emotional response inspired by a landscape is not moral. Making a judgment about the landscape is not moral. But if all three are combined, it can create a moral influence. "All things are moral," Emerson repeated, for that "which within us is a sentiment, outside of us is a law."[61] Laws were universal, applicable to all, and thus moral sentiment was "the foundation of culture, as of character," following God as "the moral ideal" of character and the first cause of all moral laws.[62]

Friedrich Schiller also offered an interpretation of this idea, in this case contributing a German application of Common Sense principles to which the Transcendentalists, given their knowledge of Schiller, were likely introduced. In Schiller's interpretation, "the contemplation of the beautiful object became not an entirely distinct mental activity from the contemplation of the moral or the political but rather a path to liberation, a way to draw people together and to renew the social order." This was a belief clearly echoed by the Transcendentalists. It was the conviction that individual "harmony between the rational and the sensible" would result in "harmony and equality to society as a whole" and thus produce "the triumph of common sense."[63] Recognizing this conception of the role that sentiment would play in character, moral life, and consequently in social and political life substantially illustrates that the Transcendentalists did not view themselves as advocating an isolated and passive lifestyle through their emphasis on self-sanctification, character development, nature appreciation, and nurturing a response based in moral sentiment to the world around them. Rather, their model of character and the relationship to nature implied an active, interventionist ethic.

This conception is reinforced by that of intuition, knowledge that is not received from the external senses. Intuition played a tremendous role in Transcendentalism. Whereas Hume had reduced intuition merely to feeling and its conclusions to subjectivism, Reid retained his classification of intuition as a sentiment and hence a form of moral realism relating it directly to judgment. He argued, and the American professor Levi Hedge repeated in his book *Logick*, that intuition was a feeling that included a judgment and thus had a definitive conclusion of truth or falsehood. Hedge wrote, "Inductive conclusions [from first principles] will amount to moral certainty, whenever our experience has been uniform, and the number of cases examined sufficiently numerous."[64] Reid explained that reason had two degrees, the first of which was the ability to "judge of things self-evident," first principles, and second to "draw conclusions that are not self-evident from those that are." The second sense could be cultivated, but the first, he maintained, was "purely the gift of Heaven, and where Heaven has not given it, no education can supply the want," though proper cultivation of a dormant faculty could be achieved.[65]

Stewart, too, maintained that intuition, moral taste, and moral beauty worked as an active power in the mind, and he encouraged literature and the use of imagination as important intellectual pursuits in discovering and applying moral improvements.[66] He did not attempt to negate Hume's position and defended him against charges of atheism. Stewart believed that it was the opposing argument, that material objects did possess a causal power and reason or empiricism could explain everything, that undermined the Christian faith "by endowing matter with an autonomy that removes its dependence upon the divine will." He counterargued that Hume was in fact defending the existence and power of God by his supposed skepticism.[67] Brown also did not believe that Hume was suggesting that we cannot have a concept of power, or cause and effect, but that he simply could not ascertain where it came from. Thus, again, it was the problem of empiricism and reason alone that he saw Hume as pointing out, and Brown concluded that the source of these unexplainable aspects of knowledge were given from intuition, "an innate disposition to believe in the uniformity of nature. . . . Stewart and Brown thus both accept Hume's arguments to the effect that reason is unable to establish the truth of basic beliefs such as that every event has a cause and that the laws of nature are uniform and unchanging."[68] In this they supported Hume against accusations of atheism and wove his views into a narrative of the inadequacy of reason alone to discern the laws of God in action and the power of intuition to discern truth even when reason failed. Both of these interpretations would be highly palatable to the Transcendentalists and one route they used to marry Scottish Realism with the German response, rather than rejecting the Scottish philosophy in favor of the German.

These views allowed for several important conclusions. First, as an active power and part of reason rather than understanding, intuition would naturally lead to deeds, not merely contemplation or internalization. Second, intuition came directly from God. Hence, intuition led to truth, not simply to utility. In this way, "intuition of larger realities like the nature of man and . . . the way we ought to think, feel, and act toward others is an experience of truth."[69] And, third, the stance that character development, including improvement in environment and opportunity as well as conscious practice, could produce character in an individual who circumstantially appeared deprived of the necessary faculties, such as enslaved Black people or women without educational resources. Emerson believed that intuition "teaches us fundamental principles which cannot be 'improved' by the 'advancement of time or knowledge." The moral sense discerned these first principles as "intuitively certain and . . . absolute. The 'moral sense' is 'coextensive and coeval' with mind" and thus absolutely knowable by the mind.[70] When understood in this way, the Transcendentalists' insistence that intuition was a valid guide to a moral life becomes a better-supported hypothesis, and so does the possibility of it becoming a driving force in social action.

These Scottish Common Sense views on epistemology and the mind in which the Transcendentalists were educated in their university formation, through parental tutelage, or self-study formed the basis of their approach to philosophical questions of the human mind and faculties, epistemology, the emotions, and their role in morals. In most of these areas, the Transcendentalists retained the Scottish framework. Some solutions the Scottish philosophy offered were not quite satisfactory, however. Questions on the origin of emotion, the perception of divinity and relation of the world with divine forces, the interconnection of humanity with the divine, and the substance of the world were issues that the Common Sense writers had left unexplored to the depths the Transcendentalists wished to pursue them. For these answers, they delved into the Idealist philosophy emerging from Germany.

Chapter Two
GERMAN PHILOSOPHY OF CHARACTER

In 1841, in his essay "The Over-Soul," Ralph Waldo Emerson pondered the difference he perceived between the philosophy of the Scottish Common Sense School and that which he was learning from the German Idealists: "The great distinction . . . between philosophers like Spinoza, Kant, and Coleridge, and philosophers like Locke, Paley, Mackintosh, and Stewart, . . . is, that one class speak *from within*, or from experience, as parties and possessors of the fact; and the other class, *from without*, as spectators merely, or perhaps as acquainted with the fact on the evidence of third persons."[1] This, for Emerson, described the deficiencies he saw in philosophies such as Scottish Common Sense that inspired him to look for further answers in the writings of the German Idealists. A sense of internal knowledge of the spiritual realm, more than external speculation on material cause and effect, was for most of the Transcendentalists even more essential for guiding life, interacting with others, and forming an understanding of the world than was knowledge of the physical world. From the metaphysics of German Idealism, they gathered greater insight into ways of viewing these aspects of the world, divinity, and human experience and expanded their philosophy into more immaterial realms. Most important, from the German writers the Transcendentalists garnered a belief in internal sources of knowledge; their interpretation of philosophical idealism; aesthetics as an act of judgment; the belief of the external world as a vital and creative energy; and the external world as a manifestation of the divine.

On the first point, that of internal sources of knowledge, Immanuel Kant set the stage. He offered the suggestion of a priori principles that formed the basis of knowledge. A priori principles, to Kant, were concepts, or "categories," for which there can be no justification found in experience but which constitute the form of experience in advance. "We can see such an a priori origin not merely in judgments, but even in some concepts," Kant stated. He argued that "if from your experiential concept of a *body* you gradually omit everything that is empirical in a body—the color, the hardness or softness, the weight, even the impenetrability—there yet remains the *space* that was occupied by the body ... and this space you cannot omit [from the concept]."[2] Kant argued that a priori forms of thought, including space, time, and the categories of substantiality, unity, causality, and necessity, among others, must be assumed for any connected experience to be possible. However, he agreed with Hume's basic stance that knowledge could only reflect the realm of experience, which Kant called the phenomenal realm, and should not seek to explain any reality beyond the world as it appears to the human mind. This reality, Kant conceded, may not be all there was to ultimate reality but must be accepted as the only reality knowable to the human mind.

Although things-in-themselves were ultimately unknowable, as Hume had contended, Kant believed that a priori principles allowed us to have objective knowledge of the "appearances" of these things, insofar as they were represented in the mind through sensory experience. "Everything intuited in space or time, and hence all objects of an experience possible for us, are nothing but appearances," he wrote, "i.e., they are mere presentations that . . . have no existence with an intrinsic basis" outside human thought.[3] The belief that objects in time and space had reality as things-in-themselves, Kant called "transcendental idealism." He clarified that he was not arguing for what he called "empirical idealism," which he believed would state that all we know "is the existence of our own minds and our temporally ordered mental states" while only inferring "the existence of objects 'outside' us in space."[4] Despite his attempts to clarify, "the meaning and significance of Kant's 'transcendental idealism' has been a subject of controversy," and the very first review of the work placed it in line with Berkeley's empirical idealism. Although Kant attempted to explain his position in the second edition of the *Critique of Pure Reason*, the details of his argument remain open to various interpretations on his exact meaning.[5]

Emerson indicated how he personally viewed Kant's statements on his theory of transcendental idealism when Emerson, after pointing out that Transcendentalism earned its name from Kant's transcendental idealism, attempted to describe what this meant. Kant illustrated, he explained, that unlike philosophers such as John Locke who believed "there was nothing in the intellect which was not previously in the experience of the senses," there was actually "a very important class of ideas, or imperative forms, which did not come by experience, but through which experience was acquired." These, as Emerson understood it, "were intuitions of the mind itself." And thus "in Europe and America . . . whatever belongs to the class of intuitive thought, is popularly called at the present day *Transcendental*."[6] It is questionable whether Kant would have agreed with this broad categorization, but Emerson's statement indicates how it was culturally understood in his time and within the Transcendentalist circle.

Emerson developed these thoughts through a discussion on the difference between "Materialists and Idealists." He stated that Idealist philosophy was founded "on consciousness" and perceived that "the senses are not final, and say the senses give us representations of things, but what are the things themselves, they cannot tell." This, Emerson concluded, emphasized "the power of Thought and Will, on inspiration, on miracle, on individual culture. . . . The idealist, in speaking of events, sees them as spirits. He does not deny the sensuous fact; by no means, but he will not see that alone."[7] Emerson understood Kant not as denying sensory experience and hence not entirely intuitive but as combining what one perceived through the senses with intuitive knowledge concerning its meaning. What begins to appear from Emerson's interpretation is a kind of Kantian recasting of Plato's Forms, of the visible world manifesting types of eternal ideas that existed above and beyond what was perceived but could be understood through this perception. For Emerson, Kant was contributing to the development of his idea of the "Over-Soul," Emerson's term for the unified life of God and each individual human and natural manifestation of this divine life. Intuitions, to Emerson, thus entered the mind from an external source where they existed independently from and antecedent to the minds that received them; they did not develop within the mind itself. Unlike Kant, who maintained that meanings and realities beyond experience could be speculated but not assumed to be actually known, Emerson believed that the meaning and spiritual nature of a Form could be reliably known through intuition after the sensory perception of it was received.

Kant, in fact, postulated a difference between the material world and the world of free action associated with the human mind, embracing a theory of duality. He believed that mind and matter must be understood in distinct ways, which Eduardo Molina has categorized as "canonical" or "practical" life, by which Kant distinguished the life of beings driven by desire; biological life as related to non-self-driven organisms; and an aesthetic definition related to the experience of feeling animation.[8] "*Life*," Kant stated, "is the faculty of a being to act in accordance with laws of the faculty of desire" and to become "*by means of its representations the cause of the reality of the objects of these representations.*"[9] What made life possible, he believed, must be intelligible and supersensible. The supersensible ground of life, freedom, and morality could not, however, be known—as it had no empirical basis—but only speculatively thought about by means of reason. According to Kant's understanding, reason could not explain its own supersensible ground because it existed outside the bounds of what was knowable.

Madame de Staël described Kant's stance in this way: "Far from rejecting experience, Kant considers the business of life as nothing but the action of our innate faculties upon the several sorts of knowledge which come to us from without."[10] From her account, the Transcendentalists acquired an interpretation that stressed the importance of the physical world and the role of the senses, but also the suggestion that the internal action of the mind acted on the world and, in some fashion, created the reality experienced. This suggestion of an eternal connection with a supersensible world clothed in visible forms resonated with the Transcendentalists. Emerson reflected on it in his statement that "philosophically considered, the universe is composed of Nature, and the Soul," with his definition of "nature" corresponding to Kant's organized beings and "soul" corresponding to Kant's categorization of canonical/practical life.[11] Kant's assertions that philosophical speculation must "explain the distinction between truth and illusion entirely within the realm of experience itself" and not stray into the metaphysical was also important for maintaining the Transcendentalists' insistence on the importance of nature and connection with the natural world so as to acquire knowledge.[12]

Where Kant differed from what the Transcendentalists would come to believe was in his argument that the knowable world was not a conscious, living force, because life in the practical sense could be experienced only as existing in the mind. The Transcendentalists, by contrast, informed by later Idealist philosophers, came increasingly to believe that the material world was a manifestation of the divine mind. In this way the material world was, in fact, a demonstration of canonical/practical life and not only of biological life, though not quite an independent canonical life in itself. However, the role of the world in unfolding the development of human reason was an idea that they carried forward, despite this modification.

Also discernible in Kant is inspiration for the Transcendentalists' shift away from pure reason as the most important faculty of the human mind. This change came from Kant's introduction of a new angle from which to approach the question of aesthetics, which played into his conception of character, particularly in relation to gender, and the role of taste, intuition, or emotion in shaping character. The philosophical debate surrounding the concept of aesthetics occurred between those who believed that aesthetics was founded on emotional perception and those who believed it issued from reason. These two schools have been designated as "aesthetic rationalism" and "aesthetic sense doctrine," or rationalists and sentimentalists.[13] Rationalists argued that objects were judged to be beautiful or actions virtuous by applying independent principles of beauty and reasoning as to whether the object or action in question aligned with those principles or whether it served a useful purpose. In contrast, Kant presented aesthetics as a matter of taste, not of reason. Taste was connected with individual interest, stemming from desire, or a judgment as to whether the object or action would be beneficial to the individual, but it did not depend on reason. For, Kant explained, if someone read him a poem that did not please him, no amount of reasoning based on a priori rules or proofs could make the poem appeal to him.[14] The feeling of animation inspired by an aesthetic perception was a distinct third definition in Kant's conception of life. As an experience unique to self-driven beings of canonical life, taste was where Kant believed aesthetics must be based, for such animation was not present in mere biological existence.[15] Aesthetic judgments were related to moral judgments, for a judgment on beauty often preceded a judgment on what was good, right, and moral.

Emerson agreed with this view of aesthetics as one of taste rather than reason, writing, "This love of beauty is Taste." And this stood in his conception as well as something necessary for the creation of true aesthetics. In his words, "The presence of a higher, namely, of the spiritual element is essential to its perfection."[16] This, in his understanding, equaled the whisperings of the divine in human consciousness, the self-driven element of a living being choosing beauty, truth, goodness, and also morality.

Inspired by Kant's writings on aesthetics and taste, Madame de Staël maintained that Kant's philosophy was acting to "re-establish primitive truths and spontaneous activity in the soul, conscience in morals, and the ideal in the arts."[17] By rejecting a Lockean worldview of the human mind as limited to sensuous input, she believed Kant was restoring autonomy to the human mind and elevating non-sensory experience through his suggestion that biological and canonical life be viewed as separate entities. The Transcendentalists, too, found inspiring hypotheses in Kant on how the human mind grasps experience that the physical senses cannot prove, that deeper meanings, or things-in-themselves, existed behind perceived objects, and that canonical, or perhaps ultimate, life took place in a realm removed from, while still connected to, the material experience of it. Several important connotations of these beliefs that the Transcendentalists would carry forward were the ability of individuals to shape the world around them, the veracity and importance of individual intuition in discovering beauty and thus morality and applying it in action, and the idea that life and the mind existed and continued outside physical forms.

The Transcendentalists' belief in the external world as a vital and creative energy is closer to the philosophy of Johann Herder than to Kant. Whereas Emerson was more heavily influenced by Kant, Herder's philosophy had a significant impact on Margaret Fuller's thinking and was an inspiration to Elizabeth Palmer Peabody. When writing his own philosophical works, Herder addressed character development more as a religious and cultural phenomenon than one of aesthetics or theories of knowledge. Following in the philosophical tradition of the Jewish-Dutch philosopher Baruch Spinoza, who argued for a single substance comprising all life, mind, and matter, Herder embraced a kind of vitalistic monism. He viewed the entire world as participating in and possessing a single, undivided, life force—that of God. In contrast to Spinoza, however, Herder treated this dynamic and intelligent substance of the world as a constantly developing and organizing force, intrinsically connected with the Christian God toward whom all life was teleologically oriented. Herder believed that the mental and physical aspects of life should not be viewed as separate substances, as Kant had contended, but as varying degrees of development, or organization, in this life force. Therefore, both the events of the natural world and the functioning of the intellectual faculties issued from the same single source and cooperated together rather than the one driving the other. This single divine life, Herder posited, was actively operating at every moment in the minutest item of creation.

Character, the concept that informed so much of the Transcendentalists' eclectic philosophical investigation and drove their political application of it, was to Herder the individual level of participation in this substantive life force—*die Kräfte*, a term for the unified and unifying powers of the world, encompassing metaphysical, physiological, gravitational, and electrical fields. The highest *Kraft* of all in Herder's conception was God himself, with the subsidiary powers being manifestations of one ultimate power. In contrast with spatial or linear concepts of time and experience as physical sensation followed by mental reasoning, Herder suggested that time was "a flow of immense depths" consisting of "layered or bundled multiple complexities" in which perception participated. Perception was neither an ocular event nor a mental reaction. It was a "comprehensive feeling" of timeless reality, in which current sense, memory, past, present, and even future coexisted. Thus, Herder argued, experience was never a single event of the senses or of reason but a holistic participation and interaction with "continuous multiplicities," and the individual was "a power in the universal system of powers, a being in the inconceivable harmony of some world of God."[18] With this suggestion, Herder moved the conception of character into greatly expanded regions, outside individual experience by a single human mind and into a fluid interaction with all life, time, and space.

Character development seen as participation in die Kräfte laid out the possibility that such development was not a singular undertaking but a cumulative effect across time and space—in Herder's words, a "chain of improvement that extends through the whole kind." This accorded with his general teleological view of history, progressing toward a discernible and achievable goal, that of the development of humanity to the full extent of its capabilities in the various landscapes and cultures of the world. This goal was also, Herder stated, an undertaking for which humans alone were responsible. For although linked with the single life force of the world, they should not expect to be aided by divine intervention through miracles or sudden transformations. Man was, rather, "what he was capable of rendering himself, what he had the will and the power to become."[19] The state of harmony was achieved through an ongoing process of "falling to the right, and to the left," or tending toward one extreme or another, until an equilibrium of powers was reached and man realized himself in harmony within his own mind, with others, and with nature.[20] In these concepts now emerged the philosophy of self-driven sanctification, *bildung*, so essential to the Transcendentalists' reform convictions.

This process of finding the balance of powers and achieving harmony of faculties that Herder described included an expansion of freedom and opportunity for non-white races and women. Herder did not believe the historical development of character and society must follow European precedents but that all peoples were provided for and guided each by their individual environment, cultures, and histories, to become exactly what they had been created to be. Regarding women's place in this teleological story, Herder thought that as men grew less rude and brutal, women required less strict protection and limitation in their sphere of activities and thus were more able to develop their own characters and talents. Both genders participated in the advancement of humanity, and when this point of full harmony was reached, it signaled the consummation of human purpose, the ultimate goal of history. The greatest achievement in life, Herder believed, lay in "the moral improvement of human minds."[21] In this way God was revealed, and humanity became fully human, their powers developed, and the objective of history achieved. In these areas, Herder's philosophy contributed toward the Transcendentalists' conception of an interconnected world, material life as participation in currents of spirit, and the joint effort of humanity in a cumulative bildung. All of these beliefs supported a reform ethos, a drive for racial equality to allow participation in this universal goal, and the important role of communion with all aspects of *die Kräfte* in the process known as bildung.

The final point of Idealism most essential to the Transcendentalists, the proposition of the external world as a manifestation of the divine, was articulated by Georg W. F. Hegel. He expanded from what Manfred Kuehn has described as Kant's "piecemeal" revision of Scottish Common Sense and Hume, advocating replacing even transcendental idealism with the concept of absolute idealism, an ideal basis of the world as a whole, with the mind, in a sense, containing its own experience.[22] Problems of thought presented themselves as conflicting ideas, material versus spiritual, unity versus diversity, and so on. The basis of Hegel's philosophy rests on the system presented in this dialectical method. In this system, he attempted to describe the process of reducing and unifying individual external entities to spiritual universal concepts and forming a unity in consciousness, the unity of *being-for-itself* with *being-in-itself*, in which the individual realized himself as totally free of any division of consciousness and consequently any reliance on external particulars. This progression moved "from consciousness to self-consciousness, to reason, to Spirit, to religion (consciousness of Spirit), and finally to Absolute

Knowing (self-consciousness of Spirit)," more often termed "absolute spirit."[23] By this pathway absolute universal self-consciousness could be achieved. Hegel described this dialectic process as beginning with the subject's perception of an object causing the reaction, or thesis, which would remain an abstract concept. This thesis is then countered by an antithesis, or opposing force, which negates the thesis. The problem is solved by a synthesis of the two opposites, which forms another abstract that together become a concrete universal. This synthesis should not be understood as abolishing one or the other particular, however, but rather forming a new reality out of them, such as father and mother are synthesized in the child or hydrogen and oxygen synthesize to become water. Once a synthesis was reached, reasoning then moves to the next, progressively higher stage of development, repeating the cycle until all forms of knowledge reach the final stage of unity, a universal in which every subject-object dichotomy is abolished and all becomes purely spiritual consciousness.[24]

"Every activity of mind is nothing but a distinct mode of reducing what is external to the inwardness which mind itself is," Hegel wrote, "and it is only by this reduction, by this idealization or assimilation, of what is external that it becomes and is mind."[25] In Hegel's thought, it was only when every concept was separated from its apparent individual materiality and recognized as unified with the universal, immaterial substance of the absolute abstract that its true reality could be understood. If the entirety of the world were already a phenomenon of thought, Hegel believed that this removed the epistemological difficulty of how material objects could be translated into perceptual experience and thus to knowledge. The Transcendentalists interpreted these propositions as suggesting that the world consisted of the activity of the divine mind and that absolute knowledge was reached through the human mind resolving the apparent conflicts of perception until the thought of the divine mind was accurately understood.

Hegel believed that involvement in the world as perceived was an essential aspect of character development, however, a concept that Walt Whitman in particular would advocate. The example of withdrawal from the world, such as that promoted by Jean-Jacques Rousseau in *Émile*, his fictionalized treatise on education, as well as the Christian monastic tradition, Hegel viewed as a hindrance rather than an aid in the pursuit of bildung, or the dialectical process as the conception became in Hegel's system. "Ultimately the discovery is made that spirit finds the goal of its struggle and its harmonization in that very sphere which it made the object of its resistance," he wrote.[26] He offered a model of character development that was applicable to the industrializing world, did not require the pastoral solitude and withdrawal from worldly concerns as did other traditions, nor an alteration in one's state of life. Human interaction, and the constant clamor of conflicting identities and interests, was necessary in Hegel's conception of the self as a dialectical *becoming*. Without the antithesis of the *other*, the externalization of consciousness, and its reunification with the self, the synthesis, the process of universalizing the concept of "I" into pure thought, or spirit, could not be achieved. The more one tried to isolate oneself from this conflict, the less progress would be made in attaining to absolute being. The fewer people achieved this state, the longer it would take for all of humanity to realize this unity in absolute spiritualized understanding and for world events, the world-historical narrative, to demonstrate these facts. In Hegel, then, there clearly surfaced the social obligation of bildung that the Transcendentalists would articulate in America.

"Character," however, was not Hegel's preferred term. Instead, he wrote of *Gemüth* or *Herz*, which can be roughly translated as "mind" and "heart," signifying a sensibility to emotions and impressions, but which has no exact corresponding term in English. Gemüth was an "undeveloped, indeterminate totality of spirit," whereas *character* was "a particular form of will and interest asserting itself" but to no specified aim.[27] Hence, "character" could be either good or bad, and the aim of "developing character" insufficient in its precision. Hegel further explained in footnotes that to develop mere "formal will or subjective freedom" was to cultivate a casual inclination toward something. On the other hand, "substantial, objective will," or "objective freedom," was dedicated to the principles that form the basis of society. This "objective will" led toward development of the pure self, distinct from any particular object and even from temporary conditions that may seem to affect it, such as "youth or age, riches or poverty, a present or a future state." Thus, while seemingly bound to "a fixed point or atom," the pure self was in fact "identical with the absolutely unlimited."[28] In this area Hegel corroborated Herder's conception of a single life force whose manifestation was not ultimately subject to matter, time, space, or material limitations.

Hegel's vision of the role of the self, the individual, in the world process was paradoxical. Whereas Herder concluded that the development of humanity— "whatever may have been the idea [each society] formed of it,"—and every individual exercising his or her faculties and acquiring "a more pleasing and free enjoyment of life,"[29] was the completion of life's purpose, Hegel suggested a view that both valued the individual as well as one that subsumed individuality into a whole. A "world-historical" character, as Hegel described it, was one that encapsulated the historical progress toward absolute spirit reached in that age.[30] The individual human being was therefore a particularized universal. The particular was responsible for furthering the universal, but the universal existed outside and beyond the particular. In this way, the particular was of the utmost importance to the universal, but as a part of the universal and not in its own self. In the context of warfare, it was thus a perspective that retained the significance of individual character even beyond death.

The transference of these philosophies from Germany into the United States was impacted by political developments within Germany itself. The Treaty of Vienna, which concluded the Napoleonic Wars in 1815, ended the French domination of Germany and created the German Confederation, a loose union that contained thirty-nine small German states. Internal political conflicts and the fragmented state of the confederation hindered industrialization, modernization, and reform. Middle-class frustration mounted and fomented democratic movements such as the Burschenschaften, young nationalist and democratic societies that formed at German colleges and universities. In 1819 the conservative Austrian chancellor, Klemens von Metternich, cracked down on the Burschenschaften with the Carlsbad Decrees, which restricted academic freedom and censored the press. Some members of the liberal student body consequently fled the country and, in the case of the subsequently influential German American intellectuals Francis Lieber and Charles Follen, found a new academic home as professors at US universities. Others caught up in these events, such as Hegel, then professor of philosophy at the University of Jena, found himself privately supporting radical policies but was constrained by external pressures to avoid public statements. He publicly reassured government officials that his philosophy contained nothing subversive while privately supporting his politically persecuted students.

In 1848, a year that saw popular revolts across Europe, German university students finally took to the streets in Vienna, joined by members of the middle and working classes, demanding progressive reforms. Despite some initial success, the reform effort largely failed and many of the disillusioned participants emigrated, becoming in the United States a radical body known as the

Forty-Eighters. They were typically well-educated and politically experienced individuals who continued their reforming efforts and political involvement in their new homeland. The number of these who sought refuge in the United States reached nearly five hundred and included such figures as Franz Sigel and Carl Schurz, who both became actively engaged on behalf of the Union cause in the Northern United States, in politics and, during the Civil War, the Union army. The American Forty-Eighters were instrumental in the Union war effort, particularly in mobilizing the larger German American population within the nation. Towns in which a single Forty-Eighter resided showed a 20 to 25 percent increase in enlistments and a 2 percent lower desertion rate than those towns that lacked the presence of a Forty-Eighter. The research also suggests, less conclusively, that the Forty-Eighters were responsible for garnering support for the newly formed Republican Party prior to the Civil War and for swaying the Midwestern states for Abraham Lincoln in the election of 1860.[31]

German philosophies also came into wide circulation in the United States through the writings of Madame de Staël. Exiled from France under Napoleon, de Staël lived for seven years in Germany, meeting many prominent intellectual figures such as Goethe and Schelling. In 1810, in close collaboration with August Wilhelm Schlegel, she completed *De l'Allemagne*, a treatment of the cultural life of Germany during Sturm und Drang, the literary and artistic movement that heralded the beginnings of Romanticism in Germany.[32] *De l'Allemagne* covered the nation's manners, customs, and morals and its geography, university system, literature, art, philosophy, and religion. It was printed in translation in the United States under the title *Germany* in 1814.

De Staël devoted one chapter exclusively to Kant and another to Herder. De Staël derived her understanding of Kant through the retrospection of the post-Kantian movement and represented his philosophy of transcendental idealism as being closer to the later absolute idealist framework than it was in actuality. This de Staëlian reading of Kant was the one that consequently took hold in the United States among American thinkers such as Emerson, a philosophical inaccuracy that scholars of the Transcendentalist movement have critiqued, and many Americans believed themselves Kantians when they actually differed considerably from his true philosophy. Kant, de Staël stated, wished to free philosophy from materialism, the "empire of external objects," "personal interest," and merely "agreeable" or utilitarian, views of philosophers such as John Locke and René Descartes.[33] She was not interested in the technical aspects of Kant's theories on knowledge and the process of knowing but focused on what she believed was the core of his philosophy, the freeing of sentiment, or intuitive feeling, from the shackles of skepticism. With this interpretation, she laid out a detailed, if not precise, account of Kant's three *Critiques*.

De Staël treated Herder in a historical and theological light, reviewing his writings in history, literature, and theology. His *Philosophy of the History of Mankind*, de Staël declared, "has more fascination in it than almost any other German production." She also praised his *On the Spirit of Hebrew Poetry*, a work of biblical historicism, and briefly addressed his theological writings. From any of his works, she concluded, one could perceive "that there never was a better man."[34] The first major work of Hegel, *The Phenomenology of Spirit*, was published a few years before de Staël left Germany, and he did not figure in her work. However, her American editor and annotator, O. W. Wight, subsequently inserted into her book a fifteen-page appendix on Hegel, his major works, the foundational concepts of his philosophical system, and the various Hegelian schools of thought that developed soon after Hegel's death, thus bringing Hegel to de Staël's American readership as well.

De Staël's *Germany* inspired a surge of interest in German culture in the United States. The year after her book appeared, the first of a coterie of students left the United States, mainly from the Northeast, to pursue higher education at the German universities she described, where they studied under the intellectual disciples of Herder and, in some cases, directly under Hegel. Between 1815 and 1850, at least 250 Americans attended German universities, among them Edward Everett, George Bancroft, Henry Wadsworth Longfellow, Frederic Henry Hedge, Joseph Cogswell, George Ticknor, James Elliot Cabot, William Emerson, and others, all of them subsequently men of intellectual stature in the Northern United States. The majority of Americans enrolling in German universities came from the Northeast, followed by the Midwest and West, with the smallest number enrolling from the South. Other prominent Americans, such as Congressman Charles Sumner and the educational reformer Horace Mann, visited Germany on various occasions to study its education, legal, or political systems, art, or scenery, independent of university affiliations.

More than 50 percent of American graduates from German universities returned to the United States to take professorships at American universities, joined by German political refugees such as Carl Beck, Charles Follen, and Francis Lieber. Harvard boasted a large share of these German-trained professors. Everett served as professor of Greek and later president of the university. Longfellow taught French, Spanish, Italian, and belles lettres. Cogswell became professor of geology and mineralogy. Cabot taught philosophy, and Hedge was professor of ecclesiastical history. German immigrants Louis Agassiz served as professor of zoology and geology, and Charles Follen became the first professor of German in the United States with his appointment at Harvard in 1825. Ticknor, Everett, and Cogswell also successfully negotiated with Goethe, with whom they had formed an acquaintance while in Germany, to donate a twenty-volume set of his works to the Harvard library. Francis Lieber taught at South Carolina College and subsequently as professor of history and political science at Columbia College in New York, where he was recruited during the Civil War to write a new military code of conduct for the Union armies and presented Lincoln with an honorary degree. In addition to their home colleges, many of these professors regularly delivered lectures, orations, and commencement addresses at other colleges in the United States, such as Williams and Brown, and in 1823, Bancroft and Cogswell organized their own private school, the Round Hill School at Northampton, Massachusetts, which enrolled a total of 293 students during its eleven years of operation. The Andover Theological Seminary and Amherst College in Massachusetts also boasted a concentration of German influence. The German political refugee Frederick A. Rauch, a former professor at the University of Heidelberg, thorough student of Kant and Hegel's writings, and author of the first American work on Hegelianism, brought much German philosophical influence into the Union Theological Seminary in New York, along with Henry Boynton Smith, Philip Schaff, and William Shedd, as well as to the German Reformed Seminary in Mercersburg, Pennsylvania, which subsequently became Marshall College in 1836 with Rauch as president.

Their prevalence in academia did not mean that these German-educated Americans and German immigrants faced no initial resistance to the reforms and the new viewpoints they wished to teach within colleges still largely aligned with Scottish Common Sense and concerned about heretical strains within Idealism. During this period, the major universities were affiliated with, or often unofficially dominated by, religious denominations, such as Harvard's relationship with Unitarianism, Yale with the Congregationalists, and Princeton with Presbyterians. The religious leanings of such colleges were initially less than welcoming of the German influence, for alongside the philosophies themselves, other aspects of German thought were penetrating

US culture, some of which the higher circles in university management deemed subversive and heretical.

Particularly concerning was the German Higher Criticism, one path within the historicist tradition, which studied the Bible as a historical text that had issued from within its contexts of ancient Hebrew culture. To many evangelical Protestant Americans, these studies seemed to desacralize the foundation of Christianity and implied that the Bible was merely a human work, full of cultural follies and prejudices. Scholars of the Higher Criticism brought out such disturbing suggestions as multiple authorship of Genesis, long believed to have been written by Moses, and the creation and insertion of books out of chronological order. Worried American Christians believed that this approach undermined their religion and encouraged questioning the divinity of Christ, and they saw the German writers as "infidels" whose influence was leading students to pantheism. Thus, despite the significant German presence among the Harvard faculty, American proponents of German thought were not always welcomed, as in the case of Ralph Waldo Emerson, whom Andrews Norton, a theologian commonly nicknamed the "Unitarian Pope," succeeded in banning from speaking on the Harvard campus following Emerson's Divinity School Address in 1838. In this address Emerson reflected the higher criticism with such concerning statements as, "Historical Christianity has fallen into the error that corrupts all attempts to communicate religion" and dwelt with "noxious exaggeration" on the "*person* of Jesus" rather than his message.[35] This was unacceptable. For, Norton wrote, "woe to our posterity, woe to the church, woe to the country, woe to the world" should "the departments of instruction ever come to be filled with transcendental infidels."[36]

Consequently, most American universities did not implement a separate class on German philosophy. Harvard was the first to do so in 1873, nearly a decade after the Civil War, listing classes in its catalog on the "schools of Descartes and Kant" and on "modern German philosophy."[37] At most, before and during the Civil War, American universities included German in their suite of courses on modern languages, allowing students to pursue reading German works on their own. The Harvard library contained at least fifteen volumes in German by the Civil War years, ranging from an "ABC" pamphlet on the German language for children, phonics, easy and intermediate German readers containing excerpts from writers including Herder, Goethe, Schiller, and Richter, as well as Goethe's own collected works, Fichte's *The Characteristics of the Present Age*, and books in the German language on Voltaire, solar clocks, and the Persian poem collection *Divan of Hafiz*.[38]

In the university curriculum, philosophy remained the final year's capstone class, being subdivided into moral philosophy and natural philosophy. The first category covered such topics as logic, ethics, metaphysics, and what was variously called intellectual or mental philosophy or psychology that included epistemology as well as the mind's functions. The second category covered the natural sciences. This latter class generally allowed students a great deal of flexibility and innovation in their studies. The German influence was also strongly felt among the scientific community, although these intellectual transformations also fell under the heading of natural philosophy. The library records from Harvard during the period of 1828 to 1845 show a spike in both the number of Idealist titles owned, and the number borrowed, alongside the writings of Cambridge Platonists such as Ralph Cudworth, along with James Marsh's edition of Coleridge's *Aids to Reflection*, indicating that professors and scholars there—including Emerson, Thoreau, and James Freeman Clarke—were reading additional philosophical works besides those required by the curriculum.[39]

The slow infiltration of these ideas and their gradual acceptance at the university level can best be discerned in some of the philosophical textbooks appearing during this transition period. Henry Tappan's 1844 text *The Elements of Logic* adopted a Kantian approach to the will, rejecting earlier texts' determinist orientation. James Walker, professor of ethics at Harvard during the 1840s, issued an edition of Dugald Stewart's *Philosophy of the Active and Moral Powers of Man*; although he was a loyal Scottish Realist and did not feel called upon to delve into the "German speculations . . . not yet naturalized amongst us," if any of his students wished to do so he recommended they read Kant's *Groundwork of the Metaphysics of Morals* and *Critique of Practical Reason*, the German theologian Friedrich Schleiermacher's writing on ethics, and Hegel's *Elements of the Philosophy of Right*.[40] The presidents of Union College and Williams College likewise demonstrated a Kantian understanding of the will, freedom, and right. Laurens Perseus Hickok, author of numerous works, including *Rational Psychology, Empirical Psychology*, and *Rational Cosmology*, relied heavily on Kant, as did Joseph Haven in his 1857 *Mental Philosophy*, which also included Herder, Goethe, and Schelling, among others. Thus, although on the surface there appeared little alteration in the instruction of philosophy at the university level, the content of the instruction itself was slowly being transformed under the influence of the German philosophers.

Outside of academia, interest in Germany's culture, literature, and philosophy continued to grow throughout the United States. Kurt Mueller-Vollmer's research found that from seven scattered annotations and one advertisement of German writings in 1809, by 1839 the appearances of German literature in American publications jumped to one hundred substantial articles, translations of German poetry, and small prose text works, featured across twenty-two different periodicals, such as the *North American Review, Western Messenger, Christian Examiner, The Dial,* and *The American Quarterly*.[41] The Library of Congress historic newspapers database reveals that by the 1840s, the name of Hegel was appearing with some regularity and familiarity. In March 1845, the *New-York Daily Tribune* ran a thorough two-column article on Hegel, which contained a biographical sketch, as well as a brief review of his dialectic and his *Phenomenology*. Aside from Fichte's, the author concluded, "no philosophy is so heroic as that of Hegel."[42] In 1847 Hegel was even being arraigned as a threat to Christianity in a review of the commencement ceremonies of the University of Vermont, where a significant German influence was being felt under the presidency of James Marsh.[43] In 1860, the *Tribune* featured an entire page review of the new publication *Humboldt's Letters to Varnhagen von Ense*, in which the writer took some pains to explain the background philosophy from whence Humboldt's dislike of Hegel, evidenced in his letters, originated. This had the consequence of providing the reader a summary of Hegel's *Philosophy of History*, in which "everything that has ever existed or happened" was reduced "to a stage in the development of 'the idea,'" in the reviewer's words.[44]

Other mentions are cursory, but by their very cursory nature they indicate that the writer expected readers to be familiar with the name of Hegel, if not the general outlines of his philosophy as well. He is referenced in connection with events occurring in Naples during the unification of Italy. A disillusioned antislavery writer quoted Hegel noting that history "is the conflict of ideas, and the victory of the deeper tho't" would at length prevail, which this writer was certain rested with antislavery forces. Other notices merely pointed out that Hegel was born in the same year as the poet William Wordsworth and an unidentified individual named Chalmers; announced the publication of a translation of Hegel's *Logic* in Paris; boasted that Hegel was included in the *New American Cyclopedia* edited by George Ripley and thrown together with a motley assortment of other famous figures ranging from Andrew Jackson and Washington Irving to Sam Houston and Archbishop Hughes; or lamented that there were no philosophers of his rank left living. A California newspaper contained a humorous poem in dialect describing a "lytenant officier" who "reasons mit Hegel und Fitche dat everydings is notting at all."[45] Herder's poem "Dragon-Fly" was translated in the *Anti-Slavery Bugle* in 1856, and four years later the same paper was extolling both Herder and Hegel as examples of the German mind to bolster their case against the immigration restrictions proposed by the Know-Nothing Party. "Would to God *Know Nothingism* knew enough not to restrict the emigration of such men and minds," concluded the author, who revealed his identity to be Parker Pillsbury, the outspoken Transcendentalist minister and social reformer from Massachusetts.[46]

Other writings that further spread knowledge of or were motivated by the German philosophers included George Bancroft's *History of the United States of America, from the Discovery of the American Continent*, a ten-volume work published between 1854 and 1878 that was indebted to Herder's and Hegel's philosophies of history. Bancroft also published translations of the writings of his Göttingen professor Arnold Heeren, a student of Herder, and a series of articles summarizing German literature. In 1833 Francis Lieber published the first volume of his *Encyclopædia Americana: A Popular Dictionary of Arts, Literature, History, Politics, and Biography*, inspired by, and indeed at times copied from, the German *Brockhaus Enzyklopädie* of a similar nature. The encyclopedia contained sixteen contiguous pages on German literature, science, and arts, in addition to separate entries on individual figures. Over time, Lieber's encyclopedia sold 100,000 copies, a similar level of circulation that Bancroft's *History* also reached. President Andrew Jackson is known to have owned a set of Lieber's encyclopedias, as did Abraham Lincoln.[47]

James Marsh, president of the University of Vermont, not only implemented German educational reform, such as the elective system that allowed students to select different course options, but also closely studied Kant and Herder, translating Herder's *Spirit of Hebrew Poetry* in the early 1820s even before his influential annotated edition of Coleridge's *Aids to Reflection* appeared, the book that prompted the first meeting of the Massachusetts Transcendentalists. George Ripley, founder of the experimental settlement of Brook Farm, also oversaw the publication of the fifteen-volume series *Specimens of Foreign Standard Literature*, which included many translations of the post-Kantian German writings. Frederic Henry Hedge's *Prose Writers of Germany* indicated the same interest, and a six-volume edition of Herder's *Zerstreute Blätter* (*Scattered Leaves*) in the original German resided in his personal library, which Harvard acquired after his death. Knowledge and availability of German ideas was not difficult to come by and was gaining in popularity.

Not only were these works circulating within the United States and being read and discussed by the Transcendentalists, but they gave the Transcendentalists a new philosophical language and interpretative slant from which to approach the standard academic fare of Scottish Common Sense. In these German Idealist perspectives, the source of intuitive knowledge was articulated, the substance of life and the world was reexamined, and the participation of the mind and spirit in this world took on new dimensions. These German ideals expanded the Transcendentalists' philosophy into a more universal and interconnected sphere and suggested deeper currents present within nature than only those perceived by the physical senses. The ways in which the Transcendentalists reconciled these two philosophical schools varied between individuals but were to carry significant impact on the country during the Civil War era.

Chapter Three
AMERICAN TRANSCENDENTALIST
PHILOSOPHIES OF CHARACTER

"Self-culture is something possible," the Unitarian minister William Ellery Channing declared in an 1838 lecture. "It is not a dream. It has foundations in our nature," in the ability to self-reflect and to self-direct. These were faculties common to every mind, making self-culture an interest applicable to every human being in any state of life. Channing recognized that he was "the first to unfold the idea of self-culture" to an American audience more familiar with beliefs of sanctification by divine intervention and the inpouring of grace, so he described for them what went into this concept and routes by which it could be achieved.[1] Self-culture, he stated, was moral, religious, intellectual, social, practical, perceptive of beauty, and competent of utterance. The development of these aspects in harmony with one another would result in "the care which every man owes to himself," Channing concluded, "the unfolding and perfecting of his nature."[2] Because he realized that this was a new concept to many of his listeners, Channing dedicated the second half of his lecture to discussing the means available to pursue self-culture. His suggestions included cultivating a strong faith both in God and in the practicality of self-culture, self-awareness, control of the "animal appetites," the society of "superior minds," reading, freeing oneself from the oppression of others' opinions and example, turning one's work into a school of self-discipline and contemplation, political involvement, and formal education.[3] Channing encouraged support of the public school system being implemented by another in the Transcendentalist circle, Horace Mann, and supported public land grants for the purpose of establishing institutes of higher education.

Channing's lecture contained the essential elements that the Transcendentalists who followed him would continue to promote. Taking abstract ideals such as intellectual improvement or receptivity to beauty, Transcendentalism brought them down into the concrete sphere of everyday life, whether that was contemplating the habits of nature at Walden Pond, joining in political activism, or pursuing university education. The Transcendentalists' approach revitalized American "ethical thought" by "convincing individuals to take up morality consciously and freely rather than unthinkingly or grudgingly" and to "organize their lives around these newly reinvigorated moral ideals."[4] The Transcendentalists merged the importance of individual sensory experience and harmonizing the faculties from Scottish Common Sense with the universal goal of advancing the world spirit from German Idealism, charting paths by which individuals might reach this ideal of self-culture, or bildung, the self-driven process of developing one's character. The reconciliation of these philosophies in the minds of Ralph Waldo Emerson, Margaret Fuller, and Walt Whitman (replacing Thoreau in this chapter for reasons explained below) illustrates three of the routes offered in Transcendentalism by which the Scottish and German philosophies were integrated and how they might be applied in individual life.

By the time these disparate philosophical stances reached the American Transcendentalists, they often appeared profoundly opposed to one another. Yet, if there was to be any final truth discoverable in philosophy, the Transcendentalists believed that they were left with the task of merging the approach offered by empiricism and that of idealism into a coherent unity. Richard Petersen points out that Common Sense itself contained many facets, and various Americans interpreted it from starting points already nearer or further from the conceptions of German philosophers. For instance, among those emphasizing the intuitive and divine origins of knowledge presented by the Scots, Petersen identifies the American educators James Walker, professor of moral philosophy and president of Harvard, and Francis Wayland, who was educated at the German-influenced Andover Theological Seminary, served as president of Brown University from 1827 to 1855, and authored one of the period's essential university textbooks, *The Elements of Moral Science* (1835). In contrast, Andrews Norton, professor of biblical criticism and sacred literature at Harvard, and James McCosh, himself from Scotland and the president of Princeton University, which had maintained its Scottish Realist ties since John Witherspoon, Petersen views as stressing Scottish Realism's empirical slant. The Transcendentalists began their philosophical inquiries from the already more intuitionist interpretation of Common Sense given by Walker and Wayland, leaving the gap between its position and the Idealist viewpoint already a smaller one to bridge. Also, as Petersen observes, there were many aspects of Common Sense that the Transcendentalists never felt called upon to challenge, and thus it continued to provide "the broad framework of thought accepted . . . in those areas where they felt no need for innovation."[5] It was the epistemological question of the source and process of knowledge that the Transcendentalists sought to solve. The construct of the mind as a division of distinct faculties, such as reason, understanding, will, and judgment, and the role of intuition as the association of particular moral feelings with certain actions, for instance, were some of the aspects they accepted from the Scottish tradition with little alteration.

How they sought to bridge the remaining gaps varied widely between the individual Transcendentalists such as Emerson, Whitman, and Fuller. These individuals offer a three-way triangulation of interpretation into or between which most of the other Transcendentalists can be fitted and which can be roughly classified as supernatural, natural, and paranormal, with Emerson exemplifying the first, Whitman the second, and Fuller the third. Other Transcendentalists who spoke less explicitly about their understanding of epistemology and philosophies of character can be categorized into these three veins of thought. Thoreau, who remained largely interested in the material realm of day-to-day sensory observation, the ways in which universal laws and morals could be identified in these observations and lived out on an individual level, falls between the interpretations of Emerson and Whitman, hence why Whitman replaces Thoreau in this section. On the other extreme, suggesting a blend of the supernatural and paranormal, the Transcendentalist poet Jones Very took the ideal of unity with divinity so far as to claim that he represented the Second Coming of Christ and was duly placed in an insane asylum for a time (though whether this institutionalization was just or unjust was and is still debated). William Ellery Channing offered a rebuttal to Hume's essay "Of Miracles," in which Hume argued against the role of miracles as proofs for faith. Many Transcendentalists, including Emerson, accepted and agreed with Hume's argument, thus placing Channing even more deeply into the supernatural than Emerson.

This wide spectrum illustrates how varied the results could be of the Transcendentalists' reading and application of the empiricist and idealist strains of philosophy. The most significant factor in determining their different conclusions for synthesizing these strains appears to be which of the German writers they most strongly resonated with or read and understood most thoroughly. For example, Ralph Waldo Emerson and Walt Whitman both followed a more Kantian and Hegelian system in their merging of the two philosophical strands, and Margaret Fuller suggested a viewpoint most indebted to Brown and Herder. Emerson, Whitman, and Fuller offer particularly thorough discussion and insights into the melding of these philosophies and therefore most clearly present these three interpretative threads—the supernatural, natural, and paranormal—for unifying the conflicting ideas to which they were exposed.

Emerson floated three main ideas for resolving the philosophical dissonance. The first was a practical approach, which suggested that philosophical truth was contained in all philosophers' attempts to capture it and that the apparent disagreements among them stemmed not so much from foundational conflict as from the necessary subjectivity of individual restatements of personal experience. The second and third ideas discernible in his writings suggest a greater debt to the theoretical outlines of Hegelian dialectic. The second was to acknowledge an eternal duality of truths, which could be found in the *is* and *is not*, mind and matter, and the body and the soul. The interplay of the two truths in each case resulted in a final synthesis of ultimate truth, experienced on a personal level and varying in manifestation and application between individual lives. Third, Emerson proposed that the discovery of truth was both an individual and communal journey, moving from a lesser truth of empiricism into a higher truth of idealism. Emerson shifted in and out of these three possibilities without a detectable chronological development throughout his life. He was often inconsistent with his statements and either preferred not to or was unable to issue a final conclusion as to which possibility was more correct, leaving the resolution undefined to occur uniquely for each individual.

Underlying these various presentations of Emerson's reconciliation, however, was one important factor that set him most significantly apart from both the position of Reid and his followers and that of Hegel: his reintroduction of a significant religious and spiritual overtone. He maintained Reid's belief in the direct imposition of God in the human mind, echoed Stewart's and Brown's support for the veracity of intuition as the action of God in the human heart, but also argued that the activity, personality, will, and attributes of divinity could be perceived in the natural world through the senses. He wrote, "My debt to my senses is real and constant" but was not an end in itself. Rather, it was the way in which to perceive "the Natural History of the soul incarnate" and see the "splendor of God . . . bursting through each chink and cranny" of the material world.[6] He steered away from the secular possibilities of Hegel's portrayal of spirituality as a synthesis of opposing positions and maintained the importance of Platonic Forms in the universe as a standard for objective truth and morality in the dialectic. The particular manifestation of a Platonic Form was what was perceivable by the senses according to the Common Sense outline, he believed, and hence the material universe of nature remained essential for knowing God and achieving any reliable knowledge. But Emerson also maintained that it required the idealism of the Hegelian dialectic to discern and reach an understanding of the universal qualities of the Platonic Form, the spiritual meaning contained in the material particular.

Emerson's first option for philosophical reconciliation stemmed from Plato. Emerson held Plato in high regard, and one of Emerson's central beliefs was that all true ideas had been present in human thought since Plato's writings. Plato had achieved the ultimate synthesis of all philosophy, Emerson contended, both European and Asian, materialist and idealist, encompassing unity, infinitude, metaphysics, and natural philosophy alike. He accomplished a "wonderful synthesis . . . the union of impossibilities."[7] Therefore, Emerson suggested that modern philosophers were merely rephrasing truths that had been explored before and previously synthesized by the Platonic philosophy of Forms, already existing in each mind as a part of the Over-Soul. Each philosopher—and Emerson listed Bacon, Spinoza, Hume, Schelling, and Kant—sought to propound a philosophy of the mind, but each was "only more or less [an] awkward translator of things in your consciousness, which you have also your way of seeing, perhaps of denominating." And if one philosopher's attempt failed to resonate, "let another try. If Plato cannot, perhaps Spinoza will. If Spinoza cannot, then perhaps Kant."[8] In each philosophy, whatever was true was likewise present in another philosophy and in the individual consciousness as a part of the divine unity. "Read in Plato, and you shall find Christian dogmas. . . . Hegel pre-exists in Proclus, and . . . in Heraclitus and Parmenides," while Swedenborg, Böhme, and Spinoza's tenets reappeared "in men of a similar intellectual elevation throughout history."[9]

Emerson therefore appears to have approached the various strains of philosophy not as being either true or untrue but as subjective efforts at capturing the subjective experience of experience itself. He stated, "Things are, and are not, at the same time.... All the universe over, there is but one thing, this old Two-Face, creator-creature, mind-matter, right-wrong, of which any proposition may be affirmed or denied."[10] Existence was a duality, he was plainly suggesting. But how, or if, one could find ultimate truth in this dualism remained a complicated issue, unless the dualism itself was the answer.

Emerson maintained that for any philosophy to survive, it must at its base describe the familiar experience of every man on the street.[11] Yet how this could be reconciled with the total diversity of philosophers' standpoints on epistemology was less easy to explain. How did both the Common Sense of Reid and the Idealism of Hegel describe the common everyday experience of humans? If Reid had experienced life as Hegel did, it would follow that he would have written a Hegelian philosophy, and vice versa. The best solution that Emerson could find was to suggest that these were, again, two sides of reality. Two facts underpinned the basis of any philosophy, he wrote, "the one, and the two. 1. Unity, or Identity; and, 2. Variety.... Oneness and otherness.... The mind is urged to ask for one cause of many effects; then for the cause of that; and again the cause, diving still into the profound; self-assured that it shall arrive at an absolute and sufficient one,—a one that shall be all." This fact was present in all philosophy, he believed. "East and west" had the same centripetence, ever "urged by an opposite necessity, the mind returns from the one, to that which is not one, but other or many.... In all nations, there are minds which incline to dwell in the conception of the fundamental Unity."[12] In this paragraph, he in effect restated the dialectical process of Hegel's philosophy, that is, the journey of the mind from oneness to otherness and back to oneness, until finally the "one that shall be all," the absolute, was reached. Thus the different philosophies can be conceived of as expressions of different points in the process. Realism can be thought of as being written from the point of otherness and Idealism from the point of oneness, making both true, but opposed, and yet reaching a synthesis in the end.

In this way, even Idealist truth did not demand a denial of the facts of sensation, Emerson contended. What it demanded was a layered vision, a vision of the Platonic Form and an understanding of its spiritual and moral meaning. One need not deny the existence or reality of a table and chairs, for example, "but he looks at these things as the reverse side of the tapestry, as the *other end*, each being a sequel or completion of a spiritual fact which nearly concerns him. This manner of looking at things, transfers every object in nature from an independent and anomalous position without [*sic*] there, into the consciousness."[13] Hence the Realism of Common Sense could accurately portray one level of experience or reality, while Hegelian Idealism described a second level—one the particularized manifestation of the Form, the other its meaning, or universal and spiritual quality. Neither was wrong, and neither was complete in itself. It required both aspects, for "who speaks not clearly to the sense speaks not clearly to the soul," as Emerson frequently quoted a statement by Goethe.[14]

This statement also resembles the resolution of faith with reason articulated at an earlier period by Jonathan Edwards. Emerson was certainly familiar with Edwards's work, as he was a prominent forerunner of Arminian religion in America. Edwards believed that "there can be no spiritual knowledge of that of which there is not first a rational knowledge."[15] Sensory perception was important to Emerson, but it required the activity of God in the individual mind to interpret this perception into its meaning and application, to synthesize it. "The act of seeing and the thing seen, the seer and the spectacle, the subject and the object, are one," Emerson wrote, blending realism and idealism into a position close to Herder's vitalistic monism but with the additional requirement of individual participation to actualize the unity.[16] In other words, God, or the "Over-Soul," in Emerson's terminology, was both the being perceiving and the thing perceived, but this fact would be realized only if the perceiving individual aligned the self with the divine perceiver. In this way, the supposed dichotomy between mind and matter, sensation and perception, could be unified because the truth of each existed within, from, and through the same ultimate existence. The perceptual universe was real and essential, but it had to be perceived by God through the human mind to be perceived correctly, not by the human mind alone.

Like Hegel also suggested, Emerson believed that the realization of and alignment with this divine mind represented a certain progression of the human experience as a whole, moving from a realist to an idealist position, collectively as well as individually. There was no point in experience that was not in some sense true at some time, but it may be nearer or further from ultimate truth. "There are degrees in idealism," Emerson contended. First, one learned to "play with it academically. . . . Then we see in the heyday of youth and poetry that it may be true, that it is true in gleams and fragments.

Then, its countenance waxes stern and grand, and we see that it must be true. It now shows itself ethical and practical. We learn that God IS; that he is in me; and that all things are shadows of him."[17] Thus, "every materialist will be an idealist; but an idealist can never go backward to be a materialist," Emerson asserted. Although he accepted that these two "modes of thinking are both natural," the latter was superior. The material view, he believed, was more apt to error, for it relied on the perhaps specious conclusion of a faulty material sense. Idealism, in contrast, he believed to rely on the divine powers placed within the consciousness.[18] Reid had suggested this also, in his assertion that reason could not explain some aspects of reason itself. As Petersen shows, this intuitionist quality of Common Sense was reflected in Transcendentalism, and for both the realists and the idealists, intuition represented the beginning point of all other mental functions.[19]

The route to ascertain this absolute truth, or first principle, was, to Emerson, the journey of self-reliance, a voyage in which an individual came to trust the complete presence and action of God within the self. It required the courage to read, to weigh, to judge, and to assimilate or discard, as seemed fit, any aspect of others' philosophical statements. "There is a better way than this indolent learning of another. Leave me alone; do not teach me out of Leibnitz or Schelling, and I shall find it all out myself," he wrote.[20] He was not concerned with philosophical exactitude or consistency and snipped, filtered, and reinterpreted as resonated with his personal experience. He went so far as to declare that because of its reliance on God to guide the individual, this was the highest philosophical approach, avowing that "dedication to one thought is quickly odious," and he saw no issue in jumping between Montaigne, Shakespeare, Plutarch, Plotinus, Bacon, Goethe, and Bettine, following whatever representation of truth and thought that fed his soul in the moment.[21]

In defending this nonsystematic system, he chose not to issue a definitive declaration as to how he saw, or experienced, the Common Sense and Idealist positions merging in his own life. It was a journey that each individual would take but one that would present differently in each life—one that, as directed by God, could be trusted without dogmatic adherence to one or another human author. Emerson suggested that each philosopher was attempting to describe this journey, and while each one's route might vary, the end goal was the same, and too great a concern with consistency and system limited, rather than assisted, an individual in discovering the truth of the Over-Soul striving for expression in each philosopher's thought.

Although he contradicted his statements concerning Plato as containing all truth for all time, Emerson also discussed the possibility that the achievements of each philosopher depended on the mass progression that humanity had reached during his particular lifetime, in addition to his personal dialectical journey, echoing the concern of Hegel for historical progress outlined in his *Philosophy of History*. Emerson stated, "The population of the world is a conditional population; not the best, but the best that could live now."[22] Thus, the philosopher of one era could believe and be accepted as if he had propounded the ultimate truth, which could be seen as surpassed by the understanding of truth reached in another age, being part of the dialectical process that happened on an epochal level, according to Hegel's vision of history. Emerson wrote, "An ingenious metaphysical writer, Dr. Stirling of Edinburgh [a biographer of Hegel], has noted that intellectual works in any department breed each other by what he calls *zymosis*, i.e., fermentation. Thus . . . the Elizabethan Age . . . culminated in Shakespeare; so in Germany we have seen a metaphysical *zymosis* culminating in Kant, Schelling, Schleiermacher, Schopenhauer, Hegel, and so ending."[23] Subjective glimpses of truth were worthy stages in the continuing progression of human understanding toward the realization of ultimate truth. If a facet of truth was not ready to be beneficially applied in certain eras, it was not yet revealed. "Whatever does not concern us, is concealed from us," Emerson wrote. "All things and persons are related to us, but according to our nature, they act on us not at once, but in succession, and we are made aware of their presence one at a time."[24] Again, this action took place on a personal and a universal level. If the Scottish Realists had not perceived a truth that the German Idealists later perceived, it was not that the Scots were less worthy or enlightened than the Germans, Emerson suggested, but because the world at the time of Reid was not prepared for the truth that Hegel revealed.

But within each of these three possibilities for philosophical reconciliation that Emerson offered, he emphasized one consistent tenet: that of the trustworthy action of God. One of the core beliefs of Transcendentalism was that God was supremely knowable and constantly communicating himself to humanity through all of existence and experience. All philosophy was an aid in growing the consciousness of this fact, an attempt to explain God's action in the human mind and the natural world. But where there was philosophical disagreement, where philosophical inquiry could not reach, or where humanity had not yet progressed in understanding an ultimate truth, Emerson believed that God could be trusted to fill in these lacks. God was the ultimate explanation and source of all truth, even when apparently unanswerable questions and contradictions confused human understanding.

While also indebted to Hegel's philosophy in his synthesis of materialism with idealism, Walt Whitman applied these ideas in a different way from how Emerson did. Emerson envisioned, and Hegel intended, the dialectic to be a journey away from empiricism into absolute idealism, whereas Whitman saw it as leading into a deeper and fuller sensuous experience of the world, the body, and humanity. Terry Mulcaire describes Hegelianism as representing for Whitman "a way to invigorate Emersonian transcendentalism, removing the lingering phenomenological barrier it left between the individual philosophical subject." Whereas Hegel and Emerson believed as "a founding assumption that the world, known truly, was most like a mind[,] Whitman's variation on this philosophical tradition was that the world, known dialectically not simply by reason, but also by physical, sensuous experience, was most like a human body."[25]

Whitman portrayed this in one of two ways. The first was to present the body as the meeting place between the mind and the world. Knowledge of either resided in and could be discovered only through the body. In a dialectical approach, the body represented the thesis, the thing first known, and the world was the antithesis, the opposition that must be harmonized with the individual body. Synthesis was reached in death, in Whitman's understanding, for with death the body no longer separated one from the world but subsumed the body into the earth and the soul into the world spirit. This perhaps explains his extensive treatment of death in his poetry and his approach to the Civil War particularly, which consistently portrayed the Hegelian dialectic becoming realized in the constant interplay of life and death, the beautiful and grotesque, "the perform'd America" growing dim, "retiring in shadow behind me" while the "unperform'd, more gigantic than ever, advance, advance upon me."[26] The material sights and experiences he described as substances that "mock and elude me." Schemes, politics, triumphs, battles, and deaths melted away, and only the "final substance" remained, the only thing sure and lasting was "the great and strong-possess'd soul," "One's-Self."[27]

The second way that Whitman approached the body as synthesis was to suggest that the two abstract concepts of good and evil were synthesized in the body and the actions carried out by the body, without which they were never incarnated, or realized. Humanity included "all life on earth—touching, including God—including Saviour and Satan." In humankind, in the general soul, was thus contained the all. "Jehovah," the abstract principle, "Christ," its manifestation, and "Satan," its opposite, were synthesized and became in humanity "spirit," these four essences becoming "the square deific."[28] This was a form of reverse dialectic, in which the universals were not taken from the perceived material realm and realized as spiritual but one where spiritual facts were moved from the abstract into the concrete and were manifested, or realized, in the material. Whitman's dialectic thus moved from idealism to realism, from something nearer the standpoint of Hegel into something resembling Reid, rather than Emerson's movement in the opposite direction.

This conception of the human body as synthesizing good and evil comes through extensively in Whitman's writings, the seeming glorification and acceptance of immorality and sin in his poetry, and his attempt to cast a shade of beauty over the most sordid images he painted. Whereas most of the Transcendentalists viewed the progressive journey of spiritualization as one of increasing holiness and nobleness, Whitman disagreed. He brought the dialectic down into the experiences of everyday life, the dirt and disease, sin and death of even the lowest members of society, the prostitutes, the insane, the enslaved. He argued that the problems of the human condition were not finally obstacles to be overcome but potential sources of beauty to be incorporated into an aesthetic view of the world, in which suffering, sorrow, and pain will always be essential moments in an endless and ultimately positive dialectical progress. Whitman strove to show the spiritual side of sexuality, procreation, injury, sin, struggle, and death and presented morality as a matter of taste and an experience of beauty, not as a duty of obligation. All things, the physical and spiritual, the moral and the immoral, were to Whitman the building blocks of the two sides of truth; body and soul, evil and good, met together and manifested in the world only through the human experience as contained within the body.

In an unpublished manuscript for a planned lecture on him, Whitman discussed Hegel's absolute spirit as being "the human soul." This, in Whitman's view, was the only real substance of the world, but the only way to experience the human soul was through the human body. Because of this unity, physical matter was spiritual, and spirit was material. In this, like Emerson, he approached a monism similar to Herder's. "Body and mind are one; an inexplicable paradox, yet no truth truer," he stated.[29] The body and soul interacted with each other. A deep experience of the body led to a spiritual experience, and a spiritual experience led to a deeper experience of the body. Whitman was unique among the Transcendentalists for particularizing spirituality in this way rather than universalizing it, perhaps because of his background as a Quaker, unlike most Transcendentalists, who were Unitarian, and his belief in the Quaker doctrine of the inner light, which Whitman understood as "the foundation of all ... the truth to which you are possibly eligible—namely in *yourself* and your inherent relations."[30] Yet, he still maintained a fundamental unity existed between all people. In speaking from his individual experience, he spoke for all. He was the wounded he cared for; he was the dead he mourned; he was the fugitive slave, the harried prostitute, the marching soldiers, and the mourning mother.

This conviction of human unity carried a unique political application. The most popular current interpretations of Whitman's writings, particularly the collection titled the *Calamus* poems, conclude that Whitman either was part of or advocated for the gay and bisexual community. However, he never agreed to this interpretation of his poetry even when explicitly encouraged to admit as much by a reader who identified as gay, John Addington Symonds, a British biographer and literary critic, with whom he carried on a correspondence for many years. If this is what Whitman was wishing to express, one would expect him to have been relieved to have found a reader who understood him and was sympathetic. Instead, he was troubled by the suggestion and consistently objected to this reading. What Whitman himself stated he wanted his *Calamus* poems to suggest was the importance of love between individuals as the basis for holding the nation together, versus reliance on political institutions, as the nation approached the crisis of Civil War. It was a search for "national unity through magnetic, passionate friendship" between men otherwise divided by region, race, political party, and social status.[31] He explained this in the preface to the 1876 edition of *Leaves of Grass*: "The special meaning of the 'Calamus' ... mainly resides in its political significance," and it was through "comradeship, the beautiful and sane affection of man for man ... that the United States ... are to be the most effectually welded together, intercalated, anneal'd into a living union."[32] This underscores another instance of the political concern the Transcendentalists communicated through the means of statements often today taken as literary or purely personal. As David Reynolds has further pointed out, the *Calamus* poems were not considered shocking at all at the time of printing, with Whitman's expressions being commonly accepted displays of friendship between people of the same sex in the mid-nineteenth century. Even the bowdlerized editions of *Leaves of Grass* that excised the *Children of Adam* poems concerning heterosexual love saw no reason to touch the *Calamus* poems.³³

Whitman's philosophical background and the ideals of unity in diversity and the spirituality of physical experience it provided supported the political unity Whitman wished to encourage. Whitman was speaking from "the universal soul" in which the experience of all sexual longing was felt, expressed, and contained within individual human bodies, and thus to capture this completeness he must write from both female and male sexual desire for the other. The bodies of all were a part of God, in Whitman's vision. As an intense physical experience, sexuality was also a spiritual experience and therefore belonged to the spiritual collective of humanity. So, too, did all intense experiences in the body, reaching from and encompassing birth to death. The body contained all the experience of God one needed and was indeed God's own experience. Again, as with Emerson, Whitman argued that the experiencer and the thing experienced were one and the same, eliminating the problematic gap left by either representationalism or empiricism and reaching a conciliation in a form of monism. For Emerson, the unity consisted in the spiritual natures of each, a second layer of meaning. For Whitman, this unity existed within the first layer, the physical world itself. Emerson's was a panentheistic type of monism; Whitman's was simply pantheistic monism. Hence, to Whitman, the physical world experienced empirically as described by Reid was one and the same with the absolute spirit, manifested as "the human soul," which he derived from Hegel. Whitman saw the very fact of living to be spiritual, to be soul, to be the absolute. Both the sense and the soul perceived, and were, the same thing.

Margaret Fuller's understanding of epistemology, although containing many similar aspects to Emerson's and Whitman's, owed more to Thomas Brown and Johann Herder's philosophies than to those of Reid or Hegel. Instead of the concept of Platonic Forms for reconciling representational knowledge with sensory perception, Fuller reflected the understanding of associationalism found in Brown's writings. The idea of association explained knowledge of unseen things as an emotional reaction that mirrored what a complementary physical perception caused. Thus flowers appeared to the eye as beautiful and evoked the same emotional reaction as did the moral beauty in virtue, and through this association one could empirically perceive and know the universal concept of physical beauty, moral beauty, and the beauty of God. Untouched snow elicited the same emotional response as innocence. The night sky raised the same response as concepts of grandeur and eternity. In this way, the material world taught humanity something concerning the immaterial, and abstract concepts could be concretely perceived. In this understanding, the empirical world and its representations in the mind were distinct, but the connection between knowledge of the one with the reality of the other was proven by emotional intuition.

According to Fuller's close friend and fellow Transcendentalist James Freeman Clarke, this emotional intuition would result in the ability to make a distinction between the *actual* versus the *real* in perception. The first layer of the physical world was perceived *actually*, in terms of "wear and tear . . . false position . . . friction of untoward circumstances," whereas the intuitional realm perceived *really*, in terms of the eternal ideal manifested, or "as God designed them."[34] Fuller similarly categorized the value of literature as lying not so much in "the accuracy of . . . facts" but in being "true to the spirit of the scene."[35] As previously noted, she further commented on this impact when discovering a field covered in brilliant wildflowers: she was unsure whether the "sort of fairyland exultation" it produced in her was due to the sensory stimulation of "the optic nerve, unused to so much gold and crimson," or whether it was produced "symbolically through some meaning dimly seen in the flowers."[36] In this she believed true perception and hence knowledge came through the perceptual and emotional interaction, the associations made in these instances, such as Brown discussed, rather than by empiricism alone.

But Fuller added a unique twist on this concept when she then wove Herder's conception of coexisting layers of existence into this associationalist background. This conception of layers was different from Emerson's, drawn from Plato. Herder's, and thus Fuller's, understanding of a layer was not that of a material appearance backed by a spiritual essence. Rather, it was the idea that the physical world itself contained layers, first a material layer, easily perceived by the acknowledged five senses, and second, a layer of electrical energy, or of magnetic fluids, perceived only by what might now commonly be called a sixth sense but what was at the time termed "animal magnetism." This phrase was coined by the German doctor Franz Anton Mesmer, who believed that all living organisms contained a universal magnetic fluid that was responsible for health, intuition, and what became known as "mesmerism," as well as paranormal phenomena.

Fuller was intrigued by this theory of magnetic forces and the paranormal. This interest was common to many Americans during the period, although Fuller's attention to the topic preceded the reported spirit communication of the Fox sisters in New York that began the major upsurge of Spiritualism across the nation. Fuller indicated interest in Spiritualism as early as 1843 and in mesmerism as early as 1838, when she consulted a mesmerist in the hopes of improving her health. She continued to consult mesmeric and magnetic doctors periodically over the following years as well for treatment of scoliosis.[37] By the time the Fox sisters began their séance career in 1848, Fuller had already departed for Italy. However, as the main body of the Spiritualist movement would also, Fuller recognized the feminist potential contained within the ideology. As popular female mediums such as Cora Scott would discover, when speaking as the voice of departed male spirits, they gained access to public speaking platforms and could convey statements that carried more weight with audiences than if spoken as a female individual. Spiritualism thus opened the door for women's involvement in public speaking, religious humanism, abolition, and many women's rights reforms. Spiritualists agreed with Fuller that susceptibility to magnetic and electrical fields was particularly present in the "female element" and that "nervous disease" could be a sign of developmental ascendency.[38]

Fuller dedicated a substantial portion of her travel diary *Summer on the Lakes* (1843) to discussing a book titled *The Seeress of Prevorst: Revelations concerning the Inward Life of Man, and the Projection of a World of Spirits into Ours, Communicated by Justinus Kerner*. The work was a biography of a German woman, Frederica Hauffe, a patient of Dr. Kerner's, who presented a case of "high nervous excitement" and the "phenomena of clairvoyance and susceptibility of magnetic influences."[39] This manifested as communication with spirits, sensitivity to the "electrical" energy of geographic locations, and the "magnetic influences from other persons" on her. She experienced conditions that Kerner described as "magnetic sleep," which transported her into a "clairvoyant state" and "magnetic trances" and existing "in so deep a somnambulic life, that she was, in fact, never rightly awake." Her own bodily energy was so depleted that the only way to revive her was by nervous "transmission from those of stronger condition, principally from their eyes and the ends of the fingers." Those who wished her ill were likewise capable of depleting her through their negative magnetic atmosphere.[40] Kerner wrote that she perceived "the spirit of things" of which others were ignorant. "She showed this sense of the spirit of metals, plants, animals, and men. Imponderable existences, such as the various colors of the ray, showed distinct influences upon her. The electric fluid was visible and sensible to her when it was not to us."[41] She described the substance of life as existing in the soul, which was pure intelligence, and the body as the "nerve-spirit."

Fuller believed that Hauffe's experience demonstrated an increased development of the brain. This followed Herder's philosophy of the ascending order of life, with higher forms assimilated from the components of the lower, from mineral, plant, animal, to human. The brain represented the highest achievement of the electrical state, evidenced in the seer being able to access the electrical layer of existence. The brain was, Fuller stated, an "immense galvanic battery that can be loaded from above, below, and around;—that engine, not only of perception, but of conception and consecutive thought,—whose right hand is memory, whose life is idea, the crown of nature, the platform from which spirit takes wing." A personal life was merely "one link in a long chain" of being that "the fashioning spirit" was drawing ever "onward to the next state of existence."[42] This electrical or magnetic susceptibility, Fuller believed, represented the next stage of humanity's progression into the deeper layers of knowledge. Fuller suggested that the electrical energy was responsible for emotion and intuition and was the essential ingredient in accurate perception, the key to accessing the deeper meaning present in the physical world, closing the break between empiricism and representationalism. Through the activity of the magnetic fluid, Fuller concluded that the mind and the external world were connected and acted upon each other.

These three Transcendentalists—Emerson, Whitman, and Fuller—each offered a unique resolution and created a distinctive way to combine the solutions reached by the Scottish Realists and the German Idealists. The differences between the approaches of Emerson, Whitman, and Fuller are apparent, with the main variation surfacing through their interpretation and understanding of divine or spiritual aspects of creation. Emerson's approach may be roughly categorized as metaphysical, Whitman's as pantheistic humanism, and Fuller's tended toward spiritualism, understood in the broad sense of "spirits" as unseen energy forces rather than solely disembodied persons. The similarities between their conclusions also rested on this tenet of spirituality, however. They took both the Realist and Idealist philosophical outlines and gave them a greater religious cast. The unity of God with creation, the immediate accessibility of the divine to the human consciousness, and knowledge as progressing toward a deeper experience of the spiritual were beliefs each one of their syntheses were founded upon and were believed to both proceed from and result in. The three affirmed the value of nature: Emerson as Platonic Form, Whitman as body, and Fuller as electrical fields. They each believed that nature contained objective moral lessons that could and would be transmitted to the human consciousness. And through their assertion of the immediate personal access to these lessons, they upheld the absolute value, freedom, and potential of all individuals to acquire moral, religious, and intellectual knowledge.

Their beliefs on how the synthesis was reached in the human mind and through which the human consciousness reconciled the empirical with the representational, the form with the substance and subjective perception with objective knowledge, can be portrayed as divided along a vertical axis. Emerson's area of synthesis existed above creation, in the spiritual Forms and the Over-Soul, and was accessed through divine intuition. Whitman's existed within and through the physical realm with no separation between it and the divine and was accessed through the unified human body-soul. And Fuller's synthesis existed below the surface of the visible world, as the magnetic and electrical impulses that controlled gravitational and energy fields, and was accessed through the nervous system and the emotions. Each from his or her own slant thus presented a similar formation of the world as an essential external creation that, although spiritual, manifested and was experienced as physical but was charged with unseen forces and powers of the divine that interpreted itself accurately in human minds attuned to its influence. These three Transcendentalists merged the Scottish emphasis on experience with the German goal of self-realization to create a focused and well-defined route for Transcendentalist bildung. Whereas Scottish philosophy had not articulated a distinct purpose to experience and German philosophy had largely divorced the method of self-realization from the importance of experience, Transcendentalist bildung created a method both practical and oriented toward a vision beyond the self alone. From individual experience grew self-culture, and out of a society of self-realized individuals came a sociopolitical climate in which all individuals could integrate themselves into these divine forces of the supernatural, natural, and paranormal; self-cultivate a universal moral character; and aid in the progression of human alignment with divine law.

These combined ideals of universal moral character from the Scottish and German philosophers played an essential, if not the deciding, role in generating the Transcendentalists' motivation for social reform and the emphasis placed on the individual experience of the Civil War. As Kent Gramm concluded, Whitman summarized this position by placing the essence of the Civil War "in the imagination."[43] In the imagination, the experience of war could be framed and processed by personal outlook. An individual was the master of his or her own imagination, not a victim, and the experience, filtered through this lens, could be used to better oneself. Bildung, the ideal of education in the broadest sense, encompassing theoretical learning, lived experience, emotional sensibility, and most of all moral character, provided the foundation for all the subsequent reforms to which the Transcendentalists devoted themselves and that so significantly shaped the Civil War era, including and encompassing the war itself.

Transcendentalists most often translated the word "bildung" as self-cultivation, or self-culture, the term brought into the Transcendentalist lexicon by William Ellery Channing in his 1838 lecture on the topic, discussion of which opened this chapter. Given the emphasis on monism and the goal of unification with a divine whole that was demonstrated in the above examination of Emerson, Whitman, and Fuller, this focus on the self initially appears at odds with their philosophy. However, this contrast was reconciled through their belief that self-culture, or bildung, was the necessary route to achieving this individual submersion into the whole and that the individual sanctification of each person was necessary to reach divinization for all. The belief that an individual had the power to create one's own self out of the given faculties of the mind, the intuition of metaphysical influences, and the progressive dialectic was a key tenet of Unitarian theology. Instead of passively waiting for divine grace, an individual could actively achieve self-sanctification. Channing and the Transcendentalists after him seized on these propositions and applied them to numerous aspects of political and social life. Self-culture became a hallmark of the period, Daniel Walker Howe affirms, as it expanded "the number of people who were entitled to an autonomous sense of self" and encouraged them "to construct an identity of their own."[44] Transcendentalist women employed it to include female bildung into the ideal of a universal moral character; notable Black Americans such as Frederick Douglass made use of the concept in shaping and presenting his rise from enslavement to gentility; and the progress of the nation itself was framed in the language of this universal moral character.

The expression, a "self-made" individual, now used to designate a successful financial entrepreneur or a rags-to-riches story, was paradoxically first coined by one of the Transcendentalists' political opponents, the great Southern Whig politician Henry Clay, to describe those whose success was to be found within their own capacities independent of outside circumstances. Although this term originated with a figure far removed from Transcendentalism, the period usage demonstrates that being "self-made" was generally accepted to mean an intellectual value. The concern for self-culture was not egocentric introspection but a powerful social force in the culture and politics of the era. As Ashton Nichols has suggested, Emerson's ideal of self-reliance actually moved the concept beyond personal identity "because each person's actions have consequences that reach far beyond their initial effects, toward what we would have to call a universal response."[45] This universality of the moral character was essential to the entirety of the Transcendentalists' vision for political, social, cultural, and religious renewal, and immersed in the depths of these philosophical outlooks, their reform activity is a natural and logical extension of their epistemology.

Evangelical Christian denominations, particularly Baptists and Methodists, experienced enormous growth during the Second Great Awakening and have been credited as responsible for initiating the antebellum reform movement. However, the Second Great Awakening was most significant in New York State, where several waves of revivals earned it the nickname of the "burned-over district." Yet this was not where the reform movement originated. Evangelical revivals were also present in the South, which nonetheless witnessed only very negligible reform activity. In the North, almost all of the major reform movements originated in Massachusetts, the home state of Unitarianism and Transcendentalism. The evangelical Christians of the period are perhaps responsible for the original oversight of Transcendentalists' and other nonevangelical denominations' involvement in the reform movement. Consistent with the belief in immediate individual conversion, abolitionists influenced by evangelical theology anticipated converting slaveholders immediately to embrace abolition if the cause were presented powerfully enough, whereas nonevangelical churches such as the Lutheran, Episcopalian, and

Catholic, as well as Unitarians and Transcendentalists, believed in a gradual course of conversion and purification. This created the divide between the gradual abolitionists and the immediate abolitionists, who thus sought to undermine the gradual abolitionists' work and contributions.[46]

However, this expectation of a gradual process for self-improvement was in some ways a more realistic and thorough approach and sought to transform circumstances just as much as personal convictions. The Transcendentalists recognized that even a sudden personal conversion was not enough to allow individuals the time and understanding to balance faculties, become in tune with the lessons of nature, and progress toward absolute spirit. It was essential that the opportunity to develop their moral character was given to them. Their environment had to be made as conducive as possible to achieve this development, but they also had to be allowed to self-cultivate for the reform to be complete and personal, not imposed on them by external suasion. The Transcendentalists' reform model was a holistic system of improvement. They believed that personal self-culture was essential for individuals to recognize the need to reform institutions, which must be reformed to enable individuals to pursue self-culture.

Educational reform was among the first, most significant, and long-lasting efforts the Transcendentalists promoted based on the model of self-culture and the belief that divine life and knowledge preexisted in the mind of every individual, waiting only to be nurtured. The first of these educational reforms began with the Transcendentalist James Marsh at the University of Vermont. It was Marsh who annotated Samuel Taylor Coleridge's *Aids to Reflection*, the book that first prompted the younger Concord Transcendentalists to begin meeting to discuss. Informed by Transcendentalism's faith in individual bildung and intuition that was developed from the philosophies of the Scots and Germans, Marsh established the elective system in American universities. The ideal of electives was to encourage students to pursue self-cultivation within the university system based on their individual interests rather than impersonal adherence to "mechanical systems" of education. Marsh believed "it was absurd to expect every young mind to develop itself in just the same way; and equally absurd to confine each one to the same kind and quantity of study." To do so was "to forget the true business of education," which was intended "to develop the mind, and to make it conscious of its own powers." Instead, "whenever a right tendency appeared" in the student, he created a system whereby it could be "allowed the freest room to unfold itself."⁴⁷ Curricula were now to become student-centered, adding discussion to instruction and focusing on the development of students' individual, self-selected bildung, and the furtherance of their individual part in the universal progression toward the absolute.

Marsh's ideal spread rapidly, and during the 1850s and 1860s, many colleges began introducing specific degrees in science or the arts, creating the differentiation between bachelor of science and bachelor of arts degrees. President of Brown University in Rhode Island, Francis Wayland, promoted the change to electives in 1850, arguing that enrollment had dropped because the university was not providing the self-development that young men were seeking. The 1852 catalog of Harvard lists elective courses as available to junior and senior classes and included offerings in German, Spanish, Italian, and Hebrew language study, botany, mineralogy, geology, modern literature, anatomy, chemistry, and zoology.⁴⁸ In 1869, Charles W. Eliot, who, unlike his predecessor, was a great friend and thorough reader of the Transcendentalists, immediately expanded the elective system at Harvard following his appointment as university president. Emerson had, in fact, been invited back to the university in 1866 with an honorary degree and an appointment to serve on the Board of Overseers, and he suggested that the curriculum be expanded to include whatever may serve to inspire men to "a finer life," such as "Language, Rhetoric, Logic, Ethics, Intellectual Philosophy, Poetry, Natural History, Civil History, Political Economy, Technology, Chemistry, Agriculture, Literary History . . . Music and Drawing . . . as well as Mathematics."⁴⁹ Not only does this quotation give an excellent representation of the expansion of course offerings that the Transcendentalist educational ideal envisioned, it also indicates the broadly practical, experiential, and versatile subjects viewed as important for bildung. The year 1870 marked a rapid spread of electives and the development of the credit system as a quantitative measure of degree equivalences. Indicating the regional spread of the method, the University of Michigan introduced the elective system in the 1870s, Yale University in Connecticut in the 1880s, and Washington University in St. Louis in the 1890s. Beginning in the 1870s, William Torrey Harris of the St. Louis Hegelians developed a general and a classical route for a high school diploma as well, which by 1890 had grown to also include a scientific, English, and business emphasis. In 1876, Johns Hopkins University was founded as the first research university in the nation.

The Concord Transcendentalists Elizabeth Peabody, Horace Mann, and Bronson Alcott were also engaged in educational reform based on the ideals of self-culture. In their work at the elementary school level, they promoted "a juvenile version of the act of spiritual reflection as proposed by Coleridge and Marsh," whom Alcott read repeatedly and included in his list for annual reading.[50] They promoted the establishment of a public school system, recognized the educational properties of play for the complete development of the child, and their teaching techniques replaced memorization with interactive methods of learning. Peabody established the first kindergartens in the United States to help foster the playful and exploratory development of young children in every aspect of their person. Margaret Fuller, during her time as a teacher at the Greene Street School in Providence, Rhode Island, took special care to create coeducational classes so her female students could see their strengths in comparison against boys and help them to develop their own creative thinking and writing.

Dorothea Dix was acquainted with several Transcendentalists, including Emerson, and was a close friend of William Ellery Channing, for whom she worked as a governess to his children for several years until founding a school out of her own home. In 1841, she undertook teaching a class in a women's prison in East Cambridge, Massachusetts, and was shocked at the conditions she witnessed there. This experience caused her focus to shift from teaching to care for the mentally ill. In 1843, Dix sent a document titled *Memorial, to the Legislature of Massachusetts*, describing the conditions she had witnessed in the women's prison and giving suggestions for reform. The legislature took note of her memorial and began to implement many of her suggestions. This work expanded into many other states over Dix's lifetime as well. She petitioned before seventeen state legislatures in all for the improvement of prison facilities, humane treatment of the mentally ill, and the recognition that they, too, could be participants in the progression of universal moral character. Samuel Gridley Howe also collaborated with Dix and Mann in education reform, founding educational institutions for children with disabilities. Howe traveled to Europe to study communication methods for those who were deaf and blind and returned to Boston to become director of the Perkins School for the Blind, for which Charles Dickens, touring the United States, had extensive praise. In his book *American Notes*, Dickens recounted the personal history of, and the teaching methods used with, Howe's student Laura Bridgman. She was the first person who was deaf and mute in recorded history who had successfully learned language communication. Dickens quoted extensively from Howe in this book, praising him as "that one man who has made her what she is."[51] Another noteworthy graduate of Perkins was Annie Sullivan, who became tutor to Helen Keller when her parents brought her to the school in 1887 having been inspired by reading Dickens's account of the school and Bridgman's success.[52] The essential Transcendentalist concern for providing opportunities for universal bildung was key to these reforms, as it opposed earlier, more Calvinist views that poverty was a punishment for moral degeneration, that people with mental illness and those who were disabled were cursed, and such populations were incapable of improvement. Mann, Dix, and Howe believed instead that such individuals were an expression of the divine and that their inclusion in universal bildung was vital for all. This conviction drove them to political action and resulted in some of the most successful reforms of the period.

The gymnasium was another movement with ties to the ideal of bildung. Part of the holistic education model emphasized in this concept was physical culture, establishing harmony between the mind and body, with each engaged but not overtaxed. In 1825, Charles Follen, a German expatriate, established the first American gymnasium for the "physical culture" of the students at the Round Hill School in Massachusetts, which had been founded by George Bancroft and Joseph Cogswell following their return from university study in Germany. Francis Lieber followed suit when he founded a swimming school in Boston two years later. Although these specific enterprises were not wildly successful at the time, the principle had been introduced and influenced American schooling and physical training thereafter, with the Transcendentalists continuing to promote physical education such as walking, rowing, riding, and skating as an important aspect of bildung. Thomas Wentworth Higginson became a major advocate of physical education after the Civil War.

The gymnasium as an aspect of self-culture is important to the ongoing historical debate surrounding ideals of manhood in North and South, and between the Civil War and the later imperialist era, for although the ideals can appear similar, the philosophical underpinnings were quite distinct. In the German philosophical context, the gymnasium assisted in creating a well-rounded character. Physical strength and health were an essential component of a fully developed human person, but they were not something to be emphasized over the intellectual faculties. Thus, it differed from Southern ideals of physical dominance to maintain one's honor and control subordinates or from the gospel of muscles and muscular manhood promoted at a later date by those such as Theodore Roosevelt as a sign of evolutionary superiority and virile prowess.

The complexity of the Transcendentalists' political and social utilization of the Scottish framework of the mind and the Idealist conception of the nature of the world and human connection expanded beyond these brief examples, as I will explore in the coming chapters. But even these few examples show that the universality of moral character was the predominant ideal that drove these Transcendentalist reformers. To be a universal ideal, it must be applicable to all, and therefore it was a moral duty not only to cultivate oneself but also to expand opportunities for those in limiting circumstances to pursue self-culture. Only in this way would the whole of humanity balance its collective faculties, connect with the metaphysical currents in the world, and progress toward absolute spirit. What emerges from this overview of the Transcendentalists' merging of Scottish Realism and German Idealism and the reforming impetus it provided them is a philosophical movement that articulated an increasingly spiritual view of the world, a progressively unified view of humanity, a growing conception of the power of thought in creating reality, and a concrete and practical approach for developing such in individuals. This understanding of the Transcendentalists elucidates the intellectual climate and the unique perspectives on the individual, the character, and the self, to which Americans of the Civil War era were heir. From this philosophical basis, the American Civil War was viewed as a time of personal and national vitality, one in which individual actions, ideals, and experiences synthesized into a unified whole and created a more spiritualized world from the elevated thought of the participants.

Chapter Four
PHILOSOPHIES OF GENDER AND FEMININITY

"Sweet sister," wrote Benjamin Brisbane into his teenage sister Addie's autograph book in 1857, "may you be ever sweet, kind, gentle and sincere; not marked by fashion's plate; but guarded in your thoughts, words, acts, and winks, by firm strict principles. . . . Aim to acquire knowledge in order to expand and beautify your own mind and person, and diffuse it to those around you."[1] His parting words, before the family left for a new homestead in the West, thus charged his sister with the importance of developing her character, a common concern referenced in writings from the period. This conceptual sphere was newly open to women. The principles of epistemology, faculties of the mind, and universal moral character from the Scottish and German philosophers guided the overarching vision for human growth and culture. But in practical application, this ideal required frameworks for promoting this growth in character and necessitated the question of how moral character ought to be formed in both men and women. Specific characteristics began to be valued in men based on these models which had not been accepted in earlier periods. Some of these had historically been denigrated in women, but with new frameworks, their presence in the feminine character was now seen in a positive light as well and provided justification for expanding the ideal of self-culture to women. This change can be traced from the Scottish Enlightenment, into Kant's writings, and then to Goethe, who provided an enormously influential model. Margaret Fuller in particular used Goethe's works to craft a detailed vision of bildung, particular to women but with universal implications. These ideals endowed women with an expanded vision of their role and contribution to the Civil War that contrasts considerably with both previous and subsequent structures for guiding feminine conduct during warfare.

That the ideal of self-culture, bildung, was extended to both sexes was a major development of the early nineteenth century and carried significant impact on the political and social culture of the United States during this period. Women strove to bolster their opportunities for self-culture in the home and in public affairs through a new discussion of the distinctive value and completeness of womanhood and its contribution to humanity. Whereas the ideal of a universal moral character of the world-soul and a world-historical character universalized these ideals, the topic of gender particularized them. This tension was ever present in the Transcendentalists' discussion and application. Although their metaphysics opened the possibility of egalitarianism, it also limited their awareness of individual needs and created inconsistencies at times in applying the ideal in daily life and the family circle.

Gender in this era was not a social science, an anthropological interest, or a nature versus nurture type of discussion as is common today. It was not a philosophical problem in the sense that its existence or classification was being challenged. Its philosophical interest was on the qualities that went into making male and female character distinct, which ones the genders were capable of, how they could best be developed, and how these served the entire social structure of human interactions. Thus, it was not an examination of gender as such but of the nuances of gendered experience and character development. In the Transcendentalist formulation of the issue, gender was interpreted as a subset within the broader intellectual movement of bildung, the ideal of self-driven education and sanctification. Gender raised the question of who was capable of bildung, what aspects of a person's character bildung could or could not change, which intellectual faculties the sexes were capable of developing, and how each sex could contribute most successfully to human society and the religious and intellectual advancement of the human race. The Transcendentalists' role in the expansion of character development to women was of great importance in laying a philosophical groundwork that argued such was not only possible but necessary.

Daniel Walker Howe, in his discussion of the role of faculty psychology in the ideals of character during this era, brings up the essential aspect of emotion in the expansion of this ideal beyond its traditional white male boundaries. Early American thinkers such as Benjamin Franklin, Thomas Jefferson, or Jonathan Edwards, he explains, had stressed emotion as a weak, instinctual, and passive power, one that should be repressed lest it distract from the achievements of reason. By the mid-nineteenth century, however, "the *right* emotions" began to be viewed "as part of the solution" rather than a problem in human character.[2] Emerson believed that emotion was essential to character, for, he wrote, "our intellectual and active powers increase with our affection."[3] Emotions were now recognized as an important aspect in the cultivation of benevolent impulses and affections rather than in mere self-interest. Passivity and emotion were thus elevated as essential aspects of character, aspects that women were still seen as possessing to a greater extent than men, but now viewed in the positive rather than negative. Emerson wrote, "In the scale of powers, it is not talent, but sensibility, which is best."[4] The cultivation of these "feminine" faculties could be as essential to the body politic as were what was seen as "masculine" reason and were part of nurturing a receptivity to divine inspiration. Whereas at the nation's founding the predominant thought pattern viewed only landholders, those who were economically self-sufficient, as being truly free and thus possessing the prerequisite for sound judgment, the ideal of self-reliance as an internal trait of character—intellectual and emotional self-sufficiency—shifted this conception. The Jacksonian revolution expanded the category of free men and thus those who were able to act from the dictates of Common Sense, to include unskilled laborers, apprentices, and servants. For the Transcendentalists, this category of freedom expanded even further to embrace "not only women but also children [and] slaves."[5] Once emotion was valued as a form of reason and sentiment as including an act of judgment, their heightened presence in a character ceased to be viewed as a sign of weakness, irrationality, and dependency. Consequently, the conception of freedom and the pool of those believed to possess Common Sense increased considerably, completely abolishing property and income requirements for voters during this period, crossing racial boundaries, and broadening the social value perceived in those formerly dismissed from civic importance.

In the writings of the Scottish thinkers, the interest in gender had viewed it as a social sign of the advancement of civilization. John Millar's *Observations concerning the Distinction of Ranks in Society* (1771) opened with this type of overview of the relationship between the sexes, beginning with the savage society and moving through pastoral cultures, to agricultural societies, and finally to commercial and industrializing nations. In this narrative, "gender relations were historically relative, related to stages of development, not divinely ordained and unchanging."[6] The experience of the individual was not emphasized in this model, which did, however, present nurturing the role and relations of the genders as a matter of national interest. In alignment with Dugald Stewart's emphasis on a general didactic enlightenment, female education was a framework laid out largely by the elite educated classes to encourage the growth of refinement and intellectual engagement among the common people and the expansion of polite culture as a cure for irrationalism.

Millar described what he viewed as the positive station of women in an industrializing society that was "advancing in improvement" and operating to direct their education, character, and manners. Such women, he wrote, "learn to suit their behavior to the circumstances in which they are placed, and to that particular standard of propriety and excellence which is set before them." They would earn respect through diligence and proficiency in the household, "look upon idleness as the greatest blemish in the female character," and be instructed in whatever was "thought conducive to the ornament of private life."[7] His use of the passive voice in these statements makes it clear that the women themselves had little to do with deciding these standards of propriety or excellence or in what topics they were to be instructed.

Still, as a result of this framework for societal progress, education in polite manners, literature, theater, and involvement in voluntary associations were opened to women as a way to encourage their education in the arts of civilized society, thereby creating a sphere in which they could become fit to be the "friends and companions" of their husbands rather than being either enslaved or idolized and become, in turn, a "school for manners" for the masculine population.[8] Although this emphasis promoted a greater degree of cultivation and attention to women's abilities and refinement, it also made women's status "dependent upon, and reflective of, the expressions of masculinity that represented man's economic, social, and moral progression." It did not stress the development of women's character for their own good or create a space in which their contributions could be valued outside their impact on masculine culture. They were "symbolisers rather than . . . agents of progress," who existed in a natural but static state of sensibility, the expression of which depended on men's progress through the stages of savagery to civilization.[9]

However, the conviction that treatment of women was a sign of civilized progress and a greater acknowledgment of the need of mutual affection and respect within marriage and the domestic sphere surely worked to improve women's situation and recognized their contributions to a rather scripted and limited vision of polite society. Most Transcendentalist women did not completely discard this kind of domestic ideal or the implication that home life and female domesticity informed the progress of civilization. But they did establish greater autonomy in their application of the ideal, emphasizing their own personal benefit from it, and expanding the promise of their involvement in self-culture beyond mere polite society into the sphere of political reform, world-historical development, and ultimately the realization of the absolute.

In the Scottish outline for masculine culture, the progression of civilization was manifested largely through industrial and commercial development. In addition to nurturing the refinement of the female character within their homes, men were expected to exchange savage customs for good breeding and manners. They ought to replace "violence with self-control" and physical prowess and honor culture with "the polite gentleman," whose social status rested on his position within commercial society and involvement with benevolent or intellectual clubs and associations.[10] The definition of virtue no longer relied on public deeds or heroic feats for the common good but on the private interaction of individuals in their everyday circle of influence. Adam Smith observed that "the man whom we naturally love and revere the most, is he who joins, to the most perfect command of his own original and selfish feelings, the most exquisite sensibility both to the original and sympathetic feelings of others" and combines amiable and gentle virtues with those that were great, awe-inspiring, and respectable.[11] Thus, he viewed self-command as the essential element of good character but also as relying on emotional sensibility and on reason. Whereas reason was governed by self-interest, sensibility was attuned to the needs and feelings of others and the demands of polite commercial society that could further the interests of the entire civilization.[12] This stance on the masculine virtues contains a closer reflection of the Transcendentalist conception of gendered character than does the Scottish view of feminine virtue, although in this area the Transcendentalists were again interested in more abstract and spiritual refinements than polite society, commercial status, or civilization for its own sake.

Furthermore, to a greater degree than in other European centers of the Enlightenment, the Scottish Enlightenment took place at the universities of

Edinburgh, Aberdeen, and Glasgow, restricting much of the philosophical conversation around gender and social improvement to the male educated classes.[13] The Transcendentalists believed that individuals with a reforming vision would be in the vanguard of self-culture and societal change, yet they also looked to innate characteristics of the people and the natural circumstances surrounding them to fuel this development. They aspired to create an organic movement of lasting social change among the population more than a didactic program to implement from above, such as the Scots envisioned in their writings on the topic of gender in character and education.

In Germany, Kant articulated one of the early discourses on aesthetics that, although not the focus of his work, contained a commentary in relation to the male and female characters and their interaction. Kant was interested in how the gendered differences between men and women influenced the feelings and how these interacted to create the social world in which both coexisted and were drawn one to the other. Thus, he did not write about how gender was shaped, whether conceptions and demonstrations of gender were fluid or static, or what influences created cultural ideals of gender. He took all such as established and approached the interaction between genders as a meeting point of the beautiful and sublime, two distinct but related sensations of taste. He framed this discussion as part of his broader work on aesthetics contained in *Observations on the Feeling of the Beautiful and Sublime* (1764), one of his early writings, produced before he developed other significant aspects of his philosophy such as transcendental idealism, and one that was significantly informed by the French writer Jean-Jacques Rousseau. Women were beautiful and men sublime, Kant concluded, based on the feelings an observer registered when confronted with an ideal manifestation of each gender. These feelings conveyed deeper meaning than mere classification, however, for Kant saw these external impressions as reflecting fundamental internal characteristics of both sexes.

Kant took men to be the standard to which his general statements applied and separated women into a special category for particular comment. To men, Kant granted worthy and profound characteristics. They possessed understanding, boldness, truthfulness, honesty, unselfish service, and courage. They ought to be independent and just. Their achievements should overcome difficulty and cost them effort. Their convictions must be established from deep reflection and prolonged consideration and be weighed carefully. Abstract knowledge belonged to the male field of speculation, he insisted, as did principles, nobility, and true moral virtue. Men inspired esteem in others, not love.[14]

The characteristics that Kant assigned to women were much more trivial and closely connected with his concept of desire in aesthetics, inspired in large part by the child-rearing treatise *Émile*, written by Rousseau. Because Kant believed that their well-being and safety were entirely dependent on men, he argued that women's development was inherently centered on learning how to be most pleasing to men. He believed that they possessed wit, cunning, jocularity, flattery, refinement, and politeness, taste, and sentiment. They had the capacity for "beautiful understanding," but that was inferior to the "deeper understanding" of which men were capable. Nor was it aesthetically pleasing for her to strive to equal him. A woman who engaged in "laborious learning or painful grubbing" and crammed her head "full of Greek" or "disputations about mechanics" destroyed the easy artfulness and grace that Kant believed essential to women. She "might as well also wear a beard," he concluded.[15] While women could display good moral qualities, they never possessed true moral virtue, of which Kant again believed only men were capable, and women were dependent on men for learning good judgment and discernment. Their achievements should be easy and pertain only to particulars, never to universals. Women could therefore never achieve full moral standing as free individuals. Women inspired love, but not the esteem owed to those of a developed moral character.[16]

These disparate characteristics were complementary, Kant suggested, because each sex was thus able to know virtues that they did not in themselves possess. Men could not be beautiful but had an instinctive inclination toward it and valued the beautiful as portrayed to them in women. Likewise, women could not aspire to be noble or sublime in themselves but were naturally drawn toward these characteristics in men. The ideal union between man and woman thus encompassed the spectrum of desirable qualities and made a complete whole. If one gender tried to emulate the characteristics of the other, Kant argued, it merely subtracted from its own nature while adding nothing to the social aesthetic of gender. "What is most important is that the man become more perfect as a man and the woman as a woman," he wrote.[17] This was the end to which the education and social opportunities of each were to be directed.

Achieving the ideal intellectual and moral development of each sex was not automatic, however, Kant suggested. The gendered tendencies must be moderate and well-balanced, in view of which he supported the ideal of a balanced character presented by faculty psychology. Deviations to either extreme were undesirable and degenerated into the grotesque, Kant stated. Thus, a man with an exaggerated taste for the beautiful and in whom the sublime was lacking became a fop or a dandy, whereas at the other extreme, unbalanced sublimity turned into merely the adventurous. Crusades, knighthood, and "subduing one's passions by means of principles" were all sublime. Adventurousness was merely an exaggerated sense of honor that led to duels, fantastic exploits, or pious extremes of vows and castigations that became grotesqueries.[18] This posture seems to contain a warning that excess civilization contained no outlets for the sublime to develop its best qualities, and one can see how antebellum Americans may have read this threat in the prosperity, peace, and growing industrialization of their era that reduced the need for skilled manual labor, physical strength, economic self-sufficiency, and masculine bravery. They feared that prosperity and peace bred frivolity and ornamentation.

Kant further elaborated on his ideal female education. He believed that women's faculties revolved around sentiment, not reasoning. Therefore, in teaching her, everything should be presented in relation to aesthetics. He argued that her moral feeling should be developed by immediate observation, not through memory, reasoning, or universal rules. She could be taught geography, but as an illustration of diverse characters, societies, and differences in "their taste and ethical feeling," especially as regarded the relation between sexes. Such education could include some "easy" explanation of climatic and political variations. However, Kant did not think the details of regional boundaries, industry, rulers, and histories suitable for women to learn. Art, he suggested, might be taught as what would now be defined as art appreciation, to elevate sentiment and breed good taste. Through instruction of this kind women would learn to avoid evil, "not because it is unjust but because it is ugly," whereas virtue produced the beautiful. They were incapable of principle, but by being taught what they should love, they would naturally do what they loved, which would never include planning, foresight, managing money responsibly, undertaking difficult labor, or propounding theological problems. As a result, they must depend on men for these things while they attended to matters of sentiment and aesthetics, such as decorating the home and fashionably imitating the forms of proper religion.[19]

Although Kant asserted that the union of sexes produced the ideal merger of virtues, faculties, and talents, it is clear that he believed men much more complete on their own. All a man needed to become the ideal man was his own experience, his own reason, and nature to serve as his guide. In contrast, women developed their character for the benefit of men and could not be complete on their own, for their education relied exclusively on the opinion of others, the teaching of others, observation of society, and a role as a mother and wife. Kant proposed to raise women solely for the role of motherhood and not as a woman in and of herself. And although at the time of writing *Observations* he spoke positively of the male role in aesthetics having its basis in taste rather than reason, by the time of his *Remarks* he wrote of this role as something of a curse, the route by which man, through lack of reasoning, was most easily deceived. However, since Kant's *Remarks* were not published in English until well into the twentieth century, in the transatlantic dialogue with which we are concerned, only the more positive treatment of man's gender relations as a subcategory of aesthetics, of taste rather than reason, would have been circulating in America.[20]

Many of these Rousseau-Kantian educational ideas were adopted by, and reached the Transcendentalists through, the Swiss educational reformer Johann Pestalozzi, whose writings in turn were read, published, and utilized by the Transcendentalist educators. In a joint book, generally known as *Conversations with Children on the Gospels*, by Elizabeth Peabody and Bronson Alcott, Peabody noted in her preface that their school's objective was to "unfold the natures of children, in the true order of their faculties."[21] The book's full title is even more illuminating, containing "*unfolding the Doctrine and Discipline of Human Culture.*" To Kant, culture meant the perfection of human nature and through this the achievement of freedom, both external, in the primacy of right, and internal, in the primacy of virtue. Developing human culture was, Alcott stated in his introduction, an art. It was the idea that each child possessed an inner dignity, a God-given preexisting personality, or character, that should be respected by the educator, who merely assisted the child in developing it.[22] It was "the art of revealing to a man the true Idea of his Being—his endowments—his possessions—and of fitting him to use these for the growth, renewal, and perfection of his Spirit. It is the art of completing a man."[23] Alcott meditated in his journals that to achieve this culture, it was the duty of a teacher to be an influence that should awaken, nurture, and guide a child, rather than forcing a child's mind down a prescribed route of reasoning.[24] His daughter Louisa May Alcott further elaborated on this idea in her autobiographical novel *Little Women* (1869). "I am not putting the thoughts into his head, but helping him unfold those already there," she narrated her fictionalized father as stating.[25] The educator would destroy, rather than develop, an individual's character if this inner life were ignored. The highest purpose of education was to raise a man, not merely to impart facts. The purpose was holistic, to develop an individual's own intellectual abilities, sensibilities, and character, not merely to export preformed knowledge to him or her in the form of data and laws, nor was it simply vocational training. In this area the Transcendentalists followed closely in the general theme of Kant's theories about educating man into the realization of spirit.

Transcendentalist women such as Margaret Fuller and the Peabody and Alcott sisters took serious issue with Kant's vision for women's sphere, however, boldly becoming religious independents, literary critics, and landscape painters; learning foreign languages; and advocating self-reliance and bildung for one's own sake, for women as well as men. Margaret Fuller wrote, "I wish woman to live, *first* for God's sake. Then she will not make an imperfect man her god, and thus sink to idolatry." She would not then feel a need to strive for "what is not fit for her from a sense of weakness and poverty" and "will know how to love, and be worthy of being loved. By being more a soul, she will not be less a woman, for nature is perfected through spirit."[26] Fuller argued that only if a woman lived first for God and for developing the richness of her own character could she even become the type of wife Kant depicted. Otherwise, out of the paucity of her own character, she would aspire to grasp for those things to fulfill her that Kant deemed uncomplimentary in a woman.

Furthermore, in the United States, with no nobility and few persons of upper class, the type of education that a woman would require was much more practical than in Europe. As Fuller pondered, "Methods copied from the education of some English Lady Augusta, are as ill suited to the daughter of an Illinois farmer, as satin shoes to climb the Indian mounds." This lack of preparation for intellectual, moral, and physical self-reliance was, she believed, a leading cause of the suffering that pioneer women experienced.[27] The demands of the frontier, often requiring women to work alongside men in any of the multitudinous tasks needed to maintain a livelihood and procure adequate sustenance, made a female model of education such as Kant's not only deficient but impossible. Thus even aside from metaphysical arguments of unity, divine expression, or bildung of the human spirit, simply the economic and social situation of the American continent itself demanded alteration. Furthermore, as many of the Transcendentalist women themselves never married, or married late, and needed to support themselves financially, an understanding of female education that did not center on pleasing a suitor or husband doubtless appeared much more pertinent for themselves and a more worthwhile and holistic model by which to educate other young women.

Margaret Fuller explicitly tied the conception of intuition and receptivity to electrical impulses discussed in the previous chapter to her views on female character. She believed that women specifically would be responsible for ushering the type of knowledge based on electrical impulses, animal magnetism, and emotion into the recognized human experience, beliefs shared by many Spiritualists as well. "The electrical, the magnetic element in woman has not been fairly brought out in any period," she wrote. Yet "every thing [sic] might be expected from it; she has far more of it than man. This is commonly expressed by saying that her intuitions are more rapid and more correct," whereas, she chided, "you will often see men of high intellect absolutely stupid in regard to the atmospheric changes." It was an awareness of these "fine invisible links which connect the forms of life around them" that women would bring to the table for the benefit of others.[28] Fuller believed that acceptance of the validity of this type of experience, rather than term it hysteria, for instance, would open the next philosophical step, and women would lead humanity in the collective to interact with the next layer of creation wherein spiritual lessons were imparted.

One of the main sources in which Fuller found ample material for building a conception of female and complementary bildung was in the works of Goethe, whose writings founded the genre of self-development novels, or "bildungsroman," with his fictional narratives focusing on the accounts of the inner workings of his characters' sentiments and their personal development in the context of an average life experience. The American Transcendentalists were thoroughly and directly familiar with the writings of Goethe. As opposed to many other European writers whose ideas they read in excerpt or through secondary treatments, and thus sometimes misinterpreted, the Transcendentalists directly studied the writings of Goethe, which suggests that his work may have carried even greater weight in their thinking than that of other philosophers. In 1850 Emerson dedicated an entire essay to examining Goethe as a "representative man" in the development of the world soul, and Emerson's published and private writings contain over sixty-two direct references to Goethe.[29] Margaret Fuller translated Goethe's *Tasso* in 1832, translated various of his poems throughout the years, and published the first English translation of *Conversations of Goethe with Eckermann* in 1839. She further published several *Dial* articles on Goethe's works and referenced him frequently in her major piece of writing, *Woman in the Nineteenth Century* (1845). Works on or by Goethe found in the Harvard Library collections that were published during or before the Civil War era in the United States include *Bettina to Goethe: An Unpublished Poem* (1861), *Goethe's Correspondence with a Child* (1861), the first (1859) and second (1860) parts of *Faust*, in addition to the 1827–34 printing of *Goethe's Werke*, published in Germany, of which Emerson was the original owner and which he donated to the library.[30]

The influence of Goethe in the thought of the Transcendentalists requires no speculation, as the connection is direct and their attribution of his works is clear. Goethe's reception by the Transcendentalists should not be taken as uncritical, however. For despite his democratic ideal of self-reliance and personal development, the reception of Goethe's works in America was not immediately a warm one. His inclusion of sexual relationships between unmarried individuals, children born out of wedlock, and most of all his 1809 novel, *Elective Affinities*, in which he portrayed a bored gentry couple experimenting with adultery, shocked the religious sensibilities of the American public. Ironically, in his personal life, Goethe was more faithful than many of the German philosophers they admired, a fact of which the Transcendentalists were seemingly unaware.[31] Nonetheless, Emerson, when he first read the translations of Goethe sent him in 1834 by Thomas Carlyle, was repelled. "The Puritan in me accepts no apology for bad morals in such as he," Emerson wrote back to Carlyle, who had predicted this and counseled Emerson to search more thoroughly to uncover Goethe's deeper meaning. Emerson appears to have followed Carlyle's advice, or else some other fascination continued to draw him back to Goethe. Six years later he was still wrestling with Goethe's total "absence of the moral sentiment," although he was beginning to discern some sagacity concerning human life.[32]

It was another five years before Emerson delivered his lecture on Goethe. Now he was ready to praise Goethe as "the soul of his century," whose vision encompassed "the past and the present ages, and their religions, politics, and modes of thinking," dissolving them "into archetypes and ideas."[33] *Faust* pleased Emerson greatly. Toward *Wilhelm Meister* he was more critical, although he believed there was good to be drawn from it. He granted that it contained "delicious sweetness . . . just insights into life, and manners, and characters; so many good hints for the conduct of life, so many unexpected glimpses into a higher sphere, and never a trace of rhetoric or dullness" that he was willing to "let it go its way." But it still left much to be desired. Wilhelm was a hero with "so many weaknesses and impurities, and keeps such bad company" that Emerson was disgusted with him, considering the book as a whole a "very unsatisfactory one" and the conclusion "lame and immoral."[34] Although he continued to dislike the morals in Goethe's writings and believed that he ranked as only a mediocre genius, what Emerson eventually grew to value in Goethe were his "universal" tendencies, and thus he could include him as a "representative man" of the era. Goethe, he concluded, had "no aims less large than the conquest of universal nature," and he expressed the essential idea of bildung, "the idea—now familiar to the world through the German mind, but a novelty to England, Old and New . . .—that a man exists for culture; not for what he can accomplish, but for what can be accomplished in him."[35] As of 1851 he observed that if you had not read Goethe, you were considered to be "an old fogy, and belong with the antediluvians."[36] Therefore, although Emerson played an important role in introducing Goethe's writings to America through his connections with Carlyle, he was not, in this instance, in the vanguard of those fostering an appreciation of Goethe but followed in the wake of others, like Fuller, who more quickly extracted value from his texts concerning the formation of character.

Goethe presented a theory of character as a dynamic process rather than a static concept. As a result, the twentieth-century German American philosopher and author, Walter Kaufmann, argued that, although generally viewed neither as a philosopher nor a psychologist, Goethe "did more than any man before him to advance the discovery of the mind." Kaufmann wrote that Goethe's understanding suggested that instead of seeking to create a theory of mind in the abstract and then impose it on the actual mind, mind itself could only be understood through observing its actions and development.[37] It was "life itself" that mattered more to Goethe than "knowledge of it," and "unless related to action, knowledge is worthless."[38] Goethe's treatment of this concept proposed that it could not be a theory of being but must be a discovery of becoming. In this way, mind must be understood as fluid, ever-changing, and depending a great deal on the surrounding circumstances to which it must react, adjust, compensate, and interpret. A theory of mind could not be formed in isolation or in abstraction, for mind did not, perhaps, even exist at all apart from its manifestation in emotion, thought, and action.

Goethe took a different stance from Kant on the question of gender, treating it neither as cultural nor aesthetic but as spiritual. He argued that in following feeling in place of reason in interactions between the sexes, men were not deceived, as Kant had suggested. Goethe proposed instead that feeling for the beautiful, the feminine, was the largest motivating factor in a man's life and the yearning that drew him toward the divine. For each gender to find completion in the soul's ultimate state in heaven, Goethe suggested that God must be androgynous. God was not only a father and masculine God, a God of reason, laws, pacts, and justice. God must of necessity also be feminine, a mother, and possess sentiment, mercy, and gentleness. Thus, each gender was drawn to God, as they were likewise drawn to the symbols of those qualities reflected in the masculine and feminine on earth. The final lines of *Faust* declare, "Wrought here in love; / The Eternal-Womanly / Draws us above."[39] Through trying to grasp and possess the earthly symbol of the feminine, Goethe's Faust was seeking to attain unity with the divine feminine. Despite his careless seductions and revels with women, Goethe presents Faust's foundational desire sympathetically. And Goethe's Margaret, whose love for Faust was pure and "who knew not she was transgressing" in allowing his sexual advances, is revealed to have been a venue of grace to him, not one of deception and ruin.[40] For, at her intercession, the Virgin Mary allows Margaret to conduct Faust to yet higher realms of heaven. The feminine, both as person and as passive sentiment, is consequently the means and the end of Faust's journey of bildung, and absolute union with the feminine represents the final consummation of his longing.

But neither did women exist solely for their spiritual usefulness to men in Goethe's writings, and his portrayal of their talents and independent virtue were much more generous than Kant's, making him a favorite authority of reference for Transcendentalist women. In *Werther*, the heroine Charlotte delights Werther with her knowledge and her astute literary criticism.[41] In *Wilhelm Meister*, the female characters present a wide range of talents and characteristics, from Mariana and Mignon, who relish their male costumes; to Aurelia, who languishes in her self-imposed dependence on and despair over faithless men; to Theresa, who manages her personal and business affairs independently and successfully, winning the respect of the men who know her through her wisdom and economy; and finally to Natalia, who rather than merely "training" her pupils, "forms them," and with whom Wilhelm is cheerfully willing to overturn traditional gender roles and subordinate himself. "I thank heaven . . . that on this occasion I am led, and led by you," he states.[42]

In *Wilhelm Meister* is also a piece titled "Confessions of a Fair Saint," in which Goethe portrayed a woman's diary recounting her spiritual journey. When offered a marriage in which she would be required to act the part of housewife alone and alter her opinions in conformity with her suitor's, she "hastened with . . . heart and mind away from this transaction."[43] She is secure in her own personal revelation of God and finds inspiration not in the ceremonies of the church but in her own being and in nature around her. "These preachers were blunting their teeth on the shell, while I enjoyed the kernel. I soon grew weary of them; and I had already been so spoiled, that I could not be content with the little they afforded me."[44] This was far removed from Kant's allowance for women to fashionably imitate religion and be instructed in what they were to believe. Goethe's "Fair Saint" existed for herself, followed her own mind concerning all aspects of life, and developed her own character independent of external guidance.

Thus, Goethe presented the role of both genders as one of equal, and simultaneously autonomous and dependent, bildung. It was a mutual apprenticeship of one to the other. The feminine served as a school in resignation and reverence for the masculine as much as the masculine was to the feminine. For both genders, the goal was the same. "He alone is worthy of respect, who knows what is of use to himself and others, and who labors to control his self-will," Goethe stated in *Wilhelm Meister*. "Each man has his own fortune in his hands. . . . But the art of living rightly is like all arts: the capacity alone is born with us; it must be learned, and practised with incessant care."[45] It was not an art that one could learn in seclusion, in denial of the world as it was, or according to carefully crafted plans of education. It was learned and practiced in the grind of everyday life, the clamor of cities and business, the irritation of inharmonious personalities, and the sins and mistakes of well-intentioned individuals. It was, in fact, the journey of life itself, and although no person could see the process as it unfolded, everything that happened in one's life left its mark and formed one's character. Character formation was happening even when one was unaware of it and did not require any particular program, location, or situation. It required only that one be open to learning the lessons that life taught and to profit from them. Hence every undertaking and every experience carried value for shaping the individual, furthering him or her toward the ultimate end goal of salvation and sanctification, and was a process that could be trusted.

Fuller immediately perceived these underlying motifs and messages within Goethe's works and was thenceforth his devotee. In addition to her translations of his works, she planned to write his biography for American readership and amassed a sizable collection of notes and sources on his life, although this dream was never completed.

Reflecting, from the vantage point of adulthood, on her own education as a child, Fuller was able to clearly identify its deficiencies. Educated by her father in "the straight-jacket Puritan manner," Fuller did not feel that she had been formed holistically. The only emphasis in her education had been "merely the development of the mental faculties," which amounted to what her fellow Transcendentalist Thomas Wentworth Higginson termed "an intellectual forcing process."[46] She was required to cram knowledge all day, recite to her father in the evening, and was all night tormented by nightmares, insomnia, and ill health. It was perhaps Fuller's story that inspired Louisa May Alcott to warn against such strenuous and limited educational methods in her novel *Little Men*. Billy Ward, she wrote of her fictional character, "had been an unusually intelligent boy, and his father had hurried him on too fast, giving him all sorts of hard lessons, keeping him at his books six hours a day, and expecting him to absorb knowledge as a Strasburg goose does the food crammed down its throat. He thought he was doing his duty, but he nearly killed the boy."[47] Although Fuller escaped with her faculties intact, she nevertheless felt that she had endured a traumatic experience. Thus, when she discovered Goethe's writings in her early twenties, she felt that he gave voice to and placed value on aspects of her being that had been repressed. In *Faust* she found this expressed in highest form, and her interpretation of the work is clearly autobiographical:

> Faust, bent on reaching the center of the universe through the intellect alone . . . which has prevented the harmonious unfolding of his nature, falls into despair. He has striven for one object, and that object eludes him. Returning upon himself, he finds large tracts of his nature lying waste and cheerless. He is too noble for apathy, too wise for vulgar

content with the animal enjoyments of life. Yet the thirst he has been so
many years increasing is not to be borne. Give me, he cries, but a drop of
water to cool my burning tongue. Yet in casting himself with a wild reck-
lessness upon the impulses of his nature yet untried, there is a disbelief
that any thing short of the All can satisfy the immortal spirit. His first
attempt was noble, though mistaken, and under the saving influence of
it, he makes the compact, whose condition cheats the fiend at last.[48]

Faust's extravagances and sins, Fuller suggested, were due not to an inherently immoral nature but to a faulty educational method. Those large tracts
of his emotional, physical, and spiritual nature that had been neglected for
so long had at last, through necessity, broken the bonds he had held them in
and demanded development. In attempting to make up for lost years, Faust
consequently overindulges what might have been realized in moderation if
nurtured and allowed to unfold slowly.

Nevertheless, Fuller suggested that Goethe regarded allowing the expression and growth of this side of nature as so essential that he made its initial
eruption from previous bonds, Faust's association with Margaret, the redemptive action of Faust's entire life. It was clearly a concept that greatly encouraged Fuller. *Faust* was, she believed, the one work that contained Goethe's
entire philosophy. It presented the "one great poetic idea possible to man, the
progress of a soul through the various forms of existence," and all his other
writings were merely more detailed illustrations of particular points that
Faust contained.[49] *Faust*, for instance, demonstrated the entirety of the ideal
of self-sanctification, while *Wilhelm Meister* was the illustration of how this
holistic education of a man was lived in daily life—"the continuation of Faust
in the practical sense of the education of man." And here Fuller recognized the
underlying principle of resignation and reverence. Wilhelm's "apprenticeship"
revealed that resignation was the virtue he was most in need of developing
to properly reverence those he encountered and his own experience of life.
"Renunciation, the power of sacrificing the temporary for the permanent . . .
is the leading idea" that Fuller extracted from Goethe's works.[50]

Furthermore, Fuller viewed *Faust* as a story not only of personal bildung
but also of society. Each of these reflected the other, she alleged, thus illustrating the social impact she believed that personal bildung would hold. "With
the progress of an individual soul is shadowed forth that of the soul of the age,"
she wrote; "beginning in intellectual skepticism; sinking into license; cheating

itself with dreams of perfect bliss . . . flying from the Byron despair . . . to schemes however narrow, of practical utility—redeemed at last through mercy alone."[51] Although Arnold Bergstraesser believed that Goethe intended *Faust* as "a symbol of the human situation rather than a model for human conduct," Fuller interpreted it differently.[52] She did not read the poem as a tale of human error but of the liberating qualities of holistic self-development. If only the entire human character were valued and cultivated, the extremes of which she spoke, the idea of humanity's progression as a "continual falling to the right and to the left," which she likely learned from her translating of Herder, would be avoided and a sustainable equilibrium achieved.[53] While writing a piece of literary critique, Fuller was, in fact, pointing out what she viewed as an ideal for personal character and for the character of human society that she found portrayed by Goethe.

In her review of Goethe for the *Dial* in 1841, Fuller hedged her praise for him owing to his often-perceived immorality, yet the tone is one of addressing her readers' expectations rather than her own conviction. This is even more probable considering the likelihood that her own later relationship with the young Italian noble, Giovanni Angelo Ossoli, was not a legal marriage and her son was conceived before any wedding ceremony, if such ever took place. In her article, Fuller even inserted a dig at those like Emerson. "The reason for Goethe's choosing so negative a character as Wilhelm and leading him through scenes of vulgarity and low vice, would be obvious enough to a person of any depth of thought," she stated bluntly. "He thus obtained room to paint life as it really is" and demonstrate how a soul in any circumstance could be led and elevated.[54] In her journal she further noted that although Wilhelm was "a milksop hero," Goethe chose to present him as such so that he could become "an ally" to undeveloped characters and demonstrate that "even arbitrary self-control" could teach the essential lesson of abnegation.[55] And whereas Emerson had difficulty getting past his disgust with Wilhelm, Fuller was much more interested in the array of female characters that Goethe painted and the depth, personality, individuality, and autonomy he gave them.

Fuller interpreted the women portrayed in *Wilhelm Meister* in two ways. First, she viewed Goethe's depictions as relating to women themselves and, second, as relating to male bildung. Goethe, Fuller observed, "always represents the highest principle in the feminine form."[56] Instead of weak, dependent, and incomplete outside marriage, Goethe's female characters were generally astute, discerning, self-governing, and self-determining, and the majority of them were not married at all. Goethe's ability to perceive women in this way was remarkable to Fuller, who credited such to a long tradition of German respect for women. "Germany did not need to *learn* a high view of woman," she wrote, for, as with the ancient Greeks, a higher ideal had already been present among them for many ages. Goethe did not strive to shape a pleasing coquette or a useful wife in his writings but aimed "at a pure self-subsistence, and free development of any powers with which they may be gifted. . . . They are units, addressed as souls. Accordingly the meeting between man and woman, as represented by him, is equal and noble, and, [even] if he does not depict marriage, he makes it possible."[57] This again appears to be a rebuff to Emerson and those like him who were too fixated on Goethe's perceived immorality to recognize the moral.

It is a notable instance of the tension between universal theories of divine equality and particular application of them in personal life that while Emerson paid lip service to the ideal of women's rights, he does not seem to have significantly implemented it in his own life. He never recorded any second thoughts about leaving his wife excluded from the intellectual meetings hosted in their home or any statements indicating that it was her wish to remain aloof. Rather, Elizabeth Peabody noted in her own journal that household duties prevented Lidian from joining her and Emerson for walks and intellectual discussion. Apparently Peabody herself felt no great concern at this unseemly situation, which suggests a divide in her own mind, perhaps regarding the proper role of a married versus a single woman rather than women as a group, but still a glaring oversight. Abigail Alcott would also complain of the intellectual exclusion and drudgery experienced by the women at the experimental community of Fruitlands, and Lidian Emerson eventually wrote a sardonic list of Transcendentalist "commandments" that included, "Never confess a fault," "It is mean and weak to seek for sympathy; it is mean and weak to give it," and "Never wish to be loved. Who are you to expect that?"[58] Thus despite the soaring rhetoric and idealism of the gender theory in this period, the actual experience of married women within Transcendentalism was indicative of a serious lack of personal follow-through of ideals into practice in the home and a failure to envision what female bildung could be within the context of marriage. As a masculine ideal extended to single women, it was easier to grasp, but Transcendentalist men such as Bronson Alcott and Waldo Emerson shrank from applying it within the marital relationship of husband and wife. Even as regarded single women, Emerson displayed some reserve, as can be seen in his concurrent polite doctoring and uncharitable disparagements of Fuller herself in the biography he jointly authored with James Freeman Clarke and William Henry Channing after Fuller's death in 1850.[59] Emerson criticized her ego and lack of physical beauty, claimed that she had inferior powers of observation to himself, and stated that, as was usual with women, her personal feelings colored her judgment in all matters. She was at the same time "sentimental" and "burly," supposedly "willingly . . . confined to the usual circles and methods of female talent" but also living a "masculine existence." Emerson, by his own admission, was shocked that men in Italy found her appealing, indicating again that his esteem for women, whatever abstract ideals he may have claimed in public lectures, rested largely on those qualities of personal appearance and lack of personal "ego" that he did not find in her.[60] And Goethe's presentation of male and female interaction that appealed so strongly to Fuller did not strike Emerson as an appealing or positive portrayal of gender relations.

According to Fuller's interpretation of Goethe's ascending female cast in *Wilhelm Meister*, Emerson would not have ranked far along the path of bildung. Neither did Goethe himself live up to his own ideal, as Fuller did not hesitate to point out. She stated of his correspondence with a young reader, Bettine, that Goethe used Bettine as a tool to further his own artistic stature, adopted the "air as of an elderly guardian flirting cautiously with a giddy, inexperienced ward," and, she concluded, did Bettine more harm than good in the interest of developing her own character.[61] Thus, if Emerson fell short of Goethe's ideals, Goethe did too at times. For it was not only feminine ability in and for itself that Fuller saw represented in his writings.

In addition to this theme, Fuller identified an application for male bildung. The women in *Wilhelm* appeared in no random sequence, she believed. Rather, they appeared in an ascending order of bildung. As Wilhelm himself advanced in his journey of self-culture and as his ability to value women in their own right improved, he befriended women progressively more developed in bildung. "As Wilhelm advances in the upward path he becomes acquainted with better forms of woman by knowing how to seek, and how to prize them when found." The chronology of his female friendships "expresses ascent in the scale of being."[62] Mariana and Philina are charming but shallow. The countess shows "genuine elegance, genuine sentiment, but not sustained by wisdom, or a devotion to important objects." Mignon and Aurelia demonstrate inspiration, mystery, and a yearning for a more intense experience of life, but they each have poorly balanced characters and succumb to the ruinous effects of a single sentiment that possesses them beyond reason. Theresa presents "practical wisdom, gentle tranquility" and domestic economy, which, although estimable, is still not adequate to fully satisfy Wilhelm's quest for companionship in the final stages of bildung. Natalia combines all the best qualities of each of these who precede her but is "enlightened by a larger wisdom" that directs each virtue to a higher purpose. And, finally, there is the mysterious character of Macaria, who possesses an "inward consciousness of a separate existence and peculiar union with the heavenly bodies" and is able to crown Wilhelm "at last with the privilege to possess his own soul," the ultimate state of bildung.[63]

Through this interpretation, Fuller wished to make her essential point clear. If men desired the successful conclusion of bildung for themselves, it was essential that they allow the same journey of character growth and self-reliance for women. If women were not granted the opportunity to pursue self-culture, there would be no Theresas, Natalias, or Macarias to assist men along their path of betterment, and neither would men be able to conceive of the highest form of womanhood if it were not displayed before their eyes, thus limiting them in their own understanding of divine completeness. "The growth of man is two-fold, masculine and feminine," Fuller wrote. They were "twin exponents of a divine thought," and "the development of one cannot be effected without that of the other."[64] This was the key argument with which she framed her appeal for expanded opportunities for women in education and the workforce, greater equality in marriage, and political rights.

A noteworthy illustration exists of the application of bildung used by women to frame their role in the Civil War. Unfortunately, the identities of the women referenced here are unknown. The letter they wrote was only discovered in 1919, and the only identifier that remained was that they resided in Knox County, Illinois, and addressed the Union soldiers from there. This in itself is significant as it indicates that these ideas were familiar throughout the Northern states, even among women still largely barred from a university education, and not confined to the Transcendentalist stronghold of Massachusetts. The words that these unidentified women wrote to their local soldiers contain a clear echo of the concept of bildung and of the interplay of genders within this model. Rather than merely as defenders of their government, these women wished to express to the soldiers their appreciation for the special role they played in their lives as men striving for a noble cause. "We are your debtors in a way not often recognized," they wrote. "You have aroused us from the aimlessness into which too many of our lives had drifted and infused into those lives a noble pathos.... Even your sufferings have worked together for our good, by inciting us to labor for their alleviation, thus giving us a work worthy of our womanhood.... You have thus been the means of developing in us a nobler type of womanhood than without the example of your heroism we could ever have attained. For this our whole lives, made purer and nobler by the discipline, will thank you."[65] They could not regret the war or the suffering it had caused in their lives. For "this war will leave none of us as it found us." Despite the hardships, they believed that the experience was ultimately beneficial for everyone involved. "Fighting for a worthy cause worthily ennobles one," they concluded. "Herein is our confidence that you will return better men than you went away. By all that is noble in your manhood; by all that is true in our womanhood; by all that is grand in patriotism; by all that is sacred in religion, we adjure you to be faithful to yourselves, to us, to your country, and to your God.... Disasters may come, as they have come, but they will only be, as they have been, ministers of good."[66] It would be difficult to find a more succinct, recognizable, and in-depth statement of the application of bildung in the culture of the Civil War as it was implemented by each gender.

The unique significance that this ideal played is heightened by contrast with a similar letter written by women to soldiers in the field during the Revolutionary War. Although the Civil War women emphasized the spiritual blessings that the soldiers' experience earned for them, the women of the Revolution listed only the material, extending their gratitude to the soldiers for the safety of their families and their family properties, their homes, fields, orchards, and barns. They would try to repay these blessings and support the cause, they promised. They would dress simply and forgo feminine adornment, cheerfully embracing the deprivations of warfare, if "the valiant defenders of America will be able to draw some advantage from the money which she may have laid out in these."[67] The interactions of gender, the role of women, and the importance of the contest were thus described in completely different terms. No mention was made of benefit to character, mutual upliftment of genders, personal growth, or spiritual improvement from the experience of war. It is also a contrast to the pin-up culture among American troops in World War II, which, Robert Westbrook has argued, framed American women as "objects of obligation," a role portrayed in propaganda as almost more important than their contribution as nurses or munitions workers. This placed gender interaction in terms of male obligation to protect their women from foreign male aggressors and female obligation to become "pin-up girls worth fighting for." It was, Westbrook concludes, "a reciprocal obligation."[68] It was, however, a quite different form of reciprocal obligation than that outlined by Goethe in works such as *Faust* and *Wilhelm Meister*, as interpreted by Fuller, and internalized by the Illinois women who valued the gendered interchange of character-building so highly, even when it came in the destructive context of war.

Thus from the Common Sense model of consciously balancing the faculties, to Kant's discussion of gender as aesthetics and character growth as the development of personal culture and freedom, to Goethe's concept of female contribution, the Transcendentalists began to articulate a vision of bildung that encompassed the entirety of the population. Those traditionally excluded based on sensibility and emotion in opposition to reason and will were embraced, and those traditionally confined to reason and will alone were encouraged to cultivate the receptive faculties. Receptivity to nature was essential to learn its deeper meanings, the definition of reason was expanded to include intuition, and the traditionally "feminine" attributes therefore had to be recognized as valid routes to self-culture. These developments would carry as crucial an impact for the male interpretation and experiential framework of the Civil War as it defined the female experience of the period.

Chapter Five
MASCULINITY AND BILDUNG IN THE CIVIL WAR

Wilbur Fisk, who had enlisted with the Union at the age of twenty-two, had not changed his mind about the war's value from the vantage point of his fifties. Delivering a Memorial Day address in 1891, Fisk still believed that the Civil War had been a beneficial discipline in self-culture and had changed soldiers for the better. The soldiers had been "made more manly, had a greater hatred of cruelty, more tenderness toward suffering and were every way more of a man" because of their experiences. "Once more," he concluded, "I am reminded by these soldiers' graves that war is sometimes right."[1] His statements were not unique. Many Union soldiers perceived the war as benefiting their characters and offering an unparalleled opportunity for personal growth in moral sentiment and integrity. From the new standards of character and the mind outlined by German writers such as Goethe, soldiers were not afraid to nurture and express emotion and sentiment as part of bildung. Such frameworks of character found their way into formal military culture through the works of Carl von Clausewitz and Francis Lieber and were presented by Herder and Hegel as extending even beyond death. Although in some instances the common rank and file were reading these works, much of this influence was diffused in the culture at large, and many soldiers were likely unaware from where their mentality originated. Nonetheless, the frequency of this framework observable in their writings suggests that the new philosophical ideal of masculinity and the concept of bildung were so widespread as to be a necessary consideration in forming an understanding of the era.

This philosophical framework for speaking of character and bildung in the war is one of the most notable and unique elements of Civil War culture and one of the least emphasized among historians. Most Union soldiers spoke of the war as a positive influence for good in their lives and the life of the nation and not as an experience that was psychologically injurious or morally degenerative. There are few accounts of soldiers stating a sense of identity loss, personal insignificance, or instances of physical abuse compared with the literature from other wars in which such mentions appear with some regularity. There have been many reasons suggested to explain the higher level of dedication among the Civil War armies, including the generally more personal nature of a civil war as well as sociopolitical, economic, and religious causes.[2] The focus on the war as a school of bildung does not discount any of these other influences but enhances an understanding of many nuances present within this high soldier motivation and positive processing of the conflict present in the Civil War, as well as the military discipline and culture during the period. The impact of the philosophical conceptions of the mind, character, and the substance of reality disseminated to the American public through the New England Transcendentalists was crucial in building this framework for viewing the war as an important stage for character development.

Civil War culture has been treated through the lens of gender and discussed in terms of both character and soldier motivation by historians such as Chandra Manning, LeeAnn White, and Reid Mitchell. These examinations proposed cultural aspects such as that Southern white men viewed the hallmarks of manhood to be "independence, courage, the right to bear arms, moral agency, liberty of conscience, and the ability to protect and care for one's family," as well as the freedom of personal mobility, without an escort or a pass such as was required of females and all Black people, whether enslaved or free.[3] The Southern view of white manhood particularly relied on the authority and the right to control subordinates believed not to possess these attributes, namely, women, children, and Black people, and thus white Southern men who did not own enslaved people still viewed slavery as a cause worth fighting to preserve. For even such Southern white men were still entrusted with the authority to command Black people and the duty to protect white women from the presumed threat of Black sensuality and violence, which they feared emancipation would unleash on the entire South.[4]

Manning also discusses how Southern white men perceived the Northern critique of slavery as an insult to their honor, a key component of Southern culture. Honor depended on social perception of the man, not concepts such as moral integrity. How he was perceived, how others spoke of him, and how effectively he exercised authority over subordinates were the linchpins of Southern honor.[5] Thus the insult from the North to their regional honor required war to defend and reestablish the South's honor in the nation, in the same way as in the South a personal insult required a duel to reestablish a man's authority, reputation, and social standing.

Although such accounts provide an important look at Southern standards of white manhood as both a character ideal and a military cause, they do little to explain the views held among the Northern populace, which were markedly different from and often in opposition to those of the South. Furthermore, gender and an understanding of manhood was also important to Black soldiers, in that slavery robbed them of the same hallmarks of manhood as white men believed in, such as independence, bearing firearms, caring for one's family, and liberty of movement and conscience. "Fighting in the Civil War offered African Americans the opportunity to display those very attributes and reclaim their identities as Black men in direct defiance of proslavery ideology's insistence that Black people were children or savages rather than real men."[6] Ideals of character were crucial in shaping Black soldiers' conduct in the war as they were required to maintain a delicate balance in their wartime service as proof of manhood and not as a confirmation of the racial stereotypes of combativeness, violence, and animalistic tendencies. Frederick Douglass, for instance, made a point to note for the public that Black soldiers fought "for principle, and not from passion."[7] Why this was so important to stress to the public of the time, and what exactly Douglass meant by principle versus passion, is left unexplained in a merely social examination of the requirements of manhood in this context, and the discussion misses much of the depth that can be uncovered when the philosophical underpinnings of character development during the era are taken into account.

Another angle to consider is that white Southern males took the abolitionist attack on slavery as an attack on the Southern household and their male position therein. This undermined a man's independence to administer his home and property as he saw fit and removed his liberty, placing him in a subordinate position equal to or below the status held by women or Black men. In this way, the Southern white man in the Civil War constructed the conflict as one of liberty and independence despite the paradox of Black slavery. It was a war for his own liberty and independence as a free, autonomous, and authoritative man in his own sphere. To white men of the North, the crisis was viewed equally in terms of a threat to their manhood. In their case, however, they believed that the unequal influence of the "slave power" in the federal government was robbing them of their manhood, understood as their independence from outside influence, and forcing them to submit to yet another form of tyranny. LeeAnn White believes that women of the time, both North and South, also generally accepted the gender hierarchy of social relations, stressing their dependence in wartime on men's service as soldiers. But women also emphasized men's reliance on them for maintaining the independence and comfort of the home in their absence, providing them with sewing and nursing assistance as well as moral support and an intimate reason for their trials in the field. Women thus expanded their own independence by painting their growing field of accepted pursuits in terms of appropriate gender interdependence.[8] These arguments address the preexisting social structures of gender in the era but do not explore the intellectual basis from which these were formed or the ideals of character-building as a particularly unique presence in Civil War culture.

Reid Mitchell touched on character when he noted how "part of masculinity was achieving the self-discipline within the institutional discipline of the army." He went on to explain, "When secession and rebellion were perceived as hot-headed and impulsive—the result of unrestrained passion—self-discipline had political implications. During the war with the emotional, treacherous—feminine, childlike—South, the son of the rational, loyal—masculine, adult—North should be manly and upright." In this he hints very strongly at the faculty psychology outlines of the mind. However, Mitchell did not explore this philosophical foundation for the beliefs he observed. Indeed, he concluded that it functioned as an unexamined social framework but "the notion that the southern states might best be understood as disobedient children, the northern ones as filial—was woefully inadequate, indeed nonsensical. I am not suggesting that anyone who seriously thought about politics entertained it for a minute."[9] By writing it off as a silly popular notion, Mitchell missed much of the philosophical background that can be uncovered by seriously examining this thought model, when the functioning of the United States government is seen as a mind writ at large, with its three branches—the legislative, executive, and judicial—mirroring the three recognized mental faculties: the understanding, the reason or will, and the conscience, such as Daniel Walker Howe suggests.[10]

Passion versus principle, physical prowess versus moral integrity, or muscular "martial manhood" versus "restrained manhood" have been other ways used to describe the regional distinctions present within the ideals of manhood during the era. Amy Greenberg offered a more nuanced division by discussing these categories as class distinctions more than simple regional disparities, because athletic development was also valued in the North as seen in the growth of the gymnasium and gentleman's sports such as rowing, wrestling, and baseball. An ideal of "muscular manhood" also surfaces in the Northern belief that war would restore the strength of the country and save it from effeminacy and degenerative civilization, which undermined male courage, independence, and hardihood. Restrained manhood first sought to fight and overcome moral challenges, such as alcohol, gambling, prostitution, and other sins, and to prove men's character through "their religious faith, their domestic virtue and treatment of family members." Martial manhood was emphasized more among working-class men and on the frontier, where, Greenberg argues, there was often neither time nor opportunity for a man to be known and respected for his character such that he sought more immediate dominance through displays of physical aggression.[11]

These generalizations still retain some problems, however, for the South would more typically represent "martial manhood," although prominent families would have been well established in the region for decades, if not centuries, and upper-class white gentleman were not manual laborers. Furthermore, Greenberg characterizes the average Northern Civil War proponent as issuing from among the "martial" men and argues that the actual experience of war discredited them for a time, for they quickly "learned how wrong their romantic expectations about war were."[12] There are two problems with this summation. First, this statement shows the typical American post–Vietnam War era predisposition to assume a significant postwar disillusionment following every conflict, when evidence of such a phenomenon is almost completely lacking in relation to the Civil War. And, second, this claim is poorly supported, for working-class Irish figure prominently in her "martial" category yet often constituted the most antiwar faction of the North. Furthermore, the majority of primary source documents from Northern Civil War soldiers represent men she would have classified as "restrained," and they frequently wrote of the war not as a demonstration of physical prowess but as a test of character. It was the Southerners they criticized for being "martial," passionate, and combative, suggesting they had not properly subordinated their passions and achieved any commendable character, whereas the Southerners, in contrast, boasted of these qualities, believing the North lethargic and incapable of carrying on a successful war. Greenberg overlooked this difference, however, because she perceived character as basically the same as physical dominance and hence only open to men during this period. She believed "manly character" to be a redundant phrase since character and masculinity were synonymous and related to patriarchy.[13]

Addressing the philosophical influence fuses the differing interpretations of gender theory during the period into a more cohesive and consistent whole. For even when historians have not engaged with issues of self, character, or gender in their treatment of the Civil War era, there surfaces with troubling regularity an underlying perplexity and incomprehension of the era's culture that can at base be traced to the period's distinctive philosophical ideas about the self, experience, and reality. Scholars have repeatedly appeared to be puzzled as to how the bloodiest, costliest war in American history produced cultural expressions in art, music, and literature that they have consistently described with adjectives like "insipid," "quaint," "sentimental," and "idealistic."[14] The unstated assumption seems to be that in contrast with "the war itself," viewed as the external material scene of battles, campaigns, casualties, and destruction, which belonged to the concrete, real, and masculine realm, the cultural expressions of the war were abstract, unrealistic, and feminine and represented a strange dissociation between the actual and the ideal. Not only does this view overlook the fact that the vast majority of the war's poetry and prose was produced by men, private citizens with no investment in producing government propaganda, it also fails to understand the ideals of manhood present during the period. The cultural expressions of the period are therefore often dismissed, when they should be used to explore the philosophical frameworks that historical actors were utilizing to shape and understand their experiences.

James McPherson observed that "our cynicism about the genuineness of such sentiments is more our problem than theirs, a temporal/cultural barrier we must transcend if we are to understand why they fought. Theirs was an age of romanticism in literature, music, art, and philosophy. It was a sentimental age when strong men were not afraid to cry."[15] Yet observing such does little to explain it, which McPherson never succeeded in doing. He was not alone in not discovering a satisfactory route to reconciling the issue. As his work demonstrated, Harry Stout could not resolve the apparent contradiction of a murderous war with idealistic portrayals. To make sense of the contrast, he could conclude only that it was denial on the part of the participants, and he thus painted even the general public as much further removed from the grisly actualities of warfare than was possible at the time.[16] For instance, battle casualties were often not of a higher percentage per population than deaths experienced in the South during prewar years in epidemics such as malaria, nor were civilians always protected from becoming casualties of the war and were certainly not far removed from its realities. Roughly 50,000 wounded soldiers were housed at hospitals in Washington, DC, at which civilians were regular visitors; battles were frequently fought across private farms and through villages, and after the Battle of Gettysburg, 22,000 wounded of both armies were cared for by the town's population of 2,400. Furthermore, the battle left an estimated 6 million pounds of decaying animal and human flesh, whose stench had barely been conquered through civilian burial efforts by the time of the battlefield dedication ceremony four months later. Yet, despite Stout's conviction that protests would have inevitably resulted if civilians had been aware of the extent of the war's destruction, the residents of Gettysburg who were forced to confront the worst of a battle's aftermath did not engage in antiwar activities following their exposure.[17]

Such approaches to the emotional aspect of Civil War culture suggest that modern historians have felt the need to explain away, overlook, or excuse Civil War soldiers for expressing what these historians clearly feel uncomfortable accepting as an aspect of masculine character. Even the seemingly innocuous divisions within published collections of Civil War songs support such a view. "Sentimental war songs" are separated from "songs the soldiers sang," as if what lachrymose women sang at the parlor pianos must of necessity be different from what hardened men would have tolerated singing in the field of destruction and death.[18] No such division can be discerned in the Civil War–era writings, however. There were actually many more instances of praise from soldiers in the field for the kind of sentimental and patriotic rhetoric that historians are uncomfortable crediting as genuine. Soldiers' writings are even found accusing civilians of lacking in patriotism and zeal. Wilbur Fisk, for example, recorded hearing the song "Brother, When Will You Come Back?," which ran in part:

Brother, dear Brother! when will you come back—
back to the hearts ever loving and true?
While your campfires are burning our fond hearts are yearning:
Brother, dear Brother! we're praying for you.

He stated that he enjoyed it very much, with no criticism of its lyrics as varnishing the experience of war or being overly sentimental.[19]

Scholars' concerns in addressing this aspect of the Civil War illustrate the need for a philosophical examination of the issue of self and experience during this period so as to understand it, one that reaches below the social roles and constructs and addresses the underlying beliefs surrounding the development and expression of human faculties, the experience of reality, and, consequently, what experience and reality consisted of. By taking for granted that the cultural philosophy of these questions has remained the same across time, historians have found no way to reconcile what they do find in the culture of the Civil War with what they expect they should find in a wartime society. Yet, considering the changes in character values discussed in the previous chapters, with the new acceptance of emotion and sensibility to aesthetic and moral impulses came new ideals of masculinity that were not at odds with the expression of sentiments.

The cultural ideal present in the North during the Civil War was informed by a framework of masculine character that was broad enough to include profuse symbolism and sentiment not seen as exclusively feminine, nor romanticized and merely allegorical, but was believed to express the basis of reality and develop one's awareness of it. "Nature is the incarnation of a thought, and turns to thought again. . . . The world is mind precipitated," wrote Ralph Waldo Emerson.[20] In his view, the mind's deliberation on the facts presented to the senses constituted the reality of a man's life, not the objects and experiences themselves that the senses perceived. Experience was not external but internal, and reality consisted of feeling, not fact. Perhaps, then, the emotional focus, the sentimental treatment of the war, and the patriotic symbolism was not a "rhetorical trap" of "moral avoidance" that "submerg[ed] the reality" of war "in a sea of romanticism," as Stout contended, nor was it an "artificial" coping strategy as Earl J. Hess suggested.[21] Instead, this perspective represented a different philosophical basis from which its participants formed their values and judged and interpreted their essential experiences. The "real war" consisted of an individual's emotional experience of it, which, for its role in bildung, was valued beyond the grim scenes the senses encountered.

◇◇◇

As with the understanding of femininity and the interaction of the genders, Goethe's work again provides insight into the values that created ideals of masculinity and bildung in the Civil War era. The environment of warfare presented a particular challenge to any philosophy that required a sheltered, structured, or utilitarian approach to nature, environment, and intentionality in the development of character, as some of the messages of early Transcendentalism did, such as was contained within Henry David Thoreau's *Walden* (1854). Soldiers in the field had no control over their environment, could not choose to what they were exposed, and were at the mercy of, rather than in control of utilizing, the forces of nature. Goethe's philosophy offered the most relevant route for handling this imperfect and always changing environment for bildung and was heavily employed by Whitman, who, unlike the older Transcendentalists, stepped into the midst of the ugliness and grime of warfare.

In his novel *Wilhelm Meister*, for instance, Goethe suggested that excessive isolation and introspection were actually unhealthy. The character of the "Fair Saint," he states, was made ill by "too much employment with her own thoughts," which prevented her from "being to the world what . . . she might have become." There was such a thing as a nature that "overcultivates itself."[22] Through these examples and Faust's unhealthy isolated state at the opening of the epic poem, Goethe sought to demonstrate that "man is not healthy if he either refuses to face the world or cuts himself off from the religious ground of his existence."[23] It required a balance of both tendencies to realize the optimal situation for personal development and growth of character. So to argue that the Transcendentalists promoted a secluded type of existence seems increasingly unlikely, given their intellectual engagement with Goethe's ideals. A balanced character required interaction with the world outside oneself. Facing and overcoming, or synthesizing, these external forces was a test of manhood.

The novel *Wilhelm Meister* also emphasized nature, although in a form different from that usually discussed. Rather than nature presented as only the natural world and its physical laws in isolation from human interaction, nature as presented in *Wilhelm* consists of the entirety of the daily ebb and flow of the natural world, social interactions, personal experiences, and religious impressions. This force does not need to be managed and controlled in Goethe's conception but merely required of one "the art of resignation," as Arnold Bergstraesser defined it. The art of resignation further required reverence—reverence for each of the three aspects of "nature" to which individuals were subjected during their journey of self-culture: God, nature, and others. Or put another way, reverence for what was above, what was beneath, and what was within.[24]

The type of resignation to events that Goethe advocated should not be understood as endorsing passivity, fatalism, or defeatism, however. Rather, the need to develop reverence was an active work. He believed that one could not simply ride the waves of life without self-examination and still profit from it. To profit, one had to examine the inner experience of life, to harmonize the emotions with reason, and to repeatedly progress through cycles of alienation, polarity, and reconciliation, or sin, repentance, and absolution.[25] These correspond to the three stages that Hegel, most likely informed by Goethe's conception, would also describe as those of separation, opposition, and unification, or thesis, antithesis, and synthesis. Whereas Hegel would universalize these concepts in *Phenomenology of Spirit* as a "*bildungsroman* of the human spirit," Goethe particularized the model in his novels as examples of individual bildung.[26] Both Wilhelm and Faust go through this cycle repeatedly in these works, by which Goethe demonstrated his conviction that, as Bergstraesser put it, "men who are capable of education arrive at truth only through error."[27] This journey through error to truth was necessary because evil, or opposition, was an essential "negating function" to stimulate growth and development. Without it, there would be no drive to action, which would prevent the very activity, manifestation, and deeds by which mind could be known, leaving existence, knowledge, and life itself an undeveloped potentiality rather than a knowable essence.[28] In *Faust*, the tempter spirit Mephistopheles serves as the personification of this negating role, but in *Wilhelm* a variety of everyday characters demonstrates its function, and increasing pressure to change his mind only solidifies the main character's resolve.[29]

Controversially, Goethe also portrayed sin as a necessary aspect of self-improvement. To protect oneself or others from error was not beneficial, he believed, for if errors were forbidden, one would linger in them with delight, but if allowed to drain error "to the dregs," individuals would find it cloying and throw it aside of their own will.[30] Goethe developed the idea that sin could, in the end, be the route itself to achieving sanctification. In traditional

German folklore, Faust was, at the end of his sinful life, carried off to Hell in accordance with the pact he had signed with the devil. Goethe, however, made a significant alteration. Earlier in the tale, Margaret, a young girl whom Faust has seduced, passes away, jailed and insane. Mephistopheles pronounces in confident satisfaction that Margaret has been condemned, but a voice from above counters, "She is saved!"[31] When Faust dies, he is carried into paradise to a chorus of angels singing, "Whoe'er aspiring, struggles on, / For him there is salvation."[32] Instead of aimless pleasure-seeking and damnation that the Faust legend was originally, Goethe now presented it as a journey of bildung progressing toward redemption, from material symbol to spiritual fact. Even those in Goethe's heaven representing babies and young children who died before earth could tarnish them occupy a lesser place than Faust, for they did not experience the struggle through error to truth.[33] Goethe suggested, then, that a man's efforts to grow through the defects of the world, even if completely misdirected, were of greater value than the effortless purity of those not exposed to its temptations.

Goethe also emphasized that it was the individual's duty to learn to accept external guidance without resenting it, as is Wilhelm's initial reaction when he finds his life has been manipulated by others to some degree. He struggles with having his own opinion condemned, his sins exposed, and is deeply hurt when his acting talent is rudely dismissed and his personal will overridden. But bildung required developing resignation toward all these factors, nature, sin, society, and the endless cycle of seeking, without expecting others to do it for one or hoping to be saved from it. Thus, Goethe was adamant that social interactions played an essential role in bildung.

Through these writings, Goethe demonstrated the ways in which the industrialized world, the paltry interactions of society, and even the faults and failings of an individual all contributed to his or her intellectual, moral, and spiritual growth. It was essential to learn to lose oneself in the masses, to live for others, and to have one's own will thwarted at times. This alone would prevent excessive introspection that led to insanity, such as he portrayed in the despair and suicide of the main character in *The Sorrows of Young Werther*, where an unhealthy passion for an unavailable woman is indulged and wallowed in rather than conquered. Rather, as in *Wilhelm Meister*, it is the guidance, criticism, and reflection of one's self found in friends and even enemies that force one to actually become acquainted with oneself. Thus a soldier thrown into the midst of armies, warfare, and the incontrollable environment of campaigns could learn the lessons of bildung as well as could be done, if not better, than in a sacred space such as Walden.

The positive emphasis on resignation in Goethe's works offers an alternative intellectual framework from which to understand Civil War Americans' cultural values. What Harry Stout interpreted as moral avoidance and Drew Gilpin Faust portrayed as fatalism can be conceived of as resignation, the willing acceptance of life events.[34] Although Stout argued that because Civil War Americans did not hold the preservation of life as the highest value, their morals declined during the war, such was not the understanding of morals that they expressed during the period.[35] The Congregational minister Horace Bushnell, in his 1866 *The Vicarious Sacrifice*, voiced clearly that to be moral was to remain firm in one's principles and to be dedicated to those principles above one's own life. Such moral dedication, he affirmed, was the lesson of the life of Christ, who "came to be the moral power of God on character." The Union soldiers of the war demonstrated this moral integrity laudably when they remained steadfast in the quest to restore the nation's harmony with divine law, "refusing to be weakened by sorrow, or shaken by discouragement, or even to be slackened by unexpected years of delay," and were "able rather to die for it than to renounce it" and the integrity of their morals.[36] It was not the bloodshed of combat that Americans wished to prolong or political absolutism that they advocated but personal moral integrity they clung to and resignation or submission to the inimitable school of bildung that they believed the war offered them.

As in the example of Wilbur Fisk, whose appreciation of the war's character-building elements was expressed at the beginning of this chapter, many soldiers valued the formative aspects of the war. After visiting Petersburg in 1882, where he had been wounded during the war, General Joshua Chamberlain wrote to his sister, "All the strifes of peaceful times [are] less noble often than those of war."[37] Another Union soldier, George Cram, even in the midst of the war, was able to recognize a similar profit from his service. "I often think, should I live to return, I shall look back with great pride upon my soldier's life," he pondered in a letter to his mother. "And I frequently say to myself now, 'It is good for us to be here.' We are learning much that could not be learned elsewhere."[38] George Burmeister also engaged very consciously with the idea of bildung during his wartime service. His diaries make frequent references to self-cultivation and a conscious effort to turn his experiences into opportunities for personal growth. He was careful to try to spend his "leisure moments in mental improvement," regretted that he was "fettered" with a "sullen temper" that he implored God's assistance to replace with a better disposition toward life, and reprimanded himself that he should exert still greater effort into self-improvement. For, he wrote, "A man's life is very short here and it is his duty to improve himself while he does live, [since] only the thoroughly educated man can enjoy life properly."[39] Every New Year's he reviewed his progress in self-improvement from the year that had ended and recorded his hopes for the year to come, both for his own bildung and for that of the nation. John Rankin of the 27th Indiana Infantry wrote following a battle, "Thank God! My higher nature has triumphed. . . . This army may be swept from the field before sunset; within a moment I may be a mangled corpse; I may sleep in an unknown grave; but, come what may, I am a victor over self."[40] The origin and professions of these select soldiers who mentioned the role of bildung in their experience and interpretation of the war ranged widely: from a rural school teacher in Vermont to a professor of rhetoric from Maine; a young Illinois college student and cartographer; a German-born Iowan rotating between country school teaching, a book store employee, and college as he could afford; and a teenage newspaper printer from the farm country of Indiana. This distribution geographically reaches from a state neighboring the Transcendentalists' Massachusetts to the northernmost state of the Union, to the home state of President Lincoln, to a state considered as the prairie frontier of the time, and to a state in the heart of the Midwest. Such a scope suggests a significant dispersal of these ideas throughout the Union and their appeal to soldiers of varied ages and backgrounds.

Even parents of Union soldiers expressed this wish, and expectation, of character development for their sons through their experience of warfare. There is little indication of a perspective of the government forcing their sons away from them as was displayed in World War I with popular song lyrics such as:

> Don't send him off to war . . .
> Who are the heroes that fight your wars,
> Mothers who have no say,
> But my duty's done, so for God's sake leave one,
> And don't take my darling boy away.[41]

Instead, we find instances like that of Jeremiah Lamson, an Oregon farmer, writing to his son on the opposite side of the continent, "Your course meets my approbation and I can truly say that I glory in having a son who is willing to risk life and all he has in this world in defence [sic] of *our country*. . . . Go on and do your duty."[42] The Transcendentalist minister James Freeman Clarke recounted that this parental disposition was not the exception but the rule, and something he never quite got used to. "I go to the house of one whose noble child has been struck down in battle . . . in fear, expecting to meet too much anguish, and almost too great a call on my sympathy," he wrote. Instead, he found mothers "happy, calm, thankful to God that he has given her such an opportunity of sacrifice for the land. . . . They gave a son; they receive back from God a saint and a hero" who died in the cause not of mere institutions but of ideas.[43]

Clarke himself saw the war in terms of self-development on a national scale. Just as everyone encountered a period in life at which the questions arose, "What am I? What am I here for? Who sent me? What can I do with myself in the world?," the Civil War represented this phase in the life of the nation. As this crisis in an individual caused him or her to become a "free being . . .—assuming self-direction, self-restraint, self-control," so it was with nations. In a very Hegelian understanding, Clarke stated that "the history of a nation is the time when it is filled with an idea, and when its life proceeds, self-directed, from that. . . . When a nation is inspired by the idea of patriotism, or of religion, or of freedom, it makes history fast." This national idea proceeded directly from God, who "when he sends an idea into the world . . . stands by it."[44] Thus, by participating in this conflict, sons were furthering the ideas of God himself within the world and dying for the national journey of bildung toward absolute idealism.

Reflections of the ideal of bildung and resignation to the lessons of war were discovered in only one instance among the Southern sources researched, when a North Carolina mother wrote to her son, a prisoner of war, to "lose no opportunity: for improvement of y[ou]r mind & character."[45] Higher scarcity of writing paper and lower literacy rates may have contributed to the significantly fewer instances of such rhetoric being recorded in writing, even if it was evoked in speech, but it is impossible to know for certain. For even well-educated and literary Southerners, such as the diarist Kate Stone, rarely displayed this focus. Stone's commentary addressed almost solely physical or social characteristics of the people she encountered, such as "beautiful," an "attractive manner," "a brilliant conversationalist," "engaging," "tall, handsome," "fresh and dainty," and "ugly."[46] It is plausible that the difference may be primarily imputed to a more infrequent circulation of German and German-inspired works such as Goethe's and of the Transcendentalists' writings among the Southern population. A study by Warren S. Tryon discovered that in the South book sales by the publishing house Ticknor and Fields, the Transcendentalists' publisher as well as the publisher of most of the German literature reaching the United States during this period, were steadily increasing from the 1840s to the 1860s. However, these sales figures were still less than half those in the Northeast, an area of equal population. Additionally, the city of Cincinnati alone, Tryon found, purchased an almost equivalent number of books from Ticknor and Fields in one year as the entire Southern region did during the same time span. He also found evidence that of the books sold by Ticknor and Fields in the South, the largest quantity was from British authors, not Americans or Germans. Although he was unable to discover most individual titles included in such shipments, Tryon did identity a few shipments of works by Longfellow and Hawthorne that reached the South in numbers between two to twelve copies to three cities in the 1850s, while a work of poetry by the British author Alexander Smith sold fifty copies in Raleigh, North Carolina, alone. Even more poorly selling in the South than American literature, he found, were religious and educational texts.[47] These figures are supported by the reading recounted by Stone. Sixty-eight percent of her listed titles were by European authors. Goethe was the only German author she mentioned, and she was "disappointed as I do not much enjoy it." She also heavily criticized Harriet Martineau's historical novel of the San Domingo revolution as "a disgusting book." Stone referenced the scarcity of reading material during the war owing to the predominance of Northern publications but also remarked that books by Yankee authors were "unreadable trash," though she did record enjoying *The Marble Faun* by Nathaniel Hawthorne and also works by Edgar Allen Poe.[48] These figures support the hypothesis that the residents of the South were by and large not acquainted with the philosophical, religious, or self-cultivation ideals being purveyed in the North during this period; if familiar, they were often unable to read them with an impartial mind, Stone's language suggests.

The absence of the primacy of a model of resignation and bildung offers an intriguing postulate for the higher desertion rates among Southern armies and the nearly constant stream of desires to return home and end the war through any compromise that appear in Confederate letters at a considerably earlier period in the war than most Union sources reveal. One Southern soldier, Francis Poteet, writing to his wife in 1863, stated that the only thing that held him in the army and prevented his desertion was her concern for his safety and reputation. But he was ready to return home and hoped there would "be peace," but did not "care how it comes," whether through victory, defeat, or stalemate. If he had known he "had to stay in the army till the war ended I would as soon be De[a]d," he concluded.[49] Daniel Revis, another Confederate soldier, also considered desertion, writing to his wife, "I hop[e] that pease [sic] will be made before long," but if the war continued "I will come eny [sic] how."[50] A third soldier, George Williams, discussed an upcoming gubernatorial election in North Carolina. The incumbent governor, Williams recounted in his letters, had been campaigning vigorously, with one of his platform planks being strong support for the continuation of the war. According to Williams, this was not well-received among the Confederate troops. "He wants to fight until hell freases over and then fight on the ice," he wrote, but they were "not willing to fight so long as that" and thus the incumbent had lost the soldier vote, Williams believed. The opposing candidate was instead "our choice by a large majoety," for he was "not for fighting that long."[51] The contrast between these statements and those of the Union soldiers cited above is striking. None of these Confederate writings demonstrates any conception like Bushnell's concerning army service as a form of Christlike moral integrity or a Goethean ideal of resignation and bildung. This raises the possibility that in the North an internalized cultural framework influenced by these ideals of character may have served not only as an individual lens through which to experience and cope with warfare but may have also played into the behavior of armies on a larger scale.

Considering the popularity of Goethe's novels and the indication that these ideas had permeated Northern society, this suggests another interpretative angle from which to view an additional notable aspect of the Civil War: the lack of personal animosity expressed toward the enemy, particularly in Northern sources. It is extremely rare to find an instance of any statements regarding wishing to kill the foe or viewing bombastic statements as proof of manhood or courage. Northern soldiers focused on their own self-offering for the cause and the rhetoric of "laying down their lives" rather than being actively killed by or killing another.[52] Drew Gilpin Faust portrays this rhetoric as a superficial coping strategy that "enabled soldiers to mitigate their terrible responsibility for the slaughter of others."[53] Yet there is scant evidence of soldiers employing the same strategy in other wars. It is difficult to imagine

Ernest Hemingway, for instance, employing such language in World War I as laying down his life on the altar of his country, in light of his statement that words such as "sacred, glorious, and sacrifice ... abstract words such as glory, honor, courage, or hallow were obscene" and an embarrassment in the context of war.[54] Goethe's portrayal of every striving as noble, the necessary and beneficial function of opposition or negation, and the Transcendentalists' interpretation of personal self-culture as embracing the entire society propose a more nuanced understanding. In such a model, even the Confederates, misguided and iniquitous as Northerners believed their cause to have been, could be acknowledged as striving for a higher goal and contributing toward the bildung of the world spirit. Union general Joshua Chamberlain, in charge of the surrender ceremonies at Appomattox, expressed this idea concisely. He believed the Confederates' bravery and character were a credit to the country as a whole. He did not approach the defeated soldiers as enemies or targets for ridicule or debasement, for he maintained that their sacrifice and courage had also contributed to the idea of world historical development, or as he phrased it "the march of man" in which even faults and sins were transmuted into an "immortal inheritance" for all.[55] And thus could the Transcendentalist minister James Freeman Clarke state that to live in such times was "something to be thankful for" because it represented a great stride forward for the human race as a whole toward the supremacy of *idea*, a very Hegelian interpretation as well.[56] Such attitudes left less room for personal blame or hatred toward Southerners than perhaps could have been expected, given the nature of civil war. In fact, a Presbyterian newssheet specifically blamed those in the Transcendentalist circle as the "namby-pamby, anti-capital-punishment, semi-universalist, semi-pantheistic clique" in Boston and New York for the toleration and leniency demonstrated in Reconstruction policies.[57] In this instance, contemporaries more clearly saw the source of the period's political philosophy than has historically been acknowledged. These Hegelian ideas also elucidate the then-unprecedented phenomenon of Reconstruction itself, that is, of the victor assisting to reconstruct the conquered region and the Northern sense of responsibility to help guide the South toward internal improvement, although such was unwelcome to many white Southerners and at times turned to self-seeking abuse of the policies among Northerners.

These elements in the military culture of the American Civil War can be significantly clarified from an awareness of Goethe's vision of bildung as an "apprenticeship" in resignation and reverence, along with his thesis of the value of even misguided striving. Each of these ideals can be seen deeply embedded in the intellectual culture of the Union armies. This philosophical framework informed individual interpretative processes and behavior during the war, the Union approach to Confederates, and the soldiers' own motivation and responsibility. Further insight into the specific characteristics that Northern soldiers strove to acquire in their application of the ideals of bildung can be found in the works of Carl von Clausewitz.

The German militarist Carl von Clausewitz authored a treatise titled *On War* (1832) that was an important text to emerge from the eighteenth- and early nineteenth-century military enlightenment in Germany, the *militärische Aufklärung*. Sara Eigen Figal has defined this movement as "a philosophical discourse" that involved the identification of self and enemy, not only in terms of intentions, logistics, and strategic mapping, as it means today, but also as "finely tuned intellectual and psychological insights into cultural difference, human rivalry, and the limits of rational control."[58] A very concrete instance of the influence of such German philosophies of character applied to the bildung of men in the Civil War is the creation of the Lieber Code. In mid-1862, General Henry W. Halleck and Secretary of War Edwin Stanton appointed Francis Lieber and Ethan Allen Hitchcock to revise the 1806 Articles of War. Hitchcock is an unsurprising choice as a graduate of West Point, a career soldier, and adviser to Stanton. He also happened to be another close acquaintance of the Transcendentalists and author of, among others, a book on the philosophers Swedenborg and Spinoza.[59] Lieber, however, is a more unexpected appointee, for although he had written extensively on issues of political science, had served in the Prussian army against Napoleon and fought with the Greek independence movement armies, he had never been involved in the US military or government. Lieber attended the University of Jena in 1820, where he learned the philosophies of Hegel and Fichte, but his involvement with the political student movement there drove him out of Germany, first to Greece and then to the United States. He eventually became the first professor of political science in the nation at Columbia College in New York City, where he authored numerous works on political science and essays on various topics.[60] He was also a friend and correspondent of the Transcendentalist James Freeman Clarke, contributed to his literary journal the *Western Messenger*, as well as corresponded with other members of the Transcendentalist circle, including Massachusetts politicians Charles Sumner and Edward Everett, reformers Julia Ward Howe and Samuel Gridley Howe and Dorothea Dix, and George Ticknor, who had studied in Germany as well.[61] These connections and influences evidence an exchange of ideas occurring between these members of the New England intellectual circle.

In addition to his personal friendship with Lieber, Halleck was also one of the few Civil War generals with a known familiarity with the work of Clausewitz. It may be possible that Halleck was interested in introducing the German militärische Aufklärung ideals, with which Lieber was acquainted, to the US military through this appointment. Lieber was thoroughly influenced by Clausewitz even before the publication of *On War*.[62] The militärische Aufklärung is particularly noteworthy for the examination of character ideals herein, for from this background Clausewitz placed great emphasis on the role of character during warfare, particularly in creating a successful commander but also as a key ingredient in the general behavior of armies, which was in sharp contrast with Napoleon, for instance, under whom Clausewitz had served. In his chapter "The Genius for War," Clausewitz laid out what he believed to be the most important characteristics for an individual to possess so as to be successful in war. What he identified were qualities that Civil War contemporaries saw present in Northern culture rather than Southern, such as calmness and stolidity, which can integrate Clausewitz's military philosophy into the broader philosophical currents of his period that I investigate—the primacy of reason and understanding over the passions.[63]

Southern citizens were convinced at the outset of the war that their culture produced the best material for soldiers. Mary Chesnut, diarist and wife of a Confederate senator, exulted in the "red-hot Southern martial spirit" of the "rash, reckless, headlong, devil-may-care, proud, passionate, unruly raw material for soldiers" that swelled the ranks of the Confederate army when war was declared.[64] Others also characterized the Southern soldiers as "fiery and reckless" and "intense, overwhelming." They were seen as "ever ready for a fight" and as possessing much "more dash . . . and more real war spirit" than the Northern soldier.[65] It was hard to envision that the Northerners, a "sordid set, fit for drudgery, but not for fighting," would ever defeat them.[66] The Northern populace was too "phlegmatic," too "dull, slow, peaceful," and had "no trace of excitability."[67] Europeans visiting the United States made the same observations. Traveling through the Confederacy in 1863, William Corsan, an Englishman, noted that the Southerners' active, outdoor lifestyle had prepared them well for army life, as opposed to the sedentary, indoor occupations of the Northern men.[68] George Templeton Strong, a native of New York, questioned early in 1861 if the Northern populace could ever be goaded "into manliness and a little moderate wrath," concluding that only their love of justice had any hope of accomplishing this goal.[69]

A principle like justice was, however, exactly what Clausewitz emphasized as necessary. A calm and reasoned intellectual cause, rather than the mere impulse of a fiery disposition, was of higher value in warfare. For, just as Chesnut observed, Southerners were "impulsive but hard to keep moving. They are wonderful for a spurt—put out all their strength and then like to rest."[70] Clausewitz observed this same tendency with any soldiers who were driven by passion. Their enthusiasm and courage blazed up "quickly and violently like gunpowder, but do not last." As a result, despite the initial deceptive appearance of more zeal for the fight, "excitable, inflammable feelings . . . are not very fit for War."[71] And although in the first half of the Civil War the Rebels did indeed perform better, by the second half, when the brief battles and frontal charges had given way to protracted campaigns and trench warfare, the balance swung in favor of the Union. A Confederate soldier from Mississippi noted with regret in 1864 that there were no longer any opportunities to charge "gloriously."[72] As Clausewitz had observed, "A brave attack, a soul-stirring hurrah, is the work of a few moments, whilst a brave contest on the battle-field is the work of a day, and a campaign the work of a year."[73] Although many factors, such as economic limitations, contributed to the higher desertion rates among Confederate soldiers, perhaps Clausewitz's observations on the role of character should not be completely dismissed when considering differences between the enculturation of stereotypical Northern and Southern soldiers, and ideals of character allowed to have played a more influential role than often credited.

Certainly, using Clausewitz's theories on the importance of character in warfare as a case study for the emphasis placed on the aspect of character by the militärische Aufklärung gives additional insight into the mindset of Northern Americans in their focus on character development and creates an intriguing line of philosophical connections, although any such direct theoretical impact behind Lieber's appointment can be only speculative. The connection with Clausewitz and the German philosophers for Lieber, however, is a certainty, and on April 24, 1863, General Orders Number 100, or the Lieber Code, officially replaced the former Articles of War. The code outlawed torture of prisoners to extract information, implemented regulations for the humane treatment of prisoners and civilians, and reminded soldiers that, despite being at war, they did "not cease on this account to be moral beings, responsible to one another and to God."[74] The provisions in the Lieber Code altered military culture significantly, even attracting international interest in the years after the war and inspiring the Hague Convention of 1907 for revisions to international treaty laws. The code can, perhaps, be viewed as the most direct importation of the militärische Aufklärung into America and places the American Civil War into a broader movement in world military history and suggests that Civil War Americans' emphasis on character within this war was a testing ground for these theories. Implementation of the code helps explain why the Northern populace in particular placed such emphasis on personal character in the prosecution and outcome of the war. The traits promoted by and associated with the Transcendentalists, such as self-reliance and self-control, introspection, and stolidity, which suggests the Transcendentalists to have been ineffective or passive members of society, are therefore the same ones that were seen as effective, aggressive, and militant traits in a wartime setting—traits that led to victory and not to defeat.

Self-control and self-discipline were particularly important qualities to the Union soldier. An ideal of nonauthoritative discipline in the raising of children as a form of instilling self-culture in the areas of self-reliance and self-control was a key tenet of Transcendentalist educational theory. By this, they strove to instill the growth of internal virtue rather than external imposition in the pursuit of morals. Bronson Alcott adopted this concept in his method of making his children punish him for their faults instead of he punishing them. His daughter Louisa portrayed this method in *Little Men* (1871), with the character of Professor Bhaer taking her father's role. To cure Nat, one of the orphan boys he and Jo have taken in, of his habit of lying, Mr. Bhaer makes Nat whip his own, Mr. Bhaer's, hand, instead of the professor whipping Nat. Nat obeys under protest, then "threw the rule[r] all across the room, and hugging the kind hand in both his own, laid his face down on it sobbing out in a passion of love, and shame, and penitence: 'I will remember! Oh! I will!'"[75] Although Louisa portrays the scene with a boy, it is critical to note that in real life Bronson was educating his daughters in the desired nonauthoritarian methods.

This ideal can be seen translated specifically into the military model of discipline prevalent in the Civil War armies of the North. It reveals a strong line of connection from Transcendentalist ideals into the culture of the Civil

War, providing an insight into both the conception of military authority in the period and the decreased loss of personal identity that soldiers recounted compared with the writings of soldiers in other American wars. In keeping with the reformist ideals already implemented in the penitentiary system, the Transcendentalist view on discipline was not a statement of belief in the depravity of human nature but in its innate ability to be improved. The combination of these two ideals, the potential for reformation and a nonauthoritarian authority, illustrates a foundation from which to examine the military discipline of the era. In contrast with the Revolutionary War, for example, when flogging or the punishment of "picketing," or driving sharp sticks into the flesh, was a frequent practice, or World War II, when sexual shaming became common, Civil War military punishments focused more on displaying the character faults of an individual as an example to others.[76] Thus, in a sense, such punishments were theoretically inflicted on the soldier not by an external authority but by his internal sense of shame so as to spur him into self-reformation.

John Pratt, a soldier in the Union army, for example, described the company's captain making "an example of some of the men who ran away, during the engagement yesterday, by marching them around camp with placards pin'd on the back of each reading as follows: 1st man 'Volunteer Skirmisher in the Rear[,]' 2d , 'I skulked to the rear[,]' 3d, 'So did I' and the 4th, 'and I too.'"[77] Though embarrassing exhibitions of character flaws like this were allowed, the Lieber Code and manuals such as Kautz's 1865 Customs of Service outlawed needlessly humiliating or debasing punishments and provided that punishments must be directly related to the nature of the offense. Common practices listed included tying soldiers up by the hands or making them carry a heavily loaded knapsack.[78] Punishments rarely strayed into physical abuse or sexual shaming for unrelated breaches of military terminology, for example, as Eugene Sledge recounted from World War II.[79] Although from the frontier army in the year after the Civil War ended, Colonel Henry Carrington's circular on discipline is illustrative. The circular read, in part: "That perversion of authority . . . which displays itself in profane swearing, verbal abuse, kicks and blows, and which violates every social, moral, and military principle, will be dealt with in the most decided manner." Equally useless and contemptible was "vulgar, profane and abusive language." Carrington was convinced that "it never can command respect. It never will prompt a cheerful obedience, where the soldier retains a spark of manhood," for that which "degrades a man, destroys the soldier, and it is perfectly compatible with strict discipline, and the highest order of military subordination, to command that the personal rights of the soldier be held as sacred as those of officers."[80] One can deduce that Carrington, who also served in the Civil War, deemed an officer's character as the deciding factor in eliciting, rather than extracting, respect from enlisted men. The common soldier's personal rights were also worthy of respect, and if esteemed, his highest character would be drawn out rather than beaten down. Such treatment would serve to benefit the army as a whole, whereas the reverse would destroy the soldier and consequently hinder any military operations in which he took part. Lieutenant Roswell Lamson similarly discussed that aboard the naval flotilla in which he served, "I always *try* to control myself, and I *very rarely* speak angrily to a man, *never* in terms of reproach or derision; and there is *nothing* that makes me so *much* out of patience as to hear an officer *abuse* a man. I do not allow one of my officers to do it."[81]

General George Meade, the highest-ranking Union military leader after Grant, evidently followed this philosophy as well. Colonel Charles Wainwright recounted an instance when Meade, in the stress and exhaustion of a campaign, slapped a soldier who had been caught stealing corn from civilians against Meade's direct orders. Wainwright related that Meade was "very much ashamed of himself" and "cleared out" to calm his temper before again addressing his troops.[82] Meade, even though upholding military order, expressed shame at losing self-control but also in trampling on the individual honor of the soldier in question. Unfortunately, the soldier who received Meade's chastisement has not been identified to allow his response to the incident to be discovered. However, other examples can be found demonstrating the weight placed on self-governance. Wilbur Fisk recorded attending a sermon by the regimental chaplain who preached on the biblical verse, "He that governeth his own spirit is better than he that taketh a city." Fisk commented that the point the chaplain made in the sermon was that "every one of us could be more heroic, wield a more difficult authority than our best and ablest officers and generals."[83] This "more difficult authority" was none other than that of creating a balanced character, of subordinating the passions, and of self-discipline. According to this line of reasoning, military authority was not something to which soldiers were unjustly subjected; the external punishment of a military commander was a sign of one's own deficiencies in character, lack of strength of will, undeveloped self-control, and a lack of self-reliance. Hence such a punishment would not be something undeserved but an aid in self-culture for the benefit of the individual, not the benefit of a politico-military machine. This theory of a nonauthoritative authority in the ideal of bildung thus comes into focus in practice and illuminates both military culture and soldier motivation in the Civil War.

Any discussion of soldier motivation and individuals' mentality toward their role within war cannot be complete without a consideration of the very real threat of death faced almost daily and their participation in the death of others. In the Civil War, this threat was presented as a much less frightful, regretful, and final event than is customary to find in later personal literature from the front lines in later wars, which coheres to the framework of bildung as well. Although few soldiers likely reasoned in philosophical depth, an overarching metaphysical outlook, conviction of the continuity of life beyond death and the continuity of their particular selves, appears to have permeated their culture. This conviction of the value of individual character as contributing toward the whole can be discerned in relation to both the living and the dead.

The Christian understanding of death had long held that it was a continuation of the life of the soul and of unity with God, which continued to be a major influence, but many aspects of such are unique to the era that cannot be traced to Christianity alone. Swedenborg's reported mystic visions, for instance, shifted the emphasis from union with God into reunion with departed family and a continuation of life like the earthly. Herder's conception of die Kräfte also presented death in a new light. Death was, Herder suggested, merely a changing of forms, not an end of existing or participating in the world. It was a "salutary opiate" during which "nature collects her powers," and although it appeared as destruction, it was progress toward new forms of life. Matter and spirit were one; there was never a severing of one from the other, merely transformation.[84] Destruction could be a conscious choice, made with an end in sight that was held in greater esteem than that which was destroyed.

Hegel's vision of the self in the world process can also illuminate particular aspects of the Northern soldiers' approach to death and their individual role in warfare. He presented a view that both elevated individuals and at the same time subsumed individuality into a whole. A "world-historical" character, in Hegel's philosophy, was one who demonstrated the state of thought, the progression toward absolute spirit, that the age, nation, and religion had reached at that particular point in time. For instance, Alexander the Great (356–323 BCE) was the world-historical figure from ancient Greece; Martin Luther

(1483–1546) of the early modern period; and Napoleon (1769–1821) of Hegel's own time. These individuals captured the essence of their particular historical epochs and were at once an individual and the mass sum of all their age, the universal in the particular.[85] One might say that an individual human being was something of a particularized universal. The universal worked within the particular for furthering its own aims, sometimes without the particular's conscious knowledge, but the universal existed outside and beyond the particular.

This conception resonates with the coexistent culture of personal value and individualism, combined with the willingness to face extreme casualty percentages, that was present during the Civil War. A soldier could be valued and honored for his individual role in furthering a cause of greater unity and universal freedom, but the cause remained of higher value than his individual life. His dedication and morale, therefore, could also remain strong for this kind of conception of the cause, without being destroyed by military blunders, payment arrears, and government failures. Likewise, the individual within the army was respected for his individual character that could be believed to contribute immeasurably toward the higher cause while still being submerged into the military whole. Although Hegel himself held that only exceptional individuals, and not the common soldier, could be world-historical, in the Jacksonian democratic atmosphere of the United States, this idea was extended to the masses. It was the responsibility of each soldier to become the world-historical individual, which required the willingness to be at the same time both more and less than the individual alone.

Without these philosophical frameworks for understanding masculinity and bildung, the impact that ideals of character held on the practical daily routines of self-cultivation, interpretation of events, and personal dedication is significantly lost, and Civil War culture remains misunderstood. But once identified and seen in application, many diverse aspects come into focus—are explicable and illuminating in understanding the war, its participants, the cultural background that shaped them and the transatlantic philosophical context that created this culture. Many of the distinctive cultural aspects of the Civil War era that have been difficult for historians to resolve find cohesion from a simple examination of the works of Goethe, the effects of Idealist philosophy on military culture in Germany in the works of Clausewitz, and the metaphysical mentality promoted by Herder and Hegel. Each of these sources emphasized sentiment, emotion, intuition, and self-control as the hallmarks of manhood, rather than bravado, virility, or physical prowess. Inspired by this outline for bildung, Northern men purposefully cultivated quieter, more introspective and measured characters, and sentiments were valued as an essential part of this character, not viewed as a detraction or weakness. The masculine ideal of the North in the Civil War was not of impassioned, violent men with a paradoxical sentimental streak but of men whose sentiments and integrity to moral convictions drove them into warfare.

Chapter Six
THE EUROPEAN INHERITANCE ON RACE AND CHARACTER

"Emerson and Thoreau are oftener in my mind, in connection with this camp life and these people, than any other writers I know," Doctor Seth Rogers, surgeon for the 1st South Carolina Colored Volunteers, wrote reflectively in the early days of the regiment in 1863.[1] He was observing in action the philosophical stance that the Transcendentalists had voiced in theory, that bildung was a universal reality. It was neither reserved to white men nor extended only to white women but was a practice that was equally applicable and valuable to other races as well, in this instance those of African ancestry. The 1st South Carolina Colored Volunteers was the locus where one of the most significant experiments in nineteenth-century racial policy was being enacted. The regiment was comprised solely of African American men, not free Black men even but "contrabands," the Black people who had escaped slavery in the American South. It was imperative for these Black Americans to prove themselves in the crucible of war as equally capable of moral character as their white counterparts. White soldiers saw combat as a field of growth in character and bildung, but for Black soldiers this was doubly true, given that the stakes based on their performance in war were even higher. If a white soldier failed, his personal character was injured. If a Black soldier failed, the character of his entire race was condemned. The shifting views of Black Americans' capabilities were again owing in part to changing philosophical currents.

Given the emphasis placed on the universal potential of moral character in the philosophical currents of the Transcendentalists' circle, it appears to be no accident that the officers of both the Union's 1st South Carolina Colored Volunteers and a like regiment recruited among the free Black men of the North, the 54th Massachusetts Volunteer Infantry, issued from the Transcendentalists' home state of Massachusetts. Thomas Wentworth Higginson, himself a Transcendentalist, led the 1st South Carolina, and Robert Gould Shaw, the son of a prominent Boston family who was close friends with many of the Transcendentalists, led the 54th Massachusetts. The obvious contradiction that existed in racialized chattel slavery could not maintain itself in the face of the Transcendentalists' argument for including all humanity in a collective progression, the bildung of mankind, toward universal moral character, unity with the Over-Soul, and with one another. The conception of humanity and the American political nation both had to include those of African descent in this vision and further the opportunities available to them for bildung, or all would suffer. Bildung demanded the political emancipation of African Americans from slavery and their inclusion in environments and education that could further the cultivation of character among those formerly deemed incapable of rational thought, moral conscience, and self-driven sanctification.

The Transcendentalists were long overlooked for their role in abolition and race relations and theory. Some historians viewed the Transcendentalists as social radicals who brought on the crisis of war through an uncompromising and confrontational approach to the question of slavery. The Transcendentalists have been accused of being "intellectuals without responsibility" who paid lip service to the belief in the humanity of those enslaved and the immorality of slavery but were so "anti-institutional, antiformal, and individualistic" that they took the moral high ground. They supposedly refused negotiation and drove the country apart through their harsh, critical rhetoric rather than promote or accept stopgap measures or compromises such as owner compensation that could have accomplished a peaceful abolition of slavery in the United States.[2] This kind of perspective on the Transcendentalists' problematic radicalism was prevalent during the Cold War and surfaced again post-9/11, with the Transcendentalists pinpointed as their era's "chief exporter of extremism, political upheaval, and uncompromising militancy."[3] More commonly, past historians portrayed the Transcendentalists as secluded scholars who ignored the social issues of their day, pretending the country was not rending at its regional seams, looking the other way when asked to lend their support to the antislavery cause, and being socially unable to cooperate with others or apply themselves to practical affairs.[4] Only recently have their contributions to and collaboration with the abolitionist movement and such Black activists as Alexander Crummell, William C. Nell, and Lewis Hayden garnered adequate attention, which now demonstrates that they were essential figures in shaping the antebellum awareness of the issues and provided a philosophical framework from which to address it.[5] Though strong proponents of abolition and generally forward-thinking for their era in their approach to race, the white Transcendentalists still retained many racial prejudices, and borrowing the insights of Ibram Kendi, their perspective can be categorized as *assimilationist*, a viewpoint that led to a "glorious struggle against racial discrimination" combined with the "partial blaming of inferior Black behavior for racial disparities."[6] They believed the Black population was capable of bildung, a significant advance in egalitarian thinking, but retained a vision of bildung that was rooted in their own white culture. The Black Transcendentalist proponents of bildung themselves were interested in drawing from the Idealist philosophers, however, so this vision was also not a white cultural imposition on and limitation of Black individuals' intellectual endeavors. Rather, this overlap emphasizes the nuanced currents present within the Transcendentalist discussion of, intersection with, and involvement in the abolitionist movement and interracial interactions.

In initially forming and subsequently defending their stance on the question of race and slavery, Transcendentalists inherited many European frameworks of racial theory, ethnic characteristics, and historical development that were woven throughout the philosophical traditions they referenced from Europe. Many of these were only dimly articulated in America but formed the major threads of interpretation that informed American ethnologists as well. The topic of race had come to the forefront of debate in the seventeenth and eighteenth centuries as increasing exploration brought European thinkers into ever-growing familiarity with non-European populations and became a theological problem when aligned with biblical accounts. There were several main theories put forth by proponents of anthropology, science, and biblical literalism during this period. Adherents of anthropology and science sought explanations in natural law to account for the racial variations of the human family, including influences of climate; varying bodily secretions; assorted theories of origins such as polygenesis, which posited several unconnected beginnings of humanity in diverse locations around the globe; and even evolution from lower animal forms in regard to some, notably those from Africa. Advocates of biblical literalism believed such natural law theories threatened the authority of Scripture and hence the foundation of Christianity itself and chose instead to trace racial differences through biblical accounts. In this view, the transmission of original sin and the universal salvation through Christ necessitated monogenesis, a single, original human family. Some commentators concluded that races could be traced from Noah's sons, with the Asian and Middle Eastern races descending from Shem, the African race from Ham, and the European from Japheth. The biblical curse of Ham's son Canaan to "serve his brothers" was thus utilized as a justification for enslaving Black people. Other views separated races as far back as Cain and Abel. The process of racial differentiation over time was explained in numerous ways. The options posited included the belief that God's curse had turned the sons of Ham Black following the flood; that God had intervened and turned Ham Black in the womb although his parents were white; that Adam had been an intermediate brown and the posterity of Cain and Abel had with time changed into greater extremes of skin tone, with Cain's descendants darkening and Abel's lightening; or that the second creation account in the Book of Genesis, where man is formed from the ground, described the origin of so-called "colored pre-Adamic races," and the first account of man as made in God's image and likeness referred solely to the creation of the white European race.[7] Whichever the theory, the one thing they had in common was justification for maintaining a social hierarchy that placed the Black population on the lowest rung and the white race at the top.

For US intellectuals, these debates held particular relevance, both in relation to the presence of racialized chattel slavery in the country and for solving the origin of the Native American populations of the American continent. The question of Native American origin featured as an especially problematic topic in biblical literalist circles before Captain James Cook's 1778 account of the proximity of continents at the Bering Strait allowing for the possibility of an original Asian migration to the American continent from which subsequent Native American peoples developed. Furthermore, with the end of indentured servitude among European Americans and the abolition of all slavery in most of the Northern United States by the close of the eighteenth century, a regional divide over the issue was coming into focus. For at nearly the same time, the economic boom of cotton following Eli Whitney's invention of the cotton gin caused racialized chattel slavery to be suddenly seen as a socioeconomic necessity by the white population of the American South, even as it was increasingly deplored among the Northern populace.

Mark Noll argues that a major cause of the Civil War crisis was the divergent scriptural interpretation present within the nation and among Christian denominations, particularly as it applied to issues of race and racialized chattel slavery. Prominent Northern denominations, he concluded, increasingly approached the Bible for its spirit rather than its letter, whereas Southern Christians clung to greater biblical literalism in their interpretation. Hence Northern Americans began to conclude that whether racialized chattel slavery was based on the curse of Ham, pre-Adamic creation, or some other ground, it was contrary to the broader message of Christianity, while Southerners continued to cite Scripture in defense of racialized chattel slavery, with one Southern author going so far as to translate the Hebrew word for Eve's tempter in Eden as "Negro gardener" rather than serpent.[8] Thus the cause, origins, and influencing factors of environment, nature, and race became a point of serious political and social debate among Americans in this era, and the Transcendentalists turned to the same philosophers that shaped their framework of universal moral character for ideas on resolution of the concerns.

Given their earlier academic acquaintance with the writers of the Common Sense School, the philosophical theories of human diversity that the Transcendentalists would have initially been exposed to would have come from among these writers. The Scottish philosophers reflected greatest interest in the topic revolving around whether racial distinctions were due to natural or intellectual causes and, consequently, whether it belonged in the realm of natural history or philosophy of mind. David Hume, in an essay titled "On National Characters" (1748), laid out a theory of human diversity and national characteristics that relied on the influence of group circumstance. He did not endorse climate as a source of cultural distinction, dismissing theories based on natural law or a search for universal systems grounded on natural law. It was human nature, he argued, that was the root cause for human diversity and human likeness. If found in the same circumstances, most people reacted the same, and this group reaction to circumstances formed the basis for societies, civilizations, and collective characteristics. But human capacity for moral character, he concluded, was gifted in greater and lesser degrees to different racial groups, with European races possessing moral superiority over those groups that happened to reside in warmer climates. Of the "four or five different" human "species" on which Hume briefly remarked, he believed they were "naturally inferior to the whites" because of an "original distinction" made by nature.[9] His argument was therefore not entirely consistent, for it removed white society from the impact of nature and climate but condemned races incidentally native to warm climates to a limited intellectual endowment that originated in nature and was consequently not something within their power to remedy whatever their circumstances.

In contrast, the Scottish philosopher and professor of moral philosophy at Edinburgh, Adam Ferguson, in *An Essay on the History of Civil Society* (1767), posited that it was climate that created the different levels of organized society witnessed between different human races. "The temper of the heart, and the intellectual operations of the mind, are, in some measure, dependent on the state of the animal organs," he wrote.[10] Cool climates resulted in better organ function, whereas heat suppressed it. The hot climate of Africa, for example, "hindered liberty and prevented the development of wise political systems." He believed that the example of the Dutch in India further proved his hypothesis, for although members of the white race were "active and productive" while in the cooler climates of Europe, they became languid and unproductive when residing in the heat of the Indian climate.[11] As opposed to Hume, his theory was at least consistent across racial categories.

Henry Home, Lord Kames, another Scottish writer and philosopher and a judge on the supreme civil court of Scotland, posited that human races were different species altogether and believed that ascribing influences such as climate or food to the regional diversity observed between people was absurd and demonstrated a mere groping for "accidental causes" that could not be supported by thorough reasoning.[12] How, he questioned, could climate create the absence of facial hair among the Indigenous population of the Americas, with continental climates that ranged from arctic to tropic? And if climate acted chiefly on the complexion, why again did Indigenous Americans present a similar skin tone across the two continents? And why did three generations of Africans living in the cool climate of Pennsylvania or Europeans residing for years in a hot climate not experience a change in skin pigmentation as a result? Polygenist origins of different human species was the only plausible answer he could reach that would stand up to scrutiny. He concluded, "God created many pairs of the human race, differing from each other both externally and internally; that he fitted these pairs for different climates."[13] Although contrary to the Genesis creation account, it was, Kames insisted, the only logical solution to an otherwise paradoxical problem.

Thomas Reid accepted what appeared as the most simple and "common sense" approach to the question: the observational classification of Carl von

Linnaeus, a Swedish naturalist. Following a scientific school of thinking, Linnaeus classified the human species into four variants—the European, the American, the Asian, and the African—and wrote of humanity "as merely one part of the natural system, legitimately classified in the same way as flora and fauna."[14] This scientific classification of races as varieties instead of distinct species could fit within the biblical framework as well and aligned with Reid's more theological focus on trusting the God-given senses. However, Linnaeus's inclusion of humanity as simply another member of the animal kingdom as opposed to a rational being removed from brute existence through intellectual exceptionality, or even at the top of the "Great Chain of Being," also made him open to theological attack, as well as criticism from other natural philosophers such as the French naturalist Georges-Louis Leclerc de Buffon, who believed Linnaeus's classification system was much too simplistic and arbitrary. If one thing in nature resembled another, that was insufficient reason to believe them related or demonstrating a universal system.[15] But Reid was not interested in these technicalities: "Of every nation and tribe, and of every individual of the human race that is, or was, or shall be, it may be affirmed that they are men."[16] That it was *the* human race, and not human races, was enough to support the idea of a universally observable and applicable system of theory, the possession of common faculties and common sense around the globe, and theological consistency. This line of thought was more acceptable to Reid than suggestions that undermined universal continuity and reliability.

From these Scottish philosophers and writers, the Transcendentalists would have been acquainted with the general options available from which to approach race theory. The German philosophers continued the debate, informed by much the same schools of thought and the same underlying problems. Questions of biblical authority, polygenist versus monogenist origins, and the effects of culture and climate also featured prominently in their treatment of the topic, which they developed in accordance with their particular philosophical focuses and the compounding insights of Idealism.

Kant's writings on race set the stage for much of the debate on racial theory that occurred in Germany during the eighteenth and nineteenth centuries and that spanned many fields ranging from linguistics and theology to aesthetics and natural philosophy. Although not the sole inventor of the modern concept of race, as Robert Bernasconi has argued, Kant nonetheless played an influential role in shaping the development of racial theory. Before Kant, Bernasconi maintains that the conception of race was fluid and undefined, a word frequently interchanged with species, class, tribe, or specimen, whose precise meaning varied according to usage. Bernasconi proposes that Kant was the first philosopher to articulate a thorough outline of racial theory based on exterior physical features, particularly that of skin color, to create a more rigid concept of race that was limited to a strictly physiological definition based on appearance.[17] However, as Stella Sandford points out, Kant most likely did not intend to articulate a philosophical justification for racism per se but sought to discover a natural system as opposed to artificial classification. He was, she argues, using the human species to explore a broader theme and reveal the secret of unity within diversity that he deemed could be demonstrated throughout the natural world. This position appears more in keeping with Kant's general philosophical focus than supposing he was solely interested in racial categorization for its own sake or for political reasons, as it was not an immediate political problem in Germany as it was in the United States.[18]

Kant wrote largely in terms of nature's provisions for human development, seeking natural laws responsible for the phenomenon of race as opposed to theories of biblical lineage. He described nature as, from the beginning, providing for the successful growth of humanity to the best advantage for developing their reason. Kant posited that nature had provided for the continued existence of the human race by originating all diverse ethnicities from a single family, an initial "stem species."[19] From a Protestant Christian perspective, upholding monogenesis not only supported the literal interpretation and wider authority of Scripture but also avoided such theological problems as the universal transmission of original sin. Philosophical ideals of universal systems would likewise be challenged if polygenesis were true, as it would appear far less certain that universal principles could be discovered if humanity had originated from diverse sources scattered around the globe.[20] Kant covered his bases on both sides, holding that from one original human family every subsequent lineage and race had developed, becoming diversified by the effects of the natural environment over time. Although he did not directly challenge a Christian understanding, Kant's interpretation of the story of Genesis did indicate significant doubt regarding biblical literalism. He never referred to the original couple as Adam and Eve, and his views on the voice of God as a natural instinct and the tempter as humans' discovery of reason were scarcely orthodox.

Kant held that, although originating from a single source, there was from the beginning a preformed germ of diversity in human nature. The original stem species contained the predispositions for all subsequent racial characteristics. Through time and with the dispersion of the human race around the globe, he believed that humanity had separated from its original unity and formed into four distinct races. Kant distinguished these races as the white race, the "Negro" race, the "Hun" race, and the Hindu race, with the first two serving as the "base races."[21] He categorized the four races by external appearance, specifically skin tones, and believed that the races were determined and defined by these physical characteristics. This dispersion and division of humanity into the four races had been predetermined by natural laws, in his view. Nature made use of human warfare, physical needs, and social tendencies to serve its own ends, scatter the population around the earth, and develop the latent racial differences that lay within the species.

This was not to say that geographic climate had *created* racial differences, Kant clarified, but that the natural environment in which the four races developed brought out the preformed germs of racial characteristics that had thitherto lain dormant. "Numerous seeds and natural predispositions must lie ready in human beings either to be developed or held back," he wrote.[22] They were inborn and responded to, rather than being developed by, the climatic conditions in which each race predominately lived. This hazy line of differentiation left more unexplained than it clarified, however, for it still failed to articulate why descendants born in racially non-native lands exhibited the same characteristics as their forebears even though absent from the "developing" climate. If Kant were correct, such people should have been some non-raced identity altogether.

The temperate region of Europe produced the "greatest riches of earth's creation," Kant concluded, and therefore caused the least divergence from what in his view constituted humanity's original form. Hence the "noble blond" stock of Northern Europe was the "first race" in the lineal roots of the human races. Because he believed that a change in climate or situation did not affect one's racial makeup, it followed that the capacity for intellectual development, the race's "original endowments," was also predetermined. In this Kant remained consistent with his search for universals, and his position reflects his interest in natural systems. But in the search for universal laws of nature, Kant fell into such sweeping generalizations as Black people being "lazy, indolent, and dawdling" as part of their unalterable makeup.[23]

This view was one that some white Southerners in America were happy to accept, such as Richard Colfax, who liberally employed it in his defense of racialized chattel slavery. Even in their native land where, without the limits of slavery, they could have developed themselves as well as any primitive European tribe had in the past, argued Colfax, Black people had only ever demonstrated "grossness of intellect, listless apathy, sluggishness, and want of national and personal pride."[24] If left to their own devices, such arguments typically concluded, the situation of free Black people in America would be worse than under slavery because they would not be able to achieve the necessary self-motivation to provide for themselves or better their condition.

Because Kant believed that races owed their characteristics to internal, inherent predispositions, he posited that races were distinct from nationalities and were created by universal natural laws, not through shared history, cultural affinity, or conscious human choice. He argued that nature had allowed a certain span of time in which the races had developed in various parts of the world but that the window for racial alteration had closed at some undetermined point when this process was deemed complete and beyond which no racial adaptation was possible.[25] The absence of any logic behind this unspecified time span or what causes would have made the process complete was a glaring oversight in his argument and suggests that, in this area, he was reduced to forcing evidence for a natural classification where there was no evidence to support it. Despite these problems, Kant was clear as to the reason why racial development had needed to cease. Nature had done this, he concluded, to discourage the migration of non-white races into the Northern regions for which they were unsuited and to prevent racial miscegenation, which he believed sapped the strength and productiveness of the pure races.[26] Kant thus blamed the ancient migration of the Indigenous American population from Asia into the foreign climates of the American continent for stunting their progress as a race, as it must have occurred after the set period for racial development. They had never successfully adapted, he claimed, and were as a result "weak, inert; incapable of any culture."[27] Kant also categorized them and African individuals in terms resonating with the classification of active and passive powers that were outlined in Thomas Reid's philosophy.

Native American and African people were, Kant believed, deficient in the active powers of the will. They were capable of working, but they lacked the ability to make themselves work. Consequently, slavery ensured they were culturally, socially, or materially productive. Kant persisted in this argument as late as 1788, when he wrote *On the Use of Teleological Principles in Philosophy*. As Pauline Kleingeld argues, however, by his later works such as *Toward Perpetual Peace* of 1795, he may have retracted his earlier support of racialized chattel slavery, stating that slavery was "gruesome" and that both slavery and colonialism were grave violations of cosmopolitan right.[28] Scholars debate whether these statements prove a suddenly egalitarian respect for other races or a growing disapproval of slavery and colonialism as it was being practiced. Or perhaps, as was not unusual in the era, Kant merely objected to slavery in a historico-political sense while condoning it in the case of African people. Or he may have condemned slavery while still maintaining strongly racist outlooks. Either of these latter combinations is the most likely and were views often found in the Americas.

Kant's theory of racial classification was supported by the work of at least two prominent natural philosophers of the period, which helped grant it popularity and legitimacy in the eyes of the public. The Dutch anatomist Petrus Camper and the German scientist and anthropologist Johann Friedrich Blumenbach both largely agreed with Kant's racial categories and classification system based on external characteristics. However, under their hands the system contained an increased emphasis on cranial structure and facial angle over skin color. This theory was further taken over by two other Germans, Franz Joseph Gall and Johann Gaspar Spurzheim, who restructured craniological study into the popular pseudoscience of phrenology, which consisted of mapping personality and intellectual capacities by measuring the areas of the skull where they believed each faculty was housed. For example, the upper forehead area contained spirituality, ideality, benevolence, and sublimity. The lower brain contained the centers for tendencies such as destructiveness, amativeness, and combativeness. These phrenological theories likely won such wide support because they fit easily within the outlines of faculty psychology.

Phrenology gained wide interest in the United States beginning around 1822, when the first phrenological essay was published, and expanded particularly after 1832 when Spurzheim arrived in the country to lecture in person. Phrenology was extensively employed as racial politics in artistic renditions of African Americans particularly but also used as proof of women's inferior intellectual abilities based on skull and brain size compared with the average white man. Because phrenology based the intellectual capacities in the forehead region of the brain and the animal instincts in the lower back regions, racial interpretations concluded that Black peoples' facial angle, often of a more reclined slant than that of Europeans, demonstrated that their intellectual capabilities were proportionately reduced. "Modern anatomists have fixed the average facial angle of the European at 80 [degrees],—negro 70,—ourang outang [orangutan] 58,—all brutes below 70," wrote the American proslavery author Richard Colfax cited above, a claim that he believed proved Black inferiority beyond all question or controversy. The only fault he found with Blumenbach's theories was that Blumenbach maintained that Black people were the same species as the white race and held with the biblical monogenesis account, a theory of origins that only encouraged the abolitionists in their extreme position, Colfax argued.[29]

Likewise, phrenology taught that the more pronounced lips in those of African ancestry corresponded with increased sensuality and licentiousness. Hence, in racist drawings and paintings of the period, these characteristics were exaggerated. This technique was employed in proslavery literature to condemn the antislavery policies of the wartime Union government and to discourage aid to the freed Black people following the war's conclusion. In contrast, literature that supported the abolition of slavery and campaigned for freedmen's aid after the war sought to demonstrate Black peoples' ability and equality with white people and shows a careful avoidance of any of these stereotypical caricatures that employed the use of the cranial angle argument in addressing racial theory. These illustrators often fell to the other unfortunate extreme, however, and presented those of African descent as devoid of unique characteristics at all. Instead, they portrayed figures that appear more as merely dark skin imposed on European features, which could present the same conclusion as the exaggerated caricatures did by suggesting that the only route to achieving equality was to erase Blackness altogether and subsume the image of moral character into a single white model.

Such racial beliefs in nineteenth-century American culture were very prominent and did not solely target non-white people. Some antislavery authors in the North also employed racial categorization as a critique against white Southerners. As a result, racism in the era should not be seen as a regional phenomenon in which Northerners were exempt and Southerners implicated. Racism targeted white ethnicities as well in both regions. Robert Knox, a Scottish author with whom Emerson was familiar, predicted that the Southern states would "become depopulated by the operation of the physiological laws laid down" and would be overrun by the "Saxon" and "Celtic" races who predominated in the Northern states. "That they will ultimately seize on them there cannot be a doubt," Knox concluded, "driving before them the expiring remains of native and Lusitanian, Celt-Iberian and Mulatto—a worthless race—effete, exhausted."[30] His argument reflects what Colin Kidd has termed the growing Aryanism that can be detected starting in the mid-nineteenth century, which ultimately led to its infamous culmination in the Holocaust. The implication of the German Idealists with some of its development gives lie to their overarching claims to universalism, although as Matthew Stewart attests, it is not "a straight line between early nineteenth-century German Idealism and early twentieth-century German fascism."[31] Nonetheless, in this era there began to be a delineation of Celts and "Latins," or southern Europeans, as the "brachycephalic," or wide-headed, lesser white races, set against the "dolichocephalic," long-headed Teutonics that constituted the pinnacle of human development.[32] In the United States, these theories manifest in the anti-immigrant, particularly anti-Irish, sentiment that was strong in the Northern states and led to the creation of the American, better known as the Know-Nothing, political party, which held that Irish Catholics were unable to understand democracy and would degrade the moral fabric of the nation.

Those such as the Transcendentalists who argued in favor of Black peoples' intellectual ability were generally opposed to this interpretation as well. Even Abraham Lincoln wrote to his friend Joshua Speed concerning this party's platform: "How can any one who abhors the oppression of negroes, be in favor of degrading classes of white people? . . . As a nation, we began by declaring that 'all men are created equal.' We now practically read it 'all men are created equal, except negroes.' When the Know-Nothings get control, it will read 'all men are created equal, except negroes, and foreigners, and Catholics.'"[33]

In some cases, however, anti-Irish sentiment and abolitionism coexisted side by side, even in the circles influenced by Transcendentalism. Robert Gould Shaw, colonel of the 54th Massachusetts Black regiment, stated that Irish soldiers seemed to him "utterly unable to learn or understand anything," and even his Black troops were "infinitely" more ready "than the Irish" to learn what he taught them.[34] Some of this antipathy was not due to racial philosophies, however, but stemmed from the opposition of many Irish to abolition and their alignment with the proslavery Democratic Party. Free Black Americans and Irish immigrants were in close contest for unskilled laborer jobs in the Northern market, which led the Irish to fear greater competition in the workplace if abolition flooded the North with free Black workers. It was a complicated and often contradictory web of racial prejudices that wove itself between ethnic and regional groups, used both to create new profiling policies or to justify preexisting ones.

The German philosophical treatment of race did not end with Kant's suggestions. Johann Herder also addressed this topic, treating it in the vein of the emerging historicist tradition in Germany that attributed a significant role to contexts such as place, time, and social constructs in shaping individuals, values, and ideology. German historicism grew largely in response to the French conviction of the universal applicability of French thought and custom, which was feared as a threat to the unique aspects of German life and culture during Herder's lifetime. A philosophy such as Kant's, which removed the formation of culture from human agency and placed it in the hands of natural law for its own ends, appeared to offer a weak defense against such encroachments as those issuing from France. John Zammito has shown that it was also during the time of Herder's break with Kant, his former professor, that anthropology was being carved out of philosophy to form its own unique field of specialization. Herder, Zammito argues, followed the anthropological wing more closely, whereas Kant turned to the more purely academic, speculative areas of philosophy.[35] Charles Taylor describes Herder as being interested in an "expressivist anthropology," a reaction against French Enlightenment views of man as an egoistic being for whom nature and society provided the means of fulfillment. This anthropological approach, however, presented man as a unified being expressing multiple forces such as reason and feeling, body and soul, society and nature, which found their balance and meaning in simultaneous expression.[36] This anthropology was not a narrative, scientific, or archaeological study of human social and cultural development but is well described by *Webster's* 1828 dictionary definition of the term as "a discourse upon human nature."[37] In this line, Herder held that each individual and each group had a unique destiny to fulfill, had "its own way of being human, which it cannot exchange with that of any other except at the cost of distortion and self-mutilation." Humanity's forms of life and culture, nationality and religion, were the means of self-expression, Herder believed, and through self-expression, self-clarification and the discovery of who they were and were intended to be. Such theory argued that "man as a conscious being achieves his highest point when he recognizes his own life as an adequate, a true expression of what he potentially is," the achievement of self-actualization.[38] Thus Herder searched for causes that remained closer to humans themselves than those posited by Kant and over which they retained some control. In this way his racial philosophy was somewhat more personally applicable than Kant's, a practical approach that individuals could implement.

The historicism and expressivist anthropology in Herder's philosophy viewed individuals from a contextual standpoint. In the historicist approach, the whole came before the individual parts. Individuals were formed by the whole, rather than forming the whole. Consequently, their identity, their self-actualization, could not be thrown off and a new one adopted simply by individual choice. It was a group process of discovery in which each individual was a vital player, an agent of the nationality's self-expression and realization, and without which that nationality's unique demonstration of humanity would be lacking. Likewise, the particular time and location of any one group of persons determined this process. Although Herder's conception of race and nationalities was closely tied to an understanding of nature and the natural environment, his approach offered a particular slant. In Herder's conception, it was not natural law in the sense of a universal principle that acted mechanically in a preformed pattern on the world. It was, rather, the active, cognitive force, *die Kräfte*, the creative power emanating as energy streams into the cosmos, in which different nations and individuals participated at various levels. This force was always acting, shaping, and providing for the increase of human happiness, not merely its own predetermined ends. Herder believed that this inseparable force of Providence and nature had expressly formed each and every national people so as to further human fulfillment and was actively forming the progression of humanity. To attempt to meddle in this was to "violate Nature" and hence do violence to one's own identity.[39] The interplay of Providence and the natural environment in Herder's view was intrinsically linked with the development of race and of national identity. To view one race or ethnicity as inhibited by its climate from reaching its potential did not follow Herder's reasoning. According to his philosophy, nature and Providence had specially formed every continent and every nationality with every geographic feature, circumstance, moment in time, and national history necessary for it to develop to its full potential.

It is not surprising, then, that Herder specifically took issue with Kant's views on racial development. He saw "no reason" to separate humanity into the four races delineated by Kant but believed that "complexions run into each other, forms follow the genetic character," and that these were merely "shades of the same great picture" that covered all space and time.[40] He likewise thought, in accord with his broader biblical historicism, that it was a worthless pursuit to engage in debates over which races descended from which sons of Noah or which nationalities stemmed from Cain or Abel, as he believed natural history plainly contradicted the Genesis accounts that had been written in the ancient Hebrew context and never intended as a precise global historical or scientific record.

Consequently, Herder was much more open and tolerant toward other ethnicities typically deemed during the period as inferior to European civilization, reminding his readers that "the Kalmuc and the Negro remain completely men" and were the brothers of Europeans, not of "the pongo nor the gibbon."[41] He stated that he believed there existed no fundamental difference between cannibals in New Zealand and European thinkers, other than their geographic location, circumstances, and historical culture. Because Herder held that "Nature and Providence have created nationalities," and not the nation-state, he granted technologically and politically undeveloped nations and non-white races as much connection and attachment to native lands and local cultures as he did to Europeans.[42] "The Negro may form his society as well as the Greek," he asserted, sharply contrasting what most Europeans viewed as the lowest ranking nationality with one of the most sublime.[43] However, he was not above repeating many assumptions that today are still clearly racist. For example, he did not question the theory that "the lips, breasts, and private parts, are proportionate to each other" and hence Africans' "thick lips are held to indicate a sensual disposition." Nature had created them, he stated, with a physiological organization aimed toward "ampler measure of sensual enjoyment" and "boiling passions" because they had been denied the "nobler gifts" of fine intellect.[44] This statement indicates that although Herder believed Black people and Black culture were equally worthy of respect, as realizing the highest they were individually able and intended to attain, they still occupied a lower rung in intellectual development than white Europeans held. However, this belief was still in harmony with the basis of Herder's philosophy of mankind: that each race and culture was responsible for actualizing its own unique identity. Other races were not created to imitate European models, as in the same way, the German people of his own time should be allowed to form their own culture and institutions rather than adopt those of the French. If each people were not allowed this freedom, Herder believed that humanity as a whole would then be lacking one of the distinct expressions of human essence that Providence, nature, time, place, and circumstance had worked together to bring into being. As a result, in his work there coexisted the potential for complete racial disparagement and the possibility of equal respect and value.

Like Herder, Hegel was a contextualist in his treatment of race, believing that time and place played a role in shaping human consciousness. But unlike Herder, Hegel viewed influences such as geography and race as just one stage in a dialectical journey toward absolute self-consciousness. Nature was a force with which humanity did not harmonize but from which it must free itself. Neither did he believe, like Kant, that racial "germs" were a distinguishing mark between individuals. Rather, he thought that individual material existence held no absolute truth. He wrote, "For mind, a specific bodily expression is an indifferent accident, it is therefore bound to be aware at once that by the so-called 'laws' discovered [by physiognomy or phrenology] it really says nothing at all," and "there is no intelligible connection between the strength or weakness of spiritual faculties and the bulging or contracted size of regions of the skull."[45] From his point of view, generalizations and outward observations could not uncover absolute reality or cause and effect. Hegel contended that even the statement of "I" was stating a universal, an abstract concept that applied to every individual and was consequently an absolute. He posited that only when humanity recognized its universal and unified nature could individuals discover their true identity, the universal "I," and their subsequent freedom from all material, physical, or geographic constraints.[46] Thus, in Hegel's philosophy, race had no bearing whatsoever on reality, because the only absolute truths were universal and applicable to the unified all. It was merely a dialectical stage, a negation of unity, through which humanity as a whole had to pass to synthesize the concepts of thesis and antithesis, to "recast" the world of sense experience into the abstract essence of thought, "transmute it into a universal," and come to realize the ultimate unity of the absolute.[47]

Despite this projection of a race-free futurity, Hegel suggested that in the initial dialectical stages of *becoming*, nature and geography did play a role as the first externality from which humanity realized its independence. He believed that those nations in the temperate zone, where nature presented the least obstacle to the life of spirit, made progress more quickly toward the self-realization of spirit. Regions that experienced either oppressive heat or cold and the resultant increased difficulty in procuring the needs of the body distracted from the ability of spirit to create a world for itself and become self-conscious. Hegel focused specifically on Africa in his treatment of this theme, arguing that "in Negro life the characteristic point is the fact that consciousness has not yet attained to the realization of any substantial objective existence," neither God, nor law, nor any other universal concept. Rather, everything remained in the sphere of the individual and particular, in both external life and religious practice. For instance, the African people had not developed any universal theory of law that stood above the individual decision of the tribal leader, and their religious practices focused only on a particular idol rather than on a universal being. Consequently, though slavery was a deplorable condition that ultimately kept both slaveholder and the enslaved person from full self-consciousness, in viewing it from a standpoint of spiritual rather than bodily freedom or bondage, according to Hegel, it represented little alteration in the existing mental state of most Africans and could even be the first step in their becoming aware of absolute freedom in the sense Hegel used the concept.[48] He was, if possible, even less sympathetic toward Indigenous nations such as Native Americans. These societies he deemed "outside of history" and as such were unable to develop spirit or freedom at all. They were simply not participants in the "universal" development of absolute spirit, whose story was unfolding in the sphere of the Asiatic and European worlds. Africa, Australia, and the Americas were ahistorical lands in Hegel's conception.[49]

It is clear that Hegel held a view that, if not explicitly racist in the typical sense, was clearly Eurocentric at best, as can also be seen in his argument that Lutheran Christianity and the German nation both represented the apex of humanity's developed spiritual understanding and political organization.[50] He did not base this belief on racial superiority, however, as much as spiritual understanding. He saw Lutheranism as stripping away the externals from religion, focusing on the pure spirituality and universal immediacy of spiritual knowledge to individuals, free of all influences outside themselves. Likewise, Hegel believed that the German nation had reached the highest understanding of political freedom, the realization of objective freedom over subjective freedom, a "totality of spirit" that recognized the only purely universal as God.[51] Although he thought that living in the temperate zone had assisted the Germanic race by freeing it from undue attention to externals, Hegel did not suggest that German progress was due to inborn characteristics, such as biblical lineage, cranial shapes, or racial germs. The importance of any earthly phenomenon to Hegel consisted in its role in the process of dialectic.

As laid out in a piece that has come to be known as Hegel's "master-slave dialectic," Hegel viewed slavery or servitude as something that could serve as a step in the dialectical process. After first emerging from a purely natural state of being into a state of consciousness and confronting another self-conscious being, Hegel believed that humans' first impulse was to attempt to negate the contradiction found in this encounter, the *me* and the *not-me*, the *self* and the *other*. This impulse resulted in either killing the *not-me* or enslaving the *not-me*. In the second situation, Hegel believed the enslaved person was at an advantage over the enslaver. Through productive activity and close contact with the natural world, the "slave" could come to a level of self-consciousness and achieve a sense of inner freedom in differentiation from the "master." In contrast, through relying on another's servitude, the enslaver "retreats to a meaningless state of leisure and consumption" in which he is dependent on the servant for knowledge of himself, the consciousness of "his *single* self-hood resulting from the suppression" of the other. Hence he could not know himself without those enslaved and was in bondage to the antithesis of *other*.[52] This imbalance naturally resulted in the enslaved overthrowing the enslaver, reaching a higher dialectical stage and making way for the next cycle of unification until eventually they each realized a mutual respect for the other as free and knowledge of the self as free *in itself*, without which neither the enslaved nor the enslaver could be free. For, wrote Hegel, "I am only truly free when the other is also free and is recognized by me as free."[53] In this mutual recognition alone could the illusion of separation be overcome and unity reach consciousness of itself, which it could not achieve in solitude.

Whether Hegel wrote of this concept as more of a theoretical proposition or a real phenomenon is a source of ongoing debate. Susan Buck-Morss, in her research on Hegel and the Haitian Revolution, argues for the latter interpretation, suggesting that the successful revolution that was occurring during his time of writing *Phenomenology* inspired Hegel's "master-slave dialectic." It was, she believes, this event that made him view the self-consciousness of those enslaved as the vital ingredient in a successful end of slavery, rather than mere legal freedom granted from without. His comments on the benighted state of Africa and acceptance of slavery as a step toward self-consciousness found in his later work, *Philosophy of History*, Buck-Morss explains in the context of growing white criticism of Haiti and Hegel's own further acquaintance with the more mainstream racial ideas of other European writers. She notes that by ignoring the historical context in which Hegel was writing, other Hegel scholars dismissed the literalism of his "master-slave dialectic." In particular, she critiques a common interpretation of Hegel as speaking broadly of subjugation found in such works of Marxist scholars as Georg Lukács,

Herbert Marcuse, and Alexandre Kojève, who she believed used unjustifiable license in interpreting this dialectic according to Marxist bias.[54]

For example, Kojève argued that Hegel's "master-slave dialectic" showed that it was "only through forced and terrified work carried out in the Master's service" that one could realize autonomous self-consciousness, and thus the truth of *being-for-itself* was realized only in the *slavish consciousness*, interpreted as a positive state.[55] By contrast, John McDowell sees the "master-slave dialectic" as an allegorical reply to Kant's theory of transcendental "apperception," a term Kant used to define the mind's consciousness of itself as the subject of its own representations.[56] Each interpretation bears merit. The historical context, and Hegel's interest, which Buck-Morss traced, in reading the newssheets reporting on the Haitian Revolution, certainly emphasize that he was not constructing his philosophical theories in a social vacuum without any actual subjects in mind. Although her initial article on the subject leaves Hegel's broader philosophical interests underrepresented, the expanded examination of its applicability to Hegel's interest in the philosophy of universal history in her book on the subject improves the scope of her argument.[57] McDowell, while stressing the purely speculative side of the viewpoint, overlooks the question of whether Hegel would have used the terms "master" and "slave" at a time when racialized chattel slavery was the status quo if he did not intend his readers to understand his meaning in relation to chattel slavery but rather Kant's transcendental apperception. Perhaps a combination of these three interpretations presents the fullest picture of the importance of the "master-slave dialectic," in that Hegel was fully aware of and inspired by the actual social events he read of and also sought an explanation within the preexisting philosophical context that could be universally applied to humanity in the abstract whole.

Hegel was equally instrumental in making the distinction between reason (*Vernunft*) and understanding (*Verstand*) briefly discussed above. *Verstand*, Hegel believed, was a better definition for what Kant and other philosophers had titled Vernunft. Hegel categorized understanding as the faculty responsible for interpreting the material world, whereas reason should be, he believed, the phenomenon of actual interest to philosophy, for reason corresponded with idea, the absolute spiritualized consciousness of reality. At its fundamental level it was the absolute absolute, the final synthesis, which was God. Thus, reason did not originate within human minds but was, to Hegel, the presence and activity of God within the individual.[58] This view opened the important possibility that even if those of African ancestry were thought to possess lower capacities for logical faculties such as comparison, causality, and calculation, such merely represented the more material, worldly, and passive faculties of reason. Other characteristics that white people more willingly acknowledged to be present among Black people, such as emotion, intuition, or spontaneity, became facets of reason, the active faculty of the will, and one spiritually oriented toward the communication of the divine. But the influence of these mitigating ideas was not enough to override the detrimental effects of racial labeling. Hegel's suggestions on a lack of understanding, which would be a prerequisite for the next dialectical stage of reason, still implies that, in his mind, African people would at least be faced with an additional hindrance to equally developing what capacities they did have, as he discussed in *Philosophy of History*.[59]

These racial philosophies from Europe were adapted in many forms by US ethnologists, with whom the general public were better acquainted. Most US ethnologists followed these general outlines, however, and with these theories on race and racial origins influencing American society, Black Southerners had two main stereotypes to fight against: the perception of Southerners in general as being ruled by passion, and those of African descent in particular as ruled by animalistic violence and passion. Frederick Douglass's assertion that Black men fought "for principle, and not from passion" becomes an important philosophical statement with a significance that should not be overlooked.[60] Douglass was making a radical statement, overturning racial stereotypes and maintaining that Black people already possessed a well-formed character and were the moral superiors of their slaveholders, who fought not from principle but from passion. As the governor of Massachusetts, John A. Andrew, predicted, the character, namely, the moral principles, self-control, and courage, that Black soldiers could maintain in combat would "go far to elevate or depress the estimation in which the character of the colored Americans will be held throughout the world."[61] It was a weight of which they were well aware. It was not enough that Black Americans be recognized as equally human, or racially equal, with white Americans. Whether the white populace would accept their participation in the war effort and in American civic society depended on their demonstration of their capacity for bildung and character.

Colonel Thomas Wentworth Higginson of the 1st South Carolina Colored Volunteers recorded the sermon delivered by the acting chaplain, Thomas Long, to his fellow Black comrades in March 1864: "If we hadn't become sojers [soldiers], all might have gone back as it was before; our freedom might have slipped through de two houses of Congress & President Linkum's four years might have passed by & notin been done for we. But now tings can never go back, because we have showed our energy & our courage & our naturally manhood."[62] Robert Gould Shaw, colonel of the 1st Carolina's sister Black regiment, was equally conscious of the pressure on his men to perform exceptionally. His tight discipline brought some "complaints from outsiders of undue severity" toward his soldiers, but it is telling that these complaints did not issue from the men themselves.[63] They understood, like Shaw, that an even higher standard of order and character was demanded of them. The Common Sense framework of character was perhaps especially relevant to this population, for a Goethean holistic acceptance of both the faults and virtues of the self could scarcely be sufficient to redeem a racial character already portrayed as too close to "nature" in a barbaric or savage sense and whose faults were certainly not seen as leading toward self-redemption. It was, instead, a strict Reidian balance of the intellectual faculties, the triumph of reason over passion and the evidence of self-command, the essential characteristic of freedom, that Black Americans had to prove.

Transcendentalists, of both African and European ancestry, were convinced that this goal was achievable if practical guidelines were applied. The achievement of character and freedom demanded both bildung of the enslaved and their emancipation from slavery so as to pursue bildung, for the benefit of the human whole. As Herder argued, every race contained the essential faculties necessary for it to reach its potential. And as Hegel contended, slavery could be a stepping stone to actualizing greater freedom than those who enslaved could become conscious of. With the support of these ideas, there grew a philosophical basis from which to endorse emancipation, make provisions for Black bildung, and integrate African Americans into civic society.

Chapter Seven
RACE AND CHARACTER IN AMERICA

In the cultural milieu of American Transcendentalism, the statements and contributions of three of the foremost figures among this group—Ralph Waldo Emerson, Henry David Thoreau, and Margaret Fuller—are noteworthy for their treatment of race. The intellectual debts and racial philosophies of these three Transcendentalists are important because of their stature in the movement and their significant corpus of writings, several of which lend themselves particularly to study on the topic of race. Furthermore, historians have frequently characterized Emerson and Thoreau, especially, as disengaged from practical action and the abolition movement.[1] As the two most historically well-known figures among the Transcendentalists, Emerson and Thoreau warrant a careful reappraisal concerning their intellectual and political involvement with questions of race and racial policy. Fuller, although one of the most practical and socially engaged of the Transcendentalists, rarely features in studies on the topic of race in antebellum America. Instead, she has garnered almost exclusive attention from historians for her feminist efforts or as the subject of biographies. Therefore, an assessment of the philosophical background and roles in racial politics of these three Transcendentalists is particularly important for reshaping the historical understanding of the Transcendentalist movement's social outlook. They drew, sometimes unconsciously, from a wide set of often contradictory European and US sources, and although they contributed at times to condemnable racial discourses, they were generally on the more progressive end of the spectrum in their era. It was their commitment to bildung that allowed them to see all people as capable of genius, morality, and self-improvement.

In addition to Emerson, Thoreau, and Fuller, there were many other Transcendentalists entrenched in the racial debates of the day, but although their debt to philosophical currents, or even their status as members of the Transcendentalist cohort, are often overlooked, their activities have been better documented. As Peter Wirzbicki observed in his research into Boston's Black Transcendentalist community, itself historically disregarded, "If anything, once one moved beyond the circle of famous celebrities into the slightly lesser-known activists and thinkers who surrounded the movement, one found even more committed abolitionists."[2] Black Transcendentalists such as Alexander Crummell and William Cooper Nell also serve as an essential reminder that the term "Transcendentalist" does not by definition mean "white." Nell was a major figure in Boston's Black Adelphic Union society that hosted Black speakers as well as white abolitionists and Transcendentalists such as James Freeman Clarke, Carl Follen, Theodore Parker, Charles Sumner, and William Henry Channing. Nell was also personally acquainted with Emerson, Bronson Alcott, and their fellow Transcendentalist Franklin Sanborn. Black intellectuals like Nell were not merely consumers of Transcendentalist thought but also important social and intellectual contributors to the movement. The Adelphic Union engaged with the same philosophies of race as did the white Transcendentalists.[3] In his speech titled "Civilization in Relation to the Physical Circumstances That Have Contributed Thereto," Black member James McCune Smith "attacked the scientific credentials of the pseudo-scientific schools of 'scientific' racism that declared African peoples incapable of civilization based on the climate in Africa or Black physiology."[4] Instead, Black Transcendentalists subscribed to the Transcendentalist ideal of bildung, self-culture, or character development, which they preferred to call "elevation," which carried specific social, political, and economic as well as moral and spiritual applications. By 1845, the city of Philadelphia alone boasted more than one hundred African American societies dedicated to mutual aid and self-improvement.[5] The Black Transcendentalists believed "the philosophy of Emerson" so powerful in their cause that in 1862 one newspaper correspondent stated that one need look no further for the inspiration behind the Union's fight than Emerson's and the abolitionists' words.[6]

Thus, the three principal figures of the movement under study here should not be taken as the sole force of the movement or as exclusively representing the entire movement's philosophy of, or approach to, racial questions. I offer them here as case studies of special significance for reevaluating the Transcendentalist impact on, contribution to, and participation with the issues of racial politics in the antebellum and Civil War era. Examining them will also assist in gaining a portrait of Northern philosophical understandings of race at large, helping explain why the issue reached a crisis point when it did, and in understanding the Transcendentalists' engagement with practical politics. This discussion shows that while economic and general religious factors played a role in driving the question of slavery to the forefront of national consciousness, the philosophical currents of the period were also responsible for contributing to abolitionist sentiment and for making the acceptance of non-European peoples into the Union's civic life appear feasible, even beneficial and necessary. The Transcendentalists believed the models offered and routes pursued by such organizations as the Anti-Slavery Society did not reach far enough and so attempted to offer a more comprehensive philosophical framework.

A selection of the popular works with which the Transcendentalists were acquainted that addressed racial theory illustrates how the European ideas were being disseminated in the United States. The work of one of the Ohio Hegelians, Johann Bernhard Stallo, titled *General Principles of the Philosophy of Nature* (1848), contains several interesting passages on racial theory and was eagerly read by New England Transcendentalists. In relation to the personal political application of these ideals by Stallo himself, his philosophical beliefs on racial egalitarianism led him to break with the Democratic Party in the 1850s and support the newly fledged Republicans. He cast his vote for Lincoln in the 1860 election and organized a German American regiment for the Union army.

In discussing race as a part of his larger focus on the philosophy of nature, Stallo referred in detail to the classifications of Lorenz Oken. A German naturalist writer and nature philosopher contemporary with Goethe, Herder, and Hegel, Oken was a professor of natural history at the University of Zurich and built on Kant's philosophy in attempting to identify a system of universal science. Rather than identifying four races based on skin color, as Kant had done, or on cranial shape, as did Blumenbach, Oken divided the human species into five races based on sensory characteristics. Like Kant, he believed that there was only one human species, which represented the whole animal kingdom developed to its highest form. But within this one genus, Oken identified "five kinds of varieties of Men, according with the development of the sensorial organs." These were as follows:

1. The Skin-Man is the *Black*, African.
2. The Tongue- " is the *Brown*, Australian—Malayan.
3. The Nose- " is the *Red*, American.
4. The Ear-   " is the *Yellow*, Asiatic—Mongolian.
5. The Eye-   " is the *White*, European.[7]

Stallo explained that in Oken's system, the anterior-positioned eye represented the highest development of animal forms, for with it "Man sees the whole Universe; whilst animals behold only individual and different parts with eyes laterally directed, so that their ideas are never brought to unity."[8] Although not directly stated, classifying the white race as the "Eye-Man," or *Homo ocularis*, then suggests that Oken viewed Europeans as the most highly developed human type, although he held that "the lowest Man is still higher than the uppermost Ape."[9] Stallo did not accept this theory of racial hierarchy, however, as he explained in a lengthy footnote. Oken's theory merely showed "one of the first attempts at determining the races from a higher point of view," but Stallo declared it was still far from satisfactory, as was the case with two other racial theorists that Stallo briefly reviewed. The first was Carl Gustav Carus, who had argued that races represented epochs of mankind's development, corresponding with the advance of day from East to West.[10] Thus, Ethiopians represented the nighttime of human development, the *nocturnal* race; Malays, Mongolians, and Amerindians represented the morning and evening twilights; and Caucasians the daytime. The other writer Stallo covered was Gustav Klemm, who had simply classified humanity into an *active race*, the Caucasian, and a *passive race*, all others.[11] This was an interesting example of both the application of Common Sense philosophy's division of the mind and the tendency to ascribe the predominance of passive faculties to non-white races.[12]

Like Hegel, however, Stallo, preferred to view race as the result of nature acting on individuals. The body, he wrote, was "the reflex of external reciprocations," determined by circumstances and by what medium an influence was carried to the senses. This shaped races, national types, and individual characteristics. But, as Hegel had also argued, these were merely natural conditions that existed prior to the soul's realization of pure ideality and freedom from external particulars. "At first," Stallo explained, "the life of the soul shares in the universal life of the planet, and is affected by variations of the seasons, &c. The more the mind frees itself from its natural psychic state, the more independent it becomes of these influences. This planetary influence particularizes itself, moreover, in the concrete terrestrial differences, and discedes into the numerous expressions of continental peculiarities, producing the varieties of race."[13] Stallo repeated Hegel's proposition that material particulars influenced individuals when they were still at the lower dialectical stages of realizing their freedom from these influences, but once they reached an understanding of the universal and unified and their concepts grasped the ideality of existence and experience, these influences would cease to affect them. In Stallo's work, the American audience was thus presented with Hegel's philosophy on racial influences as one that was much more accurate and useful than static theories of racial division such as Oken's. And, as we can also see, to Stallo personally, this philosophy of race was not a mere metaphysical matter with no practical application but the basis for his flight from the Democratic Party, the expected political home at the time for a Catholic immigrant like himself, into the Republican fold and the politics of abolition.

Another author that Emerson recorded reading, as a "rash and unsatisfactory writer" who made "unpalatable conclusions," was Robert Knox, a Scottish anatomist and ethnologist.[14] In *The Races of Men, a Fragment* (1850), Knox took basic issue with the Kant-Blumenbach line of racial development theory and with the Herder-Hegelian line of reasoning, furthered by Stallo, in rejecting climate as the key cause of racial differentiation. Although hinting at polygenesis, Knox remained safely vague on the exact time or cause of racial separation. Knox held that the fact of racial diversity had existed at least from prehistoric times and was unalterable. Every individual's character was shaped by his or her race, and every other cultural achievement stemmed from racial predispositions, he explained. "Look at the Negro," Knox wrote. "Is he shaped like any white person? Is the anatomy of his frame, of his muscles, or organs, like ours? Does he walk like us, think like us, act like us? Not in the least." Any claim that such extreme differences were due to climate or climate combined with some "mysterious law" was, he concluded, "fanciful."[15]

Using the Caribbean and American South as a prime example, Knox argued that the Europeans who inhabited the region demonstrated the inability of climate to alter their race. They suffered along "pale, wan, and sickly," and without fresh imports of new European immigrants, he believed they would soon die off. Likewise, Africans transported to other climatic regions failed to adapt or to understand any of the arts of civilization, of peace, science, literature, or justice. At best, they merely mimicked what they saw of white culture, as had occurred with the Haitian Revolution and the establishment of Liberia, but he did not believe this constituted true development. Such events were merely "a ludicrous farce." The Black president of Haiti, Knox scoffed, stood in the same relation to Napoleon as an "oran-outan [orangutan] does to . . . Apollo," whatever "sham" title he chose to assume.[16] Because of their supposed racially determined inability to conform and adapt, Knox concluded that all the dark races were dying off, although, inconsistently, he did not see in white Caribbeans the doom of the Caucasian race. There was no help for dark races, he contended, whatever "wild, visionary, and pitiable" theories "statesmen, theologians, philanthropists of all shades" put forth in their effort to convince society otherwise. All but the Saxon or, as he preferred, the Scandinavian race were "destined by the nature of their race to run, like all other animals, a certain limited course of existence, it matters little how their extinction is brought about."[17]

Curiously, Knox himself was opposed to slavery and colonization, but one would conclude it was rather more because of the detrimental effects he feared from racial amalgamation—which he termed "miscegenation"—than from egalitarian convictions. Taken at face value, Knox's speculations on racial theory could be understood on an equally practical level as those of Stallo. Somewhat paradoxically, they were likewise grounded in the transatlantic exchange of philosophic-scientific ideas, but in this case, these philosophical conjectures offered a defense of racialized chattel slavery, disparaging the belief in free Black peoples' ability to develop their character and sounding a note of extreme disinterest over the extermination of Native Americans.

Another work that addressed issues of race which the Transcendentalists made special note of reading was Harriet Martineau's *Society in America*, a three-volume social commentary on her 1834–35 travels in the United States, during which she personally met with several of the Transcendentalists. Martineau was a widely published British writer of journalism, fiction, and essays, as well as an influential feminist, abolitionist, and Whig activist. Her social critique of America consequently focused on the issues in which she was most interested, the situation of women and African slavery. Martineau's method of castigating slavery was largely political and economic. She reviewed at some length the history of the institution in the United States, from the compromise made during the constitutional conventions in the 1790s to the Nullification

Crisis that had ended just before her visit, in which South Carolina threatened to disregard federal law on the basis of states' rights and a perceived regional disadvantage regarding new import tariffs. Martineau traced the economic backwardness of the South to the effects of slavery, and she openly discussed the possibility of the dissolution of the Union over the slavery issue, the economic and social implications of continuing slavery, and the various solutions that Americans discussed with her. Among these, she noted the prominence of schemes for colonization. When she questioned why this was thought necessary, Martineau recorded a typical dialogue in which white Americans consistently referenced climate: "Unless [Black people] remain as they are, Africa is the only place for them. . . . The climate of Canada would not suit them: they would perish there. . . . There is no rest for the soles of their feet, anywhere but in Africa!" When further pressed as to why they had to relocate at all, Martineau received the reply, "They could never live among the whites in a state of freedom. . . . They would die of vice and misery."[18] She also encountered some doubt as to Black peoples' humanity. One slaveholder she met, having read the Transcendentalist Dr. Channing's pamphlet on slavery, remarked that he would agree with the implications of the argument and free those he enslaved at once if the premise that "negroes are more than a link between man and brute" and "actually and altogether human" could be proven. Martineau believed there was ample evidence to prove this to him, and she further stated that she had heard enough stories of enslaved Black people who demonstrated some special talent or virtue that she had no doubt as to their moral and intellectual capacity. Any laws or arguments put forth to the contrary, she held to be opposed to the inborn conscience of any rational human being, thus "the law of man" came into "collision with the law of God," and this unsustainable contradiction was bound to crumble.[19]

These books by Stallo, Knox, and Martineau illustrate the wide range of interpretations to which the debates on race could be subjected, even while being founded on the same philosophical systems at their base, and they suggest the scope of content on the issue being produced in and reaching the United States. The books also show that the Transcendentalists were exposed to differing opinions as to the accuracy or failings of the European philosophical systems on race and were apparently interested in investigating all sides of the debate, not distancing themselves from the practical implications of racial theory in their own time and place but conducting a focused reading on the issue. As they were exposed to competing theories and as the events in the country unfolded, their responses to the question of race underwent some alterations. Their philosophical approach to racial politics was not formed in isolation from the outside world but was a response to the political and social events and concerns that surfaced across the span of several decades. Consequently, the Transcendentalists were not always consistent in their literary treatment of race or their political responses, and they did not always agree among themselves.

The Transcendentalists' statements on the topic of race can appear paradoxical and at times disturbingly cavalier. It is of little surprise that their stance has produced interpretations at each end of the spectrum: they are found in one sentence condemning the abolitionists and in another faulting those who failed to speak out against slavery. They praised Native Americans' nobility at the same time as resigning themselves to their destruction and hoping for a national institute to procure a collection of their skulls. One day they wrote of being content to go in search of wild raspberries where the state was nowhere to be seen, and the next they were overflowing with grief and anger at the failure of John Brown's seizure of the federal arsenal at Harpers Ferry.[20] Hence a systematic review of their positions in relation to the transatlantic intellectual contexts that shaped their thinking on this issue clarifies their approach and provides new insights into the ways in which these philosophical models shaped their viewpoints and actions over time.

Emerson in particular demonstrated quite a thorough familiarity with the topic of racial theory. In his early years—and unfortunately those years most frequently focused on in historians' treatment of his life and thought—he was disengaged on the issue of slavery. As a teenager, he even pondered the question of whether Black people were human or beast, evidently shaken in his views somewhat by Harvard classmates from the South. However, he was also never proslavery. And while the argument of whether Emerson was racist or not has generated a debate of its own, the focus here is not to become embroiled in this dispute but to situate his views into their transatlantic philosophical context to understand them, and his subsequent actions, more fully.

Emerson's section entitled "Race" from his long essay on the characteristics of the English people contains the fullest account of his thought and gives a good indication of the extent of his knowledge of other writers on the topic. Robert Knox's *The Races of Men* was the work with which Emerson opened his discussion. "An ingenious anatomist," he noted, "has written a book to prove that races are imperishable, but nations are pliant political constructions, easily changed or destroyed."[21] Emerson was not, however, convinced by the premise of the work. He did not believe that Knox had founded his "assumed" races on any necessary natural or metaphysical law, and furthermore, he judged any division of races as being clearly arbitrary, as everyone produced a different number. "Blumenbach reckons five races; Humboldt, three; and Mr. Pickering, who lately, in our Exploring Expedition, thinks he saw all the kinds of men that can be on the planet, makes eleven." Then there was the additional problem that no one agreed on what characteristics were the property of any one race, for as soon as someone outlined such a division, "the best-settled traits of one race are claimed by some new ethnologist as precisely characteristic of the rival tribe." Such efforts at racial delineation and claims to unalterable racial characteristics were, Emerson suggested, largely the result of vanity: an attempt to make success, wealth, or civilization a hereditary attribute inseparable from the very genetics of those who claimed it. But in reality such arguments of pure races were mere legends created to "flatter the self-love of men and nations," Emerson concluded, and had little basis in fact.[22]

Emerson found climatic theories of ethnic differentiation, such as Herder or Hegel presented, more plausible than pure racial lines. The suggestions he made as to climatic influence were a curious blend of these two philosophers' views. He did not fully accept the belief that environment worked to create a national identity, as Herder had argued, or that nature was only a force from which one realized one's freedom, as Hegel's philosophy held. Rather, Emerson suggested something more interactive. As an American in a nation composed of a diverse range of ethnicities, it would have been difficult to wholly accept Herder's conviction that a nationality was indebted to its natural environment for its formation. If this were so, then the Native American populations and lifestyles were that which the American continent had produced and which were destined to form out of any who inhabited the region for sufficient periods of time. European settlers would clearly be, and forever remain, the misguided impostors that Herder accused them of being.[23] The logical political implications of this would demand the land be returned to Indigenous peoples, and European-Americans, ill-fitted for the environment, should return to Europe. Emerson did not follow this line of logic, and Indigenous peoples figured sparely in his writings. Nevertheless, the idea of nature as a divine influence and creative presence in the life of mankind was a far too strong influence in Emerson's thought for him to dismiss altogether the belief that nature was a determining entity. What he proposed, therefore, was a solution in which nature resonated with and brought out certain qualities in different individuals but which higher faculties in humanity could mitigate. These higher faculties could, as Hegel had suggested, overcome climatic or cultural barriers altogether and thus free any individual from external constraints. But nature also worked to develop these higher faculties and to launch any individual who was attuned to its influence to the highest intellectual and spiritual plane that individuals of any race had ever ascended.

Thus, while the British "race" was of the same stock on both sides of the Atlantic, Emerson explained national differences by a concept not of natural selection but of temperamental selection. Political liberals of England were drawn to American shores, whereas conservatives flourished in Britain, and those believed to be representative of the English were really only those who congregated in London and excluded the Irish, Scottish, and Welsh, he suggested. Just as "out of a hundred pear-trees, eight or ten [varieties] suit the soil of an orchard, and thrive, whilst all the unadapted temperaments die out," so it was with humanity.[24] The natural environment nurtured human development in ways that complemented its purposes, and nature drew to itself those who harmonized with its unique environmental expressions around the globe. Echoing Kant, Herder, and Hegel, Emerson saw the temperate zone as the region responsible for elevating the highest sentiments in the human race. "The highest civility has never loved the hot zones," he wrote. "Wherever snow falls, there is usually civil freedom. Where the banana grows, the animal system is indolent and pampered at the cost of higher qualities, the man is sensual and cruel."[25] Emerson here clearly implies a preference for European civilization, and although an overtly racist slur, one can equally conjecture that Emerson also had in mind white slaveholders and overseers in his classification of men in southern latitudes as sensual and cruel. For, as with Hegel, Emerson did not believe this consequence to be uniformly or inescapably true. In other words, it was not the *race* of the individuals who lived in these regions that "arrested" their growth, even if Emerson saw such "arrested" growth manifested in the race as a group. He traced such characteristics instead to the limitations imposed on them by climatic factors. These factors, however, could be overcome through the self-cultivation of the individual. And those who lived in harmony with nature, unhindered by the false and unnatural states of society, could even have an advantage in understanding divine law. Emerson suggested in one of his wartime poems that the free and enslaved Black people who answered the call to serve in the Union army demonstrated that they had

> ... avenues to God
> Hid from men of Northern brain,
> Far beholding, without cloud,
> What these with slowest steps attain.[26]

In other words, because of their closeness to the state of nature, they could intuitively see divine laws at work in the world and were quicker to respond to them and reach spiritual understanding than were those whose perception had been dulled by artificial systems.

The key factor that decided whether a race or culture was either hindered or aided by nature, Emerson suggested, was its perception of the spiritual idea, on which Hegel had based his philosophy of history. Emerson wrote of how "high degrees of moral sentiment control the unfavorable influences of climate," and he pointed to the cultures of Egypt, India, and Arabia as examples of warm regions that had produced high intellect and profound spiritual faiths. Then, continuing to reflect Hegel's philosophy of history, Emerson contemplated what this meant: "The evolution of a highly destined society must be moral," and to be moral meant to act toward universal ends. "Hear the definition," Emerson specified, "which Kant gives to moral conduct: 'Act always so that the immediate motive of thy will may become a universal rule for all intelligent beings.'"[27] As a result, he concluded that a Hegelian conception of universals, the spiritual facts true to all beings, was necessary to neutralize any constraints imposed by an unfavorable climate, enabling any race to advance toward high levels of civilization.

Certain races had had an advantage in this process, according to Emerson, and thus made it easy to credit their race as the reason for their achievements. He did not grant equal development to all races, for he believed that the "Negro" and "Arab" character of his day were identical to those in the days of Herodotus or Pharaoh, and that the "Jewish" character had remained the same across millennia and under every climate. He was even uncertain as to whether the cephalic classification of Celts and Saxons carried a grain of truth, the classification that, he mentioned, "alleged" that all Celts were Catholics and loved unified power, and all Saxons as Protestants demonstrated the "representative principle." He could even believe that he saw great similarities to the ancient Roman historian Tacitus's account of the Germanic tribes in the German immigrants he met in America.[28] So what, then, was the explanation for the disparity he perceived in different cultural developments, if it were not due to race itself?

The conclusion Emerson reached was actually quite broad-minded for his time. It was an ideal conclusion for encompassing all the contradictions present within the United States and its ever-expanding melting pot of ethnicities. Just as one could trace the similarities presented by the races he reviewed above, Emerson pointed out, so, too, one found a similarity in appearance among the adherents of different religious sects, political affiliations, trades, and professions. Such similarities could not, therefore, be traced to one's racial makeup. Rather, it was "credence" that etched itself into the character and lineaments of any population; the foundational beliefs held by any race, nationality, religion, or trade were reflected in the exterior life and features of the group. It was this "main element," according to Emerson, that determined the observable phenomena of racial and national differences that other philosophers had striven to explain by race. "'Tis said," Emerson clarified, "that the views of nature held by any people determine all their institutions. Whatever influences add to mental or moral faculty, take men out of nationality, as out of other conditions, and make the national life a culpable compromise."[29] Again discernible in this statement is the echo of Hegel's proposition that knowledge of either the particular and material, or the universal and absolute, determined a nation's development and history, as well as the individual's journey toward complete self-consciousness.

A key element in developing the beliefs of any one group was, as Emerson viewed it, exposure to other peoples and systems of thought. It was not race as much as proximity to the sea and thus to extensive navigation and the exploration of remote regions that accounted for a civilization's success. The Phoenicians, Greeks, Incas, and British, in Emerson's examples, flourished because of exploration. Through this they learned "the secret of cumulative power, of advancing on one's self" and incorporating into their own systems of thought the universal aspects found in the beliefs of those they encountered.[30] This explains Emerson's enthusiasm for the United States Exploring Expedition of 1838–42, which he followed closely and often mentioned in his writings, an event otherwise seemingly at odds to the interests of the stereotyped recluse of Concord.

The importance of cultural and racial encounters of this kind was even broader than intellectual exposure alone, however. Emerson suggested that racial intermingling was also an element for success. The immense global power of the British peoples, Emerson concluded in a statement that must have shocked contemporary ears, was not due to their racial purity but to racial multiplicity. The English character was a composite of numerous ethnic backgrounds. English customs, language, and beliefs were the fusion of "three or four nations" that no one was able to trace to its origins with any degree of certainty. "Who can call by right names what races are in Britain?" Emerson queried. "Who can trace them historically? Who can discriminate them anatomically, or metaphysically?" British dominance in world affairs was thus not due to any pure racial "stem," such as Kant had proposed, but to the very mixed nature of the inhabitants of Britain that had produced "a better race" than any single race would have developed in isolation. "Effecting a worldwide mixture, is the most potent advancer of nations," Emerson concluded.[31] In this way, the best traits of every people, the highest thoughts, and the most universal concepts would be unified. It was a necessary conclusion as far as the future of the United States was concerned and one strikingly contrary to the common fears of racial miscegenation among white Southerners and Northerners alike and the Northern anti-immigration Know-Nothing Party, or the belief that Native Americans and Europeans could not successfully assimilate with one another that had driven the Cherokee removal policy.

Furthermore, by emphasizing the achievements of exploration by nations of non-European races such as the Incas and the benefits of racial intermingling, Emerson was acknowledging the ability of every race to pursue and achieve self-culture. The expansion of the Scottish Realist model of balancing the intellectual faculties to self-create the ideal character was an important development occurring during this period. Formerly reserved for white men, the belief in an individual's ability to construct the ideal character was now being granted to other races. It was in this vein that Frederick Douglass shaped his account of his own life, *A Narrative of the Life of Frederick Douglass* (1845). It was, he related, only upon hearing his "master" at the time, a Mr. Auld, impressing on Auld's wife the grave risks of teaching those he enslaved to read, that Douglass understood how racialized slavery had been accomplished and was maintained. It was only by suppressing enslaved Black peoples' intellects that the white race preserved their authority over them. "From that moment, I understood the pathway from slavery to freedom," wrote Douglass, and from that time he began to teach himself to read. His life was proof of the fact that a Black man had sufficient active powers of will to apply himself to education and useful work and had adequate reason and could achieve self-driven intellectual culture and a high moral character. Douglass's book demonstrated "how a slave was made a man" entirely through his own efforts.[32]

Margaret Fuller, too, recognized Douglass as a proof of Black ability in the review she wrote for his autobiography in the *New-York Daily Tribune* in June 1845. Douglass's book was, she affirmed, "to be prized as a specimen of the powers of the Black Race." When liberated from the intellectual limitations of slavery, Douglass had been "free to develop the powers that God had given" and gave the country an incontrovertible demonstration of what those powers were. Fuller wished everyone to read the work so as to "see what a mind might have been stifled in bondage."[33] In addition to being a manifestation of Black ability, Douglass's life and character were of value to the entire nation, Fuller suggested. Like Emerson, she believed it possible that a fusion of racial qualities in the United States was to be a central ingredient for the country's success. It could be that "the African Race had in them a peculiar element, which, if it could be assimilated with those imported among us from Europe, would give to genius a development, and to the energies of character a balance and harmony beyond what has been seen heretofore in the history of the world," she wrote.[34] And, privately, she also commented that she believed that "the African and Irish will I think temper our blood advantageously."[35] The source for this idea she attributed to another of her close friends in the Transcendentalist circle, William Ellery Channing, who, being from the older generation of Transcendentalists, may well have originated the concept before Emerson also adopted it.

Similarly, an underlying theme in Harriet Beecher Stowe's 1852 best-selling novel *Uncle Tom's Cabin* was the slaves' morals and success in self-culture even under the most trying circumstances. They were, in her portrayal of "romantic racialism," harbingers of a unique utopia because of their cultural and spiritual identity as a "natural" race, close to the divine forces of nature.[36] Uncle Tom himself was presented as the ideal man, who had successfully subsumed his lower faculties to the higher and was more attuned to the divine truths presented in nature than were the white slaveholders. These "masters," in contrast, by maintaining control over their slaves by physical force, nurtured the lower faculties of aggressiveness, destruction, and passion of all forms. Stowe also made certain to note that after the fictional Harris family escaped slavery to freedom in Canada, "the same zeal for self-improvement" that had always motivated the head of the family, George, "still led him to devote all his leisure time to self-cultivation."[37] This continuing cultivation of the self ensured the family's success in the novel and argued in favor of the belief in Black people possessing the necessary active powers of self-motivation to provide for themselves, better their condition, and become honorable members of society. In fact, Frederick Douglass eventually distanced himself from the American Anti-Slavery Society of William Lloyd Garrison and drew closer to the Transcendentalists largely because the Garrisonians did not wish him to cultivate himself too much. If he did, no one would believe he had actually been a slave, they argued, and wanted him to "retain 'a little of the plantation' in his speech."[38] Douglass resented the implication that he could never completely transform himself into more than merely an escaped slave. He was striving to prove that as a Black man he could create the ultimate cultivated character, with all his faculties as well-balanced and his civilization as complete as any white man could boast. The Transcendentalists who emphasized self-cultivation and self-reliance over public argument were more open to this ambition than were the Garrisonians, who wished to use Douglass more as a tool of propaganda than allow him the power over his own self-development.[39]

Additionally, Emerson emphasized the ability of Native Americans to pursue self-culture in his 1838 protest letter on the removal of the Cherokee Nation from Georgia. In this letter, he specially noted the Cherokee peoples' application to industry and civilization, writing: "Even in our distant State some good rumor of their worth and civility has arrived. We have learned with joy their improvement in the social arts. We have read their newspapers. We have seen some of them in our schools and colleges. In common with the great body of the American people, we have witnessed with sympathy the painful labors of these red men to redeem their own race from the doom of eternal inferiority, and to borrow and domesticate in the tribe the arts and customs of the Caucasian race."[40] Thus, although their initial culture had indeed been, he inferred, inferior to that of European civilization, the Cherokee people were proving themselves worthy of the government's respect and care because they were demonstrating themselves as capable of entertaining the same aspirations and style of intellectual development as were white citizens.

Although Emerson's stance emphasized Indigenous people's equal capabilities, it still reflected a view today seen to retain considerable racism within it, such as the assumption that adopting white culture was the goal and ideal and only this made them worthy of the government's respect. The people of the Cherokee Nation themselves were divided on their best course of action, with one faction in favor of relocation to better retain their unique culture and the other faction proud of those intercultural achievements such as Emerson listed and incensed that white people still ostracized them. Given the intellectual climate of his times, Emerson was on the progressive front of racial egalitarianism in a situation such as this. While many white people wished to exclude the Cherokee people from the state even if they were living exactly the same as their white neighbors, Emerson's views on the capacity of any individual for bildung, the self-driven development of moral character, at least helped him consider the possibility of an interracial society. He held in high esteem whatever individual or racial group demonstrated growth in their awareness of universal spiritual concepts, whether they were Cherokee, Inca, or British. Ethnicities whose moral character as a group had, in his assessment, remained the same across millennia, he held less respect for, and one can recognize echoes of Hegel's dismissal of such groups as ahistorical.[41] Problematic demands to erase aspects of Native culture and adopt European value systems were still entailed in Emerson's vision. At the same time, his views allowed for the possibility of assimilation into American civic society for people of any race who did desire this outcome, which was more than could be said of many participants in the political discussion surrounding the Cherokee Nation. Hence, despite evident cultural bias, Emerson's racial philosophy pushed his era's usual boundaries in acknowledging the intellectual and moral ability of non-white people and offered them a place in American life if they applied themselves sufficiently to self-culture. His ideas thus suggested not only a vision but also a practical program for how to reach that goal.

Thoreau, in his writing of the deep enjoyment he found in hunting for arrowheads, displayed an appreciation for Indigenous culture that went beyond Emerson's acknowledgment of the Native Americans' abilities to cultivate themselves according to white culture and echoed more closely Herder's conviction of every culture's innate value. The arrowheads, Thoreau wrote, bore "crops of philosophers and poets" and inspired in him a new thought each time he discovered one. They were, to Thoreau, a "mind-print," a "fossil thought," left on the earth by the individual who had created it, and thus to Thoreau his interest was more than a hobby or a pastime. It was to be "on the trail of mind"

and to commune with the spirits of the departed Indigenous peoples that he believed were never far off—spirits that, he declared, never failed to set him right in his pursuit of knowledge of the divine action in nature, knowledge that would translate into an understanding of how to live human life aright in accordance with these same principles.[42] Any degradation observed in Native American life was not the result of their own culture, in Thoreau's view, but only the result of colonization, similar to the effects of slavery. White traders, seeking only monetary profit, quickly abandoned Christianization efforts, becoming "a vast rat-catching" operation rather than missionaries, and instead of trying to uplift the Indigenous people they encountered tempted them "to become mere vermin-hunters and rum-drinkers." In this relation, neither party was above the other. "Savage meets savage, and the white man's only distinction is that he is the chief," Thoreau concluded.[43]

However, like Emerson, Thoreau subscribed to the belief that the temperate zone was the ideal climate for the development of culture and intellect. "One might at first expect that the earth would bear its best men within the tropics, where vegetation is most luxuriant and there is the most heat," he commented. "But the temperate zone is found to be most favorable to the growth and ripening of men. This fruit attains to the finest flavor there." And as with fruit, where neither the stem nor blossom end contained the best flavor and appearance, so it was with the earth. The midrange, where America and Europe lay, was the "rosy cheek" of nature.[44] This did not mean in Thoreau's thought that Europeans and European Americans were better than the people of torrid regions. And he entertained no question as to whether a Black man was fully a man, ridiculing the notion that a mere human judge could determine the humanity of enslaved peoples. Instead, his philosophy of nature as presented in his works such as *Walden* suggests that he believed it was because of the divine laws reflected in the process of the seasons found in temperate latitudes, the cycles of growth, death, and regrowth, that nature offered her complete canvas in these regions, and thus the full operation of divine laws was presented before the eye and understanding of humanity. In this way it was easier for one to draw close to the divine, or the universal absolute of Hegel's thought, in temperate regions, but still only for the mind open to seek and discover these truths and to apply them in one's own life. Once again, the concept of bildung was essential. Nature in itself did not do the work of perfecting man. One had to apply the lessons learned therein.[45]

An examination of Thoreau's antislavery work suggests that he was one of the most vocal, active, and zealous abolitionists of the Concord Transcendentalists. He was among the first to become involved with the Underground Railroad and promotion for abolitionist speakers. In contrast with Emerson, who was lukewarm if not skeptical toward John Brown's raid at Harpers Ferry, that event induced Thoreau's most avid outpouring of rhetoric on the topic of slavery. "This most hypocritical and diabolical government looks up from its seat upon four millions of gasping slaves and inquires with an assumption of innocence, 'What do you assault me for? Am I not an honest man?' 'Ah, sir, but your seat—your footstool—my father and mother—get off!—get off!'" Thoreau raged. "But there sits the incubus with all his weight, and stretching ever more and more, and for all reply answers, 'Why won't you cease agitation upon this subject?'"[46]

To make matters worse, in Thoreau's mind, even the avowed abolitionists shied away from supporting Brown. Garrison and *The Liberator* ran no articles praising him, and the Republican party rushed to wash its hands of him, as if, Thoreau scoffed, any "intelligent person will ever be convinced that he was any creature of yours."[47] While other Americans were content to wish for good to triumph, for slavery to end, but above all to look after their own comfort, Thoreau saw Brown as the exemplar of the true meaning of Transcendentalism, the triumph of the ideal over material concerns. He was, as Thoreau extolled him, "a Transcendentalist above all, a man of ideals and principles,—that was what distinguished him." Because of him, the North was awakened from its lazy and comfortable repose, it became "suddenly all Transcendental. It goes behind the human law, it goes behind the apparent failure, and recognizes eternal justice and glory."[48] That slavery was an injustice and incompatible with the ideals of the United States, Thoreau had no doubt. It did not matter what the Constitution allowed or did not allow; that slavery was evil was written in every man's conscience and reflected a higher law, a divine mandate.[49] This disregard for the Constitution was a radical and risky position, as much of the slavery debate centered on what power lay within the government to enforce slavery or abolish it, and even many abolitionists believed the Constitution did permit it. The approach that Thoreau adopted removed the topic from the jurisdiction of government altogether, placing it on the basis of higher law, which was the very same divine action presented in nature, and in the process of understanding it, one also came to understand how this law operated in human life. If slavery could not be found in nature, it was contrary to true human life itself and, if lived out, was in direct opposition to the forces of bildung that would bring humanity into harmony with nature and with God, an inseparable entity.

Thoreau's racial views were thus similar to Emerson's in that he believed the individual application of universal truth to be an essential element in self-cultivation, but he stressed that such knowledge came from nature and was thus intrinsically connected with every race's development. It did not rely on exploration, exposure to cosmopolitan ideas, reading, or historical agency but came solely through the natural world, accessible and comprehensible to all. In this way his vision carried less insinuation that alteration from one's native culture was necessary than did Emerson's view, and *Walden* laid out a practical program for attaining the familiarity with nature required for successfully applying its lessons to an individual life.

Fuller expressed both agreement and disagreement with Emerson and Thoreau on various points of racial philosophy. She was the most clearly polygenist of the three, a view also espoused by Louis Agassiz, the German scientist and professor at Harvard who was also a member of the Boston Transcendentalists' discussion group, the Saturday Club, and supported a Platonic conception of nature as existing to demonstrate the idea or as a type of the divine mind. In planning for her Midwestern journey that she recounted in *Summer on the Lakes*, a book that sold better than Emerson's *Nature* at seven hundred copies in its most expensive edition within a year and earned Fuller praise even from critics generally disparaging of Transcendentalism, Fuller read other travel accounts of the region to prepare herself to assess their merits.[50] One such book was written by a Jonathan Carver, *Travels through the Interior Parts of North America in the Years 1766, 1767, and 1768*, which she cited as merely "*Carver's Travels*." In his book, Carver included a discussion of the probable migrations of Asian people to the American continent, perhaps the Tartars and Scythians specifically, who, he assumed, were the ancestors of Indigenous Americans. "The inhabitants of both hemispheres are certainly the descendants of the same father," he wrote. "The common parent of mankind received an express command from heaven to people the whole world, and accordingly it has been peopled."[51] Fuller was unconvinced and considered Carver's observations on any similarities between Tartars and Native Americans trivial and cursory. The origin of the latter was an ongoing and interesting topic of speculation, she wrote, but she personally believed "it seems most probable, that a peculiar race was bestowed on each region."[52] However, even as Agassiz had aligned himself with the polygenesist school, he had clarified that he did not interpret this position to be one of racial superiority or denying the human nature of each race. "All men shared a spiritual and moral unity" that overshadowed any biological diversity, and thus institutions such as slavery remained an "immoral abomination."[53] Fuller included a similar qualification to her polygenesist statement. Man had two natures, she maintained, "one, like that of the plants and animals," influenced by climate, race, and origin, and the other a spiritual nature that, like Hegel and Emerson also believed, rose above these limitations. Hence it was not a complete contradiction that she also praised Edward Everett's speech to the Sauk and Fox Nations, in which he stated that both the Indigenous and white races were "all one branch, one family, it has many branches and one head."[54] Fuller believed such to be true in spiritual unity, yet the animal natures of man may have been of separate origins. Despite retaining her era's troublesome delineation of "civilized" and "savage" that could raise questions about the depth of her convictions, Fuller did not endorse one nature over the other in her writing. Each state of being had its unique demonstration of the divine life within it, for although the cultivated mind contained more knowledge of spiritual facts, closeness to the original state of nature also represented an intuitive cooperation with the universal laws of Providence. As a result, Fuller saw mankind as losing "in harmony of being what he gains in height and extension; the civilized man is a larger mind, but a more imperfect nature than the savage."[55] In other words, she saw both forms of life as demonstrating different attributes of God.

In her journey through the Great Lakes region, then the western frontier of the United States, Fuller combined several strands of transatlantic influences. In addition to engaging with the debate of racial origins, government policy, nature philosophy, and copious quotations from Goethe, she was also contributing to a specific literary type. Like Thoreau's *Walden*, Fuller's travelogue was not intended merely as an account of events but was also written in the genre of the bildungsroman, a form that German travel writers were championing. This style combined observations, expectations, literature, emotions, and personal experience into an account of "the affective response to outside circumstances." The result of this genre of writing was a tangled and spotty narrative intended to communicate the journey of the individual "developing myself as I am" through the experiences encountered.[56] Fuller was thus interested not only in anthropological observations of Indigenous lifestyles but also their interconnection with the environment and their effect on her own inner life of experience and sentiment.

Her interest explains writings by Fuller that at first scarcely appear to be serious statements of racial theory. For instance, when she asserted, "The Indian cannot be looked at truly except by the poetic eye," the statement gains in breadth when understood in the broader intellectual context in which she wrote. Fuller was not interested in their supposed "filthy" habits and "treacherous" nature that had been recounted in a work she cited as "Murray's travels." Viewing them from a higher point of view, she posited that one would discern "more beauty and dignity" than had Murray from a purely exterior survey.[57] Fuller was interested in the interior nature of Indigenous peoples, the individuals' interconnection with their natural environment, and comparing what she saw of their lifestyle with the customs of white Americans. The Native Americans, she believed, experienced the same sentiments of local attachment, love of home and family, and faith in God. They believed in immortality, in an objective standard of right and wrong, reward and punishment, truth and fidelity. These they had received from knowledge of divine laws inborn in their own consciousness and from what they saw in the natural world. And in some areas, Fuller believed that white culture could take a useful lesson.[58]

But she did not gloss over Indigenous culture either and disparaged those writers who "either exalt the Red man into a Demigod or degrade him into a beast."[59] Native Americans displayed both good and bad tendencies, just as did white settlers of the region, whom she also did not shrink from describing as "slovenly" and "repulsive" in their abodes compared with those of their Indigenous counterparts. She felt that white women did occupy a more revered place in their respective cultures than Native American women did, despite her serious complaints about the former as well. Fuller even hinted at a phrenological understanding of Indigenous peoples' capacities in her discussion of a painting of a Native American woman, Flying Pigeon, which she had seen in an art gallery. She described, this time without qualification, a fellow observer of the portrait commenting to her, "If you cover the forehead, you would think the face that of a Madonna, but the forehead is still savage; the perceptive faculties look so sharp, and the forehead not moulded like a European forehead."⁶⁰ This reference she presently followed with her statement of hoping for an institute to collect skulls from around the country. These references are too brief to conclusively deduce from them whether Fuller believed in phrenology, as she also mentioned in a somewhat humorous tone a shabby phrenologist at the wharfs busily measuring the heads of "half-conceited, half-sheepish" clients.⁶¹ Her acceptance of the theories of animal magnetism and the effects of magnetic currents on susceptible beings suggests that Fuller may have been more open to the theories of phrenology than either Emerson or Thoreau betray. Such acceptance may have led to her either looking down on Native Americans or subscribing to the Spiritualist belief in Native Americans' receptivity to magnetic and electrical impulses that increased their spirituality and ability to interact with the spirit of nature. Perhaps she held a combination of both views.

As with her Transcendentalist cohorts, Fuller ascribed much of the worst of Indigenous life to white traders. She was disgusted at the sight of Native Americans in a Christian church and thought white missionaries would be much better employed converting themselves and the traders than attempting to force a hypocritical religion on the Native population. "Oh, my heart swelled when I saw them in a Christian church!" she wrote. "Better their own dog-feasts and bloody rites than such mockery of that other faith. . . . 'You say,' said the Indian of the South to the missionary, 'that Christianity is pleasing to God. How can that be?—Those men at Savannah are Christians.' Yes! Slave-dealers and Indian traders are called Christians, and the Indian is to be deemed less like the Son of Mary than they!"⁶² If the white settlers had truly been Christianized, civilized, or even humanized, Fuller believed that the conflict of races on the continent could have been avoided. But pride and selfishness had driven their actions. With the banishment of the Cherokee Nation from Georgia that Emerson had protested, Fuller believed the last chance of a sincere experiment in interracial peace had vanished. The white Americans had never made a wholehearted effort to either "civilize" or live in peace with the Native inhabitants of the continent. The chance was now lost, to her view, and she saw no solution to the slow but steady eradication of the race. Amalgamation would be the only possible route, but unlike Emerson or Channing, who hoped to see a strong and advanced race result from an ethnic blending, Fuller believed it hopeless. "Those of mixed blood fade early, and are not generally a fine race," she stated, and thus the Native American would still die out in the end. As for "liberalizing the missionary, of humanizing the sharks of trade, [or] infusing the conscientious drop into the flinty bosom of policy," Fuller despaired of that occurring in time to save the Indigenous peoples from extinction.[63] As McGarry discussed in relation to the Spiritualists, it was much easier to romanticize and value the guidance of Indigenous peoples located conveniently in the next realm than to value and cooperate with those still living and occupying physical space and not mere spirits to be conjured and dismissed at will.[64] Unfortunately, the Transcendentalists displayed a similar approach.

Yet, like Thoreau with his arrowheads, Fuller did maintain the continuing value of the lost civilizations of Indigenous Americans. Although "few of the every-day crowd have hearts to feel" it, the Indigenous peoples embodied a "beauty and grandeur" that would "leave in the world its monuments, to inspire the thought of genius through all ages."[65] Without them and the example of Native life, none would be able to entirely appreciate the full majesty displayed in the continent's natural environment. One was intensely bound up in the other. "I realized," Fuller wrote, when standing before the falls at Niagara, "the identity of that mood of nature in which these waters were poured down with such absorbing force, with that in which the Indian was shaped on the same soil."[66] And even while partially destroyed by the march of white settlement, Fuller could still perceive "the soul of this race; I read its nobler thought in their defaced figures. There *was* a greatness, unique and precious."[67] Fuller clearly valued the irreplaceable culture of Indigenous peoples, despite its variance from European norms. Herder himself could scarcely have written a sentence that better summarized this philosophy of history.

Fuller's perspective on African Americans was similar, but her political stance somewhat different. Irritated by the self-righteousness of the abolitionists, Fuller saw the antislavery cause as intrinsically bound up with the broader cause of expanding freedom and discovering the unity of all races and genders with one another. Her complaint with the movement rested on the fact that the leaders of abolitionism assumed a tone of "excess and exaggeration" that turned too frequently into mere "invective and denunciation" as opposed to anything constructive.[68] Furthermore she felt that they too often implied there was no other cause worthy of attention, including her own pressing interest in women's rights. She criticized Harriet Martineau, otherwise a compatriot in her work for women's rights, for making her travel account of the United States into "an abolition book" with this cause alone "haunt[ing] almost every page."[69] Likewise, from Italy in 1847, she wrote to the *New-York Daily Tribune* that while at home, she could "never endure" the abolitionists because they were "so tedious, often so narrow, always so rabid and exaggerated."[70] From the perspective of distance, however, she perceived that this cause was one and the same with the cause of freedom around the world, whether the wars for Italian Unification in which she was then caught up, the liberation of Poland, or the US war against Mexico. If abolition of American slavery was not "the only thing worth thinking of," she conceded that it was nonetheless "really something worth living and dying for" and demonstrated a high and eternal motive.[71] Sounding a Hegelian note, she further stated that although slavery made a mockery of the statement in the Declaration of Independence that "all men are born free and equal," she believed this statement was still the first clarion call to a higher perspective that would eventually triumph in the world. For, she asserted, "that which has once been clearly conceived in the intelligence cannot fail sooner or later to be acted out."[72] Sooner or later, throughout the world and in respect to every cause of greater human liberty, the highest truths would be realized, and once realized, they could never again be retracted or erased from human memory.

Fuller further explored Black rights in an 1846 piece for the *Tribune* titled "What Fits a Man to be a Voter? Is It to Be White Within, or White Without." Considering her reticence concerning the abolitionists, it is surprising that she went so far as to argue on behalf of equal civic participation for Black Americans, something that even many antislavery Northerners shied away from advocating. But Fuller was more progressive in this regard than other abolitionists because she realized that even white women were unlikely to be granted full civic participation if Black men were not. This particular piece of writing was formatted as a vague kind of allegory. Its setting was an undefined council, at which men were arguing about the attributes of assorted varieties of nuts and whether their usefulness or flavor could be judged from their shells. Into this council entered two people of "darker complexion," a beautiful and grand woman, and a handsome youth carrying a white banner bearing the words, "Peace and Good Will to Men." "I came hither," the youth announces, because the inscription above the doors read, "All men born Free and Equal," and he hoped to find a home within. He takes up the walnuts, chestnuts, and others and found them all white within, "fresh from the bosom of the earth," except for the walnuts that had been kept in the cellar. The youth advised the council to plant all the nuts together, lest the walnuts, from their unnatural preservation, fail to grow. "Has not Heaven permitted them both to grow on the same soil? And does not that show what is intended about it?" the youth inquires. The council members resist his suggestion, arguing, "But they are black and ugly to look upon." Fuller's youth replies with a biblical line of reasoning, intended to counteract the proslavery defense of Ham's curse. Fuller then pulls in the story of Judas, who betrayed Jesus to the Jews and Romans to be put to death, "Yet all the others" of Jewish descent were not "put under ban because of his guilt," as the claim of Ham's curse held Black people to have been because of the guilt of one. The council members reply with another reference to Scripture that they are bidden therein to exile whatever is black and unseemly, with the qualification, or so "our teachers tell us."

At this point Fuller reveals her youth to be the Christ in disguise when he cries out, "Have I been so long among ye and ye have not known me?" Shocked, the council members for a moment do not know how to react. Then one begins to conservatively reason that perhaps they have taken their understanding of the evil of Blackness too far. A painting of the Last Supper that portrayed Judas as Black was taking liberties with Scripture, he acknowledges, and though he supports the Constitution and feels the strongest "personal antipathy" toward "Negroes," he concedes that perhaps it would be best after all to plant the black nuts among the others so that if the walnuts failed they might at least "make use of this inferior tree." Here Fuller finishes her story by recounting that at this reluctant concession there "arose a hubbub, and such a clamor of 'dangerous innovation,' 'political capital,' 'low-minded demagogue,' 'infidel who denies the Bible,' 'lower link in the chain of creation,' &c. that it is impossible to say what was the decision."[73] It is also difficult to determine exactly what point Fuller intended to make in this allegory.

Fuller's piece contains several implications. Despite the obvious problems with her usage of colors as values, the title of the story itself is a radical statement, as in 1846 the most pressing issue was the abolition of slavery and not the wider status of Black people in civic society. Perhaps this may have been a statement against the abolitionists for not taking their reform efforts far enough or a statement against the American Colonization Society, which sought to repatriate Black people to Africa rather than let them remain in America and participate in US politics. The statement of her Black youth in the story, that Heaven had ordained all varieties of nuts to grow on the same soil, indicates that perhaps this latter meaning was the case, especially when read alongside her review of Frederick Douglass's work referencing Dr. Channing's idea that the Black population contributed something unique and important to the society of America. But one wonders if the inclusion regarding the strong personal antipathy toward Black people was also Fuller's view.

The specific mention that the black nuts came fresh from the earth, whereas the walnuts were spoiled by having been kept in the cellar, strikes another central note. As with the Indigenous Americans and her discussion of the civilized man losing the qualities of the natural man, Fuller again appears to be suggesting that, although less "civilized" than white people, Black peoples' closeness to nature, when nature was viewed as a second scripture after the Bible for the revelation of divine law, gave them a more spontaneous and intuitive knowledge of divinity than given the white population, whose only knowledge came through their, evidently mistaken, teachers who distorted the divine law revealed in the written Scripture. Those in the story who accuse the man of being an "infidel who denies the Bible" when he has conceded to let the black nuts grow, when the Black youth has just been revealed to be Christ himself, highlights the contradiction that Fuller apparently wished to make.

The view of Christ as the culmination of bildung was shared among the Transcendentalists. Thoreau used the Christ metaphor when speaking of the enslaved Black population and of John Brown. "A government that pretends to be Christian and crucifies a million Christs every day!" he fumed. "A church that can never have done with excommunicating Christ while it exists."[74] For Thoreau, Jesus Christ and John Brown represented two ends of the same rope that stretched across the ages, linked by all the martyrs and heroes who had sacrificed themselves for the ideal of truth. This was not the same thing as saying that Black enslaved people, John Brown, Abraham Lincoln, or the Union soldiers, who were also cast in the role of Christ once the war had begun, were the fullness of God in human form. The Transcendentalists had a different understanding of the historical person of Jesus and the spiritual conception of Christ than traditional Christianity had taught. The Transcendentalists betrayed a view both reflective of the biblical historicism of those such as Herder, who read Scripture in context of ancient Hebrew culture, and the conception of God more resonant of Hegel, described as the absolute, the *nous* or world-soul of Plato's thought, the divine mind, or, in Emerson's favorite phrase, the Over-Soul. This view has been defined as panentheism, the belief that God was both immanent and transcendent in relation to the world. It was opposed to theism, which held that God was distinct from creation, as well as to pantheism, which taught there was no God outside creation. The Transcendentalists' views thus portrayed God less as a divine personality who resided in Heaven and more as a divine energy flowing through, and fully present in, creation, although emanating from an outside source. As such, Transcendentalism maintained that each individual had immediate and personal access to God. In this complete unity of creation with creator, the divine nature of Christ existed and was not exclusive in the historical figure of Jesus. It was true of everyone who progressed far enough along the routes of bildung. Every individual was thus part of the one Christ, the single divine idea of humanity. The Transcendentalist poet Walt Whitman displayed a vision of this in his poem "To You":

> Painters have painted their swarming groups and the centre-figure of all,
> From the head of the centre-figure spreading a nimbus of gold-color'd light,
> But I paint myriads of heads, but paint no head without its nimbus of gold-color'd light.[75]

In this imagery, he emphasized that the Christ-nature was dispersed through all and not concentrated in only one. In seeking absolute self-consciousness such as Hegel described, every individual could achieve the same insight and understanding as Jesus. In this vein, Emerson admonished his readers, "Be to them a Plato; be to them a Christ, and they shall all be Platos, and all be Christs."[76] Just as Plato and Christ had raised the level of spiritual consciousness for humanity by their example, Emerson, Thoreau, and Fuller believed that anyone, of any race, could have the same effect in the world.

The fullest demonstration of this spiritual consciousness was to be faithful to its dictates even in the face of external and material threats, something the Transcendentalists did their best to do, as can be seen by their risky social and political statements and actions. The American Congregational minister Horace Bushnell, who was heavily influenced by the liberal theology issuing from Germany during this period, offered one of the most clear and thorough explanations of this view in his 1866 book *The Vicarious Sacrifice*. The crucifixion of Jesus, Bushnell explained, was not necessary because God demanded a blood sacrifice to atone for man's sins. Rather, it was demanded of Jesus by his own awareness of his moral obligations to himself, the moral obligation to be obedient to the principles of God and the dedication to upholding these moral truths to the death. Bushnell did not believe that this moral integrity was a "monstrosity of goodness" applicable to Christ alone but rather that all Christians were able and expected to do the same. It was this complete commitment to living the moral laws of God that made Christ's sacrifice central to human history, not the facts of Christ's bodily suffering and death, Bushnell argued. It was in this type of moral integrity that all people were called to make a vicarious sacrifice for the benefit of others, not for their salvation after death, as traditionally understood, but to participate in the work of restoring humanity's consciousness to order and harmony with the metaphysical laws of the divine universe.[77]

It was in this way that Thoreau understood John Brown to be again the Christ, and a man of Transcendental principles, which were, in fact, the same thing. It was to "not value his bodily life in comparison with ideal things" but to hold to the ideal, the spiritual idea, of man and man's unity above all other considerations.[78] Thus, even behind their specific discussions of physical race, of monogenesis or polygenesis, miscegenation or racial purity, civilization or savagery, and their own cultural biases and personal prejudices, the Transcendentalists had a view of an ideal. Despite the petty faults and obnoxious methods of reformers, Emerson recognized that they represented a striving of the Over-Soul to "have its way through us."[79] Human life was a process of realizing unity, as Hegel described it, of solving the contradiction between the *me* and the *not-me*. In Emerson's words, it was with the understanding that "the heart and soul of all men being one, [the] bitterness of *His* and *Mine* ceases. His is mine. I am my brother, and my brother is me."[80] Emerson reflected in his lecture notes about Hegel's conception of the dual limitation of slavery in the "master-slave dialectic," jotting "Chain Slave Chain Master," a law that would "execute itself."[81] Fuller likewise believed that "while any one is base, none can be entirely free and noble," for as humanity had but "one soul and one body, any injury or obstruction to a part, or to the meanest member, affects the whole. Man can never be perfectly happy or virtuous, till all men are so." Humanity as a whole, across time and space, race and gender, had to come into true freedom and develop itself in full for any single individual to achieve the absolute demonstration of divine life. It was impossible to achieve in a single life, she believed, but would be accomplished through a cumulative effort by all, "the sum of the lives of men, or man considered as a whole."[82] If man thus included every individual that had in the past, was currently, or would ever walk the earth, then those of other races were necessarily integrated into the entire teleology of the world, whatever personal preferences or prejudices the Transcendentalists retained regarding other cultures.

At base, then, the Transcendentalists argued that the solution to ending slavery, uplifting the enslaved person, and overcoming external differences of race, culture, or climate was to be found in the internal actions of the mind and required the dedication to bildung from everyone. Emerson's "Lecture on the Times" gives the clearest outline to the action he believed imperative. If all material institutions, laws, and customs were seen as the unreal phantoms he believed they were, what was left were the ideas of the heart and the mind. Therefore, he reasoned, if "I am selfish, then is there slavery, or the effort to establish it, wherever I go. But if I am just, then is there no slavery, let the laws say what they will. For if I treat all men as gods, how to me can there be any such thing as a slave?" Battling against exterior circumstances was, he stated, a futile and trivial approach. It merely made slaves to materiality out of the "denouncing philanthropist" who endlessly emphasized a conflict between himself and an other who was at fault. No unity or interior freedom could be realized in this situation, leaving the abolitionist, the slaveholder, and enslaved people victims of a mistaken worldview. The solution was to be found instead, Emerson suggested, in elevating the religious sentiment of one's self and others. Given this understanding, even the "slave" was no longer a slave but now the "master," as was laid out in Hegel's "master-slave dialectic." For sentiment was not a mere feeling but the action of the divine energy in the individual's consciousness. It was the same force manifesting itself internally as that which externally manifested itself as moral law.[83] Fuller likewise concluded, "Could you clear away all the bad forms of society, it is vain, unless the individual begin [sic] to be ready for better."[84] The beginning of any reform must occur within the individual consciousness before it could be successfully carried out. Seeing the opposition as a concrete *not-me* with which to contend, either to convince of an opinion or alter an exterior situation, these Transcendentalists did not view as an effective strategy.

What Emerson, Thoreau, and Fuller offered was not indifference or lack of sympathy with abolitionism but an alternative approach to abolition. It was no less intended as a practical program than that which other abolitionists followed. But it was based on an in-depth philosophical platform and required self-culture of the individual, asking for a more profound change in one's perception of the natural world, the divine, and humanity's cooperation with both, than did simple monetary contributions to the antislavery or colonization societies, participation in political campaigns, or antislavery rallies. The Transcendentalists participated in these efforts as well, but such were not the trademark of their activity or what they viewed as the most essential element. What they sought to accomplish was an intellectual revolution, a national bildung, transforming a materialistic worldview into a metaphysical one that would necessitate the outward transformation of political, social, and individual relationships in harmony with the new truths perceived and bring about a greater and more thorough reform than they believed merely the legal abolition of slavery could accomplish.

It is true, however, that when they first began their discussion club and started to articulate and clarify their individual systems of thought in the 1830s, many of the Transcendentalists were not engaged in public reform. Nevertheless, emphasis on this decade alone as the heyday of the Transcendentalists has led to a skewed view of their social involvement. It was not by any means the high point of Transcendentalism but only the genesis of the movement. Not only were many of the major Transcendentalists just beginning their formation of an intellectual identity, but most also were still in their twenties and likely unprepared to take leading roles in social reform. However, this changed as they matured. Most of the Transcendentalists were engaged in public reform by the 1840s, and by the 1850s, they were willing to take the title of "abolitionist" despite their differences with the Garrisonians or the American Colonization Society founded by Robert Finley.

One of the first political events in which Emerson became involved was concerned with racial policy. He was thirty-five years old when he addressed the open letter to President Martin Van Buren remonstrating against the deportation of the Cherokee Nation from their ancestral homeland in Georgia to the present State of Oklahoma as discussed above. In 1844, two years before the Mexican-American War brought increased attention to the issue of slavery, Emerson gave his first lecture denouncing slavery to the Women's Antislavery Society of Boston, in which his second wife Lidian had long been a member. Many abolitionists celebrated this move as Emerson's conversion to their position, although "it might be closer to the truth to say that they had joined him," for he was among the first to portray the cause of abolition as an unassailable spiritual idea, certain in its triumph, as opposed to merely personal effort exerted against an equally powerful opposition, as earlier abolitionist crusaders had typically done.[85]

The Transcendentalists increased their abolitionist activity around the time of the Mexican-American War (1846–48), demonstrating the political implications of their philosophical thought. Thoreau defended his refusal to pay his poll tax as a stance against the government for its participation in expanding slavery. Wendell Phillips, one of the harshest and most controversial abolitionist speakers, came to the Concord Lyceum three times to lecture at Thoreau's invitation. When the church sexton declined to ring the bells to call audiences to these and other antislavery lectures held at the Concord church, Thoreau himself would do so. When the Fugitive Slave Law was revived as part of the Compromise of 1850, the Transcendentalists' involvement in the issue spiked. Thoreau, Emerson, the Alcott family, and Theodore Parker sheltered fugitives on the Underground Railroad. Parker also led the Boston Vigilance Committee that worked to thwart the Fugitive Slave Law by preventing the recapture of enslaved and free Black people. In 1854, Anthony Burns, a fugitive slave, was arrested in Boston. The Transcendentalists' response proves that they were ready to practice what they preached, for they did not sit by the sidelines. Thoreau, Alcott, Parker, Lewis Hayden, and Thomas Wentworth Higginson petitioned the authorities to release Burns, and when this failed, they risked arrest themselves by attempting to break into the jail to free him. They were unsuccessful but somehow escaped repercussions from their actions. When the Supreme Court issued the Dred Scott Decision three years later, ruling not only against the Scotts but further declaring that African Americans were not and never could be American citizens, the Transcendentalists were gravely disappointed. The decision was nothing but blasphemy, according to Emerson, who viewed it in the same light as "Indian removal," an immoral action that cut away at the moral fabric of the nation.

The Transcendentalists cited compliance with a higher law than that of the land with regard to slavery, but this did not preclude political involvement. Many Transcendentalists supported the abolitionist Liberty Party, Free Soil Party, and, later, the new Republican Party, even actively campaigning for their candidates at times. When political tension in Kansas escalated into violence between the proslavery and antislavery settlers vying to sway the state's constitutional stance on slavery, then under construction, the Transcendentalists strongly supported the antislavery side. The funds raised for this purpose in Concord alone equaled $1,300, equivalent to $49,384 in 2024 currency.[86] Henry Ward Beecher in New York raised money from his church congregation to purchase a shipment of Springfield repeating rifles and sent them to antislavery forces in Kansas. Theodore Parker's congregation similarly sent donations of money and supplies. Emerson attended aid meetings gathering relief for Free-Soilist Kansans and delivered lectures in support of the Free Soil cause. Thomas Wentworth Higginson personally traveled to Kansas to join the antislavery faction. In contrast, despite their historical record as being much more politically involved and essential to the abolition movement than were the Transcendentalists, William Lloyd Garrison and the Antislavery Society condemned the events of Bleeding Kansas, citing pacifism, and did not extend any support or assistance to the Free Soil settlers there.[87]

Through these connections with the Free Soil faction in Kansas, the Concord Transcendentalists became acquainted with John Brown, of whom, despite his violent tendencies, they gained a favorable impression. Some, including Theodore Parker, Thomas Wentworth Higginson, and Samuel Gridley Howe, became members of Brown's Secret Six, an informal committee that operated from 1858 to 1859 for the purpose of orchestrating a violent overthrow of slavery, subsidizing Brown's abolitionist activity as well. The other three members comprised Franklin Benjamin Sanborn, Gerritt Smith, and George Luther Stearns. Each of these members were also acquainted with the Transcendentalist circle. This committee assisted Brown in preparing for the raid of the federal armory at Harpers Ferry, by which he hoped to arm a slave revolt. Although most of the North strongly disapproved of Brown's method, Thoreau was a staunch supporter. In his public "Plea for Captain John Brown" delivered to the citizens of Concord, Thoreau acclaimed Brown for being "a transcendentalist above all, a man of ideas and principles."[88] Emerson appreciated Brown's reckless dedication for the fact that it proved a man could love "an idea better than all things in the world, that he is thinking neither of his bed, nor his dinner, nor his money, but will venture all to put in act[ion] the invisible thought of his mind." Still, Emerson remained more critical of the action than Thoreau and privately commented that Brown, though a true hero, had "lost his head" at Harpers Ferry.[89]

Even after Brown was executed, the Transcendentalists did not revoke their support. *Echoes of Harper's Ferry* (1860), a book of speeches, poems, and letters that was published soon after the execution took place, featured many contributions from the Transcendentalists. They held a memorial service for Brown in Concord, despite threats from fellow townspeople that they would fire a cannon at the church if they dared to ring the bells, and the Emersons boarded Brown's two daughters in their home in order for them to attend

Franklin Sanborn's school. It was a hazardous stance to support a convicted criminal, a position that was unpopular with many, even abolitionist Northerners, and one that risked not only the Transcendentalists' careers but also their safety and that of their families. These cases evidence that Transcendentalist philosophical outlooks were not by any means passive, disengaged, or opposed to practical action and that many of these Transcendentalists and their followers were willing to put their reputations and lives on the line for the cause of abolition.

Certainly, Southerners of the period frequently perceived the Transcendentalists as a threat and a prominent voice among, or even the cause of, the abolition movement. Mary Chesnut, the wife of a South Carolina politician, for instance, cited in one sentence Harriet Beecher Stowe, Horace Greeley, Henry David Thoreau, Ralph Waldo Emerson, and Charles Sumner as the stem of New England abolitionism.[90] She did not include in this list William Lloyd Garrison, John Brown, the Grimké sisters, or other figures now more specifically associated with antislavery agitation. George Fitzhugh, a lawyer in Virginia who was a distant relative of General Robert E. Lee and wrote numerous proslavery tracts, blamed the North's "New Philosophy" as the root cause of their social innovation and biblical infidelity, which he thought had resulted in their "fanciful" ideas regarding abolition. A southern gentleman, he avowed, would sooner be caught practicing the black arts than reading a book by Robert Owen or Charles Fourier, two of the leading thinkers behind the Transcendentalists' utopian socialist community experiments, Brook Farm and Fruitlands.[91] In 1865, the *Daily Dispatch* of Richmond, Virginia, ran an editorial observing that in the past New England had been notoriously fond of the Old Testament, but it had been surpassed by "the philosophical productions of Ralph Waldo Emerson," for the Bible did not condemn slavery, the editorial claimed, but Emerson certainly did.[92] By implication, this editorial aligned itself with the belief that the Bible supported racialized chattel slavery and demonstrates that many Southerners of the time perceived Emerson's writings to be vocally antislavery, which they believed accounted for Emerson's appeal to Northern readership.

When war was declared, the Transcendentalists were some of the North's most enthusiastic supporters, for they viewed the abolition of slavery as its underlying goal earlier than did many of the wider population, who took time to publicly accept this position. The Concord Transcendentalists actively supported the war in the ways they were able, whether through writings, lectures, sermons, and fundraising for soldier aid or, in the case of younger members of the circle, such as Walt Whitman and Louisa May Alcott, going to serve as nurses, or like Charles Russell Lowell, Charles Anderson Dana, William Greene, and James Kendall Hosmer, enlisting in the Union army. Thomas Wentworth Higginson, a disciple of Emerson and related by marriage to the Channing family, led the first army regiment recruited from among former slaves, the 1st South Carolina Colored Volunteers, and Robert Gould Shaw, a former pupil of Elizabeth Peabody and whose family was friends with many of the Concord Transcendentalists, led the first regiment of free Black men, the 54th Massachusetts. Emerson traveled to Washington in 1862 at the invitation of Senator Charles Sumner to deliver a public lecture held at the Smithsonian Institution promoting the cause of emancipation as a war aim. While there, Secretary of State William Seward introduced Emerson to President Lincoln at the White House. When on January 1, 1863, the Emancipation Proclamation took effect, the Transcendentalists were responsible for hosting a celebration of the event in the Boston Music Hall. These facts illustrate that the common perception of the Transcendentalists as idle, withdrawn, and complacent naturalists is a caricature of their story.

When he thought of the writings of Emerson and Thoreau in relation to his camp life as doctor with the 1st South Carolina Colored Volunteers, Seth Rogers drew on both the physical and the metaphysical aspects of the Transcendentalists' reflections on race. The Black men were undeveloped intellectually, he believed, but they were nonetheless "intensely human." And, despite their lack of civilization in some respects, owing to the absence of cultural impediments on their innate capacity for spiritual perception, they were closer to the unadulterated state of nature than was the white population. "They have a boundless conception of the divine spirit and a more intense trust in the fatherhood of God than have the cultivated whites of my acquaintance," Rogers concluded, thus proving that they were also "intensely divine" and were the "children of God." Although white readers complained that they did not understand Emerson's poetry because it was too abstract and mystical, Rogers noted that the Black soldiers seemed to understand it easily and recorded that they responded with great enthusiasm to Emerson's poem "Boston Hymn," which he had written to honor the other Black regiment, the 54th Massachusetts.[93] The 1st South Carolina's colonel, Thomas Wentworth Higginson, likewise echoed Rogers's observations. The Black soldiers' philosophizing was, he found, "often the highest form of mysticism; and our dear surgeon [Rogers] declares that they are all natural transcendentalists."[94] They were Transcendentalists, it may be surmised, because they demonstrated their unity with the moral laws of nature, their common humanity, and their depth of understanding for and dedication to the universal ideal of humankind in spiritual unity with the divine. Rogers and Higginson, at least, found the Transcendentalists' philosophical platform to be proven true, applicable, and practical, even in the crucible of war.

There were limits to Emerson's willingness to sacrifice for abolition and the war effort, however. Following Robert Gould Shaw's death, Emerson was asked to allow his one surviving son, Edward Waldo Emerson, to lead the 54th Massachusetts. Emerson excused his son, citing the need for him to complete his education at Harvard. Edward himself wished to serve in the Union army but never did so because of his father's opposition. Still, the elder Emerson did not sit philosophizing on the sidelines. In his biography of his father, Edward Waldo stated that "from the beginning of the anti-slavery struggle Mr. Emerson stood for Freedom," admitted abolitionists to speak from his pulpit when he was still a minister in Boston, and always, if possible, accepted invitations to speak against slavery. "He would speak, or at least sit on the platform, at large meetings in the cities, especially if the meeting promised to be stormy," his son recalled, feeling "bound to give the sanction of his presence" to the cause, "whether the speakers were good or bad."[95] Emerson's earliest antislavery address was delivered in 1837, followed by another in 1844. The following year he joined a committee protesting the treatment of a Massachusetts lawyer, Samuel Hoar, in South Carolina, when that state's legislature blocked Hoar's negotiation efforts to prevent the seizure and enslavement of free Black sailors during voyages to the US South. Also in 1845, the African American Transcendentalist, abolitionist leader, and Boston intellectual, William Cooper Nell, praised Emerson and Charles Sumner for boycotting the New Bedford Lyceum over its segregation policies.[96] Following the Fugitive Slave Law of 1850, Emerson publicly advocated breaking the law, a statement that could well have landed him in trouble and brought an investigation into him and his Concord neighbors participating in the Underground Railroad. During the capture of two fugitives in Boston, Thomas Sims and Anthony Burns, Emerson actively worked for their release. He braved speaking to a shouting mob in Boston, although forewarned that they had determined to break up the antislavery meeting. He was deeply distressed when the great Northern politician Daniel Webster reneged on his abolitionist stance. Edward Waldo Emerson further recounted a time when he had been assigned a school essay on the topic of building a house. "You must be sure to say that no house nowadays is perfect without having a nook where a fugitive slave can be safely hidden away," his father reminded him.[97]

Despite these actions in support of the abolition movement, his son quoted from Emerson's journal in 1852, "I waked last night and bemoaned myself because I had not thrown myself into this deplorable question of Slavery." The elder Emerson felt that he could not devote all his time to this cause alone, when the broader demands made on him by the "imprisoned spirits, imprisoned thoughts" his other writings addressed still needed attention as well.[98] Still, he continued to write and speak on behalf of abolition, to donate to John Brown, and to encourage his neighbors to vote for antislavery candidates, and he attended political meetings, although his son recalled that with his shy, introverted nature, it was "a discipline of courage" for Emerson to do so.[99] When the war came, Emerson was in full support of it, short of allowing Edward to enlist, believing separation of the Union was better than allowing the cancer of slavery to continue festering and trusting that a war fought for divine principles would ennoble the country.[100] During Reconstruction, following the Confederates' defeat, Emerson supported the policies of the second phase, when those in Congress known as the "Black Republicans" or "Radical Republicans" spearheaded the Reconstruction program and vastly increased the civil rights and protections granted to the freed slaves. "We have seen the most healthful revolution in the politics of the nation,—the Constitution not only amended, but construed in a new spirit," he rejoiced.[101]

Thoreau did not live to see the end of the war but he threw himself into abolitionism with more fervor than Emerson. He lectured before the Concord Lyceum in early 1849, recounting his views on the power of what was to become known as "civil disobedience." His house was a refuge for slaves on their way to freedom in Canada on the Underground Railroad, whom, recounted his fellow Transcendentalist Moncure Conway, he watched over with "singularly tender and lowly devotion."[102] Thoreau allowed a free Black woman to board with him while she worked to raise funds to buy her husband out of slavery. In 1854 he attended a meeting at Framingham with other abolitionists, including William Lloyd Garrison, and delivered his speech "Slavery in Massachusetts," which was reprinted in Garrison's *Liberator* and in Horace Greeley's *New-York Daily Tribune*, a newspaper with one of the highest subscription rates in the country at the time. Three years later, Franklin

Sanborn introduced Thoreau to John Brown, who visited at length and delivered a speech on his antislavery activities in Kansas at the Concord Town Hall. Thoreau, who had refused to contribute to a memorial statue of Horace Mann, the Transcendentalist educational reformer, gave money to support Brown's activities, along with Emerson and Sanborn. And when Brown's Harpers Ferry raid ended in Brown's arrest, Thoreau booked the Town Hall on the night of October 30, 1859, for his own purposes this time, ringing the bell to call an audience, against direct orders, and delivered his impassioned plea for Brown. He was then invited to Boston and Worcester to lecture in Frederick Douglass's stead, as Douglass temporarily fled to Canada because of his connections with Brown. When one of Brown's accomplices stumbled into Concord, Sanborn and Thoreau smuggled him to safety on a train bound for Canada, and when authorities attempted to arrest Sanborn himself for his role in the Secret Six committee supporting Harpers Ferry, Thoreau joined in the Concord mob that drove the deputy marshal out of town. By the time the Civil War began, Thoreau was too ill to leave any significant written records of what his thoughts were, and he passed away in early 1862 just as the more important Union victories were being won in the West. Yet even as his health was declining, Conway recorded that when he visited Thoreau following the Union defeat at First Bull Run, he found Thoreau ecstatic in his confidence that the war heralded the moral regeneration of the nation.[103]

Fuller had a more complex relationship with the abolitionist movement than either Emerson or Thoreau. Harriet Martineau, whose work Fuller had criticized for being solely an abolition book, wrote Fuller off in her own autobiography, in stinging words, as being taken up with "fanciful and shallow conceits" rather than practical solutions and for looking "down upon persons who acted instead of talking finely."[104] While the other Transcendentalists defended her in their biographies by pointing out that the abolitionist movement was barely entering its active phase by the time Fuller left the country as a newspaper correspondent, the charge continued to haunt her reputation regarding abolition.

The limitations imposed on Fuller by her gender is another issue to consider. For instance, whether public speaking was an acceptable platform for a genteel woman was still a contested topic during her lifetime, a problem she somewhat managed to maneuver by labeling her lectures as "conversations" with mostly female attendance. Consequently, what activities she would have undertaken if not restrained by custom cannot be known. Furthermore, the abolitionist and feminist movements had always had a strained relationship. Feminists such as Fuller justly hoped that the abolitionists would champion the rights of women as well as Black people for civic participation and legal protections, but the abolitionists often feared that embracing this additional cause would distract and detract from their own movement and hence held feminists at arms' length. Writing was, therefore, perhaps the best venue in which Fuller could influence the public mind. And in her writings it is clear that while she privately deplored much of the abolitionists' invective and self-righteous confidence that their cause was the only one worthy of attention, hence detracting from her own special cause, she thoroughly supported ending slavery and viewed Black rights as one and the same with the cause of greater freedom for women, Jews, Irish, and all Americans. She begged her female readers to stand against the annexation of Texas in 1845 that added slaveholding territory to the Union, because "this cause is your own, for as I have before said, there is a reason why the foes of African slavery seek more freedom for women; but put it not upon that ground, but on the ground of right."[105] Her review of Frederick Douglass's work for Horace Greeley's *New-York Daily Tribune* further contains cautious praise for the noble aims of the abolitionists, despite her annoyance with their personal faults. Other topics she covered for the *Tribune* included commentaries on public charities, mental health institutions, common courtesy to the poor, and, finally, the Wars of Italian Unification.[106]

Fuller also gained much appreciation for the abolitionists while abroad, and thus whether she would have become more involved in the movement upon her return to the United States is another question that cannot be answered. It was 1850, the year of the Compromise and Fugitive Slave Law that goaded the other Transcendentalists into greater political and social action, that Fuller was lost in a shipwreck upon her return voyage from Italy. Still, considering the additional constraints on her participation in the movement as a woman and the reach of her writings, particularly in the *New-York Daily Tribune*, her influence on the public mind should not be discredited.

Thus, although the Transcendentalists suggested intellectual and moral routes to begin the process of national regeneration other than abolition, their emphasis did not preclude active involvement in that political and social movement. From Thoreau's Underground Railroad activity to Emerson's lectures and Fuller's newspaper column, each of these three Transcendentalists, according to their ability, were putting into practice a philosophical view of race that relied on the concept of bildung to acknowledge the abilities and contributions of non-white peoples. Because they generally chose to approach the issue from a different slant than the Garrisonian abolitionists does not automatically mean that they were not active in the practical platforms available to them to work for the abolition of slavery. Through their emphasis on bildung, for both white and non-white individuals, they were suggesting a practical program of their own for individual and racial uplift. This examination of the transatlantic philosophical background of the Transcendentalists' thoughts and actions also suggests that the distinct philosophical blend that developed in the United States during this period provides an important key for understanding why these strains of thought appeared at this particular moment, spurred the unfolding of racial freedom, made a multiracial politic appear feasible, and brought the slavery issue to a crisis.

Chapter Eight
THE POLITICAL CHARACTER OF THE NATION

The American Transcendentalists' views on the question of nationhood and statecraft present a circuitous, at times inconsistent, and quite variable picture. Two main philosophical threads, however, influenced the Transcendentalists' view on nationality and government: the role of the nation and its citizens as world-historical actors, and the conception of the state as the manifestation of a national spiritual principle. These ideas were interwoven and created a kind of metaphysical nationalism in which the nation was expressed through the political, social, and natural forms but existed beyond them. Indebted to Scottish jurists on the moral sense and to Fichte and Hegel for metaphysical nationalism, the Transcendentalists believed the principles that drove national events took place in an ultimate reality outside space and time yet also occurred within a national history confined both spatially and temporally. In these ways, their political perspectives contributed to an authentic culture of sentiment and patriotism during the Civil War.

Three primary schools of political thought present during the Civil War era have been identified, which Daniel Malachuk has defined as the originalist, aspirationalist, and proceduralist. The first camp, which most notably included Daniel Webster, believed the Founding Fathers to have been inspired by the divine will and thus all questions of statecraft must be referred back to their original writings. The second camp included Lincoln, the Republican Party, Frederick Douglass, and John Brown. These aspirationalist thinkers held that the nation was steadily progressing toward the realization of the

City of God on earth. And the third camp, the proceduralists, exemplified by the important Democratic politician Stephen Douglas, believed that popular sovereignty, the conviction that the will of the people gave government its legitimacy, was bringing the nation into alignment with higher law. Malachuk concluded that the Transcendentalists were exceptional because they subscribed to none of these common interpretations. Instead, he posited, they held the philosophical conception of the City of God and the City of Man "in productive tension rather than coincident" and sought to "sacralize persons, desacralize democracy."[1] However, over time, with the dawn of the Civil War, and especially once emancipation was espoused as a war aim, Malachuk understood the Transcendentalists as shifting into the aspirationalist camp. "The United States metamorphosed into a state overlapping with the City of God," and the Transcendentalists lost their vision of the two cities as separate and distinct.[2] Malachuk's book provides an important insight into one framework from which to interpret the Transcendentalists' political position. His observation of the productive tension present within their political thought is certainly borne out in their political statements and actions. Many political frameworks have been offered between the time of Augustine of Hippo (354–430) and the Transcendentalists, however, and some of their more contemporary transatlantic political theorists offer insight into the intellectual currents that shaped their views.

Questions such as the teleological orientation of government and the role of nature in national development were only two aspects of the broad question of nationality, what it was and what caused and created nationalities, which was a topic of interest throughout the European world in the eighteenth and nineteenth centuries. The Transcendentalists were participants in this much larger transatlantic conversation. Philosophers in both Scotland and Germany delved into this topic, offering various speculations as to what caused the phenomenon of national cultures and characteristics. Hume argued that a national people was formed through the imitative behaviors of a group once a political structure was already in place. Kant, in contrast, portrayed a nation as a kinship of people who consciously entered into a social contract with one another to form a state, though their kinship existed before, and distinct from, the political state they formed. Fichte posited that a nationality was made distinct by an intangible spirit that led a nation toward a cosmopolitical destiny. Political divisions, foreign conquests, or even internal disputes could not extinguish this spirit. Under these circumstances, a national spirit may appear to exist only in fractured individuals, but it was "a universal and national self" that would draw itself together again and remain the nation's "exclusive possession," to continue "whole and undiminished in spite of infinite division."[3] This view was very much shared by Hegel, albeit with an additional emphasis on statecraft as the manifestation of the people's national ethic and as the vehicle to carry this destiny forward. Herder, however, argued it was the shared geographic, climatic, and historical-linguistic influences on a people that made them into a nation, existing separately from, and in fact sometimes hindered by, the political organization of the state. Thus, the options for considering the nature of nationality that were available to the American Transcendentalists were many and quite diverse.

The American Civil War itself sits in a global context of civil wars and revolutions and the search for national reform, unification, and identity creation with the Mexican Revolution, the 1848 Revolutions spreading across Europe, the Wars of Italian Unification, partition of Poland, and, just a few years after the close of the American Civil War, the Franco-Prussian War and the consolidation of the German states. Each of these wars brought up questions of cultural continuity and change, national identity, and the interaction of government and citizen. Thomas Bender categorizes the nationalism of the United States in the mid-nineteenth century as most closely reflecting the Fichte-Hegelian view that was at once "romantic and idealistic" and one where the "cultural nation" was "identical with the political nation" in which "a people realized themselves."[4] In other words, a cultural identity without a political nation was an unrealized potentiality, and a political structure corresponding with national culture was essential for the participation of a people in an overarching teleology of representative world history.

This framework was crucial in the ideological construction of the Civil War in the minds of nineteenth-century Americans. As Lincoln stated, the issues at stake in the war reached far beyond the "fate of these United States" alone to influence fundamental issues for the "whole family of man."[5] This paradigm embraced the conception of the nation as "something bridging the empirical and the non-empirical" and creating what Oisín Keohane has termed "cosmo-nationalism," the belief that one nation best embodies the universal interests of humanity and "uses the apparatus of the nation . . . as a vehicle to accomplish a given set of cosmopolitical aims."[6] This phenomenon was not present only in the United States in this period but was embraced by many European nations as well. It was strongly present in Germany, informing the work of Hegel in particular, who believed that Germany was "the spirit of the new world," but its aim was a universal aim, "the realization of absolute truth as the unlimited self-determination of freedom," which was the essence of history itself.[7]

Bender illustrates the similarities present within Germany and the United States at this time. "These national peoples, conscious of having a national culture, were living in pieces of a nation rather than a consolidated whole.... Washington was more like the headquarters city of an agglomerated league that shared cultural and economic interests, much like the German Confederation," and thus German political philosophy was easy to apply to the situation of the United States. Hegel dismissed the Indigenous nations and enslaved Africans altogether from the historical narrative, but he saw even the Euro-American immigrant society of the United States as "a people developing spatially rather than politically."[8] This, Hegel believed, showed that they were not yet a fully developed nation and thus unable to take their place in the world-historical progression of human history toward the spiritual and universal absolute. It was, instead, "the land of the future, where, in the ages that lie before us, the burden of the world's history shall reveal itself—perhaps in a contest between North and South America."[9] Although his prediction was inaccurate, it was near enough to the truth that it was easy for contemporaries to apply his insight to the Northern and Southern states of North America instead.

The progression of world spirit, Hegel believed, was triumphing in his own nineteenth-century Germany and flowering in Lutheran Protestantism. Although the Transcendentalists did not go this far in favor of Germany and Lutheranism, they and the St. Louis Hegelians adopted Hegel's views both as a spur to the cultural development of the United States so as to participate in the world spirit and in the usurpation of Germany's leading position in this concept. Even Henry Clay Fish, a Baptist minister in New Jersey, can be found displaying this Hegelian type of viewpoint during the Civil War, stating that "in this struggle we stand for the world, we represent the world. *For the world freedom lives or dies here and now!*"[10] The Transcendentalists believed that the United States, not Germany, could hold a position as the site of realization of the world-historical achievement of absolute spirit.

These views represented a shift from the Scottish conceptions of nationality that had been essential in the ideology of the American Revolution and the early republic. David Hume assessed the incidence of commonalities among the people of nations in his essay "Of National Characters" (1752). What he termed "moral" causes were the essential defining foundation of a nation, he argued. The proximity and similar interests of people in one locality in regard to defense, commerce, and government, would naturally lead them to "acquire a resemblance in their manners, and have a common or national character."[11] Arguments for physical causes such as climate and latitude were baseless claims that did not survive scrutiny.

Likewise, to Hume, it was moral influences that grew to form the basis of government. Governments were founded on the majority "opinion of interest" and "opinion of right." Interest rested on the perceived benefits and advantages of the particular government in question, and "opinions of right" upheld a belief in that government's right to power and, second, individuals' right to property. These rights, according to Hume, were the original principles of government. His analysis of these questions rested on circumstance, utility, and opinion. Nations formed from common interest among groups of people who perceived a net benefit to the group from creating a government, agreeing on the source of power within said government, and having their interests sufficiently served by the government they had created.[12] In his essay on the perfect commonwealth, Hume laid out his vision of ideal government, with details such as the division of counties, election process, and number of officials elected to a senate. "'Tis needless to enquire whether such a government would be immortal," he concluded. What mattered was whether the ideal would be "a sufficient incitement to human endeavors" if it were to last merely many ages and not presume to aspire to "that immortality, which the Almighty seems to have refused to his own productions."[13] Purely pragmatic, there were no abstract ideals of a unique folk spirit or national destiny contained within Hume's treatment of the matter.

Another option offered from Scottish political thought was that of Henry Home, Lord Kames, of the supreme civil court of Scotland. He approached the question of governance and law from a position influenced by the moral sense philosophy of Shaftesbury and Hutcheson. Justice and law were not derived from precedent or rational deliberation, Kames held, but rather "justice was derived from the sense of duty" that discerned beauty and virtue in actions.[14] Because this sense was, like the other external and internal senses in Common Sense theory, given to all mankind, with its source in the divine, it could be trusted to judge rightly. Although Kames identified the failure in Shaftesbury's writings to prove that virtue was a duty, he in turn failed to make a clear distinction between moral obligations and legal obligations in his own work. "MORAL duties," Kames wrote, "originally weak and feeble, acquire great strength by refinement of manners in polished societies. . . . Promises and covenants have full authority among nations tamed and disciplined in a long course of regular government: but among Barbarians it is rare."[15] In this he suggested that moral duty was nearly synonymous with legal duty, for without legal duty he implied that moral duty was scarce if not impossible to find or cultivate. Thus, in his political thought, government became a vital component of personal morality and the nation an important vessel in the growth and cultivation of virtue.

Kames's conviction that the moral sense could rightly discern legal duty was put into action during the 1778 Court of Session's ruling in the case of *Knight v. Wedderburn*. After four years of deliberations in lower courts in which Joseph Knight, a Jamaican slave, was suing for his freedom from Sir John Wedderburn, the case was heard in Scotland's supreme court on which Lord Kames sat. The case elicited a similar set of questions and examinations as the Dred Scott case later did in the United States, such as whether the law of the nation supported slavery to begin with, whether men of all races were equal, if slavery was compatible with Christianity, and slavery as property rights. Lord Kames stood on the side of Knight in this case, basing his argument on the conviction that slavery was not found in the state of nature and was thereby a forced and unnatural state, contrary to both humanity and Christianity.

Although trained in the English rather than the Scottish legal tradition as Kames was, the same type of emphasis on intuition and feeling as a form of legal judgment can be found in the writings of the English jurist William Blackstone, whose *Commentaries* on British common law remained the foremost book on law in America through the nineteenth century. His commentaries formed the bulk of legal training for most American lawyers, including Abraham Lincoln. What can appear as sentimentalism or providentialism to a modern reader would thus have carried legal weight to the contemporaneous audience. A reference to either Kames or Blackstone would reinforce the Transcendentalist emphasis on these aspects of character as a political force, for Blackstone urged his readers "to feel as well as think their way to justice," and, like Kames, depicted that "adhering to the law was natural."[16] Dugald Stewart, too, emphasized that moral philosophy held an important role in creating what he termed "rational patriotism." The French Revolution demonstrated the negative possibilities of "instinctual patriotism" that relied on cultural prejudice, ignorance, and "national vanity."[17] Stewart saw the solution to this type of threat as the careful cultivation of the moral sense in the lower classes of society as well as in the upper ranks. Such discernment required the development of the moral faculty throughout the nation, which Stewart hoped to achieve through a program of moral education, including lectures, publications, and philosophical and literary societies. Not only were Stewart's methods for achieving this moral education closely imitated by the Transcendentalists, but these concepts are also critical in understanding the Transcendentalists' approach to intuition and the moral sense as a political element of character.

If morality and law could be rightly discerned and judged through sentiment, then the basis of Transcendentalist abolitionist activity and defiance of constitutional law in favor of "higher law" comes into focus. The Scottish legal tradition that Kames relied on in forming his vote in the *Knight* case was founded on the belief in first principles rather than legal precedent; even if a nation's laws had originally supported an institution such as slavery, legal duty required adherence to first principles foremost. Thoreau, for example, considered it a mistaken approach to the question of slavery to debate whether it was constitutional. "The question," he declared, "is not whether you or your grandfather, seventy years ago, did not enter into an agreement to serve the Devil, and that service is not accordingly now due; but whether you will not now, for once and at last, serve God . . . by obeying that eternal and only just CONSTITUTION, which He, and not any Jefferson or Adams, has written in your being."[18] Intuition and sentiment, he thus argued, were better routes to discerning what constituted justice than bare logic or historical precedent. He was also following in an Americanized interpretation of Common Sense first promoted by Thomas Paine. Unlike Reid, who had emphasized the universality and timelessness of Common Sense, Paine introduced the possibility that Common Sense might be rightly discerned only when "mass prejudice, misinformation, and inequity recede," and "what is antithetical to the common" in the moment could become "familiar and agreeable at another" time. To reach this future state, what was needed was "the voice of the clear-sighted, prophetic individual who intuits what the people should be able to grasp but cannot by themselves."[19] This hypothesis of Paine's strongly reflects the position of Transcendentalists such as Thoreau, who called on the Common Sense he believed to have been written into everyone's innermost being but not heeded due to the influence of prejudice and misinformation.

This context for approaching the emotions sheds light on the nuanced understanding of freedom as promoted by the Transcendentalists and expressed in the Northern wartime rhetoric of freedom and the role of character in assuring its triumph. Reid, in a letter to Lord Kames, laid out an ideal of freedom based on the model of balanced character, which would have been highly acceptable to the Transcendentalists. "The proper exercise of liberty is," wrote Reid, "to be determined, not by the strongest motive, but by that which has most authority . . . the part that is decent, that is manly, that is virtuous, that is noble, has always authority upon its side. Every man feels this authority in his own breast."[20] And one was only truly at liberty if he exercised "power over the determinations of his own will."[21] Thus could Thoreau write with conviction, "That government is best which governs least," or better yet, "That government is best which governs not at all." And, Thoreau maintained, "when men are prepared for it, that will be the kind of government which they will have."[22] This key phrase, "when men are prepared for it," illustrates how Thoreau referred to the model of character development in preparing men for self-government through balanced faculties. It again reflects Paine's belief that true Common Sense on certain matters could come to be recognized even by those who currently did not believe a particular stance was aligned with Common Sense.

Recalling the regimental chaplain employing Proverbs 16:32, "'He that governeth his own spirit is better than he that taketh a city,'" to preach on the importance of governing one's own spirit, Wilbur Fisk believed that this individual self-governance, if practiced by a sufficient number, would spill over into forming the political nation. For, Fisk discussed, when these perfected characters were "put into the balance" with those of undeveloped character, he believed that it would tip as if "between a pile of froth and a wedge of gold."[23] Thus, he trusted, would the nation itself be slowly perfected and the Union party of Lincoln would prevail over the Peace Democrats in the North. Other Union soldiers employed the same conviction in regard to the South. George Burmeister was appalled at the lack of refinement he observed in Confederate soldiers, noting in his diary that they were "extremely dirty, and very ignorant, the majority cannot converse with any degree of intelligence or propriety. They do not know really why they are engaged in this war." And he questioned: What would "become of this people if they do not receive a better mental and moral culture?"[24] Napoleon had allegedly held the opinion that the worse the man, the better the soldier, Fisk commented, but he did not believe this to be true. If it were, he feared that the Union army would be in serious trouble, for he felt that the majority of soldiers he had encountered were fine men. He was instead convinced that men of high character not only made better soldiers but that their character would serve to tip the balance in favor of their cause.[25] Roswell Lamson, a cadet from Oregon studying at the Naval Academy at the start of the war, expressed the same conviction, writing, "I have no doubt of the final triumph of the *Union* cause any more than I have of the final triumph of true principles."[26] The two, he suggested, were one and the same.

If freedom consisted of a self-regulated character, which meant the subordination of passions to principle, the Northern conviction that they fought for white Southerners' best interests in addition to those of enslaved people is also illuminated. "The Southerner talks of *whipping*," wrote Emerson in disdain. "He has yet no other image of manly activity & virtue, charity none; endurance, perseverance, none; attainment of truth none."[27] Roswell Lamson described in a letter to his cousin that the "warm Southroners [*sic*]" among the cadets attempted verbal debate to prove to him that the Bible and the Constitution both supported slavery. When they failed to convince him by reasoned argument, he recounted, they fell back on the threat that they could "whip the Northerners five to one."[28] The South, if seen as driven by passion rather than reason, became something in need of assistance in enabling the higher faculties to triumph over the lower. As Reid Mitchell has concluded, according to a typical Northern viewpoint, the Southerner was "hot-headed and impulsive—the result of unrestrained passion," whereas the Northerner was rational and loyal.[29] Daniel Walker Howe, in a more sophisticated analysis, contended that the three branches of American government—legislative, executive, and judicial—had initially been created to mirror the three mental faculties recognized by Reid and faculty psychology: the understanding, the reason or will, and the conscience.[30] With the South in the majority in the legislative branch, this could mean, according to the Northern perspective, that passion was overpowering understanding in the national government.

Even the usual phrase in the North to describe the South's legislative majority, "the slave power," bears a possible connotation with this designation of the mind as intellectual powers. A piece from the *Kansas Herald of Freedom* in 1858 remarked on "the ruling passion of the slave power." The *National Era* berated another newspaper for serving "the interest of the Slave Power, and its appeals to the passion for plunder." And in 1865, the *Chicago*

Tribune remarked that these destructive "passions of the slave power" were still in action, sacrificing even the life of President Lincoln to its uncontrolled impulses.[31] In *History of the Rise and Fall of the Slave Power in America* (1872), Henry Wilson, Massachusetts senator and chairman of the Senate Committee on Military Affairs, described the situation of the South and the danger it held to itself and the country at large, as follows: "With ignorance so profound, with prejudices so unreasoning, and with passions so inflammable, it was not difficult to hoodwink and commit such people to purposes and plans not only dangerous to others but destructive to themselves."[32] The framework of balanced powers in character easily applied to a framework of balanced powers in government, and a region's perceived lack of self-control became an issue within the national character, a matter of concern for the national body, and it was therefore the duty of reason, the North, to subdue passion, the South, so as to retain true freedom.

The German philosophers shifted and expanded the conception of the nature and role of government. Writing during the turbulent political period of the late 1700s, Kant viewed the state as necessary for the advancement of human and universal aims. He described the development of nationality in terms of a social and political phenomenon, one that served as a positive good although it was brought about through the negative tendencies in human nature. Kant believed that their "antagonism," or "asocial sociability," drove humans together and became the basis of all lawful order and civic society. In its "quarrelsomeness," "enviously competitive vanity," and "insatiable desire to possess or to rule," Kant held that humanity was almost tricked, as it were, into forming political nations.[33] But he thought that nature, in turn, used these negative traits to refine and goad humans into the full development of their higher function as rational beings. Without the context of a just civic constitution, Kant did not believe that mankind would achieve any successful development of its higher faculties and would therefore fail to serve the end in the order of creation to which it had been assigned. The creation of such just civic constitutions, Kant argued, was the intention of nature and the goal of all human history.

In contrast, Herder, reacting to the enlightened despotism of the European monarchies on the eve of the French Revolution and the encroaching French political and cultural influences in Germany, concluded that while the state could serve a negative good, it was not natural or necessary for the existence of a nation. Indeed, Herder believed that governments, leaders, legislatures, and judges were unknown to the "original dispositions of Nature" and were artificial institutions imposed on the natural alliances of people bound together by history and culture.[34] Striving to defend German cultural identity and cohesion in the face of French power, Herder did not view a nation as stemming from or relying on forms of government or political organization at all. Rather, he considered it to be intrinsic to the people themselves, regardless of the political state in which they lived. Moreover, Herder delineated the people as a group defined by the physical geography of their homeland, their historical development as a group, and their distinct folk character.[35] Grassroots movements within a population, local customs, and personal achievements were consequently esteemed by Herder as of great value and viewed as essential in protecting against the encroaching demands of conformity to concepts of universal systems of natural law, such as those promoted by the French.

Despite differing considerably from Kant's ideal of history as the progression of reason, history still retained immense significance to Herder. He believed that rather than the development of the rational human mind alone, history was the canvas on which multiple layers of human nature were expressed—the artistic, emotional, and spiritual, as well as the rational.[36] He viewed history as a force that lived on within each individual and thus shaped the present, rather than existing merely as a dead and distant past that could be studied only for its demonstration of universal systems. No individual and no nation could have a meaningful identity apart from its historical experience, Herder posited, because cultural identity created the individual rather than the individual creating culture and identity. For instance, he asserted that the culture of the Greeks and Romans was not created by the famous individuals of their history but that these individuals "were precisely what they were capable of becoming" in the context of "the genius of nature, their country, their way of life, the period in which they lived, and the character of their progenitors."[37] Herder concluded that local cultures and local histories, whether personal or national, should be respected as the very foundation from which individual identity emanated and should not be subsumed into a rigid, legal, codified system built on the assumption of universal laws. These views were easily assimilated into the American intellectual milieu as an endorsement of popular government and faith in the common man, but they also help explain why both Northerners and Southerners were adamant in their claims during the Civil War that their cause built on the legacy of the Founding Fathers.

In his treatment of history, Herder identified "the education of the human race" in the discovery of its humanity in all areas of human identity and culture, a life in which "every one might exercise his faculties," learn to subordinate the passions to understanding, and thus accomplish "the symmetry of his powers," in which true happiness lay.[38] Each national history was seen as the story of this process.[39] But Herder did not believe that this happened as linear "progress," or *Fortschritt*, culminating in one era, or region, or in a predefined celebration of European political organization, as Kant had suggested. Rather, Herder argued for "progression," or *Fortgang*.[40] This more nuanced approach allowed for each nationality to achieve its own path of development rather than portraying a single route to a single goal. It also accounted for periods of growth, bloom, and decline in nations, without destroying faith in an overseeing Providence working out its own ends. The progression of history, Herder believed, was the system that Providence had provided for humanity in order to develop "in the human heart little by little certain inclinations and forces for which people previously and on another path saw no clear trace."[41] But he cautioned that Providence's designs were for the most part beyond human awareness, and thus no nation could judge as *progress*, or lack of progress, the individual and unique *progression* of other national peoples toward the ultimate development of their humanity. He believed that each nationality had its own route, ordained by the provisions of Providence, to discover and develop the humanity of its national people, and in this progression no other group had any justification to meddle. The implications of this on colonialism in the American context and interactions with Indigenous nations were certainly not emphasized by the Transcendentalists. They seized instead on the general ideal of progression and growth of character in humanity that Herder portrayed.

Perhaps because he wrote in the period following the Treaty of Vienna when Germany was relatively stable and not subjected to foreign rule, Hegel held the most optimistic view of the state as a political organization of any of these three German philosophers. This view resonated most strongly with Americans in the Northern states during their own struggle for the Union during the Civil War, which was somewhat contradictory to Hegel's emphasis on stability for the optimal functioning of government. On the subject of history, Hegel's view was, like Herder, that it was a process and, like Kant, also a story of progress. The structure of Hegel's philosophy of history rested on the assumption that world history is a rational process, but not rational in the sense that Kant used the word. To Hegel it was not "speculative cognition" as a faculty of the human mind that directed the course of world events; rather, he held that the underlying force of universal development was reason. Reason, as defined by Hegel, is "substance," "infinite power," and the "entire essence and truth" of all created things.[42] The history of the world, according to Hegel, was thus the story of a universal consciousness coming to know itself. "It may be said of universal history," he wrote, "that it is the exhibition of spirit in the process of working out the knowledge of that which it is potentially."[43] In other words, by acting and manifesting itself in the world, spirit moved from the abstract realm into the concrete and thus came to self-awareness. Hence world history was the stage on which reason, or spirit, can be observed in action. Hegel did not portray history as an uninterrupted, linear story of progress; nor did he deem all cultures as equal. He was interested instead in showing how humans throughout time had striven, with greater or lesser success, toward the goal of spiritualization and unity with the absolute. It was not "this or that specific occurrence or achievement" or "the contingencies of race or geographical location" that featured in Hegel's philosophy of history but "a civilization's mode of *understanding* the world and itself."[44] To Hegel, outward events were only the emanation of the inward consciousness of particular nations and specific time periods. Hegel believed that "the history of the world is none other than the progress of the consciousness of freedom," but his concept of freedom was also different from that of either Kant or Herder and was one he developed more fully than either.[45]

Kant had viewed freedom as a supersensible property that we attribute to reason, insofar as reason has purposes and acts in the world. Hegel argued that this Kantian sense of "reason" actually meant "understanding," a type of knowledge constrained to the material world. Herder had viewed freedom as allowing humanity to discover itself in all cultural expressions. Hegel, by contrast, defined freedom as the realization of spirit as free from any dependence on material substance, intermediaries, other humans, rituals, or rules and morals imposed on one from outside of oneself. Spirit, he maintained, "has not a unity outside itself, but has already found it; it exists *in* and *with itself*.... Spirit is *self-contained existence*." Spirit did not rely on any outside substance, or other entity, for its existence or its knowledge of itself, and, Hegel stated, "This is freedom, exactly." His conception of spirit, and hence of freedom, was synonymous with God himself, his nature, his will, and his absolute being.[46]

Because Hegel viewed God as the absolute self-existent spirit, he believed that God's nature was of necessity one of freedom, and the realization of God's own nature, spiritual freedom, was God's will for the world. It was humanity's development of an awareness of this self-contained freedom that Hegel deemed as the purpose, scheme, and final cause of world history. "God governs the world," Hegel stated. "The actual working of His government, the carrying out of His plan, is the history of the world."[47] If understanding this divine freedom constituted the plot of history, Hegel posited that awareness of this freedom was best traced through the religious practices of any given people, which was where they demonstrated comprehension of God, absolute spirit, and hence freedom. Hegel followed this approach in *Philosophy of History* (1837). Through an examination of select nations' religious beliefs, covering ancient Greece, Rome, the Zoroastrians of Persia, Chinese Confucianism, Judaism, Catholicism, and Protestant Christianity, Hegel assessed what the people regarded as the truth. It was only, he argued, when they recognized "God, as unity of the universal and the individual," that they reached a true understanding of freedom.[48] Hegel consequently treated progress as the development of humanity's understanding of this freedom and its extension to all individuals, an interpretation that naturally resonated with Northerners in the United States during their campaign for abolition. "The Eastern nations knew only that *one* was free; the Greek and Roman world only that *some* are free; while *we* know that all men absolutely . . . are free," Hegel wrote.[49] While Hegel believed that Christianity, particularly his own denomination of Lutheranism, presented the highest understanding of freedom as the realization of God's will, so long as it remained particularized in a church, he considered it still a limited demonstration because it was not yet universal.

To attain universality, Hegel believed that the political construct of the state was necessary because the state was the only form in which universal abstract reason, will, or spirit was joined with the individual and concrete, ideally demonstrated in a constitutional monarchy, which visibly contained the union of the objective universal idea with the subjective individual personality of the monarch. His conclusion was obviously not in accordance with American views but was easily reshaped to support a democracy, understood as the individual subsumed into a totality, and the basic argument lent itself to sacralizing the Union of the United States among the Northern populace during the Civil War. Thus, in sharp contrast to Herder, who believed political organization was an unnatural, though necessary, imposition, Hegel contended, "The state is the divine idea as it exists on earth."[50] Hegel structured his political treatise, *Philosophy of Right* (1820), as a dialectical problem that began with the abstract right, not yet realized. From there, it moved into morality, understood as the private realization of right. But he held it was only through the state that the final synthesis of the abstract and the personal could be demonstrated as universal ethical life. In the state, Hegel explained, right could become "a structure of objective mind" with universal application and the power to dialectically cancel out wrongs through the synthesis of universal and individual rights under the law.[51]

The political state, in this conception, was responsible for actuating people's rights, property, and culture, and the spiritual height that a people's religion had reached was defined by the constitution of their state and was demonstrated in their art and philosophy, with all these aspects springing from the single foundation of their understanding of spiritual freedom. Without each one of these aspects, there could not be a nation and, consequently, no history. Those people without such a political state organization, Hegel classified as ahistorical, an undeveloped potentiality, outside the bounds of history and of little importance in the world narrative.[52] It was only when individuals belonged to the state that they could be truly moral and realize universal principles. This was not a loss of natural freedom, Hegel argued, but the only true freedom. By belonging to a state, its laws and policies belonged to the people, the geographic features belonged to them, and its history belonged to them. "All is their possession, just as they are possessed by it; for it constitutes their existence, their being," Hegel concluded. This unity created the "spirit of a people" and determined their being. He considered each individual as a unit of the whole, and as a result, "none remains behind it, still less advances beyond it." With this unity in mind, Hegel presented nations' famous characters as "world-historical" figures who summed up and demonstrated the entire spirit of their age and their individual nation, an idea that the American Transcendentalists adopted and that flourished in the emphasis on personal heroism during the Civil War.[53]

Hegel also differentiated between the active spirit of a people and mere custom. Customary life, he believed, was a mindless cycle, as a watch continuing to run after being wound. If a nation lived merely by custom, it had already entered its decline and was passing out of the world-historical narrative. Many Americans expressed this fear in the early nineteenth century once the impetus of the Revolution and political formation stages had passed, to which they believed the Civil War offered a solution, as Hegel held that actual endeavor, the intentional striving toward self-realization of spiritual freedom, was the principle that drove national development. Just as individuals passed through various stages of development while remaining a single entity, "in like manner does a people, till the spirit which it embodies reaches the grade of universality," Hegel stated. Once this stage was reached, the world-historical striving passed on to another people, who then claimed the universal spotlight as the demonstration of spirit's self-realization. This process was "the soul, the essential consideration, of the philosophical comprehension of history."[54] As with all of Hegel's philosophical investigations, true reality was a process of becoming, never a static beginning or ending point. And political organization was yet another, if not the most important, demonstration of humanity's growing awareness of spiritual universality. Consequently, Hegel held a much more positive view of political government and the forces that drove human societies to form it than did either Kant or Herder. In large part, Americans of the Civil War era appear to have rejected theories such as Kant's, although similar views had shaped the thought of the Founding Fathers, and instead adopted the positive threads of Herder's popular nationality and Hegel's sacred state. Thomas Bender has suggested that this combination created Americans' compound model of a "nation-state" and particularly guided the Republican Party's cultural and socioeconomic platform prior to and during the Civil War, if not beyond.[55]

The St. Louis Hegelians, the small Western offshoot of Transcendentalism that coalesced in Missouri, placed the Civil War conflict squarely into the middle of this understanding of a nation-state. Henry Brokmeyer, the founding member of this group, believed that "the laws of the land expressed the current Folk-Soul," and it was Lincoln, a "world-historical character," who grasped this soul of the nation and harnessed it within the construct of the government. Brokmeyer and his cohort members, William Torrey Harris and Denton Snider, believed that the Civil War represented the dialectical "elimination of the dualism introduced into the Union at its birth" with slavery and freedom and was "a manifestation of a profound development in the World-Spirit, a decisive advance in the movement of world history toward the actualization of concrete freedom."[56] Thus "Union" was not a noun only but a verb as well. Fighting for "the Union" was to fight for the existing Union of governmental states, but also for a dialectical union of ideas, for the sake of Euro-Americans, African Americans, and the world as a whole.

Margaret Fuller, who did not live to see the Civil War, could not interpret the war to be fulfilling this growth, but she recognized the need for continued development of the American idea. "Books which imitate or represent the thoughts and life of Europe," she wrote, "do not constitute an American literature. Before such can exist, an original idea must animate this nation and fresh currents of life must call into life fresh thoughts along its shores." Although she did not see this happening before the continent was traversed and settled and the hyperactivity of exploration and settlement ceased, she had faith that in "that riper time national ideas shall take birth," which would define the nation's principles.[57] She also echoed this belief in a *New-York Daily Tribune* article, writing that the cause of the 1848 Revolutions and the Wars of Italian Unification was that "still Europe toils and struggles with her idea, and, at this moment, all things bode and declare a new outbreak of the fire."[58] For the realization of a national idea was like human nature that "goes not straight forward, but by excessive action and then reaction in an undulated course," alternating between one extreme to another until the perfect balance was reached and maintained.[59]

Emerson also related to the framework of a national idea, stating in his essay "Circles" that "our culture is the predominance of an idea which draws after it this train of cities and institutions."[60] He also believed that "we have yet not genius in America. . . . Our log-rolling, our stumps and their politics, our fisheries, our Negroes, our Indians, our boats, and our repudiations, the wrath of rogues, and the pusillanimity of honest men, the Northern trade, the Southern planting, the Western clearing Oregon and Texas, are yet unsung. Yet America is a poem in our eyes; its ample geography dazzles the imagination, and it will not wait long for metres."[61]

This was the role that Walt Whitman appointed himself to fill, stating that his creative genius had been simmering until Emerson brought it to a boil. Emerson was impressed by Whitman's results, declaring his *Leaves of Grass* "the most extraordinary piece of wit and wisdom that America has yet contributed."[62] Whitman indeed encapsulated just the kinds of details that Emerson mentioned, weaving images and personalities of American life into his poetic acclamations of the American people, the American spirit, and the American nation as a nation built of these individual blocks, yet forming a unified whole. Adam Gurowski, a Polish immigrant and astute social and political commentator, likewise wrote in his diary in the summer of 1861, "These freemen of America . . . incarnate the loftiest principle in the successive, progressive, and historical development of man. . . . Nations, communities, societies, institutions, stand and fall with that principle . . . whereof they are the incarnation."[63] This conception of the nation as the incarnation of a principle was shared by many Northern Americans during the Civil War.

The Union, one of the most common causes for which Northern soldiers stated they fought, carried many layers of meaning beyond the mere incorporation of thirty-four states that made up the United States of America during the 1860s. It has been an unending historiographical debate as to whether the North fought the American Civil War for the abolition of slavery, economics, or maintaining the Union. The full answer to this question lies not in one or the other of these suggestions, but in the view that Gurowski summarized above: The North fought as the incarnation of a principle. Its cause was "to save and preserve pure self-government in principle and in its direct application," and as a principle, these causes were inclusive of one another and not separate or exclusive.[64] Self-government meant freedom for personal agency, for the free market, for the realization of human fullness, for alignment with divinity, and freedom in the Hegelian sense of the dialectical synthesis. Each of these threads in the Union cause grew out of theoretical frameworks regarding nationality and government that had changed significantly by this time from the Founders' sources of inspiration in English law, the writings of Locke, and the Roman Republic. Bender notes that during the nineteenth century, the prevalent political theory in the United States had shifted away from the Lockean model that placed the origin of individual rights in the people themselves, into a German-inspired understanding that placed these rights as derived from the state.[65] Although he placed this shift as the responsibility of John W. Burgess during his time as professor of law at Columbia University from 1876 to 1912, it is likely to have begun influencing American political thought with the first significant wave of Americans who studied in Germany and became American policymakers, such as Francis Lieber, Carl Schurz, and Edward Everett in the 1840s to 1860s. "We must think of the nation-state as a compound of nation and state," Bender concludes, "crudely Herder's cultural nationalism and Hegel's state structure. Because Germans did not have a territorial state, Herder turned to culture and language, arguing that a national identity was achieved through cultural production. For Hegel, social and political developments were central." The Lincoln administration, Bender believed, "brought together both the cultural and socioeconomic elements, Herder and Hegel."[66] Both of these philosophers viewed nations as a furthering of a universal ideal.

Hegel argued that the national structure of government, built successively up from the family and social order, led to the status of citizen in a political nation. In the duties that citizenship entailed, he wrote, "the individual finds his liberation" from "natural impulse" and depression over his individual helplessness to cause things to be as he believed they ought. This was liberation as well from "indeterminate subjectivity" which caused him to remain "self-enclosed and devoid of actuality."[67] Duty to the government, the Union, and the duty to participate in the war effort during the American Civil War, then, could be viewed in higher terms and understood as striving for one's personal freedom as well as that of the national state, rather than being viewed as unjustified limitation of personal freedom and external coercion, as soldiers from other wars expressed more frequently. "In whatever way an individual may fulfill his duty, he must at the same time find his account therein and attain his personal interest and satisfaction," Hegel wrote. Furthermore, the state was defined as "the actuality of the ethical Idea," not as "external appearances—i.e. contingencies such as distress, need for protection, force, riches, &c."[68] This conception illustrates how it might not be the actual government itself or its political functions to which Union soldiers were loyal but the idea or the ethics that they believed their nation was founded for and embodied. This thought perhaps helps explain why Union soldiers maintained high levels of dedication and loyalty to the cause, even when criticizing the government or the political handling of the war effort, and so consistently used the abstract term "Union" to describe that for which they were fighting.

The American Transcendentalists, while accepting the framework of a national idea, were careful to make a distinction between the government as the vessel of that idea and the government merely as a secular construct. Emerson believed that a reliance on property, and government to protect that property, was a "want of self-reliance," and he consistently, especially in his earlier years, poked fun at the excessive faith his fellow citizens had in political organizations. "The delegation from Essex! The Democrats from New Hampshire! The Whigs of Maine!" were all lauded as saviors of society, and yet, he observed, "nature will not have us fret and fume.... When we come out of the caucus, or the bank, or the Abolition convention, or the Temperance meeting, or the Transcendental club, into the fields and woods, she says to us, 'So hot? my little sir.'"[69] The true representation of a national idea was, instead, to be found in the individual who lived by, embodied, and stood by this idea, for they were "themselves the country which they represent."[70] Thomas Wentworth

Higginson stated after the Anthony Burns affair, "The way to make principles felt is to assert them—peaceably, if you can; forcibly, if you must. The way to promote Free Soil is to have your own soil free; to leave courts to settle constitutions, and to fall back (for your own part,) on first principles: then it will be seen that you mean something."[71] In this way, individuals were the original source of all government and law, which "sprung . . . from the character and condition of the people," where "governments have their origin in the moral identity of men."[72] Because of this, Emerson maintained, "the less government we have the better,—the fewer laws, and the less confided power. The antidote to this abuse of formal government is, the influence of private character, the growth of the Individual." The nation was barely breaking ground into what it ought to be, Emerson believed. "We think our civilization near its meridian, but we are yet only at the cock-crowing and the morning star. In our barbarous society the influence of character is in its infancy."[73] Emerson emphasizes once again that, through the means of individual betterment, he was envisioning political implications and addressing political issues within the nation. As the North consistently grew stronger in its resolve to end slavery and elected abolitionist officials, and the national government became apparent as the only route to achieving this end, Emerson's appreciation for the role of the federal government in furthering the national moral ideal also increased from that expressed in earlier statements.[74]

Neither did Transcendentalists view the war in as negative a light as might be expected. The German writer Fichte had opined in his influential work on nationality, *Addresses to the German Nation* (1808), that when a nation reached a point of decline, subjugation, or unrest, it must save itself "by means of something completely new and never previously employed, namely, by the creation of a totally new order of things." A nation was to discover what this new order should be based on "the reason why . . . [the old] order had inevitably to come to an end" in the first place. Whatever was the opposite of the cause of decline was the new element that "must be introduced into the age, in order that by its means the fallen nation may rise to a new life."[75] This reason, in the United States, was clearly traceable to slavery. As Lincoln stated in his famous speech in 1858 when campaigning for the Senate, "A house divided against itself cannot stand. I believe this government cannot endure, permanently half slave and half free."[76] The antithesis of freedom was plainly slavery, so it was the abolition of slavery that must be the foundation stone for a completely new order of things of which Fichte spoke.

As national events plunged toward the outbreak of war and emancipation became increasingly accepted as a war aim, dedication to this conviction and to the conception of the nation as the vessel for progression and moral duty that Hegel had articulated meant that suddenly the Transcendentalists found themselves not only becoming increasingly supportive of the federal government but even actively accepting politically motivated armed violence. It is difficult to reconcile their militant attitude with the common conception of them as withdrawn intellectuals who advocated nonresistance and individual reform, as well as presenting the problem of their defending violence and the destruction of human life. Two common routes exist to reconcile the Transcendentalists with this controversial stance. One is to argue, as Randall Fuller has done, that they were veiling their remorse for an ideological inflexibility that they recognized as having driven the country to war by maintaining a false front of support.[77] Another is to argue that, as in the case of Bleeding Kansas, the Transcendentalists were "unaware or deliberately overlooked the full extent of Brown's violence in Kansas" and viewed him through a "distorted lens" of romanticized fiction.[78] Given their personal acquaintance with John Brown, the Secret Six Harpers Ferry conspirators' connection with Transcendentalism, and Henry Ward Beecher's sending rifles to Brown in Kansas, this conclusion is much too simple. On the surface, the fact that the Transcendentalists did not hold the preservation of an individual life as the highest good appears to contradict their promotion of the individual above the collective, self-culture above institutional change, and private reformation over public social upheaval. The development of political events over their lifetime certainly altered the Transcendentalists' approach to political and social problems, as they perhaps came to embrace an aspirationalist political philosophy, as Daniel Malachuk argues.[79] Yet the threads of a worldview elevating moral integrity above the preservation of physical life were clearly present in their earlier writings as well, as they were within the sources from which the Transcendentalists were creating their philosophical framework. The Transcendentalists supported the Civil War, although aware of its destructive nature through graphic newspaper accounts, photographic evidence, the loss of family and community members, and personal involvement. That they supported the resort to violence for what they were convinced was a worthy cause is an undeniable fact, and it obscures their complexities and humanness to force a consistent image of them as contemplative intellectuals who preached only nonresistance, as Thoreau's influence in particular has been interpreted to have impacted later activists like Martin Luther King Jr. and Mahatma Gandhi. In actuality, the moral foundation of government and the state, the role of conscience, limited government power over citizens, and the duty to disobey unjust laws were all aspects of Thoreau's philosophy.

Thoreau was the most vocal Transcendentalist in support of John Brown, and Emerson decisively stated his belief that "the war with all its defeats & uncertainties is immensely better than what we lately called the integrity of the Republic, as amputation is better than cancer."[80] "Our culture," Emerson further wrote, "must not omit the arming of the man. . . . But warned, self-collected, and neither defying nor dreading the thunder, let him take both reputation and life in his hand, and with perfect urbanity, dare the gibbet and the mob by the absolute truth of his speech, and the rectitude of his behavior. . . . To this . . . we give the name of Heroism."[81] Fuller regretted that "the effect of continued prosperity is the same on nations as on individuals,—it leaves the nobler faculties undeveloped," and thus, though deceased by the time of the Civil War, she lamented America's complacent prosperity and delighted in the tumult of the Italian Unification for this very reason.[82] Stances such as these caused Harry Stout to castigate Civil War–era Americans on both sides for immorality in their conduct of the war and what he viewed as their refusal to admit the extent of destruction or accept responsibility for the loss of life that they inflicted on their countrymen.[83] Americans of the Civil War era did not commonly express this view themselves, however. The fear of cowardice was given precedence over reservations concerning destroying lives. But this stance was not understood as an immoral but rather a moral one. Moral integrity, as discussed in depth by Transcendentalist-leaning minister Horace Bushnell, was the quality held in highest esteem and meant that one could face any trial, challenge, fear, or even death without giving up or compromising moral convictions.

As I discussed previously, Bushnell argued in *The Vicarious Sacrifice* that sacrifice for a moral cause, even to the point of death, was an internal requirement that grew out of individual character and was not imposed by external forces or governmental policies. This, Bushnell believed, Americans already fully understood:

> What meaning there may be in this ought, henceforth, to be never a secret to our American people. In our four years of dreadful civil war, what immense sacrifices of blood and treasure have we made; refusing

to be weakened by sorrow, or shaken by discouragement.... Nothing could meet our feeling but to ... forever establish the broken order of the law. All the stress of our gigantic effort hinged on this and this alone.... The victory we sighed for, and the salvation we sought, were summed up in the victory and salvation of law. Failing in this every thing would be lost. Succeeding in this all sacrifice was cheap, even that of our firstborn. What now do we see in the sacrifice of Christ, but that he, only in a vastly higher and more grandly heroic devotion of his life, is doing all for the violated honor and broken sovereignty of law.[84]

Bushnell was convinced that the Union soldiers, by their determination to uphold the moral principles of the cause even at the cost of their own lives, had participated in the ongoing work of Christ to bring the world back into harmony with the law. Bushnell did not reference the laws of the American government but the "higher law," the law of God accessible within nature and the human mind.

The imagery of the war as a participation in Christ's passion was driven home even more strongly by the sequence of the war's final days. It was Palm Sunday 1865 when Confederate general Robert E. Lee surrendered, and the day on which President Lincoln died fell on Good Friday. On the Easter Sunday following Lincoln's assassination, Maria Lydig Daly, a prominent New York woman, noted in her diary that on "Easter morning, instead of the Resurrection and Christ has Arisen, the clergyman began with Abraham Lincoln, mentioned that he was sacrificed on Good Friday, and it seemed to me that they gave Our Lord only the second place in his own house."[85] This minister probably did not view this as giving Christ second place but, given the typical views of the soldiers during the war already, as aligning Lincoln and the war dead with Christ's universal work of bringing the world back into harmony with the moral law. But Daly, as a Democrat, had never been a supporter of Lincoln and was more than a little displeased with the comparisons made.

Some Union soldiers themselves confidently spoke of their role as Christ-like and salvific. John W. Darby, writing amid the battle at Spotsylvania in May 1864, pondered in a letter to his brother, "I have thought that if I should be killed it might be the means of your salvation." Seeing as he had survived, however, a redemptive word would, he hoped, effect the same conversion in his brother, if his brother would allow it an opportunity to work on him.[86] This letter suggests that Darby, like Bushnell, was speaking of the sacrifice of life as the demonstration of absolute moral integrity and not as a purgation of evil through blood. William Ball, a soldier from Wisconsin, compared the loyal Southern civilians who had been killed by secessionists to the martyrs of the early church. They had, he stated, displayed "as much true courage and heroism" in dying for their country as any martyr had displayed in dying for Christ.[87] Less directly, but still reflective of this perspective, other Union soldiers consistently described their sacrifice as one of passively, like Christ, laying down their lives for the principles at stake in the Union cause or for the nation. Examples of this view include Theodore Ayrault Dodge, who assured his family that he was "happy to lay down my life for my Country if need be," and George Washington Beidelman, who wrote of his comrades who "lay down their lives on the altar of their country."[88] These soldiers did not speak of being killed against their will but of freely, like Christ, "laying down their lives" for the moral benefit of the nation and the universal cause of human freedom.

Earl J. Hess asserted that Civil War participants became "not victims, as twentieth-century authors tend to portray soldiers in all wars, but victors over the horrors of combat."[89] Acknowledging the moral power of an identification with Christ and participation in the universal salvation of humanity clarifies the understanding of morality and the convictions that upheld the Civil War population as they faced an unprecedented national tragedy. They did not value "'honor' at the expense of morality," as Stout interpreted their actions, but rather believed that honor and integrity were the highest form of morality.[90] For, as Philip Cafaro concludes, from their interpretation of Kant, the Transcendentalists created an understanding of morality as the "free expression of our true (or highest) nature."[91] And steeped in the philosophy of Idealism that placed life on a different plane than individual mortal lives, Civil War participants believed that this true and highest nature could be preserved only through absolute integrity to moral principles, not merely by the preservation of bodily life.

Individual life in the life of the nation and historical progression were inseparable ideas in Hegel's thought, as the nation was the structure through which the maturation of the world-historical idea was being carried forward. With world history understood as the "progress of the consciousness of freedom," life was a progression toward consciousness of self-contained spirit that relied on no external property. To Hegel, matter, on the contrary, relied for its existence on "gravity in virtue of its tendency toward a central point" distinct from itself. As a result, Hegel wrote, matter "seeks its unity; and therefore exhibits itself as self-destructive, as verging toward its opposite. If it could attain this, it would be matter no longer, it would have perished. It strives after the realization of its idea; for in unity it exists *ideally*."[92] For this reason, armed combat could be seen as displaying this dialectical striving toward unity. Combat was the result of the inherent draw toward self-destruction present within the contradiction of matter with spirit, and it was this end toward which it was directed. Thus destruction was not inflicted externally but, in a sense, sought internally. "As a living thing man may be coerced," Hegel wrote, but "the free will cannot be coerced at all," which agreed with Bushnell's conception of the sacrifice of self in warfare as being demanded from within, not inflicted from without.[93] Such a view also accounts for the frequent passive rather than active language regarding killing and the lack of personal culpability applied to the killer demonstrated in Civil War literature, for example, "died for the Union" rather than "killed by a Rebel." It could perhaps be argued that it was the killing of fellow Americans in the Civil War that required this particular coping strategy, but this language was not present in the Revolutionary War, which was also a war against compatriots. Neither did German- or Japanese-born Americans use this strategy during World Wars I and II. In an important commentary on the invention of gunpowder, Hegel discussed its role in furthering the spiritual idea. It was an agent of the mind, he suggested, that removed the killing of individuals from the realm of material opposition, of personal hatred or revenge, and placed it on a more spiritualized plane. It was, he stated, "one of the chief instruments in freeing the world from the dominion of physical force."[94] No longer was it particular minds and material bodies that contended with one another on the battlefield but an impersonal force, the use of which no longer relied on muscular strength but on mental strategy, on "spiritual valour" and the willingness to sacrifice oneself for the common good. Consequently, the enemy was not individual combatants but an abstract enemy that one was required to defeat through "intelligence, the generalship, the character of the commander," not through "the heat of personal feeling."[95] Although the depersonalization of killing can also be a troubling development, it was, to Hegel, seen as a progression toward spirit in warfare and world history.

Hegel believed humanity's true or highest nature to be that of divine union, and it was therefore a spiritual existence that did not rely on physical matter for life, for "matter itself has no truth," Hegel stated, and even physicists were discovering that matter grew "thinner in their hands" upon greater inspection.⁹⁶ The willingness to stake one's life on the recognition of this ideal was the ultimate dedication to this stage of the dialectic. Yet Hegel cautioned that such an ideal was not, still, the ultimate solution to the problem, for it involved the destruction of the thesis or the antithesis rather than them being truly synthesized. But, he reasoned, since it may solve the paradox in the consciousness of those involved and because all humanity was united, any individual's sacrifice of his individual "I," for the sake of seeking unity with the universal "I," furthered humanity toward realization of the absolute.⁹⁷

Although writing before his known familiarity with Hegel's ideas, Emerson voiced a similar stance when he considered there to be "one mind common to all individual men." History was the record of this mind, for "the thought is always prior to the fact. . . . Epoch after epoch, camp, kingdom, empire, republic, democracy, are merely the applications of his manifold spirit to the manifold world," and each individual was "one more incarnation" of this mind.⁹⁸ The critical element, then, was the idea, the divine mind, through which every individual came out of and returned to, connected and eternal in an individually manifested progression of a spiritual unity. When a manifestation ceased, the essence of the individual in this mind did not end, was not destroyed. And if engaging in combat, in violence and warfare, was the highest, most visible, and missionary action that an individual could take to manifest the Over-Soul, the mind, the absolute, then it was the action morally required of him, one that he took on at the demand of his own moral integrity, and was not an unfortunate accident, a destruction of life by an external party, or an immoral disregard of life. It was an action upholding the universal life, universal moral law, and carried forward the idea of the moral into the entire future unfolding of the truth, the absolute, in human history and in the American nation.

These views on universal moral progression, unity, and identification with Christ help us understand statements such as that of Union soldier John Rankin, who gloried in the fact that his "higher nature" was "a victor over self," although "within a moment I may be a mangled corpse."⁹⁹ Conquering the "natural being," as Hegel described it, ensured that Rankin's higher nature could triumph; it was an idea that seems to have considerably bolstered Rankin's resolve in facing death. Walt Whitman also recounted that a doctor with whom he worked in the military hospitals in Washington, DC, stated that he had never encountered a soldier who was afraid to die in the whole six months he had served there. Whitman reached a similar conclusion during his work as a nurse there and witnessing hundreds of military deaths himself. Following his experiences in the hospitals, Whitman wrote in a letter to friends in New York, "This then, [is] what frightened us all so long. Why, it is put to flight with ignominy—a mere stuffed scarecrow of the fields. Oh death, where is thy sting? Oh grave, where is thy victory?" George Frederickson, too, has recognized that Hegel's vision that every death "contributed to a cosmic whole" was central to Whitman's ability to reconcile strident patriotism with the carnage of the war.[100] Similarly, on Easter Sunday in 1864, Henry Ward Beecher opened the service with a prayer of thanksgiving for all the fallen Union soldiers, convinced that "the dying who die nobly enrich life more than they impoverish it. Then, when they are dead, there spring up a thousand powers; and being dead, they yet speak. We cannot mourn them that depart who do not go out in darkness, but rather rise into light unapproachable." In his 1867 novel *Norwood*, Beecher presented his character, Rose Wentworth, as able to rejoice upon news of her beloved's death that "since God has taken him into heaven, he will send over all things that the heavens cover, something of his nobleness and honor. The sun shall be brighter to me for his sake; the earth, and all that grows upon it, shall have new meaning now." William Henderson from Iowa, while on furlough from the Union army and visiting the families of his comrades who had died in battle, noted that they "feel the loss of their son very much but don't regret his sacrifice."[101] If historians dismiss the Civil War culture of sentiment and patriotism as inauthentic or fabricated to conceal the true nature of war, it is a significant failure to provide an account of such reports as these that demonstrate such language and cultural narrative was not destroyed for many families, even by the death of loved ones.

Thus, despite interpretations that portray the philosophy of Transcendentalism as failing to provide a meaningful framework for Americans' experience during the Civil War, the postwar years show the Transcendentalists growing in popularity, more widely accepted, and held in higher esteem than they had been before the war.[102] Such interpretations also fail to recognize the tragedies that had occurred in the Transcendentalists' own lives, prior to or coexisting with their philosophical development. Loss of family members often served as the catalyst for the beginning of the Transcendentalists' introspection, deliberation, and ultimately the formation of their philosophical identities. Emerson's father died while Emerson was a boy, and over the years, he lost his three brothers, his first wife Ellen, and his young son Waldo. Emerson even returned after several years and reopened the graves and coffins of his wife and son to contemplate the sight and confront the idea of mortality. Thoreau lost his older brother John to tetanus from a cut while shaving, and four years later Thoreau was creating his haven at Walden Pond, diving into philosophical speculation and application and writing his most famous work on the experience. Bronson Alcott lost his twenty-two-year-old daughter Lizzie, and her older sister Louisa May spent several years caring for her before her death that occurred three years prior to the Civil War and Louisa's wartime service as a nurse. It is thus a considerably problematic assumption that these historians have made in assuming a confrontation with death was a late development for Transcendentalist philosophy and one it could not withstand, when, in fact, it grew out of the quest for answers that the Transcendentalists began after they had experienced a loss. The convictions they reached on the ultimate goodness of humanity, the unreality of death, and the spiritual, immortal quality of the universe were the answers they found, not fanciful illusions that were destroyed by the harsh experiences of war and death.

Emerson's belief in the spiritual substance of the universe was also supported by his scientific interests. When traveling in Europe in 1848, Emerson attended a lecture by the English scientist Michael Faraday, who spoke on the atomic theory suggesting that what the physical senses perceived as material substance actually comprised energy. This lent scientific credence to the ideas that the Transcendentalists were developing, and the indestructible nature of such a composition of the universe carried important possibilities for a new way of viewing life and death. Emerson paraphrased an older presentation of this idea from the Katha Upanishad:

> If the slayer thinks he slays
> If the slain thinks he is slain
> Both these have no knowledge
> He slays not, is not slain.[103]

And Bronson Alcott reflected a similar understanding, stating that "neither matter nor death are possible."[104] Energy or spirit could not be destroyed by death or decay, and in this, a person's true life and substance resided.

Walt Whitman repeated this understanding of death many times in his poetry. "I know I am deathless," he declared. The natural world itself proved this, he believed, for "the smallest sprout shows there is really no death, and if ever there was it led forward life." And thus it also was with human life.

"Not a grave of the murdered for freedom but grows seed for freedom."[105] The rural cemetery movement, of which the postwar rural battlefield preservations were a part, was built on this belief. Such cemeteries were intended to serve as the visible manifestation and proof of the renewal of life. Nature, in its repeated cycles of life and death and new life, demonstrated this tangibly to mourners. Whitman, furthermore, believed that there was a universal quality to all sacrifices made in the name of a higher principle and that an individual's death would lift all humanity incrementally closer to the truth. James Harris, a Confederate soldier, when writing to a friend about Pickett's Charge during the Battle of Gettysburg in 1863, stated that it had been a fatal, but not a regrettable, event. For although it failed, that did not detract from its demonstration of humanity's capacity for heroism and chivalry.[106] In their true spiritual natures, the dead had not ceased to exist, this belief maintained, for spiritual energy did not depend on a physical body. "I do not think seventy years is the time of a man or woman," Whitman wrote, "nor that seventy millions of years is the time of a man or woman, nor that years will ever stop the existence of me or any one else." Life was not "chaos or death," he asserted, but "form and union and plan . . . it is eternal life . . . it is happiness."[107] And in the Over-Soul, every heroic deed colored the experience and understanding of all humanity for all time. The nation, and the cause of Union, was then immersed in a wider context of the spiritual and a human unity above and beyond the physical nation and even the physical world.

It should again be recalled that Whitman did not write these statements in a sheltered study where they were abstract concepts. He wrote them from his personal experiences in the hospitals and on the battlefields of the war itself. He was as familiar with injury, illness, death, and decay as anyone could be. Yet he never compared the battlefields, like Hemingway did in World War I, to "the stockyards at Chicago if nothing was done with the meat except bury it." Nor did he conclude that if a man shed his blood for his country, "only the flies benefited," as it seemed to Eugene Sledge in the midst of World War II.[108] Whitman continued to believe that every man's sacrifice held an eternal value and benefited all.

The Transcendentalists' conception of the national cause, grounded in these broader themes, contributed significantly and in unexpected ways to the political understanding and the conduct of Northern armies in the Civil War. These ideas supported a dedication to victory at all costs when the cause was presented as a cosmological struggle that would either further the world-historical idea of spiritual freedom or hinder it and betray one's own nature. In this way, Randall Fuller may have had a valid point that the Transcendentalists contributed to the violence and carnage of the Civil War by emphasizing moral integrity over physical preservation. But he neglected to account for the fact that this philosophy viewed death in terms different from a mere termination of life and enabled the war's participants to frame their experiences in a less traumatic and more productive way than might be expected, willingly choosing to make the sacrifice, and striving for spiritual progress while helping to secure the Union victory and the abolition of slavery.

Chapter Nine
THE NATION'S GEOGRAPHIC CHARACTER

In the Transcendentalists' political philosophy, the government constituted only a portion of what made up a nation. Even more essential, they believed, were the geographic landscapes provided for a people. Here, they were convinced, was where the City of God resided and where one could experience and inhabit it "not every millennium but nightly" by the mere sight of the stars.[1] In this natural geographic sphere, the higher law was primarily present as God's direct manifestation and was demonstrated daily. The landscapes of the continent, the Transcendentalists held, were given to the nation for an express purpose, and if the principles they demonstrated were contradicted, the nation would fail to fulfill its destiny. It thus required minds open and oriented toward nature and the divine present within it, to perceive, interact with, and implement the proper harmony and order of the higher laws displayed in the geographic nation into the body politic. Transcendentalist philosophy presented nature as an interactive and cognitive presence that was actively cooperating with the moral cause of abolition, which view can be found reflected in many writings of the common rank and file of the Union armies as well as the public literature and art of the period. Such a view lent conviction and comfort to many soldiers in the field and presented individuals as powerful political agents in creating and maintaining a moral nation. The understanding of the importance of geography to nationhood and individual ability to recognize and apply moral law from the nation's natural geography was developed first in much of Herder's writings.

Whereas Hegel wrote in a time of relative peace and prosperity, Herder lived against a backdrop of almost constant warfare in which the German Confederation strove to consolidate its power and gain ascendency in the region. During his travels in France, Herder witnessed the reign of Louis XVI firsthand, and by the last decade of his life, Europe was facing the repercussions of the French Revolution. Conflicts during his lifetime included the War of the Austrian Succession, the Seven Years' War, the partitions of Poland, and the Revolutionary and Napoleonic Wars. The fragmented state of the German nation, ongoing wars of conquest and expansion, and the "enlightened absolutism" of Frederick the Great shaped Herder's philosophic standpoint on identity and cultural belonging. With political divisions and rulers constantly in flux, Herder could not assign the phenomenon of nationality to the state government as Hegel would do. Instead, Herder believed that national character sprang from the common people themselves, regardless of any current government. Godfried van Benthem van den Bergh claims that Herder was the first to apply "the modern concept of 'nation' to describe the whole of a particular society."[2] From Herder's experience and observations of the monarchies in Germany and France, he was, additionally, deeply critical of government itself. He viewed it as an unnatural imposition on the state of nature, which had amply provided for the realization of human happiness and fulfillment.

Thus, the unique context in which Herder lived enabled him to articulate a conception of nation, government, and people that played a significant role in shaping the nineteenth-century understanding of nationality. He believed that humanity's differences were formed by time, place, and circumstance alone and argued that these factors created the distinct nations and nationalities throughout history. All nations, and all human history, consequently contributed to the whole store of knowledge of mankind in its search for the proper balance, or harmony, of personal and political powers. Failures were lessons for those who followed, and successes continued advancing the next phase of society, until ultimately the ideal balance was reached, which was not to be accomplished from the top down by any hierarchy of government or church, Herder maintained, but rather by and among the common people themselves.

From this philosophic standpoint, it is not difficult to understand why Herder's model of nationality found widespread acceptance in the United States. As a young, diverse nation—and categorized by Hegel as still uncovering and growing toward its successful manifestation of national principle—the concept that a common people could create a national identity from the ground up, inclusive of the diverse races and religions in their midst, was applicable and encouraging. George Bancroft, the Transcendentalist historian of America and statesman who spent several years studying in Germany, was an especially strong proponent of the nationalist enthusiasm inherent in Herder's philosophy. Bancroft's multivolume *History of the United States*, published between 1834 and 1860, was virtually a manifesto of the Herderian paradigm of history as applied to the United States. In his book, Bancroft credited the American Revolution to the environmental influences of mountains and sea on the continent. He viewed these landscapes as always being across the world the "favorite home" of freedom. From these lessons in nature and the cumulative growth toward freedom occurring in humanity from its beginnings among the Hebrews to the Greeks and Romans and through Christianity, Bancroft believed that the American colonists "deduced from universal principles" the Bill of Rights, "as old as creation and as wide as humanity," that would ensure that "every faculty have the unlimited opportunity for its development and culture," the height of Herder's vision for historical development.[3] An 1835 address to the Adelphi Society of Williamstown College further encapsulates Bancroft's debts to Herder. "German literature," Bancroft eulogized, "is almost entirely a popular creation. It was fostered by no monarch; it was dandled by no aristocracy. It was plebeian in its origin, and therefore manly in its results." The cultivation of such popular culture, Bancroft stressed, was not merely a fine wish but also a duty for every individual because it was only through "the moral and intellectual powers of the people" that the society could advance.[4] Some scholars have credited the influence of such proponents of a Herderian conception of nationality and history in the United States to the significant upsurge of American cultural works and the break with European precedents that occurred between the late 1810s and the Civil War.[5]

Herder maintained that the true aim of national identity was to ensure the full development of humanity. He described the ideal nation as one that realized as its purpose the provision of a situation in which "everyone might exercise his faculties," learn to subordinate the passions to understanding, and accomplish "the symmetry of his powers."[6] Herder drew out two faculties in particular to accentuate, reason and justice, which he viewed as the cornerstones of humanity by which the laws of nature were brought to fruition and created the necessary symmetry. Herder believed that nature had placed in humanity the laws of reason and justice, which also governed the universe at large, and consequently, humanity needed no external venues to learn these laws. "A head stuffed with knowledge, even of golden knowledge," was only "a morbid burden to the life of him who bears it," he observed.[7] All that was necessary to learn was present within one's self and the laws of nature. Thus Herder maintained that even if only one man had ever walked the earth and no forms of government or church had ever been created, human existence would have been complete in that one man if he had achieved this goal of harmony of reason and justice within himself and with nature. If the most essential teacher of virtue was nature, then it was imperative to connect with nature and to protect it from influences that would distort or prevent the manifestation of the lessons it had to offer. Without nature, there would be no civil society, no nationality, and no nation.

Herder's views on nature rather than government as nurturing human society were important for the American Transcendentalists' approach to the role of the continent's natural environment in shaping the character of the nation. Nature, Herder stressed, had already put in place all the prerequisites of success and happiness for human society, and if they were properly implemented, humanity would find the same harmony of powers in a completely savage state as under the most sophisticated government on earth. With little political history and an untamed continent before them, the Transcendentalists understood this concept to denote that nature itself was participating in forming the American nation. The natural landscapes of the continent were seen to contain within themselves the secrets for the successful utilization of the land, and the nation's prosperity was already written into the fabric of its natural territory, which acted as a living, inspiring presence among the people. Nineteenth-century Americans' enthusiasm for the idea of "Manifest Destiny" is usually treated in terms of a Calvinist faith in Providence. However, Herder's philosophy surely contributed as well. Throughout his work he repeatedly concluded that everything able to happen in a certain time, place, and circumstance would happen, and the geographic location of a people was an essential ingredient in their national development. It was not difficult for the population of the United States to believe that because the country could expand across the continent, it would do so. But Herder also emphasized that nature's gifts could be truly enjoyed only by cooperating with its demands, which were, in his words, "exercise, toil, and labor."[8] Hence the campaign to prevent the expansion of slavery into the American West, as well as the emphasis on Free-Soil and Free Labor promoted by antebellum politicians of the North, can be viewed in light of Herder's philosophy. Living off the labor of others, namely, slavery, was in Northern Americans' minds a misuse of the country that nature had provided and would inhibit the development of a national people.

Emerson had much to say regarding the proper disposition of man toward nature. If it were not approached with reverence and an inquiry into its own ends, he believed that interaction with nature became merely a trade, turned for man's own ends. It became a parody of truth. "Astronomy to the selfish becomes astrology; psychology, mesmerism . . . and anatomy and physiology become phrenology and palmistry."[9] It required the additional component of divinity to truly learn the lessons of nature, not just its material laws but also the lessons it offered as symbols, or "types," of higher laws. Only then could an individual use nature and become a "natural man" in a profitable manner. For then could "the currents of the Universal Being circulate through me" and the lessons of nature be assimilated into the mind, "not for barren contemplation, but for new creation."[10] Emerson's "natural man" was not a passive recipient of sensory information, so as to utilize it for his own needs. Instead, Emerson painted a vision of an individual's character as an active creator of experience, as one with both matter and mind, in which character development in conjunction with nature would be neither brutish nor selfish but intimately related to the good of the whole. For as "part or parcel of God," one would be unavoidably devoted to the "general will."[11] The will of God would constitute the most general will that one could conceive of, a truly universal will that would work for the good of the entire nation and even the world. From this foundation, the Transcendentalists sought to identify a national ethic, which was in turn closely interwoven with the role of nature, understood as the unity of God with his visible creation, in revealing what these principles were to be.

The phrase "higher law" only came into common usage in US English in 1850 and peaked as the Civil War conflict exploded, its use plummeting again after the war ended in 1865. Thoreau employed this term frequently, writing that what was wanted in the abolition and Free-Soil struggle was "men, not of policy, but of probity,—who recognize a higher law than the Constitution."[12] Emerson was explicit about where this law originated and where it could be discovered. "The universe becomes transparent," he wrote, "and the light of higher laws than its own shines through it." It was these higher laws, as written in nature, that determined the course that a people should pursue. It was these higher laws of nature that contained the seed of national character and national destiny. When reason was "stimulated to more earnest vision," Emerson maintained, "outlines and surfaces become transparent, and are no longer seen; causes and spirits are seen through them."[13] In nature, therefore, the true cause of freedom and the true spirit of the nation were made manifest. If these were heeded, the nation would align itself with higher law, which the Free-Soil movement maintained was indisputably on the side of abolition. Higher law thereby sanctioned the activity against slavery criminalized by man-made laws. This stance was epitomized in John Brown, which the Transcendentalists recognized. In his actions in Kansas, Brown was, wrote Thoreau, "in obedience to an infinitely higher command" than any earthly authority.[14]

In his polarizing speech to Congress that elicited his beating by Senator Preston Brooks, Charles Sumner also employed many of these idioms. The beauty and climate of Kansas, he declared, was "calculated to nurture a powerful and generous people, worthy to be a central pivot of American institutions." The Kansas-Nebraska Act of 1854 that opened Kansas to the curse of slavery was the mere action of a mortal man, whereas the principle of freedom was immortal, infinite, inborn, ineradicable, and invincible. It was a principle for which nature fought "in all her subtle forces." The introduction of slavery would be a violation of the "organic law of the Territory" and a "*Crime against Nature* from which the soil recoils."[15] In this, Sumner explicitly utilized the idea of nature as a cognitive force that was fighting on the side of Free-Soilism and employed it for political purposes, rallying the North and incensing the South.

Margaret Fuller, a reader and translator of Herder, in her journey through the Midwest, wrote of the settlers drawing from the landscape some dim conception of "its moral and its meaning" and of striving herself to "woo the mighty meaning of the scene." She had to do so through "daily and careless familiarity" with nature, asserting that its moral lessons could not "be seen by being stared at" but through a kind of spiritual communion with it—one that would importantly shape the viewers, or rather participants, who experienced it.[16] Fuller's belief in the power of electrical forces in nature to provide inspiration and knowledge also factors into the importance of maintaining the country's natural landscape untainted by negative electrical influences, which would be a setback in humanity's progression toward increasing spiritualization. Henry Brokmeyer of the St. Louis Hegelians also took up this strain, writing in May 1856: "Yes, that sun that reveals that stream [the Mississippi] to the outer eye, creates that stream for the inner eye, and it takes both the outer and the inner to ask and to answer the question" of its deeper meaning. It was for this "inner eye" that all streams were created "and with them the chain of causation that stretches from the first rude labors of erosion, where mountain is ground into plain, and plain is furrowed into mountain, and the home of the flora and the fauna is prepared, up to the very birth of intelligence in man—the very birth of the inner eye, that transfigures the external, the many, the apparent heterogeneous, into one interdependent, harmonious totality."[17] In this passage, Brokmeyer laid out the Hegelian problem of two truths that must be synthesized, the perceptions of the outer eye and those of the inner eye, the physical landscape and its spiritual meaning.

Thoreau relied heavily on nature to reveal the moral lessons that should guide the nation. To Thoreau, it was absurd to imagine nature being a supporter of the Missouri Compromise, to suppose that slavery accorded with moral nature in one region and not in another, or to imagine that a water lily would still smell sweet if it were engaged in foul deeds. Likewise, if humans' actions were at variance with the lessons taught in nature, nature itself would be cheated of its fullness, and both its lessons and its beauty would not be perceived. Thoreau's reference to the Missouri Compromise, which admitted Missouri as a slave state and Maine as a free state to maintain the balance in Congress, is a striking instance that demonstrates a definitive political application and an envisioned outcome if these philosophical ideals were to be applied and lived. He retreated to Walden to learn from nature how to live—individually, socially, and politically.[18]

Transcendentalism's interpretation of nature as a source for the revelation of divine laws served as an inspiration for reforming efforts additional to abolition as well. The landscape architect Frederick Law Olmsted read the works of Transcendentalists such as Emerson and Thomas Carlyle, which inspired him to introduce natural spaces back into the cities for the benefit of city dwellers and particularly the laboring classes. If individuals could reconnect with nature, he believed, they would discover "a sense of enlarged freedom," the "unbending of the faculties" by engaging the imagination, and growth in "health, strength and morality."[19] With this goal in mind, he undertook his first significant project, Central Park in New York City, which was completed in 1857. Over the following decades, Olmstead was responsible for creating hundreds of city parks and college campuses across the country. With the similar goal of using nature to teach lessons of divine truths, Transcendentalist philosophy promoted the rural cemetery movement, inspiring the creation of the first such cemeteries, namely, Mount Auburn and Sleepy Hollow in Massachusetts, Rose Hill in Chicago, and Oak Ridge Cemetery in Springfield, Illinois. The latter was where Lincoln chose to have his son Willie buried and where, after his assassination, the president himself was laid to rest. These rural cemeteries and the battlefield parks and graveyards preserved following the war were intended to remind mourners through the regenerative cycles of nature of the promise of eternal life.

Louis Agassiz and George Perkins Marsh, two important American scientists and members of the Saturday Club with Emerson, which discussed many of the founding texts of Transcendentalism, also played an interactive role in the Transcendentalist approach to nature. They were an inspiration for, and likewise encouraged by, the Transcendentalists' natural philosophy and view of nature as a second scripture. The cultural support that Transcendentalists such as Thoreau gave to scientific discovery and conservation encouraged the agitation for national parks. Theodore Roosevelt, Gifford Pinchot, and John Muir usually receive credit for the concept of conservation, but little attention is paid to them as readers of the Transcendentalist literature and, in the case of Muir, a correspondent and friend of Emerson whom Emerson visited in Yosemite. It was these earlier Transcendentalist naturalists who were among the first to promote the idea of conservation, and their advocacy resulted in 1872 in the creation of Yellowstone National Park under President Ulysses Grant.

In contrast, John Witherspoon, one of the most influential university presidents of the colonial and early republic period, advised his students that there should be no thoughts of beauty in nature without a "reflection on their utility" for mankind's use, so as to "curb the excesses of the imagination."[20] George Bancroft, while studying abroad in Germany, perceived the mark left by this approach on the American mind and lamented the "unfortunate tendency of national character in America . . . to seek the useful to the neglect of the beautiful" and to constantly inquire, "to what purpose? To what use?" He believed this perspective was a sign of selfishness and a regrettable lack of "high idealism."[21] Fuller, too, wrote with disdain of a man who looked into Niagara Falls and after a moment's pause, "with an air as if thinking how he could best appropriate it to his own use, he spat into it." And it grieved her, she stated, "to hear these immigrants [to the West] who were to be the fathers of a new race, all, from the old man down to the little girl, talking not of what they should do, but of what they should get in the new scene. It was to them a prospect, not of the unfolding nobler energies, but of more ease, and larger accumulation." Such as these, she hoped, "will not . . . be seen on the historic page to be truly the age or truly the American."[22] They were, she trusted, an unfortunate exception to a people overarchingly eager to obtain a more elevated understanding of their national landscapes.

John Charles Frémont, a lieutenant in the Army Topographical Corps, led several exploring expeditions throughout the West during the 1840s, and his descriptions of the Great Plains as an area filled with valuable aesthetic impact on the perceiver was instrumental in shifting the public perception of the American West from one of aridity and utilitarianism into one of more intuitive appreciation and even pilgrimage.[23] The new intellectual framework through which Frémont was able to approach and portray landscape in the West owed itself to Herder's conception of the role of the natural environment in shaping nationhood and was also indebted to some of the aesthetic frameworks within Kant's *Observations on the Feeling of the Beautiful and Sublime*, namely, his differentiation of two types of aesthetics. The first type, "beauty," was that which was accessible, useful, and pleasing. In this category, he included beauty such as the tame landscape of meadows and forests, the daytime, and the sunshine. The second type of aesthetic form Kant called the "sublime," using examples of the nighttime, violent weather such as a thunderstorm, and untamed, rugged landscapes such as deserts and mountain ranges. He described it as a quality that commingled in the perceiver with a sense of awe.[24] This shifted the value scale applied to landscapes such as those of the American West from being judged as merely not beautiful or useful into a recognition of their "sublimity" and of inherent value in the perceiver's emotive experience of them.

This philosophical framework can be found applied to the West by diverse writers in addition to Frémont. For instance, William Gilpin, an explorer who accompanied Frémont on his California expedition, used the word "sublime" three times in a short piece describing the Sierra Madre that was printed in the *Kansas Herald of Freedom* in 1858. In an address he delivered in Kansas City a few months later, he again spoke of the sublimity of the Western landscape that "elevated" Americans' inspiration to establish and nurture "divine principles" in the civilizations they established in the region.[25]

These ideas enjoyed a wide circulation even in the Western territories themselves to a surprising extent given stereotypes of an unintellectual frontier population. Again in 1858, the *Kansas Herald of Freedom* can be found running an excerpt from the well-known New York clergyman Henry

Ward Beecher. Beecher was "America's most prominent 19th century liberal preacher and a major spokesperson for New England Transcendentalism."[26] Although today he is not regularly counted among the Transcendentalists, at the time Beecher was consistently considered one of them, and he never protested the designation. When toasted by a convention of self-titled "infidels" at Cincinnati as one of the "heretic clergy," along with the Transcendentalist ministers Theodore Parker, Ralph Waldo Emerson, and Moncure Conway, Beecher gloried in the incident.[27] In the piece in the *Herald*, Beecher spoke of the natural world and the proper relationship of humankind with it. He wrote, "Nature comprises in herself all the effects which she causes upon the *senses*, and all that she causes upon the *mind*. He will see the most without who has the most within; and he who only sees with his bodily organs sees but the surface. . . . He that reads Nature reads God's language."[28] This excerpt from Beecher is both a good example of the way in which Americans were interpreting the ideas on nature that Herder promoted and had been adopted by the Transcendentalists and also explicit evidence that this philosophy of nature was being disseminated in Kansas, the hotbed of proslavery and Free-Soil conflict, during the 1850s.

A certain otherwise unidentified Miss Fannie J. Barbour prayed in her editorial to the same newspaper on September 3, 1859, that the West may "ever consecrate to God, to whom she is indebted for so many blessings, her simple hearted and brave sons and daughters that they may rise up and call her blessed, and emulate her virtues!"[29] It may strike a modern reader as strange to speak of a geographic region as something possessing virtues, as demonstrated here, yet this phraseology was not unusual in the mid-nineteenth century. The context of this editorial suggests that it was the geographic landscape of the region itself, as well as the human legacy of courage and perseverance in interacting with the landscape, to which Barbour referred. Americans like the Transcendentalists reasoned that if those who refused to look for, perceive, and live by the moral laws they found present in nature were to settle the West and bring the institution of slavery with them, it would be detrimental to the moral fiber of the nation and would squander the Western landscape. In failing to perceive nature's lessons and treating as nonexistent its divine revelations, the nation would relinquish part of its destiny. In another editorial in the *Kansas Herald of Freedom*, Gilpin commented: "The fact of it is, that the sight of these broad prairies so lately consecrated to freedom, and the scent of the mountain breezes sweeping over them bearing the fragrance of flowers, is of itself enough to infuse new life and energy into any person not entirely lost to the grand and glorious in nature."[30] The *Kanzas News* from Emporia, on September 25, 1858, published an excerpt from the *Scientific American*, stating that "lessons may be learnt by studying the workings of the natural forces, and by imitating the economy of nature, we shall ever be healthy, happy and content."[31] If these lessons were not learned and institutions that did not accord with nature were followed, that is, slavery, the reverse was assumed to be true: Kansas, the broader West, and the nation as a whole would not be healthy, happy, or content.

The Independent, on September 12, 1860, similarly reprinted an article from the Transcendentalist newspaper *Spirit of the Age* that declared, "At some period of life, all mankind is prompted by nature to be natural; to find beauty in the mountain, the forest, the river, and no longer delude themselves with false ideas of happiness." Just as "a noble statue is an object of physical beauty to all; but to the true lover of art, its ideal value is inestimable; for, in surveying it, he builds up within himself a statue poem, an idea as distinct and glorious as the statue itself," so it was with the true lover of nature.[32] Only those who truly loved it, appreciating its value as a divine revelation of metaphysical facts, would become like it. Emblematically the Twin Mound Harmonic College, established in Douglas County, Kansas, in 1858, listed as one of its principal aims "to instruct in the universal School of Nature, and in the facts and laws of the Constitution of Man; and as the result, to harmonize Man *with* Nature and his own Constitution, and thus develop him into the highest perfection of his humanity."[33]

One of abolitionist John Brown's sons, John Brown Jr., recollected, "During the years 1853 and 1854 most of the leading Northern newspapers were not only full of glowing accounts of the extraordinary fertility, healthfulness, and beauty of the Territory of Kansas, then newly opened for settlement, but of urgent appeals to all lovers of freedom who desired homes in a new region to go there as settlers, and by their votes save Kansas from the curse of slavery."[34] He suggests that the idea of the fecundity of Kansas was closely tied up in the desperation to "save" it from slavery. It reached beyond solely the free labor ideology, which Eric Foner identified as the basis of Western tensions prior to the Civil War.[35] Such ideology would have implied saving Kansas *for* free laborers or saving Kansas to add a free state to the legislative balance. Brown's statement suggests instead the wish to save Kansas for the sake of the natural essence of Kansas and to save the region for people who would perceive and imitate the moral lessons offered therein. Although he did not directly employ the philosophy of nature in his writings like the Transcendentalists and others did, John Brown Sr. did avail of the theory of higher law to justify sometimes extreme acts of violence in support of the Free-Soil and abolition cause.

The fact that the Transcendentalists supported Brown and participated in the fight for free soil, while other abolitionists, notably the Garrisonians, did not, implies the possibility that they were driven not only by the humane considerations of the slavery struggle but also by how nature and landscape in the West played a role in their concerns. The prevalence of a nature-centric rhetoric and a type of symbiotic nature-human ethical and moral relationship purveyed by the Kansas newspapers from the era further suggests that Transcendentalist nature philosophy was embraced by the inhabitants of the West and was a philosophical paradigm they used to frame, if not inform, their approach to the struggle of Free-Soil versus slavery in the state of Kansas and the West beyond. For the impact of these ideas was not felt in Kansas alone. The Unitarian minister Thomas Starr King from Boston, a close associate of the Transcendentalist circle, carried these ideals with him to California in 1860. King was a prominent lecturer who campaigned heavily against the Pacific-Republic secession movement in California that sought to create an independent but pro-Confederate nation on the West Coast. In his lecture titled "Lessons from the Sierra Nevada" in 1863, he wrote of bowing "reverently before the mountains that guard the eastern frontier of our State," for "love of nature has its root in wonder and veneration, and it issues in many forms of practical good. There can be no abounding and ardent patriotism where sacred attachment to the scenery of our civil home is wanting."[36] King's Unionist influence in California was so significant that General Winfield Scott credited him with having "saved California to the Union," in which sentiment he was joined by Abraham Lincoln.[37]

Every application of this philosophy of a geographic nation in the West was not praiseworthy, however. While the greatest focus among the Transcendentalists and those influenced by their views regarding the West does not appear to have been racially driven toward keeping Black Americans out of the region, it was nonetheless a vision centered on white agriculturalists. Starkly lacking from their discourse was any discussion of what intellectual or spiritual value Black Americans might bring into the territories or whether they believed them capable of perceiving and implementing the moral lessons present in nature. From their discussions on race, it appears that they believed the influence of nature would have an ameliorating effect on African Americans, and that once removed from the languid and sultry climate of the South to the clean, invigorating air of the West, they would likewise be improved in self-culture. However, no such explicit reference could be found in regard to Bleeding Kansas.

A further omission within the Transcendentalist discourse on the role of nature in shaping the national "American" character was the lack of any consideration of the Indigenous peoples' claim to the land before European settlement and Western expansion. As Joshua David Bellin has concluded, "The Transcendentalists' attempts to 'speak for the Indian' were far from praiseworthy" and rarely translated into any concrete action.[38] The Transcendentalists did support the rights of Native Americans in theory and at times protested their treatment by the US government, such as with Emerson's involvement in campaigning for the rights of Native Americans concluding with his 1838 public letter to President Van Buren defaming the removal of the Cherokee Indian Nation from the state of Georgia. Margaret Fuller also expressed sorrow over the treatment of Midwestern Indigenous nations she observed in the Great Lakes region, and she equated the majestic and rugged landscape in which they lived with the majesty and strength she observed in Native Americans, similarly crediting the lands' spiritual qualities for the best in Native American culture and lauding the ability of Indigenous nations to create their settlements in harmony with the surrounding landscape. However, Fuller, Emerson, and other Transcendentalists, including Thoreau, Convers Francis, Christopher Cranch, James Freeman Clarke, and Bronson Alcott, generally spoke with resignation and romanticization of the projected destruction of Indigenous peoples and their civilizations. When they met living Native Americans, their experience failed to meet Transcendentalist expectations. Lydia Maria Child confessed, "I have to struggle with considerable repugnance toward them," and her support of their cause was "mere duty-work."[39] It appears that Transcendentalists often followed the same route as the Spiritualists' approach to Native Americans: although they lauded the "'magnetic forces' of spectral Indians for séance communion" and an Indigenous role as "spiritual forebears and teachers," their concern did not extend past the departed to their living descendants.[40] Idealized "noble savages" of the past in spiritual communion with nature, imparting legends of wisdom and simplicity to the nation's history, were palatable and convenient. They had laid in the nation's past the foundation of spiritual awareness, examples of courage, austerity, and harmony with nature, and their lives contributed toward the progression of history. But in that vision of historical progression, Transcendentalists "failed to envision, much less to advocate, alternatives to the beliefs and policies that deprived Indian peoples of their homelands, lifeways, and lives."[41] Instead, they lamented that progress was wiping them out and advocated preserving the artifacts of their lives but believed their elimination was inevitable and therefore exerted little to no effort to stop it. In this they represented a much more Hegelian attitude toward this population than a Herderian one. They accepted that world history would continue its preordained progression without the Indigenous nations rather than demonstrating a concern for Indigenous cultures developing and reaching their own ultimate potential for themselves.

It is clear that, in relation to expansionist and imperialist ambitions for the nation, the Transcendentalists demonstrated a significant lack of awareness on racial diversity for the West and did not include African, Asian, or Native Americans in their vision of an enlightened and spiritual population for the region. Emerson, in his 1838 Indian removal letter, also echoed the typical nineteenth-century American belief that the rightful owners of land were those who would develop and cultivate it, writing that the Cherokee had earned their worthiness to retain their land because they had worked hard to "redeem their own race from the doom of eternal inferiority, and to borrow and domesticate in the tribe the arts and customs of the Caucasian race."[42] Yet he confessed in his journal that he hated this letter, that it had issued from his friends who dictated it to him, and it was "not my impulse to say it & therefore my genius deserts me."[43] Whether because of uncertainty as to his own convictions, stated views he partially disagreed with, or time pressures merely resulted in a piece he was not happy with is difficult to know. Whatever the case, his concern with Indigenous affairs was clearly tainted by widely accepted prejudices and was short-lived. The fate of Native Americans in the West never featured in his lecture discourses. Thus, the Transcendentalists' nature philosophy was a powerful argument in favor of keeping slavery out of Kansas, but their vision for the region was clearly Eurocentric, supporting the displacement or exclusion of Native Americans. And, perhaps unconsciously, the picture they painted for an ideal citizenry for Kansas was quite recognizably one of white agricultural communities.

During the Civil War in the East, many of the wartime diaries of Northern soldiers correlate to the Transcendentalist perception of nature. George C. Burmeister, a Union soldier who had been born in Germany and emigrated with his family to Iowa, penned a New Year's prayer for 1864 as it dawned, praying that the nation would "learn more of nature's hidden powers." Later in the year, on Easter Sunday, he recorded that "the source of light sends his beams to us to cheer and strengthen us, all nature smiles, and reminds us in its vernal beauty, that it is again assuming its most gorgeous robe, a fit type of Christ's resurrection which this day . . . should recall to our minds."[44] Soldiers described their role as one that was releasing nature from immoral uses, protecting it from the contamination of slavery, and they understood nature in turn as a presence that was cognizant, protective, and participating in their crusade. George Cram wrote home to his mother in 1863 that if he could prevent the Confederacy from acquiring "one inch" of Illinois soil, he would willingly remain a soldier even if the war took another three years. George Burmeister described the Union soldiers of the "glorious young state of Iowa" as having "shed a halo of glory around it that shall last forever" from their loyalty and courage.[45] He was confident that Iowa as well as their individual characters would reap the benefits of their heroism, growing in splendor and nobility.

Union soldiers also wrote of freeing the Southern landscapes from the curse of slavery, but they lamented the destruction that the war caused to nature. Andrew F. Davis, an officer from Indiana, mourned the sights of devastation in Bowling Green, Kentucky, as the Union troops entered after the Confederate withdrawal. He admitted in his diary, "It almost makes one shed tears to see the beautiful and costly dwellings thrown open to the mob to pillage and destroy and their once beautiful grounds and yards turned out to the commons." George Cram felt that nature itself seemed to mourn, observing as he moved South with the army, that "the trees seem to have a sad expression as they wave their branches over a desolated country."[46] Writing a letter to his hometown newspaper in Vermont while seated on a hill in Virginia overlooking the landscape, Wilbur Fisk philosophized on what he saw: "God must have made a great many acres of handsome forest here in Virginia for nothing, or else he made it to look at himself. . . . One can hardly suppress a feeling of regret, to see land so fair so ruthlessly destroyed." But slavery had already cheated the land from being worked under moral conditions, and now the land itself must go through a purification, for "the day of her retribution" had come. At another time, he noted "an ominous black looking cloud of huge dimensions [that] loomed up from the Southwest. It had a dark and angry appearance. Perhaps it reflected the political condition of the country over which it had just passed."[47] These examples suggest that many Union soldiers understood the themes of Free-Soilism, the Union, and abolition through a lens reflective of the Transcendentalist approach to nature, though unlikely aware of its source. They viewed slavery and disunion as a sin against the land that God had provided to be the home of freedom and morality. Slavery was therefore a blight on the earth in a very literal sense, for it ignored the lessons of nature, undermined its revelations of divine truth, and refused to cooperate with it in realizing the divine laws nature was created to demonstrate. If slavery continued to exist in the Southern states or spread into the West, it threatened to destroy the complete revelation of nature, the second scripture, that God had presented for the people of the continent to follow.

This approach to nature found in Union soldiers' personal writings further illustrates that the nature imagery so frequently used in the public literature of the war was not a tactic used to conceal the true experience of war but a reflection of a pervasive belief system that was percolating throughout the culture. If nature was a manifestation of divinity, then it followed that it should be a participating force in humanity's struggle for moral improvement, protecting, mourning, and caring for soldiers in the field. Fisk described without qualification the "moon keeping vigil over our unconscious hours."[48] Specific elements of nature like the moon appeared with particular regularity, for instance, in a song titled "The Little Major": "See! the moon that shone above him, / veils her face, as if in grief; / And the skies are sadly weeping—/ Shedding teardrops of relief."[49] A poem recounted a battle from the perspective of nature:

> Still, in the cannon's pause, we hear
> Her sweet thanksgiving psalm;
> Too near to God for doubt or fear,
> She shares the eternal calm.
>
> She knows the seed lies safe below
> The fires that blast and burn;
> For all the tears of blood we sow
> She waits the rich return.

> She sees with clearer eye than ours
> The good of suffering born—
> The hearts that blossom like her flowers,
> And ripen like her corn.[50]

The poem suggests that nature held promises untouched by the doubts, fears, and tragedy of the human scenes enacted on it and that victory for the Union was as certain as the eternal moral laws demonstrated within nature. As Burmeister stated, "As certain as the sun shines on our earth, so certain shall [victory] come to pass. Departed heroes, your sacrifice has not been in vain, your blood helped to cleanse our nation, and our land shall rise regenerated, the true home of Liberty."[51] This promise was, as he saw it, renewed every morning in the reliable cycles of nature. Soldiers could rely on nature to aid them in the battle, to care for them when abandoned by fleeing armies, and nature would be supporting the cause of freedom, even when human eyes could not discern its progress. These nature references do not seem to have been simply sentimental rhetoric but to have carried real meaning for the people who employed them. The imagery of Romantic art, such as weeping willow trees to signify mourning and crowns of laurel for victory, also reflect these views of nature as a participant in the human drama. Significantly, the Northern armies typically named battles after the natural landmarks near which they took place, whereas Confederate accounts used the names of nearby towns to identify battles, such as Bull Run versus Manassas and Stones River versus Murfreesboro.

Emerson felt that Faraday's atomic theory, discussed previously in relation to understandings of death, also corresponded to a conviction that nature, as divine energy and the very presence of God, was necessarily working for the realization of justice, freedom, and morality. It was a force that could be harnessed by those who realized this truth. Emerson based one of his wartime lectures on this premise, arguing that humans were far too timid in asserting their moral, spiritual influence, when "we are made of it, the world is built by it, things endure as they share it; all beauty, all health, all intelligence, exist by it.... The motive force of life, and of every particular life, is moral. The world stands on our thoughts.... The source of all the elements, is moral force."[52] Charles Sumner had much praise for the lecture, and it was warmly received by the audience at large.

This scientific element of Transcendentalist thought on nature suggests a much more serious approach to it than has been credited by many historians, who have frequently criticized such nature references. The twentieth-century editor of Alfred Bellard's diary, for instance, praised Bellard for being an unsentimental writer in general but faulted him for occasionally succumbing to "such wartime clichés as 'the sacred soil of Virginia.'"[53] Whether it was a cliché to Bellard or a sincerely felt statement was not apparently considered. The writings of another Union soldier, George Washington Beidelman, evidence sincere conviction behind like statements, for he pondered on the anniversary of several friends' deaths at the battle of Ball's Bluff in 1861 that the soil of Virginia was, "if not before sacred, now surely made so by the outpouring of the blood of many patriots" who had laid down their lives "on the altar of their country."[54] Mere clichés would not be expected to survive personal tragedy.

These views on nature and the nation-state as vitally connected to, and partially stemming from, the natural environment were novel during this period. These suggestions are not found present in the writings of the country's Founders. A more abstract and nuanced approach to what constituted the nation is one area in which a quite radical change can be observed between the early republic and Civil War eras. That early law allowed only landholders to vote, as the "owners" of the country in the very literal sense of the topography itself, strongly indicates this difference. While Revolutionary War soldiers' diaries are typically very prosaic regarding environment and nationhood, Civil War soldiers reflected a much more abstract and idealized appreciation for what the nation encompassed and what nationhood meant.

The Transcendentalist interest in nature was never intended to remain in the sphere of a solitary walk or personal contemplation of nature. It became, instead, an impetus for political action. From the Transcendentalists' appeals against the Mexican-American War to their support for John Brown in Kansas and Sumner's impassioned speech to Congress, the conviction that nature was holding forth a divinely appointed national character, visible to the discerning citizen, carried weight in shaping the Free-Soil narrative and the ideal of an indivisible Union. The natural environment was not there to be employed in a utilitarian manner but cooperated with, its spiritual manifestation of higher law followed, and its full promise for the nation uncovered. In most areas of political concern and ideals of national identity, this philosophy contributed to a more positive, equal and inclusive, abstract, and morally goal-oriented understanding of the nation. It encouraged responsible citizenship and social activism, as well as respect for the natural environment. On the other hand, the Transcendentalists' understanding of these political philosophies countenanced politically motivated violence and the destruction of human life, the "progression" of Anglo-American culture and the white agrarian ideal at the expense of the Indigenous population, and subtly encouraged the mindset of American exceptionalism and Manifest Destiny. In both areas, the egalitarian and the imperialist, however, the Transcendentalists were clearly involved in a political discourse that informed their own actions, the intellectual framework on nationhood and statecraft, and the implementation of the war effort of many Americans. At stake was not only the political nation and the national populace but also the geographic nation whose destiny lay written by the hand of God within its landscapes.

CONCLUSION

On April 19, 1867, Ralph Waldo Emerson stood before the citizens of Concord, Massachusetts, to speak at the dedication ceremony of a Civil War monument to the area's fallen soldiers. "The armies mustered in the North were as much missionaries to the mind of the country as they were carriers of material force," he stated. And he was convinced that wherever they had borne the Union banner, they had carried with them "a higher civilization."[1] It had been two years since the Confederate surrender at Appomattox. The process of relocating and reburying the war dead was still a work in progress. An outpouring of literature on the war continued to appear—novels, memoirs, poetry, and songs—and like Concord, many towns and organizations across the country were erecting memorials and monuments to the war's dead. The Radical Republicans in Congress continued pressing for racial equality and political rights for the Black citizens across the South, and optimism was high. Even as the nation processed the crisis through which it had passed, the narrative did not undergo any alteration but remained among the Northern populace one of pride and patriotism. The Transcendentalist ideals were not discarded in a postwar reassessment of values, nor patriotic, sentimental, or romantic rhetoric revoked. In 1867, there were no indications that the Northern population felt they had been led astray by propaganda or wartime highs or duped into inauthentic representations of their experience. Nor was there an immediate postwar decline in moral society, little evidence of the mass exodus toward pragmatism that Louis Menand described in relation to several select individuals, or a haunting guilt and retreat from Idealist ideology that Randall Fuller has posited.[2]

Far from a fading influence by the time of the Civil War, the philosophical frameworks for approaching issues of character, gender, race, and nationhood that the American Transcendentalists were responsible for promoting in the United States had become so integrated and essential to the outlook of many Americans that they had, perhaps, ceased to recognize the source or the uniqueness of these ideas. Yet even as personal figures, the Transcendentalists remained in the forefront of American culture and political dialogue into the Civil War, and their popularity reached its peak in the years after the war's conclusion. Many soldiers continued to speak of their experience in a language reflective of the influences of Transcendentalism. One such soldier, Union general Joshua Chamberlain, was charged with overseeing the surrender ceremonies at Appomattox. He expressed no feelings of glory over the defeat of his enemies. Instead, he viewed the conquered Confederates through a belief that echoed the Hegelian collective progression of character wrought through the experience of war. Like their Union counterparts, the Confederate men were "the embodiment of manhood," whose character and valor would become a legacy of pride and a credit for the whole country, and not for one region alone. They were not in Chamberlain's eyes worthy of contempt, degradation, shame, or punishment. He was convinced that despite their misguided cause, they had also contributed to the "immortal inheritance [of] all pure purpose and noble endeavor, humblest service and costliest sacrifice" that even "mistaken martyrdoms offered . . . for the sake of man."[3] Because of the Transcendentalist worldview, Chamberlain and many other Northerners viewed the defeated enemy as also participating in the Over-Soul and believed that they had merely played their part in the cosmic dialectic toward the absolute. They were not destroyed and blotted out but subsumed into a greater, truer, and deeper Union than that which had existed prior to the war.

Most Northerners continued to believe that the character of the nation had been purified and moved closer toward spiritualization because of the war. Observing the grand review of the Army of the Potomac in June 1865, Horace Porter, aide to General Grant through the last years of the war, noted that nothing moved the crowds so deeply as did the battle flags. He described people running out into the street as the flags passed them to press "their lips upon the folds of the standards."[4] Even looking back from the vantage point of years, Wilbur Fisk believed in the moral benefit of the war. It had, on the whole, been a valuable time of growth in character for him and his comrades. Through their military service, they had been "made more manly, had a greater hatred of cruelty, more tenderness toward suffering and were every way more of a man."[5] It was rare to find any Civil War participants, soldiers or civilians, who repudiated the wartime rhetoric of Idealism, wrote with regret on their experience, or believed themselves victimized by their service. They did not look back and condemn the philosophical currents that had shaped the war and their understanding of it. Rather, they continued to view the war with pride and devotion, and Transcendentalist understandings of the war remain in their literature for the remainder of the century, even as younger generations began reflecting instead the growing secularism of the Gilded Age and new threads of philosophy such as pragmatism.

The Union victory in the Civil War was in some ways the culmination of the Transcendentalist movement, "the climax of Transcendentalism . . . as far as its political and economic agenda was concerned."[6] Most historians date the end of Transcendentalism long before the Civil War, usually in the 1830s, but such was not the case. Emerson delivered his greatest number of lectures ever in 1867, with a record eighty lectures delivered in one year. John Wesley Powell carried a volume of Emerson's essays down the Colorado River and read from it to his companions on his second exploration of the Grand Canyon in 1871. The Concord School of Philosophy that Bronson Alcott founded in 1879 gained around four hundred attendees. James Freeman Clarke's book *Self-Culture: Physical, Intellectual, Moral, and Spiritual* (1880) reached twenty-one editions before the turn of the century. Mary Baker Eddy authored a work on spiritual healing, *Science and Health with Key to the Scriptures*, in 1875, which Bronson Alcott declared to be a Transcendentalist gospel, and her Boston Metaphysical College remained open through the 1880s. Eddy's book remains in wide circulation today, and her Church of Christ, Scientist, continued to expand and attract members even after her death in 1910, continues today, and teaches many metaphysical ideas it shared with Transcendentalism.

The predominance of Transcendentalism as a sole philosophical influence began to fade in the early 1880s. The language of dialectic, spiritualization, bildung, and Over-Soul become scarcer in the sources left by individuals, replaced with more typical expressions of Protestant Christianity, the material progression of the nation, and self-made individuals in today's definition of economic entrepreneurs. This time frame also aligns with the regression that Black rights began to witness during this decade, when racial philosophy shifted away from theories of bildung and human interconnection into more physical-based "evidence" for scientific racism and eugenics. This shift resulted in political decisions such as the invalidation of the 1875 Civil Rights Act by the Supreme Court in 1883 and the court decision in *Plessy v. Ferguson* in 1896 that constitutionally defended racial segregation. A mere twenty-two years later, anti-German sentiment from the First World War ensured the end of German Idealism in America and almost eradicated the awareness of any philosophical properties of Transcendentalism owed to such. The Cold War climate that followed the Second World War created the strong influence of anticommunism and led historians to paint the Transcendentalists as social radicals who were the exception among a generally harmonious American society, whereas a post-9/11 fear of ideological extremism faulted Transcendentalist political optimism for inciting political violence.

From these trends and with the progression of other philosophical, intellectual, and political developments in American culture that influenced the succeeding generations of historians, the recognition of any philosophical orientation present in the Civil War era was largely overlooked and often missed entirely. The Transcendentalists came to be mainly portrayed as literary figures alone, and divorced from its source in Idealist philosophy, even Romantic literature itself ceased to be understood. Because of this problematic oversight of the immense cultural influence of the Transcendentalists and the Scottish and German philosophies they married, the essential political implications that their philosophical milieu held have also been missed. This gaping vacuum leaves the Civil War culture almost incomprehensible.

The philosophical currents of the nineteenth century were as essential in shaping the worldview and political actions of Civil War participants as had been the earlier philosophical schools in shaping the understanding, prosecution, and political actions of their Revolutionary War–era forebears. Far from being merely a limited literary circle in one small town of Massachusetts, the Transcendentalists' ideas and political reform activities reached across most of the United States and even traveled back to their sources in Europe. This cohort invented and disseminated a novel American philosophy. They were a formative influence and actively engaged in driving the reform efforts and intellectual and political culture of the antebellum era, particularly in the area of growth of character in gender, race, and nationhood. Transcendentalism was not a vanishing philosophy that failed Americans during the Civil War: the war was a crucible in which to test these theories, and Transcendentalism emerged as a more vibrant force than ever at the war's end. The worldview created by Transcendentalist philosophy influenced the culture until at least the 1870s and only slowly diminished over the remainder of the century. Historians must cease dating the movement to the 1830s alone, or the historical significance of Transcendentalism is lost as this time frame fails to account for the most politically and socially active years of the Transcendentalist individuals, as well as neglects their impact on one of the most important historical events in the development of the United States.

Furthermore, it is essential to grant sincerity and genuine meaning to the language of the era's culture. Even if many modern historians do not understand the faith and idealism that Civil War soldiers expressed, they should not be written off as therefore inauthentic. It is a regrettable historical inaccuracy to elevate soldiers who were the exceptions rather than the rule and present the accounts from those who "had an aversion for . . . high-flown language" or "star-spangled rhetoric" as portraying the true experience of the war, while assuming that the considerable majority who resonated with such expressions were glossing over their experience.[7] Louis Menand used the examples of Charles Russell Lowell, William James, and other pioneers of pragmatism who lost faith in Transcendentalism during the war as representative of the population as a whole, without recognizing their rarity from among the sources left of wartime and postwar reflections. His account of their own individual philosophical journeys is insightful and to all appearances accurate.[8] Yet they were not the majority. Likewise, works on the Civil War by authors such as Ambrose Bierce and Stephen Crane have survived as classic literature from the period, when the outlooks expressed by these authors were again atypical of the era, while the popular works of the period are neglected and dismissed as too sentimental to be authentic accounts. Yet Bierce was almost alone among Civil War veterans in writing of his wartime service as a disillusioning and traumatic experience, and Crane did not serve in the Civil War at all. Crane's famous novel, *The Red Badge of Courage*, was published in 1895 when pragmatism was overtaking Transcendentalism as the predominant American philosophy, and the book was not well-received by at least one Civil War veteran, Richard Ashhurst, who was offended and disheartened by the book's philosophical vapidity.[9] Crane served as a journalist during the Spanish-American War, and his poems from this conflict stand in stark contrast to anything produced during the Civil War in the futility and doubt they expressed in statements such as "God lay dead in Heaven."[10] That these writings of Crane's from an era whose culture was already distinctly different from the Civil War have been purveyed as more authentic Civil War writings than those produced during the actual conflict is a failure in historical presentation. This elevation of secondary over primary sources testifies to grave misunderstandings by historians of the Civil War's unique culture. It is a misunderstanding so significant that many have refused to accept the evidence before them and looked elsewhere for a more familiar paradigm with which to overlay the words of the actual participants in the historical event they study. This does not mean there were no exceptions, such as those identified by Menand, but to consider them as shaping the outlook of the era is granting them too much cultural influence, as an examination of the literature shows that they were decidedly in the minority.

Thus, in this book I have striven to remedy this common historical oversight by illustrating that applying the Transcendentalists' philosophical influence to specific areas in American culture during the Civil War greatly increases the understanding of political developments during the era, explains the reasons these political movements emerged when they did, and evidences the personal convictions and worldviews of participants that shaped the experience and prosecution of the Civil War. In philosophical understandings of character, gender, race, and nationhood that it offered from the blending of Scottish Realism and German Idealism, Transcendentalism provided to participants in the Civil War a firm belief in their individual agency in shaping the world around them, their contribution toward universal spiritualization, and their ability to self-sanctify themselves and others, while stressing their metaphysical identity, untouchable by material events and even death. These beliefs proved strong enough to withstand the onslaught of war and were able to uphold soldiers and civilians alike through the conflict with high levels of faith and optimism. The political impact of Transcendentalist philosophy had created a culture in which each individual was viewed as an essential participant in a cosmic movement toward freedom, truth, and virtue, and as such, the idealism they displayed issued from these deep-seated convictions.

An emphasis on a philosophical understanding of the war does not rule out the other influences historians have researched and written about throughout the years, including the religious, economic, political, or social aspects of the war and its culture, and many limitations to my research remain that were outside the scope of this book. There are many areas that deserve further research and discussion: the contribution of the Cambridge Platonists to the philosophical theories investigated here, the role of Thomas Carlyle in shaping the Transcendentalists' thought on these issues, the impact of other contemporary German thinkers not covered here, the minor Transcendentalists, and comparative work on the philosophical culture of the South, to name a few. I hope this book will inspire further scholarly investigation into these areas. What I have sought to achieve is a sufficient demonstration that the philosophical undercurrents impacting the era's perspective provide greater richness and depth to the understanding of the period as a whole. Transcendentalism explains many areas that have puzzled or been dismissed by historians in the past. It created a view of the individual as a powerful agent of transcendent progress toward goodness and divinity, of genders as sacred expressions of divine androgyny, and race as a varied manifestation of awareness and attunement with divine currents, while the Union could be read as reaching beyond government or politics and existing in spiritual realms and in nature as the source of the nation's destiny and world-historical development. These beliefs nurtured political responses that sought increased opportunities for an individual's growth in character and recognition of the universal sanctity of the human person and of every racial lineage, encouraging respect for the individual soldier in the military, dedication to the preservation and value of the natural environment, and commitment toward national improvement. Transcendentalism emphasized the spiritual quality of life and a unity with the Over-Soul, the divine, or God, which precluded even beliefs that death would separate people from the world with which they were familiar. This view removed the Civil War from a framework of destruction, victimization, or political gain and presented it as a great human striving toward goodness and moral excellence and as a universal crusade that depended on each individual's character and effort. Though the Transcendentalists' vision often fell short in personal application and in relation to those of African ancestry and Indigenous peoples by today's standards, their stance was oftentimes on the progressive front of promoting inclusiveness in their era.

Recognizing a unique philosophical presence during the Civil War era also clarifies the reason why the war has retained such importance in historical memory and its continuing impression on the minds of many Americans. Tony Horwitz researched this modern interest in the Civil War, concluding that it is the most well-known and studied event in the history of the United States. The number of books published on the Civil War each year far exceeds those on any other event in American history. In the 1990s when he wrote, subscriptions to Civil War history magazines were around 250,000, and the number of Civil War reenactors numbered roughly 40,000.[11] The Transcendentalists, a main voice of philosophy in the United States during the era, presented Americans with a unique conviction of their individual role in a timeless sphere of universally accessible principles that continues to attract and speak to many modern Americans.

"Anyone who is not sentimental has no chance of understanding" the Civil War, mused Kent Gramm in his work on the historical memory of the war.[12] In light of the philosophical basis of the war's culture I have covered, this observation contains a great deal of truth. It was in the sentiments, the mind, and the spirit that these philosophies maintained that life and reality existed, after which experience followed. Thus, in the accounts left behind by participants, one can discover their ideals, thoughts, sentiments, and journeys of bildung, which can be experienced, can resonate, and can be conveyed through the written word, transporting the mind into the regions from which they issued. One does not have to witness the physical realities experienced by the Civil War populace to catch a glimpse of their inner lives. The material circumstances of Civil War battle can never be recreated, but through the cultural emphasis on immaterial experiences that can be, the soul of the Civil War, as it were, is left accessible to posterity. Primary sources from the Revolutionary War generally contain factual accounts of events with little personal input, and correspondence in World Wars I and II consisted of personal relationships and life at home or general events, often downplayed for the home front audience and focused on the lighthearted or humorous. The culture of character improvement during the Civil War that grew out of the European philosophies of Common Sense and Idealism and their American presentation in Transcendentalism, however, created a wartime literature that was serious, introspective, and filled with the individuals' thoughts, emotions, interpretations, allegories, symbolism, religious experience, and self-assessment. Hence it created a rich historical account that continues to resonate with Americans. Perhaps it is the very "sentimentality" of the war to which Americans have been innately drawn, despite at times an intellectual lack of full understanding as to what these values meant or the philosophical foundations from which they sprang. Perhaps, as Emerson believed, the Union armies were indeed and have remained missionaries to the mind of the country, felt though not always understood by the Americans who experience the draw of "battlefield mysticism" that hovers around the

Civil War. Instead of being mawkish, unrealistic, or ineffective, Transcendentalism not only elucidates an essential element of Civil War culture and the continued interest in the war today but also contains a coherent framework from which to understand the world and holds a well-demonstrated record for spurring political action and social reform in the Civil War era and for successfully upholding these Americans' intellectual, emotional, and spiritual well-being through one of the worst crises in the nation's history.

We are again today living in an era of a highly politicized public. Many diverse social groups are impassioned and mobilized but oftentimes insufficiently educated on the issues that drive them, nor are they articulating a clear vision for the social and political outcomes for which they agitate. We are again divided, not by region but by deep moral questions present within the political discourse. Election follows election, and rather than reaching federal resolution to our conflicts, the division, hostility, and violence continues to grow deeper for us as it did for the antebellum populace. It is worth recalling what the Transcendentalists offered to a situation eerily comparable. As Brian Wolfel phrased it, they offer to the modern American "a third way" between secularism and dogmatism, conservatism and liberalism, racism and ethnocentrism, capitalism and socialism, fascism and communism.[13] They issued a call to action for the individual to cease looking and agitating for outside forces to reform the world according to the platform of their political affiliation, but to be the change they wished to see, beginning within themselves and only then expanding, first to their own neighborhood, their state, and finally their nation. Although this program was not enough to prevent the nation of their day in continuing down the path of division and into civil war, it did provide the populace with a vision of the world and their place within it that was able to uphold them with surprising vigor, peace, conviction, and forgiveness during the crisis. Political resolutions have failed and continue to fail us today. But each one of us is capable of turning to ourselves and our communities, to take up the discipline of bildung, and to try to live by the universal laws revealed to us in nature and in morally developed characters. As the Transcendentalists' countercultural movement sought to become mainstream, we ought not to scoff at small steps. Their philosophical musings emerged from the shady groves of Concord to ignite the mind of the nation toward a vision that was higher and nobler than the daily grind they witnessed in the street and the political stalemate gripping the government. It is a vision still held before us. A vision worthy of seizing and making our own.

Appendix

The following is a list of prominent figures in Northern society that I have identified as being involved with, influenced by, or in association with Transcendentalism under some form, whether through reading, lectures, church attendance, correspondence, or personal acquaintance:

The Major Transcendentalists:
The Alcott family, including A. Bronson (1799–1888) and Louisa May (1832–88)
Ralph Waldo Emerson (1803–82)
Margaret Fuller (1810–50)
Henry David Thoreau (1817–62)

Principal Northern Reformers:
Orestes Brownson (1803–76), whose passion lay in labor reform
Susan Burley (1822–1907), hostess of Transcendentalist "conversations" meetings and a literary patron in Massachusetts of writers such as Nathaniel Hawthorne (1804–64)
Caroline Healey Dall (1822–1912), feminist and author
Dorothea Dix (1802–87), advocate for mental health
Frederick Douglass (1818–95), active in abolition

John Sullivan Dwight (1813–93), first American music critic; introduced the works of Beethoven and Bach to the United States

Marianne Dwight (1816–1901), engaged with mesmerism and women's rights

George B. Emerson (1797–1881), an educational reformer

Octavius Brooks Frothingham (1822–95), an early abolitionist

William Lloyd Garrison (1805–79), abolitionist

Julia Ward Howe (1819–1910) and Samuel Gridley Howe (1801–76), gender and disability reformers

Ednah Littlehale (1824–1904), who financially supported and personally lectured in and outside New England on reforms ranging from political equality for women and African Americans to women's education and served as director of the Free Religious Association of Boston

Horace Mann (1796–1859), education reformer

Samuel J. May (1797–1871), a labor, education, women's rights, and abolition reformer

Anna Parsons (1796–1878), engaged with mesmerism and women's rights

The Peabody sisters, Elizabeth (1804–94), Mary (1806–87), and Sophia (1809–71), who were among the early proponents of Romanticism and women's engagement with cultural development

George Ripley (1802–80) and Sophia Ripley (1803–61), founders of the utopian community of Brook Farm

Franklin Sanborn (1831–1917), a journalist, teacher, and abolitionist

Elizabeth Cady Stanton (1815–1902), women's rights

Politicians, Lawyers, and Army Officers:

Charles Anderson Dana (1819–97), assistant secretary of war, coeditor of the *New-York Daily Tribune*, a philanthropist and businessman

William Herndon (1818–91), Lincoln's law partner at their practice in Illinois

Thomas Wentworth Higginson (1823–1911), commander of the 1st South Carolina Volunteers; also a minister, author, and abolitionist

James Kendall Hosmer (1834–1927), a pastor, author, historian, and corporal of the 52nd Massachusetts Regiment color guard who declined several promotions to maintain this post

Abraham Lincoln (1809-65), president of the United States

Wendell Phillips (1811-84), attorney

Robert Gould Shaw (1837-63), colonel of the 54th Massachusetts

Charles Sumner (1811-74), senator from Massachusetts

Ministers:

Cyrus Bartol (1813-1900)

Henry Ward Beecher (1813-87)

Charles Timothy Brooks (1813-83)

Horace Bushnell (1802-76)

William Ellery Channing (1780-42)

William Henry Channing (1810-84)

James Freeman Clarke (1810-88)

Moncure Conway (1832-1907)

Mary Baker Eddy (1821-1910), founder of the Church of Christ, Scientist

Convers Francis (1795-1863)

Isaac Hecker (1819-88), a onetime Brook Farm member and eventual founder of the Paulist Fathers, a Catholic order of priests

Frederic Henry Hedge (1805-90)

Sylvester Judd (1813-53), minister and novelist

Theodore Parker (1810-60)

Parker Pillsbury (1809-98)

Writers and Artists:

Louisa May Alcott (1832-88)

Lydia Maria Child (1802-80)

Christopher Pearse Cranch (1813-92), a painter of the Hudson River School

Emily Dickinson (1830-86)

Nathaniel Hawthorne (1804-64)

Eliza Buckminster Lee (1792-1864)

James Russell Lowell (1819-91)

Herman Melville (1819-91)

Sampson Reed (1800–1880)
Edwin Percy Whipple (1819–86)
Walt Whitman (1819–92)
John Greenleaf Whittier (1807–92)
Jones Very (1813–80)

Notes

INTRODUCTION

1. Henry Conrad Brokmeyer, *A Mechanic's Diary* (Washington, DC: E. C. Brokmeyer, 1910), 12.
2. Ralph Waldo Emerson, "History," in *Works of Ralph Waldo Emerson, 12 vols.* (Boston: Houghton, Mifflin, 1903), 2:4.
3. George M. Frederickson, *The Inner Civil War: Northern Intellectuals and the Crisis of the Union* (New York: Harper & Row, 1965); Earl J. Hess, *Liberty, Virtue, and Progress: Northerners and Their War for the Union* (Bronx, NY: Fordham University Press, 1997); Earl J. Hess, *The Union Soldier in Battle: Enduring the Ordeal of Combat* (Lawrence: University Press of Kansas, 1997); Harry S. Stout, *Upon the Altar of the Nation: A Moral History of the Civil War* (New York: Viking, 2006); Drew Gilpin Faust, *This Republic of Suffering: Death and the American Civil War* (repr.; New York: Vintage, 2009).
4. René Wellek, "The Minor Transcendentalists and German Philosophy," *New England Quarterly* 15, no. 4 (December 1942): 652–80; Régis Michaud, "Emerson's Transcendentalism," *American Journal of Psychology* 30, no. 1 (January 1919): 73–82; Henry A. Pochmann, *German Culture in America: Philosophical and Literary Influences, 1600–1900* (Madison: University of Wisconsin Press, 1957); Henry A. Pochmann, *New England Transcendentalism and St. Louis Hegelianism: Phases in the History of American Idealism* (Philadelphia: Carl Schurz Memorial Foundation, 1948).
5. Ethan J. Kytle, *Romantic Reformers and the Antislavery Struggle in the Civil War Era* (New York: Cambridge University Press, 2016), 4, 20, 26, 32, 120, 140, 173.
6. Manfred Frank, "What Is Early German Romantic Philosophy?," in *The Relevance of Romanticism: Essays on German Romantic Philosophy*, ed. Dalia Nassar (New York: Oxford University Press, 2014), 24.

7. Frederick Beiser, "Romanticism and Idealism," in Nassar, *Relevance of Romanticism*, 36.
8. Charles Taylor, *Hegel* (Cambridge, UK: Cambridge University Press, 1977), 9.
9. Taylor, *Hegel*, 21.
10. Charles Taylor, *Sources of the Self: The Making of the Modern Identity* (Cambridge, MA: Harvard University Press, 1989), 27, 104, 159, 250, 372.
11. Gerald N. Izenberg, *Impossible Individuality: Romanticism, Revolution, and Origins of Modern Selfhood, 1787–1802* (Princeton, NJ: Princeton University Press, 1992), 6.
12. Peter Wirzbicki, *Fighting for the Higher Law: Black and White Transcendentalists against Slavery* (Philadelphia: University of Pennsylvania Press, 2021).
13. Matthew Stewart, *An Emancipation of the Mind: Radical Philosophy, the War over Slavery, and the Refounding of America* (New York: W. W. Norton, 2024).
14. Kytle, *Romantic Reformers*; Philip F. Gura, *Man's Better Angels: Romantic Reformers and the Coming of the Civil War* (Cambridge, MA: Belknap Press of Harvard University Press, 2017).
15. Harry S. Stout, *Upon the Altar of the Nation: A Moral History of the Civil War* (New York: Viking, 2006), 110.
16. Randall Fuller, *From Battlefields Rising: How the Civil War Transformed American Literature* (New York: Oxford University Press, 2011); John A. Buehrens, *Conflagration: How the Transcendentalists Sparked the American Struggle for Racial, Gender, and Social Justice* (Boston: Beacon Press, 2020).
17. Robert A. Gross, *The Transcendentalists and Their World* (New York: Farrar, Straus and Giroux, 2021).
18. See George C. Rable, *God's Almost Chosen People: A Religious History of the American Civil War* (Chapel Hill: University of North Carolina Press, 2010); Timothy Wesley, *The Politics of Faith during the Civil War* (Baton Rouge: Louisiana State University Press, 2013); Elizabeth Flower and Murray G. Murphey, *A History of Philosophy in America* (Indianapolis: Hackett, 1977); Pochmann, *German Culture in America*; Pochmann, *New England Transcendentalism and St. Louis Hegelianism*; George M. Frederickson, *The Inner Civil War: Northern Intellectuals and the Crisis of the Union* (New York: Harper & Row, 1965); Hess, *Liberty, Virtue, and Progress*; Hess, *Union Soldier in Battle*; Paul Boller Jr., *American Transcendentalism, 1830–1860: An Intellectual Inquiry* (New York: G. P. Putnam's Sons, 1974); and Anne C. Rose, *Transcendentalism as a Social Movement, 1830–1850* (New Haven, CT: Yale University Press, 1979).
19. Bernard Bailyn, *Ideological Origins of the American Revolution* (Cambridge, MA: Harvard University Press, 1967); Gordon Wood, *The Creation of the American Republic* (Chapel Hill: University of North Carolina Press, 1998); C. Bradley Thompson, *America's Revolutionary Mind: A Moral History of the American Revolution and the Declaration That Defined It* (New York: Encounter Books, 2019).
20. Charles Bradford Bow, "Reforming Witherspoon's Legacy at Princeton: John Witherspoon, Samuel Stanhope Smith and James McCosh on Didactic Enlightenment, 1768–1888," *History of European Ideas* 39, no. 5 (2021): 2, 5.
21. Michael Brown, "Dugald Stewart and the Problem of Teaching Politics in the 1790s," *Journal of Irish and Scottish Studies* 1, no. 1 (January 2007): 87–126.
22. Charles Bradford Bow, "In Pursuit of 'Moral Beauty' and Intellectual Pleasures:

Dugald Stewart and Edinburgh's Literary Culture, 1762–1810," in *The Scottish Enlightenment and Literary Culture*, ed. Ralph McLean, Ronnie Young, and Kenneth Simpson (Lewisburg, PA: Bucknell University Press, 2016), 166.

23. Andrea Wulf, *Magnificent Rebels: The First Romantics and the Invention of the Self* (New York: Alfred A. Knopf, 2022), 417.

24. 1860 Census, Minnesota Population Center, National Historical Geographic Information System: Version 11.0 Database (Minneapolis: University of Minnesota, 2016), http://doi.org/10.18128/D050.V11.0; *American Slavery: A Protest against American Slavery: By One Hundred and Seventy-Three Unitarian Ministers* (Boston: B. H. Greene, 1845).

25. Susan Belasco, "The *Dial*," in *The Oxford Handbook of Transcendentalism*, ed. Joel Myerson, Sandra Harbert Petrulionis, and Laura Dassow Walls (New York: Oxford University Press, 2010), 381.

26. Daniel Walker Howe, *What Hath God Wrought: The Transformation of America, 1815–1848* (New York: Oxford University Press, 2007), 614; Henry Steele Commager, *The American Mind: An Interpretation of American Thought and Character since the 1880's* (New Haven, CT: Yale University Press, 1950), 167; Merle Curti, *The Growth of American Thought* (New Brunswick, NJ: Transaction, 1981), 336.

27. Ralph Waldo Emerson, *Journals and Miscellaneous Notebooks*, vol. 12, ed. Linda Alladrt (Cambridge, MA: Harvard University Press, 1976), 175, 264, 267; Howe, *What Hath God Wrought*, 620; 1860 Census, Minnesota Population Center; Curti, *Growth of American Thought*, 347.

28. Pochmann, *New England Transcendentalism and St. Louis Hegelianism*, 12, 15; Brokmeyer, *A Mechanic's Diary*.

29. Loyd D. Easton, "Hegelianism in Nineteenth-Century Ohio," *Journal of the History of Ideas* 23, no. 3 (July–September 1962): 355–78.

30. Robert D. Richardson Jr., *Emerson: The Mind on Fire* (Berkeley: University of California Press, 2015), 472–76.

31. George Bancroft, *The History of the United States of America from the Discovery of the Continent* (Chicago: University of Chicago Press, 1966), 137.

CHAPTER 1

1. "Special Orders No. 57} Head Qrs. Dist. of Washington, July 25th, 1865, Officers and Men of the 1st Division, 9th Army Corps," copy preserved in Lewis Crater Diary, 1864–1898, University of Iowa Digital Library, https://digital.lib.uiowa.edu/node/829624.

2. James McPherson, *For Cause and Comrades: Why Men Fought in the Civil War* (New York: Oxford University Press, 1997); Thomas E. Rodgers, "Billy Yank and G. I. Joe: An Exploratory Essay on the Sociopolitical Dimensions of Soldier Motivation," *Journal of Military History* 69, no. 1 (January 2005): 93–121.

3. Henry Steele Commager, *The American Mind: An Interpretation of American Thought and Character since the 1880's* (New Haven, CT: Yale University Press, 1950); Christopher S. DeRosa, *Political Indoctrination in the U.S. Army from World War II to the Vietnam War* (Lincoln: University of Nebraska Press, 2006); Paul Fussell,

Wartime: Understanding and Behavior in the Second World War (New York: Oxford University Press, 1989); Robert B. Westbrook, *Why We Fought: Forging American Obligations in World War II* (Washington, DC: Smithsonian Books, 2004); J. Glenn Gray, *The Warriors: Reflections on Men in Battle* (New York: Harcourt, Brace, 1959).

4. David Hume, *A Treatise of Human Nature* (1739, repr.; London: Longmans Green, 1878).
5. Philip F. Gura, *American Transcendentalism: A History* (New York: Hill and Wang, 2008), 45.
6. David Hume, *Enquiry concerning the Human Understanding* (1748, repr.; London: J. B. Bebbington, 1861), 25.
7. Hume, *Enquiry*, 11, 10, 31.
8. Richard Petersen, "Scottish Common Sense in America, 1768–1850: An Evaluation of Its Influence" (PhD diss., American University, 1963), 22.
9. Claire Etchegaray, "Reid on Our Mental Constitution," in *Common Sense in the Scottish Enlightenment*, ed. Charles Bradford Bow (New York: Oxford University Press, 2018), 73–74; Manfred Kuehn, *Scottish Common Sense in Germany, 1768–1800: A Contribution to the History of Critical Philosophy* (Montreal, Can: McGill-Queen's University Press, 1987), 21.
10. Thomas Reid, *Essays on the Intellectual Powers of Man* (1785), in *The Works of Thomas Reid, D.D.; Now Fully Collected, with Selections from His Unpublished Letters*, ed. Sir William Hamilton (Edinburgh: Maclachlan and Stewart, 1852), 434, 416.
11. Ryan Nichols and Gideon Yaffe, "Thomas Reid," *Stanford Encyclopedia of Philosophy*, summer 2021 ed., ed. Edward N. Zalta, https://plato.stanford.edu/archives/sum2021/entries/reid/.
12. Reid, *Essays on the Intellectual Powers*, 411.
13. Bernard E. Rollin, "Thomas Reid and the Semiotics of Perception," *Monist* 61, no. 2 (1978): 257–70.
14. Rollin, "Thomas Reid," 257–70.
15. Dugald Stewart, *Elements of the Philosophy of the Human Mind*, vol. 2 (Boston: Wells and Lilly, 1814), 46.
16. Charles Bradford Bow, "In Pursuit of 'Moral Beauty' and Intellectual Pleasures: Dugald Stewart and Edinburgh's Literary Culture, 1762–1810," in *The Scottish Enlightenment and Literary Culture*, ed. Ralph McLean, Ronnie Young, and Kenneth Simpson (Lewisburg, PA: Bucknell University Press, 2016), 160–63.
17. Scott Philip Segrest, *America and the Political Philosophy of Common Sense* (Columbia: University of Missouri Press, 2009), 5.
18. Douglas Sloan, *The Scottish Enlightenment and the American College Ideal* (New York: Teachers College Press, 1971), 238–39.
19. David K. Nartonis, "Louis Agassiz and the Platonist Story of Creation at Harvard, 1795–1846," *Journal of the History of Ideas* 66, no. 3 (July 2005): 439.
20. Levi Hedge, *Elements of Logick; or a Summary of the General Principles and Different Modes of Reasoning* (Cooperstown, NY: H. &. E. Phinney, 1843), ix–xi, 13–30.
21. Merrell R. Davis, "Emerson's 'Reason' and the Scottish Philosophers," *New England Quarterly* 17, no. 2 (June 1944): 219, 226–27.
22. Ralph Waldo Emerson, *Two Unpublished Essays: "The Character of Socrates,"* and, *"The Present State of Ethical Philosophy"* (Boston: Lamson, Wolffe, 1896), 68–69.

23. Gordon Graham, "Scottish Philosophy in the 19th Century," *Stanford Encyclopedia of Philosophy*, winter 2015 ed., ed. Edward N. Zalta, https://plato.stanford.edu/archives/win2015/entries/scottish-19th; George Spring Merriam, *Noah Porter: A Memorial by Friends* (New York: C. Scribner's Sons, 1893), 211.
24. Ralph Waldo Emerson, *Journals and Miscellaneous Notebooks of Ralph Waldo Emerson, 1822–1826* (Cambridge, MA: Harvard University Press, 1961), 212–13.
25. Margaret Fuller to Susan Prescott, 11 July 1825, in *The Portable Margaret Fuller*, ed. Mary Kelley (New York: Penguin, 1994), 479; *Memoirs of Margaret Fuller Ossoli*, vol. 1, ed. William Henry Channing, Ralph Waldo Emerson, and James Freeman Clarke (Boston: Philips, Sampson, 1852), 18, 125.
26. Reid, *Works of Thomas Reid*, 242.
27. Thomas Reid, "Paper on Constitution," Papers of Thomas Reid, GB 0231 Special Collections, MS 3061/8, University of Aberdeen.
28. Emerson, *Journals and Miscellaneous Notebooks*, vol. 12, ed. Linda Alladrt (Cambridge, MA: Harvard University Press, 1976), 257.
29. Reid, *Works of Thomas Reid*, 244.
30. Ralph Waldo Emerson, "Divinity School Address," in *Works of Ralph Waldo Emerson, 12 vols.* (Boston: Houghton, Mifflin, 1903), 1:129 (hereafter cited as *WRWE*).
31. Emerson, "Nature," in *WRWE*, 1:40.
32. Emerson, "Eloquence," in *WRWE*, 8:117.
33. Ralph Waldo Emerson to Miss Lydia Jackson, January 24, 1835, folder 3, letter 17, Ralph Waldo Emerson additional papers collection, Houghton Library, Harvard University, New Haven, CT.
34. Daniel Walker Howe, *Making the American Self: Jonathan Edwards to Abraham Lincoln* (New York: Oxford University Press, 1997), 64–65.
35. Daniel Walker Howe, *The Unitarian Conscience: Harvard Moral Philosophy, 1805–1861* (Cambridge, MA: Harvard University Press, 1970), 36.
36. Emerson, "The Over-Soul," in *WRWE*, 2:269.
37. Reid, *Essays on the Intellectual Powers*, 496; Thomas Reid, "Paper on Body and Mind," Papers of Thomas Reid, GB 0231 Special Collections, MS 3061/19, University of Aberdeen.
38. Dale Tuggy, "Reid's Philosophy of Religion," in *The Cambridge Companion to Thomas Reid*, ed. Terence Cuneo and René Van Woudenberg (New York: University of Cambridge, 2004), 293.
39. Reid, "Paper on Body and Mind."
40. Emerson, "Nature," in *WRWE*, 1:23.
41. Emerson, "Nature," 50.
42. Thomas Reid, *Essays on the Active Powers of Man* (London: John Bell and G. G. J. & J. Robinson, 1788), 238.
43. Charles Bradford Bow, "Introduction: Scottish Philosophy in the Nineteenth-Century Atlantic World," *History of European Ideas* 39, no. 5 (November 2012): 605–12.
44. Francis Hutcheson, *Inquiry into the Original of Our Ideas of Beauty and Virtue* (London: D. Midwinter, 1738).
45. Howe, *Unitarian Conscience*, 46–48; Nichols, and Yaffe, "Thomas Reid."
46. Kenneth P. Winkler, "Hutcheson's Alleged Realism," *Journal of the History of Philosophy* 23, no. 2 (April 1, 1985): 182–83.

47. David Fate Norton, "Hutcheson's Moral Realism," *Journal of the History of Philosophy* 23, no. 3 (July 1, 1985): 416.
48. Thomas Reid, *An Inquiry into the Human Mind on the Principles of Common Sense* (Glasgow: W. Falconer, 1819), 126–27.
49. Reid, *Inquiry into the Human Mind*, 129–30.
50. Peter Kivy, *The Seventh Sense: Francis Hutcheson and Eighteenth-Century British Aesthetics* (New York: Oxford University Press, 2003), 170–71.
51. Dan Robinson, "Reid on the Principles of Morals," recorded lecture, Oxford University, Fall 2013, posted May 14, 2014, https://podcasts.ox.ac.uk/reid-principles-morals.
52. Terence Cuneo, "Reid's Ethics," *Stanford Encyclopedia of Philosophy*, winter 2016 ed., ed. Edward N. Zalta, https://plato.stanford.edu/archives/win2016/entries/reid-ethics.
53. Terence Cuneo, "Reid's Moral Philosophy," in *Cambridge Companion to Thomas Reid* (New York: University of Cambridge, 2004), 263.
54. Thomas Brown, *Lectures on the Philosophy of the Human Mind* (London: McCorquodale, n.d.), 162.
55. Brown, *Lectures*, 255.
56. Dugald Stewart, *The Collected Works of Dugald Stewart*, ed. Sir William Hamilton, vol. 5 (Edinburgh: Thomas Constable, 1855), 247.
57. Margaret Fuller, *Summer on the Lakes*, in *The Portable Margaret Fuller*, ed. Mary Kelley (New York: Penguin Books, 1994), 89.
58. Fuller, *Summer on the Lakes*, 85–86.
59. Henry D. Thoreau, *A Yankee in Canada, with Anti-Slavery and Reform Papers* (Boston: Houghton, Mifflin, 1892), 116.
60. Emerson, "Nature," 40.
61. Emerson, "Compensation," in *WRWE*, 2:102.
62. Emerson, "Progress of Culture: Address before the ΦBK Society at Cambridge, July 18, 1867," *WRWE*, 8:228; Emerson, *Journal and Miscellaneous Notebooks*, 12:257.
63. Sophia A. Rosenfeld, *Common Sense: A Political History* (Cambridge, MA: Harvard University Press, 2011), 225.
64. Hedge, *Logick*, 82.
65. Reid, *Essays on Intellectual Powers*, 425.
66. Charles Bradford Bow, "In Pursuit of 'Moral Beauty,'" 154.
67. James A. Harris, "The Reception of Hume in Nineteenth-Century British Philosophy," in *The Reception of David Hume in Europe*, ed. Peter Jones (London: Bloomsbury, 2013), 316.
68. Harris, "Reception of Hume," 316–17, 318.
69. Segrest, *America and the Political Philosophy of Common Sense*, 49, 54.
70. Davis, "Emerson's 'Reason,'" 217, 228.

CHAPTER 2

1. Ralph Waldo Emerson, "The Over-Soul," in *Works of Ralph Waldo Emerson*, 12 vols. (Boston: Houghton, Mifflin, 1903), 2:6.

2. Immanuel Kant, *Critique of Pure Reason* (1781), trans. Werner Pluhar (Indianapolis, IN: Hackett, 1996), 47.
3. Kant, *Critique of Pure Reason*, 506.
4. Nicholas F. Stang, "Kant's Transcendental Idealism," *Stanford Encyclopedia of Philosophy*, spring 2021 ed., ed. Edward N. Zalta, https://plato.stanford.edu/archives/spr2021/entries/kant-transcendental-idealism/.
5. Stang, "Kant's Transcendental Idealism."
6. Ralph Waldo Emerson, "The Transcendentalist: A Lecture Read at the Masonic Temple, Boston, January 1842," in *Works of Ralph Waldo Emerson*, 1:340.
7. Emerson, "Transcendentalist," 330.
8. Eduardo Molina, "Kant and the Concept of Life," *CR: The New Centennial Review* 10, no. 3 (Winter 2010): 21–36.
9. Immanuel Kant, *Critique of Practical Reason* (1788), trans. Thomas Kingsmill Abbott (New York: Cosimo, Inc., 2008), 8.
10. Madame the Baroness de Staël-Holstein, *Germany, with Notes and Appendices by O. W. Wight*, vol. 1 (Cambridge, MA: Cambridge University Press, 1859), 164.
11. Emerson, "Nature," in *Works of Ralph Waldo Emerson*, vol. 1:4.
12. Frederick C. Beiser, *German Idealism: The Struggle against Subjectivism, 1781–1801* (Cambridge, MA: Harvard University Press, 2002), 72.
13. Peter Kivy, *The Seventh Sense: Francis Hutcheson and Eighteenth-Century British Aesthetics* (New York: Oxford University Press, 2003), 169–70.
14. Immanuel Kant, *Critique of Judgement* (1790), trans. J. H. Bernard (London: Macmillan, 1914), 157–58.
15. Molina, "Kant and the Concept of Life."
16. Emerson, "Nature," 1:23, 19.
17. Madame de Staël, *Germany, with Notes and Appendices by O. W. Wight*, vol. 2 (New York: Hurd and Houghton, 1864), 159.
18. Beate Allert, "The Natural and the Virtual in Herder's Approach to Temporality," presentation to the American Society for Eighteenth-Century Studies, Denver, Colorado, March 22, 2019; Johann Gottfried von Herder, *Outlines of a Philosophy of the History of Man* (New York: Random Shack, 2016), 5. Reprint edition of translation by T. Churchill, London, 1800.
19. Herder, *Philosophy of the History of Man*, 196, 377.
20. Herder, 389.
21. Herder, 197.
22. Manfred Kuehn, *Scottish Common Sense in Germany, 1768–1800: A Contribution to the History of Critical Philosophy* (Montreal, Can: McGill-Queen's University Press, 1987), 12.
23. Clare Thérèse Pellerin, "The Philosophies of History of Herder and Hegel" (master's thesis, University of Saskatchewan, 2005), 62.
24. Georg W. F. Hegel, *Phenomenology of Spirit*, trans. A. V. Miller (New York: Oxford University Press, 1977), 483; Michael Allen Fox, *The Accessible Hegel* (Amherst, NY: Humanity Books, 2005), 22, 43; Joseph McCarney, *Routledge Philosophy Guidebook to Hegel on History* (London: Routledge, 2000), 17, 29; Tom Rockmore, *Before and After Hegel: A Historical Introduction to Hegel's Thought* (Berkeley: University of California Press, 1993), 58, 61.

25. Georg W. F. Hegel, *Philosophy of Mind*, trans. William Wallace, with the *Zusätze*, trans, Ludwig Boumann (repr.; London: Oxford University Press, 1971), 11.
26. Georg W. F. Hegel, *The Philosophy of History* (Chicago: University of Chicago Press, 1952), 321.
27. Hegel, *Philosophy of History*, 319.
28. Hegel, 319–20.
29. Herder, *Philosophy of the History of Man*, 375–76.
30. Hegel, *Philosophy of History*, 166.
31. Christian Dippel and Stephan Heblich, "Leadership in Social Movements: Evidence from the 'Forty-Eighters' in the Civil War," *American Economic Review* 111, no. 2 (2021): 472–505.
32. Andrea Wulf, *Magnificent Rebels: The First Romantics and the Invention of the Self* (New York: Alfred A. Knopf, 2022), 435.
33. De Staël, *Germany*, 1:163.
34. De Staël, 2:88.
35. Ralph Waldo Emerson, *Divinity School Address* (London: Philip Green, 1903), 43–44.
36. Andrews Norton, *A Discourse on the Latest Form of Infidelity, Delivered at the Request of the Association of the Alumni of the Cambridge Theological School on the 19th of July, 1839* (Cambridge, MA: John Owen, 1839), 21.
37. *The Harvard University Catalogue, 1873–1874* (Cambridge, MA: Charles W. Sever, 1873), 78.
38. Harvard Library, "Reading: Harvard Views of Readers, Readership, and Reading History," CURIOSity Collections, https://curiosity.lib.harvard.edu/reading/about/collection-overview.
39. David K. Nartonis, "Louis Agassiz and the Platonist Story of Creation at Harvard, 1795–1846," *Journal of the History of Ideas* 66, no. 3 (July 2005): 440–45.
40. Dugald Stewart, *The Philosophy of the Active and Moral Powers of Man*, revised with omissions and additions by James Walker, 6th ed. (Boston: Phillips, Sampson, 1858), 450.
41. Kurt Mueller-Vollmer, *Transatlantic Crossings and Transformations: German-American Cultural Transfer from the 18th to the End of the 19th Century* (New York: Peter Lang, 2015), 88.
42. "Hegel," *New-York Daily Tribune*, March 27, 1845.
43. "Commencement Anniversaries of the University of Vermont," *Burlington Free Press*, August 6, 1847.
44. "New Publications," *New-York Daily Tribune*, May 5, 1860.
45. "Italy—Federation," *New-York Daily Tribune*, November 17, 1859; "Triumph of the 'National'" *True American*, February 4, 1857; "Pairs of Great Men," *Penny Press*, February 10, 1860; "The New American Cyclopedia," *Randolph County Journal*, May 21, 1860; "There Were Giants in Those Days," *Daily State Sentinel*, November 9, 1864; "A New Deutsch Ballad" *Trinity Journal*, September 15, 1860.
46. "John Gottfried von Herder and Ralph Waldo Emerson," *Anti-Slavery Bugle*, December 20, 1856; Parker Pillsbury, "Communications," *Anti-Slavery Bugle*, April 7, 1860.
47. Robert J. Scholnick, "Boston and Beyond," in *The Oxford Handbook of Transcendentalism*, ed. Joel Myerson, Sandra Harbart Petrulionis, and Laura Dassow Walls (New York: Oxford University Press, 2010), 502; Daniel Walker Howe, *What Hath*

God Wrought: The Transformation of America, 1815–1848 (New York: Oxford University Press, 2007), 614; Henry Steele Commager, *The American Mind: An Interpretation of American Thought and Character since the 1880's* (New Haven, CT: Yale University Press, 1950), 167.

CHAPTER 3

1. William Ellery Channing, *Self-Culture: An Address Introductory to the Franklin Lectures, Delivered at Boston, September 1838* (Boston: Dutton and Wentworth, 1838), 12, 15.
2. Channing, *Self-Culture*, 11.
3. Channing, 30–57.
4. Philip Cafaro, "Transcendental Virtue," in *The Oxford Handbook of Transcendentalism*, ed. Joel Myerson, Sandra Harbert Petrulionis, and Laura Dassow Walls (New York: Oxford University Press, 2010), 538.
5. Richard J. Petersen, "Scottish Common Sense in America, 1768–1850: An Evaluation of Its Influence" (PhD diss., American University, 1963), 190, 195.
6. Ralph Waldo Emerson, "Prudence," in *Works of Ralph Waldo Emerson, 12 vols.* (Boston: Houghton, Mifflin, 1903), 2:223 (hereafter cited as *WRWE*).
7. Emerson, "Plato," in *WRWE*, 4:54.
8. Emerson, "Intellect," in *WRWE*, 2:345.
9. Emerson, "Quotation and Originality," in *WRWE*, 8:180–81.
10. Emerson, "Nominalist and Realist," in *WRWE*, 3:245.
11. Emerson, "Success," in *WRWE*, 7:301.
12. Emerson, "Plato," in *WRWE*, 4:47–49.
13. Emerson, "The Transcendentalist," in *WRWE*, 1:330–31.
14. Ralph Waldo Emerson, *Journals and Miscellaneous Notebooks of Ralph Waldo Emerson, 1832–1862*, ed. Linda Allardt (Cambridge, MA: Harvard University Press, 1976), 202.
15. Douglas Sloan, *The Scottish Enlightenment and the American College Ideal* (New York: Teachers College Press, 1971), 52.
16. Emerson, "The Over-Soul," in *WRWE*, 2:269.
17. Emerson, "Circles," in *WRWE*, 2:309.
18. Emerson, "The Transcendentalist," 1:330.
19. Petersen, *Scottish Common Sense in America*, 183.
20. Emerson, "Greatness," in *WRWE*, 8:307; "Literary Ethics: An Oration Delivered before the Literary Societies of Dartmouth College, July 24, 1838," in *WRWE*, 1:161.
21. Emerson, "Experience," *WRWE*, 3:55.
22. Emerson, "Fate," in *WRWE*, 6:16.
23. Emerson, "Eloquence," in *WRWE*, 8:131; James Hutchison Stirling, *The Secret of Hegel: Being the Hegelian System in Origin, Principle, Form and Matter* (London: Longman, Roberts & Green, 1865).
24. Emerson, "Nominalist and Realist," in *WRWE*, 3:243.
25. Terry Mulcaire, "Dialectic," in *Walt Whitman: An Encyclopedia*, ed. J. R. LeMaster and Donald D. Kummings (New York: Garland, 1998), 180.
26. Walt Whitman, "Years of the Unperform'd," in *Drum-Taps* (New York, 1865), 53.

27. Whitman, "Quicksand Years That Whirl Me I Know Not Whither," in *Drum-Taps*, 30.
28. Whitman, "Chanting the Square Deific," in *Leaves of Grass* (San Diego: Word Cloud Classics, 2015), 409.
29. J. P. Craig, "Walt Whitman and Hegel," *International Journal of Liberal Arts and Social Science* 3, no. 5 (June 2015): 137–38.
30. Lawrence Templin, "The Quaker Influence on Walt Whitman," *American Literature* 42, no. 2 (1970): 165–80.
31. David S. Reynolds, "'Affection Shall Solve Every One of the Problems of Freedom': Calamus Love and the Antebellum Political Crisis," *Huntington Library Quarterly* 73, no. 4 (2010): 640.
32. Reynolds, "'Affection,'" 640.
33. Reynolds, "'Affection,'" 634–35.
34. *Memoirs of Margaret Fuller Ossoli*, ed. William Henry Channing, Ralph Waldo Emerson, and James Freeman Clarke (Boston: Philips, Sampson, 1852), 115.
35. Margaret Fuller, *Summer on the Lakes*, in *The Portable Margaret Fuller*, ed. Mary Kelley (New York: Penguin, 1994), 87.
36. Fuller, *Summer on the Lakes*, 89.
37. Megan Marshall, *Margaret Fuller: A New American Life* (Boston: Houghton Mifflin Harcourt, 2013), 115, 247–48.
38. Molly McGarry, *Ghosts of Futures Past: Spiritualism and the Cultural Politics of Nineteenth-Century America* (Berkeley: University of California Press, 2008), 42, 45, 52, 126.
39. Fuller, *Summer on the Lakes*, 146.
40. Fuller, 154, 158.
41. Fuller, 159.
42. Fuller, 167.
43. Kent Gramm, *Somebody's Darling: Essays on the Civil War* (Bloomington: Indiana University Press, 2002), 90.
44. Daniel Walker Howe, *Making the American Self: Jonathan Edwards to Abraham Lincoln* (New York: Oxford University Press, 1997), 109.
45. Ashton Nichols, "Emerson, Thoreau, and the Transcendentalist Movement," lecture series transcript (Chantilly, VA: Great Courses, 2006), 57.
46. Barry Hankins, *The Second Great Awakening and the Transcendentalists* (Westport, CT: Greenwood, 2004), 90.
47. James Marsh, *The Remains of the Rev. James Marsh, D. D. Late President, and Professor of Moral and Intellectual Philosophy in the University of Vermont; with a Memoir of His Life*, ed. Joseph Torrey (Boston: Crocker and Brewster, 1843), 79–80.
48. *A Catalogue of the Officers and Students of Harvard College, for the Academical Year 1852–53. Second Term. Second Edition.* (Cambridge, MA: John Bartlett, 1853), 44–46.
49. Hazen C. Carpenter, "Emerson, Eliot, and the Elective System," *New England Quarterly* 24, no. 1 (1951): 13–34.
50. Martin Bickman, *Minding American Education: Reclaiming the Tradition of Active Learning* (New York: Teachers College Press, 2003), 51–52; Marjorie Stiem, "Beginnings of Modern Education: Bronson Alcott," *Peabody Journal of Education* 38, no. 1 (1960): 7–9.

51. Charles Dickens, *American Notes* (London: Hazell, Watson & Viney, 1843), 29–42; Kimberly French, *Perkins School for the Blind* (Mount Pleasant, SC: Arcadia, 2004), 13–14, 35.
52. French, *Perkins School*, 35.

CHAPTER 4

1. Benjamin L. Brisbane to his sister P. Adeline Brisbane, "Cherished Fragments: Autograph Book of P. Adeline Brisbane, Arena, Wisconsin, 1857," William Henry Brisbane Papers, box 1, folder 8, Wisconsin Historical Society, Archives Division, Madison.
2. Daniel Walker Howe, *Making the American Self: Jonathan Edwards to Abraham Lincoln* (New York: Oxford University Press, 1997), 66–67, 69, 121.
3. Ralph Waldo Emerson, "Friendship," in *Works of Ralph Waldo Emerson*, 12 vols. (Boston: Houghton, Mifflin, 1903), 2:191.
4. Emerson, "Success," in *Works of Ralph Waldo Emerson*, 7:295.
5. Sophia A. Rosenfeld, *Common Sense: A Political History* (Cambridge, MA: Harvard University Press, 2011), 163–64.
6. Sue Innes and Jane Rendall, "Women, Gender, and Politics," in *Gender in Scottish History since 1700*, ed. Lynn Abrams, Eleanor Gordon, Deborah Simonton, and Eileen Janes Yeo (Edinburgh: Edinburgh University Press, 2006), 49.
7. John Millar, *Observations concerning the Distinction of Ranks in Society* (London: John Murray, 1773), 86.
8. Innes and Rendall, "Women, Gender, and Politics," 49–50.
9. Rosalind Carr, *Gender and Enlightenment Culture in Eighteenth-Century Scotland* (Edinburgh: Edinburgh University Press, 2014), 11, 12.
10. Katie Barclay, *Love, Intimacy and Power: Marriage and Patriarchy in Scotland, 1650–1850* (Manchester: Manchester University Press, 2011), 64.
11. Adam Smith, *The Theory of Moral Sentiments; to Which Is Added, a Dissertation on the Origin of Languages* (London: George Bell & Sons, 1892), 214.
12. Carr, *Gender and Enlightenment Culture*, 19–20.
13. Carr, 9.
14. Immanuel Kant, *Observations on the Feeling of the Beautiful and Sublime, and Other Writings*, ed. Patrick Frierson and Paul Guyer (New York: Cambridge University Press, 2011), 18, 22, 37, 85.
15. Kant, *Observations*, 37.
16. Kant, 18, 22, 37, 85.
17. Kant, 48.
18. Kant, 21.
19. Kant, 38–39.
20. Patrick Frierson and Paul Guyer, introduction to Kant, *Observations*, xxix–xxxiv.
21. A. Bronson Alcott, *Record of Conversations on the Gospels, Held in Mr. Alcott's School; Unfolding the Doctrine and Discipline of Human Culture* (Boston: James Munroe, 1836), iii.
22. Ashton Nichols, "Emerson, Thoreau, and the Transcendentalist Movement," lecture series transcript (Chantilly, VA: Great Courses, 2006), 259.

23. Alcott, *Conversations on the Gospels*, xxix, xxx.
24. Bronson Alcott, "Journals," in *Selected Writings of the American Transcendentalists*, ed. George Hochfield (New York: New American Library, 1966), 92–93.
25. Louisa May Alcott, *The Works of Louisa May Alcott* (Stanford, CT: Longmeadow, 1995), 407.
26. Margaret Fuller, *Woman in the Nineteenth Century*, in *The Portable Margaret Fuller*, ed. Mary Kelley (New York: Penguin, 1994), 330.
27. Margaret Fuller, *Summer on the Lakes*, in Kelley, *Portable Margaret Fuller*, 107.
28. Fuller, *Woman in the Nineteenth Century*, 285.
29. Frederick A. Braun, "Goethe as Viewed by Emerson," *Journal of English and German Philology* 15, no. 1 (January 1916): 27.
30. Horace Biddle, *Bettina to Goethe: An Unpublished Poem* (Cincinnati: Moorse, Wilstach, Keys, 1861); Bettina von Arnim, *Goethe's Correspondence with a Child* (Boston: Ticknor and Fields, 1861); J. W. Goethe, *Faust: A Dramatic Poem* (Boston: Ticknor and Fields, 1859), and Goethe, *Faust: A Tragedy* (Boston: Ticknor and Fields, 1860); J. W. Goethe, *Goethe's Werke* (Stuttgart: J. G. Cotta, 1827–34). Also present in Harvard's collection is an English novel on Goethe, H. Noel Humphreys, *Goethe in Strasbourg: A Dramatic Nouvelette* (London: Saunders, Otley, 1860).
31. See Andrea Wulf, *Magnificent Rebels: The First Romantics and the Invention of the Self* (New York: Alfred A. Knopf, 2022).
32. Braun, "Goethe as Viewed by Emerson," 25, 26.
33. Emerson, "Goethe," *Works of Ralph Waldo Emerson*, 4:273.
34. Braun, "Goethe as Viewed by Emerson," 26.
35. Emerson, "Goethe," 285.
36. Emerson, journal quoted in *Works of Ralph Waldo Emerson*, 4:373.
37. Walter Kaufmann, *Discovering the Mind: Goethe, Kant, and Hegel* (New York: McGraw-Hill, 1980), 6, 25.
38. Arnold Bergstraesser, *Goethe's Image of Man and Society* (Chicago: Henry Regnery, 1949), 293.
39. Johann Wolfgang von Goethe, *Faust*, trans. George Madison Priest (Chicago: Encyclopaedia Britannica, 1952), 294.
40. Goethe, *Faust*, 293.
41. Johann Wolfgang von Goethe, *The Sorrows of Young Werther*, 1774, trans. R. D. Boylan, ed. Nathen Haskell Dole, https://www.gutenberg.org/files/2527/2527-h/2527-h.htm.
42. Johann Wolfgang von Goethe, *Wilhelm Meister's Apprenticeship and Travels: Three Volumes in One*, trans. Thomas Carlyle (London: Chapman and Hall, 1907), bk. 8, 219, 223.
43. Goethe, *Wilhelm Meister*, bk. 6, 90.
44. Goethe, bk. 6, 102.
45. Goethe, bk. 1, 58.
46. Frederick Augustus Braun, *Margaret Fuller and Goethe* (New York: Henry Hold, 1910), 23.
47. Louisa May Alcott, *Little Men*, in *Works of Louisa May Alcott*, 448.
48. Margaret Fuller, "Goethe," *Dial*, July 1841, 13.
49. Fuller, "Goethe," 12–13.

50. Quoted in Braun, *Margaret Fuller and Goethe*, 183.
51. Fuller, "Goethe," 14.
52. Bergstraesser, *Goethe's Image of Man and Society*, 158.
53. Johann Gottfried von Herder, *Outlines of a Philosophy of the History of Man* (New York: Random Shack, 2016), 389. Reprint edition of translation by T. Churchill, London, 1800.
54. Fuller, "Goethe," 15.
55. S. Margaret Fuller autograph manuscript journal, 1840, undated entry, MS Am 1086 (85), Margaret Fuller Family Papers, Harvard University Houghton Library Collections, Cambridge, MA.
56. Fuller, "Goethe," 16.
57. Fuller, *Woman in the Nineteenth Century*, 256, 300.
58. Megan Marshall, *Margaret Fuller: A New American Life* (Boston: Houghton Mifflin Harcourt, 2013), 193–94.
59. William Henry Channing, Ralph Waldo Emerson, and James Freeman Clarke, eds., *Memoirs of Margaret Fuller Ossoli* (Boston: Philips, Sampson, 1852).
60. Channing, Emerson, and Clarke, *Memoirs of Margaret Fuller Ossoli*, 215, 263–64, 279, 280–81, 322.
61. Fuller, "Bettine Brentano and Her Friend Günderode," review of *On "Goethe's Conversations with a Child,"* in Kelley, *Portable Margaret Fuller*, 25.
62. Fuller, *Woman in the Nineteenth Century*, 300.
63. Fuller, "Goethe," 15–16.
64. Fuller, *Woman in the Nineteenth Century*, 229, 326.
65. "Messages of Love and Encouragement: A Reminiscence of the Civil War," *Journal of the Illinois State Historical Society (1908–1984)* 11, no. 1 (1918): 59–61.
66. "Messages of Love and Encouragement," 59–61.
67. James Thatcher, *Military Journal, during the American Revolutionary War* (Hartford, CT: Silas Andrus & Son, 1854), 289.
68. Robert B. Westbrook, *Why We Fought: Forging American Obligations in World War II* (Washington, DC: Smithsonian Books, 2004), 69, 84.

CHAPTER 5

1. Wilbur Fisk, *Hard Marching Every Day: The Civil War Letters of Private Wilbur Fisk*, ed. Emil Rosenblatt and Ruth Rosenblatt (Lawrence: University Press of Kansas, 1992), 352.
2. For works on soldier motivation, see Thomas E. Rodgers, "Billy Yank and G. I. Joe: An Exploratory Essay on the Sociopolitical Dimensions of Soldier Motivation," *Journal of Military History* 69, no. 1 (January 2005): 93–121; Robert B. Westbrook, *Why We Fought: Forging American Obligations in World War II* (Washington, DC: Smithsonian Books, 2004); Earl J. Hess, *Liberty, Virtue, and Progress: Northerners and Their War for the Union* (Bronx, NY: Fordham University Press, 1997); George M. Fredrickson, *The Inner Civil War: Northern Intellectuals and the Crisis of the Union* (New York: Harper & Row, 1965); Mark A. Noll, *The Civil War as a Theological Crisis* (Chapel Hill: University of North Carolina Press, 2006); and James

McPherson, *For Cause and Comrades: Why Men Fought in the Civil War* (New York: Oxford University Press, 1997).
3. Chandra Manning, *What This Cruel War Was Over: Soldiers, Slavery, and the Civil War* (New York: Vintage Civil War Library, 2008), 37, 129.
4. Chandra Manning, "Wartime Nationalism and Race: Comparing the Visions of Confederate, Black Union, and White Union Soldiers," in *In the Cause of Liberty: How the Civil War Redefined American Ideals*, ed. William J. Cooper Jr. and John M. McCardell (Baton Rouge: Louisiana State University Press, 2009), 90–92.
5. Manning, "Wartime Nationalism and Race," 92.
6. Manning, *What This Cruel War Was Over*, 129.
7. Quoted in Jim Cullen, "Gender and African American Men," in *Divided Houses: Gender and the Civil War*, ed. Catherine Clinton (New York: Oxford University Press, 1992), 81.
8. LeeAnn White, *The Civil War as a Crisis in Gender: Augusta, Georgia, 1860–1890* (Athens: University of Georgia Press, 1995).
9. Reid Mitchell, "Soldiering, Manhood, and Coming of Age: A Northern Volunteer," in Clinton, *Divided Houses*, 46, 53.
10. Daniel Walker Howe, *Making the American Self: Jonathan Edwards to Abraham Lincoln* (New York: Oxford University Press, 1997), 92–93.
11. Amy S. Greenberg, *Manifest Manhood and the Antebellum American Empire* (New York: Cambridge University Press, 2005), 11, 140.
12. Greenberg, *Manifest Manhood*, 275.
13. Greenberg, *Manifest Manhood*, 139.
14. See Paul Negri, ed., *Civil War Poetry: An Anthology* (Mineola, NY: Dover, 1997), preface, back cover; Irwin Silber, ed., *Songs of the Civil War* (New York: Dover, 1995), section introductions; Harry S. Stout, *Upon the Altar of the Nation: A Moral History of the Civil War* (New York: Viking, 2006); and McPherson, *For Cause and Comrades*, 100.
15. McPherson, *For Cause and Comrades*, 100.
16. Harry S. Stout, *Upon the Altar of the Nation: A Moral History of the Civil War* (New York: Viking, 2006).
17. Drew Gilpin Faust, *This Republic of Suffering: Death and the American Civil War* (repr., New York: Vintage, 2009), and George A. Coco, *A Strange and Blighted Land—Gettysburg: The Aftermath of a Battle* (Gettysburg, PA: Thomas, 1995).
18. Silber, *Songs of the Civil War*, 113, 165.
19. Fisk, *Hard Marching Every Day*, 202.
20. Emerson, "Nature," in *Works of Ralph Waldo Emerson*, 12 vols. (Boston: Houghton, Mifflin, 1903), 3:196.
21. Stout, *Upon the Altar of the Nation*, 116, 110, 241; Earl J. Hess, *The Union Soldier in Battle: Enduring the Ordeal of Combat* (Lawrence: University Press of Kansas, 1997), 128–29.
22. Johann Wolfgang von Goethe, *Wilhelm Meister's Apprenticeship and Travels, Three Volumes in One*, trans. Thomas Carlyle (London: Chapman and Hall, 1907), bk. 8, 207.
23. Arnold Bergstraesser, *Goethe's Image of Man and Society* (Chicago: Henry Regnery, 1949), 169.

24. Bergstraesser, *Goethe's Image of Man and Society*, 24, 284; Goethe, *Wilhelm Meister*, bk. 2, 70.
25. Bergstraesser, *Goethe's Image of Man and Society*, 138.
26. Walter Kaufmann, *Discovering the Mind: Goethe, Kant, and Hegel* (New York: McGraw-Hill, 1980), 231.
27. Bergstraesser, *Goethe's Image of Man and Society*, 257.
28. Bergstraesser, 42; Kaufmann, *Discovering the Mind*, 30, 261.
29. Goethe, *Wilhelm Meister*, bk. 5, 7.
30. Goethe, *Wilhelm Meister*, bk. 7, 187.
31. Johann Wolfgang von Goethe, *Faust*, trans. George Madison Priest (Chicago: Encyclopaedia Britannica, 1952), 114.
32. Goethe, *Faust*, 290.
33. Goethe, *Faust*, 294.
34. Faust, *This Republic of Suffering*, 122.
35. Stout, *Upon the Altar of the Nation*, 338, 347.
36. Horace Bushnell, *The Vicarious Sacrifice, Grounded in Principles of Universal Obligation* (New York: Charles Scribner, 1866), 20, 183, 301–2.
37. "Joshua Chamberlain to his sister Sarah, Jan. 29, 1882," in *War Letters: Extraordinary Correspondence from American Wars*, ed. Andrew Carroll (New York: Washington Square, 2001), 122.
38. George Cram, *Soldiering with Sherman: The Civil War Letters of George F. Cram* (DeKalb: Northern Illinois University Press, 2000), 67.
39. George C. Burmeister Diaries, Jan. 20, 1861, Dec. 2, 1861, Feb. 27, 1864, MSC0906, Civil War Diaries and Letters, University of Iowa Special Collections Department, Iowa City, Iowa.
40. Quoted in Earl J. Hess, *Liberty, Virtue, and Progress: Northerners and Their War for the Union* (Bronx, NY: Fordham University Press, 1997), 43.
41. William A. Dillon, "Don't Take My Darling Boy Away," composed by Albert Von Tilzer (New York: Broadway Music Corporation, 1915), https://www.loc.gov/item/2013569497/.
42. Jeremiah D. Lamson to Roswell Lamson, July 6, 1861, in *Lamson of the Gettysburg: The Civil War Letters of Lieutenant Roswell H. Lamson, U.S. Navy*, ed. James McPherson and Patricia McPherson (New York: Oxford University Press, 1997), 21–22.
43. James Freeman Clarke, *Discourse on the Aspects of the War, Delivered in the Indiana-Place Chapel, Boston, on Fast Day, April 2, 1863* (Boston: Walker, Wise, 1863), 10.
44. Clarke, *Aspects of the War*, 4–6.
45. Anna Greenough Burgwyn to William H. S. Burgwyn, January 4, 1865, North Carolina Digital Collections, https://digital.ncdcr.gov/documents/detail/590365.
46. Kate Stone, *Brokenburn: The Journal of Kate Stone, 1861–1868*, ed. John Q. Anderson (Baton Rouge: Louisiana State University Press, 1972), 70, 89, 91, 102.
47. Warren S. Tryon, "The Publications of Ticknor and Fields in the South, 1840–1865," *Journal of Southern History* 14, no. 3 (August 1948): 305–30.
48. Stone, *Brokenburn*, 332, 314, 51, 270, 357.
49. Francis Marion Poteet to Martha Hendley Poteet, Nov. 22, 1863, Aug. 21, 1864, North Carolina Digital Collections, https://digital.ncdcr.gov/Documents/Detail

/letter-francis-marion-poteet-to-martha-hendley-poteet-nov.-22-1863/602605; https://digital.ncdcr.gov/Documents/Detail/letter-francis-marion-poteet-to-martha-hendley-poteet-aug.-21-1864/605008.
50. Daniel W. Revis to Sarepta Revis, Nov. 8, 1862, North Carolina Digital Collections, https://digital.ncdcr.gov/Documents/Detail/letter-daniel-w.-revis-to-sarepta-revis-nov.-8-1862/604754.
51. George A. Williams to his family, April 5, 1864, North Carolina Digital Collections, https://digital.ncdcr.gov/Documents/Detail/letter-george-a.-williams-to-his-family-april-5-1864/577027.
52. George Washington Beidelman to his father, October 15–21, 1862, MS-043: George Washington Beidelman Collection, Special Collections and College Archives, Musselman Library, Gettysburg College, Gettysburg, PA; Theodore Ayrault Dodge, *On Campaign with the Army of the Potomac: The Civil War Journal of Theodore Ayrault Dodge*, ed. Stephen W. Sears (New York: Cooper Square Press, 2001), 7.
53. Faust, *This Republic of Suffering*, 6.
54. Ernest Hemingway, *A Farewell to Arms* (New York: Charles Scribner's Sons, 1929), 184–85.
55. Joshua Lawrence Chamberlain, *The Passing of the Armies: An Account of the Final Campaign of the Army of the Potomac, Based upon Personal Reminiscences of the Fifth Army Corps* (New York: G. P. Putnam's Sons, 1915), 260, 271.
56. Clarke, *Aspects of the War*, 5–6.
57. "Glory and Perils of Victory," *American Presbyterian*, April 13, 1865.
58. Sara Eigen Figal, "The Point of Recognition: Enemy, Neighbor, and Next of Kin in the Era of Frederick the Great," in *Enlightened War: German Theories and Cultures of Warfare from Frederick the Great to Clausewitz*, ed. Elisabeth Krimmer and Patricia Anne Simpson (London: Camden House, 2011), 21.
59. Ethan Allen Hitchcock, *Swedenborg, a Hermetic Philosopher. Being a Sequel to Remarks on Alchemy and the Alchemists, Showing That Emanuel Swedenborg Was a Hermetic Philosopher and That His Writings May Be Interpreted from the Point of View of Hermetic Philosophy. With a Chapter Comparing Swedenborg and Spinoza* (New York: D. Appleton, 1858).
60. See, for instance, Francis Lieber, *On Civil Liberty and Self-Government* (London: Richard Bentley, 1853).
61. Charles B. Robson, "Papers of Francis Lieber," *Huntington Library Bulletin*, no. 3 (February 1933): 135–55.
62. John Fabian Witt, *Lincoln's Code: The Laws of War in American History* (New York: Free Press, 2012), 185.
63. Carl von Clausewitz, *On War*, trans. Col. James John Graham (London: N. Trübner, 1873), bk. 1, chap. 3, https://www.clausewitz.com/readings/OnWar1873/TOC.htm.
64. Mary Chesnut, *Mary Chesnut's Civil War*, ed. C. Vann Woodward (New Haven, CT: Yale University Press, 1981), 57, 128.
65. William Carson Corsan, *Two Months in the Confederate States: An Englishman's Travels through the South*, ed. Benjamin H. Trask (Baton Rouge: Louisiana State University Press, 1996), 101; Henry Ward Beecher, *Norwood; or, Village Life in New England* (New York: Charles Scribner, 1868), 386; Mrs. Burton Harrison, *Recollections*

Grave and Gay (New York: Charles Scribner's Sons, 1911), 94, http://docsouth.unc.edu/fpn/harrison/harrison.html; Letter of a lieutenant from the 12th New York Infantry, quoted in J. McPherson, *For Cause and Comrades*, 96.
66. Beecher, *Norwood*, 355.
67. George Templeton Strong, *Diary*, vol. 3, ed. Allan Nevins and Milton Thomas (New York: Macmillan, 1952), 101; Beecher, *Norwood*, 386; Horace Porter, *Campaigning with Grant* (New York: Century, 1897; repr., New York: Bantam, 1991), 58.
68. Corsan, *Two Months in the Confederate States*, 103.
69. Strong, *Diary*, 114, 3.
70. Clausewitz, *On War*, 71; Chesnut, *Mary Chesnut's Civil War*, 366.
71. Clausewitz, *On War*, 58–59.
72. An unnamed Mississippi soldier, quoted in David J. Eicher, *The Longest Night: A Military History of the Civil War* (New York: Touchstone Books, 2001), 680.
73. Clausewitz, *On War*, 59.
74. General Orders No. 100: The Lieber Code: Instructions for the Government of Armies of the United States in the Field, prepared by Francis Lieber, LL.D., Originally Issued as General Orders No. 100, Adjutant General's Office, 1863 (Washington, DC: Government Printing Office, 1898), http://avalon.law.yale.edu/19th_century/lieber.asp.
75. Louisa May Alcott, *The Works of Louisa May Alcott* (Stanford, CT: Longmeadow, 1995), 471.
76. Jeremiah Greenman, *Diary of a Common Soldier in the American Revolution, 1775–1783: An Annotated Edition of the Military Journal of Jeremiah Greenman*, ed. Robert Bray and Paul Bushnell (DeKalb: Northern Illinois University Press, 1978), 73, 141; Eugene B. Sledge, *With the Old Breed: At Peleliu and Okinawa* (New York: Ballantine, 1981), 10.
77. John W. Pratt Diary, 1865, University of Iowa Digital Library, https://digital.lib.uiowa.edu/node/86694/.
78. General Orders No. 100; August Kautz, *The 1865 Customs of Service for Officers of the Army: A Handbook of the Duties of Each Grade Lieutenant to Lieut.-General* (Mechanicsburg, PA: Stackpole, 2002), 231.
79. Sledge, *With the Old Breed*, 10.
80. Frances C. Carrington, *My Army Life: A Soldier's Wife at Fort Phil Kearny* (Boulder, CO: Pruett, 1990), 111.
81. Roswell Lamson to Katie, April 2, 1863, in McPherson and McPherson, *Lamson of the Gettysburg*, 90.
82. Charles S. Wainwright, *A Diary of Battle: The Personal Journals of Colonel Charles S. Wainwright, 1861–1865*, ed. Allan Nevins (New York: Harcourt, Brace & World, 1962), 116.
83. Fisk, *Hard Marching Every Day*, 128.
84. Johann Gottfried von Herder, *Outlines of a Philosophy of the History of Man* (New York: Random Shack, 2016), 9, 96, 109. Reprint edition of translation by T. Churchill, London, 1800.
85. Georg W. F. Hegel, *The Philosophy of History* (Chicago: University of Chicago Press, 1952), 166.

CHAPTER 6

1. War-Time Letters from Seth Rogers, M.D. Surgeon of the First South Carolina Afterwards the Thirty-Third U.S.C.T. 1862–1863, Florida History Online, https://history.domains.unf.edu/floridahistoryonline/projects-proj-b-p-html/cir-index-htm/war-time-letters-from-seth-rogers.
2. Stanley Elkins, *Slavery: A Problem in American Institutional Life*, 3rd ed. rev. (Chicago: University of Chicago Press, 1976), 147–48.
3. Randall Fuller, *From Battlefields Rising: How the Civil War Transformed American Literature* (New York: Oxford University Press, 2011), 38.
4. Arthur M. Schlesinger Jr., *The Age of Jackson* (Boston: Little, Brown, 1945), 382; George M. Fredrickson, *The Inner Civil War: Northern Intellectuals and the Crisis of the Union* (New York: Harper & Row, 1965), 87, 90, 172–78; Philip F. Gura, *Man's Better Angels: Romantic Reformers and the Coming of the Civil War* (Cambridge, MA: Belknap Press of Harvard University Press, 2017).
5. Peter Wirzbicki, *Fighting for the Higher Law: Black and White Transcendentalists against Slavery* (Philadelphia: University of Pennsylvania Press, 2021).
6. Ibram X. Kendi, *Stamped from the Beginning: The Definitive History of Racist Ideas in America* (New York: Nation Books, 2016), 3.
7. Colin Kidd, *The Forging of Races: Race and Scripture in the Protestant Atlantic World, 1600–2000* (New York: Cambridge University Press, 2006), 22–25, 34–37, 139.
8. Mark Noll, *The Civil War as a Theological Crisis* (Chapel Hill: University of North Carolina Press, 2006), 74; Kidd, *Forging of Races*, 149.
9. David Hume, *The Philosophical Works*, ed. T. H. Green and T. G. Grose, 4 vols. (London, 1882), 3:252–53.
10. Adam Ferguson, *An Essay on the History of Civil Society* (Dublin: Boulter Grierson, 1767), 175.
11. Silvia Sebastiani, *The Scottish Enlightenment: Race, Gender, and the Limits of Progress* (New York: Palgrave MacMillan, 2006), 42.
12. Lord Henry Home Kames, *Sketches of the History of Man*, vol. 1 (Edinburgh: William Creech, 1807), 19.
13. Kames, *Sketches of the History of Man*, 59.
14. Bruce R. Dain, *A Hideous Monster of the Mind: American Race Theory in the Early Republic* (Cambridge, MA: Harvard University Press, 2002), 24; Nicholas Hudson, "From 'Nation' to 'Race': The Origin of Racial Classification in Eighteenth-Century Thought," *Eighteenth-Century Studies* 29, no. 3 (Spring 1996): 253.
15. Dain, *Hideous Monster of the Mind*, 11–13.
16. Thomas Reid, *Essays on the Intellectual Powers of Man* (1785), in *The Works of Thomas Reid, D.D.; Now Fully Collected, with Selections from His Unpublished Letters*, ed. Sir William Hamilton (Edinburgh: Maclachlan and Stewart, 1852), 391.
17. Robert Bernasconi, "Who Invented the Concept of Race? Kant's Role in the Enlightenment Construction of Race," in *Race*, ed. Robert Bernasconi (Hoboken, NJ: Wiley-Blackwell, 2001), 14.
18. Stella Sandford, "Kant, Race, and Natural History," *Philosophy & Social Criticism* 44, no. 9 (November 2018): 950–77.
19. Pauline Kleingeld, "Kant's Second Thoughts on Race," *Philosophical Quarterly* 57, no. 229 (October 2007): 579.

20. Kidd, *Forging of Races*, 25, 106.
21. Immanuel Kant, "On the Different Human Races," in *Kant and the Concept of Race*, trans. and ed. Jon M. Mikkelsen (Albany: State University of New York Press, 2013), 55–71.
22. Kant, "On the Different Human Races," 65.
23. Kant, 58, 67.
24. Richard Colfax, *Evidence against the Views of the Abolitionists; Consisting of Physical and Moral Proofs, of the Natural Inferiority of the Negroes* (New York: James T. M. Bleakley, 1833), 29.
25. Kleingeld, "Kant's Second Thoughts on Race," 579.
26. Immanuel Kant, "*On the Use of Teleological Principles in Philosophy*" (1788), in *Anthropology, History, and Education*, ed. Günter Zöller and Robert B. Louden (Cambridge, UK: Cambridge University Press, 2007), 209–11 (trans. Mary Gregor).
27. Kleingeld, "Kant's Second Thoughts on Race," 574.
28. Kleingeld, 588.
29. Colfax, *Evidence against the Views*, 25, 8.
30. Robert Knox, *The Races of Men: A Fragment* (Philadelphia: Lea & Blanchard, 1850), 80–81.
31. Kidd, *Forging of Races*, 192; Matthew Stewart, *Emancipation of the Mind: Radical Philosophy, the War over Slavery, and the Refounding of America* (New York: W. W. Norton, 2024), 317; Anthony Quinton, "Idealists against the Jews," *New York Review*, November 7, 1991, https://www.nybooks.com/articles/1991/11/07/idealists-against-the-jews/.
32. Kidd, *Forging of Races*, 172, 192–94.
33. Abraham Lincoln to Joshua Speed, August 24, 1855, Abraham Lincoln Online, Speeches & Writings, https://www.abrahamlincolnonline.org/lincoln/speeches/speed.htm.
34. Robert Gould Shaw to Mother, May 25, 1861, and March 25, 1863, in *Blue-Eyed Child of Fortune: The Civil War Letters of Colonel Robert Gould Shaw*, ed. Russell Duncan (Athens: University of Georgia Press, 1992), 104, 313.
35. John H. Zammito, *Kant, Herder, and the Birth of Anthropology* (Chicago: University of Chicago Press, 2002), 1–11.
36. Charles Taylor, *Hegel* (Cambridge, UK: Cambridge University Press, 1977), 15.
37. *Websters Dictionary*, 1828, under "anthropology," http://webstersdictionary1828.com.
38. Taylor, *Hegel*, 15–17.
39. Beate Allert, "The Natural and the Virtual in Herder's Approach to Temporality," paper presented at 50th annual meeting of the American Society for 18th Century Studies, Denver, Colorado, March 21–23, 2019.
40. Johann Gottfried von Herder, *Outlines of a Philosophy of the History of Man* (New York: Random Shack, 2016), 141–42. Reprint edition of translation by T. Churchill, London, 1800.
41. Herder, *Philosophy of the History of Man*, 141.
42. Carlton J. H. Hayes, "Contributions of Herder to the Doctrine of Nationalism," *American Historical Review* 32, no. 4 (1927): 735.
43. Herder, *Philosophy of the History of Man*, 389.
44. Herder, 128–29.

45. Georg W. F. Hegel, Philosophy *of Mind*, trans. William Wallace, with the *Zusätze*, trans. Ludwig Boumann (1830; repr., London: Oxford University Press, 1971), 349; Georg W. F. Hegel, *Phenomenology of Spirit*, trans. A. V. Miller (New York: Oxford University Press, 1977), 538.
46. Hegel, *Zusätze*, 11.
47. Michael Allen Fox, *The Accessible Hegel* (Amherst, NY: Humanity Books, 2005), 69.
48. Georg W. F. Hegel, *The Philosophy of History* (Chicago: University of Chicago Press, 1952), 190, 196, 198–99.
49. Hegel, *Philosophy of History*, 199.
50. Hegel, 349–53.
51. Hegel, 319, 350.
52. Simon Blackburn, ed., *Oxford Dictionary of Philosophy*, 2nd ed. rev. (New York: Oxford University Press, 2008), 225.
53. Hegel, *Zusätze*, 172.
54. Susan Buck-Morss, "Hegel and Haiti," *Critical Inquiry* 26, no. 4. (Summer 2000): 821–65.
55. Alexandre Kojève, *Introduction to the Reading of Hegel*, assembled by Raymond Queneau, ed. Allan Bloom, trans. James H. Nichols Jr. (New York: HarperCollins, 1969), 26–29.
56. John McDowell, "The Apperceptive I and the Empirical Self: Towards a Heterodox Reading of 'Lordship and Bondage' in Hegel's *Phenomenology*," in *Hegel: New Directions*, ed. Katerina Deligiorgi (New York: Routledge, 2014), 33–48.
57. Susan Buck-Morss, *Hegel, Haiti, and Universal History* (Pittsburgh: University of Pittsburgh Press, 2009).
58. Tom Rockmore, *Before and After Hegel: A Historical Introduction to Hegel's Thought* (Berkeley: University of California Press, 1993), 69–70; Joseph McCarney, *Routledge Philosophy Guidebook to Hegel on History* (London: Routledge, 2000), 26, 49.
59. Hegel, *Philosophy of History*, 190, 196, 198–99.
60. Jim Cullen, "Gender and African American Men" in *Divided Houses: Gender and the Civil War*, ed. Catherine Clinton (New York: Oxford University Press, 1992), 81.
61. Luis Fenollosa Emilio, *History of the Fifty-Fourth Regiment of Massachusetts Volunteer Infantry, 1863–1865* (Boston: Book Company, 1891), 3.
62. Thomas Wentworth Higginson, *The Complete Civil War Journal and Selected Letters of Thomas Wentworth Higginson*, ed. Christopher Looby (Chicago: University of Chicago Press, 2000), 209.
63. Shaw to Mother, March 25, 1863, in Duncan, *Blue-Eyed Child of Fortune*, 313.

CHAPTER 7

1. See Arthur M. Schlesinger Jr., *The Age of Jackson* (Boston: Little, Brown, 1945), 369; Stanley Elkins, *Slavery: A Problem in American Institutional and Intellectual Life*, 3rd ed. rev. (Chicago: University of Chicago Press, 1976), 151–52.
2. Peter Wirzbicki, "Black Transcendentalism: William Cooper Nell, the Adelphic Union, and the Black Abolitionist Intellectual Tradition," in "The Future of

Abolition Studies: A Special Issue," ed. Manisha Sinha, *Journal of the Civil War Era* 8, no. 2 (June 2018): 269–90.
3. Peter Wirzbicki, *Fighting for the Higher Law: Black and White Transcendentalists against Slavery* (Philadelphia: University of Pennsylvania Press, 2021), 55–60.
4. Wirzbicki, "Black Transcendentalism," 277.
5. Daniel Walker Howe, *Making the American Self: Jonathan Edwards to Abraham Lincoln* (New York: Oxford University Press, 1997), 152.
6. Wirzbicki, *Fighting for the Higher Law*, 60.
7. Lorenz Oken, *Elements of Physiophilosophy*, trans. Alfred Tulk (London: Ray Society, 1847), line 3579, Project Gutenberg, http://www.gutenberg.org/files/49196/49196-h/49196-h.htm.
8. John Bernhard Stallo, *General Principles of the Philosophy of Nature: With an Outline of Some of Its Recent Developments among the Germans, Embracing the Philosophical Systems of Schelling and Hegel, and Oken's System of Nature* (Boston: Wm. Crosby and H. P. Nichols, 1848), 325.
9. Oken, *Elements of Physiophilosophy*, line 3582.
10. Carl Gustav Carus, *An Induction to the Comparative Anatomy of Animals: Compiled with Constant Reference to Physiology, and Elucidated by Twenty Copper-Plates* (London: Longman, Rees, Orme, Brown and Green, 1827).
11. Gustave Friedrich Klemm, *General Cultural History of Mankind* (Leipzig: Teubner, 1852).
12. Stallo, *General Principles*, 325–26.
13. Stallo, 121, 485.
14. Ralph Waldo Emerson, "Fate," in *Works of Ralph Waldo Emerson*, 12 vols. (Boston: Houghton, Mifflin, 1903), 6:16 (hereafter cited as *WRWE*).
15. Robert Knox, *Races of Men, a Fragment* (Philadelphia: Lea & Blanchard, 1850), 161, 14.
16. Knox, *Races of Men*, 303–4.
17. Knox, 7, 163, 302.
18. Harriet Martineau, *Society in America, in Two Volumes* (New York: Saunders and Otley, 1837), 352–53, Project Gutenberg, http://www.gutenberg.org/files/52621/52621-h/52621-h.htm.
19. Martineau, *Society in America*, 41.
20. Ralph Waldo Emerson, "Lecture on the Times," in *WRWE*, 1:280; Emerson, "Spiritual Laws," in *WRWE*, 2:36; Margaret Fuller, *Summer on the Lakes*, in *The Portable Margaret Fuller*, ed. Mary Kelley (New York: Penguin, 1994), 223, 212; Henry David Thoreau, *The Writings of Henry David Thoreau*, vol. 12, *Journal, March 2, 1859–November 30, 1859*. (Boston: Houghton Mifflin, 1906), 43 (hereafter cited as *Journal*); Henry David Thoreau, "A Plea for Captain John Brown," 1859, Project Gutenberg, https://www.gutenberg.org/cache/epub/2567/pg2567.txt.
21. Emerson, "Race," in *WRWE*, 5:44.
22. Emerson, "Race," 44, 49, 54.
23. Johann Gottfried von Herder, *Outlines of a Philosophy of the History of Man* (New York: Random Shack, 2016), 145. Reprint edition of translation by T. Churchill, London, 1800.
24. Emerson, "Race," 52.

25. Emerson, "Civilization," in *WRWE*, 7:25–26.
26. Emerson, "Voluntaries," in *WRWE*, 9:207.
27. Emerson, "Civilization," 26–27.
28. Emerson, "Race," 47–49.
29. Emerson, 49.
30. Emerson, "Civilization," 20.
31. Emerson, "Race," 51.
32. Howe, *Making the American Self*; Frederick Douglass, *Narrative of the Life of Frederick Douglass, an American Slave. Written by Himself* (Boston: Anti-Slavery Office, 1845), 33, 66.
33. Margaret Fuller, "*New-York Daily Tribune* Columns," in Kelley, *Portable Margaret Fuller*, 379, 381.
34. Fuller, "*New-York Daily Tribune* Columns," 379.
35. S. M. Fuller, autograph manuscript journal, 1840, undated entry, Harvard University Houghton Library Collections, Cambridge, MA.
36. Josephine Donovan, "A Source for Stowe's Ideas on Race in *Uncle Tom's Cabin*," *NWSA Journal* 7, no. 3 (Autumn 1995): 24–34.
37. Harriet Beecher Stowe, *Uncle Tom's Cabin: Or, Life among the Lowly* (Boston: J. P. Jewett, 1852), 14, 147.
38. Howe, *Making the American Self*, 150.
39. Howe, 150.
40. Ralph Waldo Emerson, Letter to Martin Van Buren, President of the United States, 1838, https://emersoncentral.com/texts/miscellanies/letter-to-president-van-buren.
41. Georg W. F. Hegel, *The Philosophy of History* (Chicago: University of Chicago Press, 1952), 199.
42. Henry David Thoreau, *The Writings of Henry David Thoreau*, vol. 18, Journal, March 2, 1859–November 30, 1859, (Boston: Houghton Mifflin, 1906), 90–91 (hereafter cited as *Journal*).
43. Thoreau, *Journal*, 18:124.
44. Thoreau, *Journal*, 18:334–35.
45. Henry D. Thoreau, *A Yankee in Canada with Anti-Slavery and Reform Papers* (Boston: Houghton, Mifflin, 1892), 98, 115.
46. Thoreau, *Journal*, 18:409.
47. Thoreau, 413.
48. Thoreau, 420; Thoreau, *The Writings of Henry David Thoreau*, vol. 19, Journal, December 1, 1859–July 31, 1860, (Boston: Houghton Mifflin, 1906), 7.
49. Thoreau, *Yankee in Canada*, 110–11.
50. Megan Marshall, *Margaret Fuller: A New American Life* (Boston: Houghton Mifflin Harcourt, 2013), 213.
51. Jonathan Carver, *Travels through the Interior Parts of North America in the Years 1766, 1767, and 1768* (London: C. Dilly, H. Payne, J. Phillips, 1781), 197.
52. Fuller, *Summer on the Lakes*, 205.
53. Colin Kidd, *The Forging of Races: Race and Scripture in the Protestant Atlantic World, 1600–2000* (New York: Cambridge University Press, 2006), 141. See also Josiah Nott, George Gliddon, Samuel Morton, Louis Agassiz, Usher William, and Henry Patterson, *Types of Mankind, or Ethnological Researches: Based upon the Ancient*

Monuments, Paintings, Sculptures, and Crania of Races, and upon Their Natural Geographical, Philological and Biblical History (Philadelphia: J. B. Lippincott, Grambo, 1854).
54. Fuller, *Summer on the Lakes*, 188.
55. Fuller, 205.
56. Kurt Mueller-Vollmer, *Transatlantic Crossings and Transformations: German-American Cultural Transfer from the 18th to the End of the 19th Century* (New York: Peter Lang, 2015), 221; Sarah Vandegrift Eldridge, "A Survey of Perspectives: Karl Philipp Moritz's *Reisen eines Deutschen* in England," paper presented at 50th annual meeting of the American Society for 18th Century Studies, Denver, Colorado, March 21–23, 2019.
57. Fuller, *Summer on the Lakes*, 87. "Murray's travels" was probably one in the British series of *Murray's Handbooks for Travellers*, but I have been unable to identity an edition on the Americas.
58. Fuller, *Summer on the Lakes*, 176–77, 197.
59. Fuller, 176–77.
60. Fuller, 210.
61. Fuller, 225.
62. Fuller, 182.
63. Fuller, 190, 213–14.
64. Molly McGarry, *Ghosts of Futures Past: Spiritualism and the Cultural Politics of Nineteenth-Century America* (Berkeley: University of California Press, 2008), 77.
65. Fuller, *Summer on the Lakes*, 190.
66. Fuller, 72.
67. Fuller, 179, 223.
68. Francis E. Kearns, "Margaret Fuller and the Abolition Movement," *Journal of the History of Ideas* 25, no. 1 (1964): 123.
69. Margaret Fuller, William Henry Channing, Ralph Waldo Emerson, and James Freeman Clarke, *Memoirs of Margaret Fuller Ossoli* (Boston: Philips, Sampson, 1852), 194.
70. Fuller, "*New-York Daily Tribune* Dispatches," in *The Portable Margaret Fuller*, ed. Mary Kelley (New York: Penguin, 1994), 414.
71. Fuller, "*New-York Daily Tribune* Dispatches," 414.
72. Margaret Fuller, *Woman in the Nineteenth Century*, in Kelley, *Portable Margaret Fuller*, 237.
73. Fuller, "*New-York Daily Tribune* Columns," 387–90.
74. Thoreau, *Journal*, 18:404.
75. Walt Whitman, "To You," in *Leaves of Grass* (San Diego, CA: Word Cloud Classics, 2015), 218.
76. Ralph Waldo Emerson, *The Journals of Ralph Waldo Emerson: 1820–1872*, vol. 3 (Boston: Cambridge Riverside, 1910), 476.
77. Horace Bushnell, *The Vicarious Sacrifice, Grounded in Principles of Universal Obligation* (New York: Charles Scribner, 1866), 301–2.
78. Thoreau, *Journal*, 18:408.
79. Emerson, "The Over-Soul," in *WRWE*, 2:271.
80. Emerson, "Compensation," in *WRWE*, 2:124.

81. Ralph Waldo Emerson, *The Journals and Miscellaneous Notebooks of Ralph Waldo Emerson, 1835–1862*, vol. 12, ed. Linda Allardt (Cambridge, MA: Harvard University Press, 1976), 92.
82. Fuller, *Woman in the Nineteenth Century*, 233, 325.
83. Emerson, "Lecture on the Times," in *WRWE*, 1:280; Georg W. F. Hegel, *Phenomenology of Spirit*, trans. William Wallace (New York: Oxford University Press, 1971), 174–76; Emerson, "Compensation," 2:102.
84. Fuller, *Woman in the Nineteenth Century*, 269.
85. Philip Cafaro, "Transcendental Virtue," in *The Oxford Handbook of Transcendentalism*, ed. Joel Myerson, Sandra Harbert Petrulionis, and Laura Dassow Walls (New York: Oxford University Press, 2010), 539; Albert J. von Frank, "Mrs. Brackett's Verdict: Magic and Means in Transcendentalist Antislavery Work," in *Transient and Permanent: The Transcendentalist Movement and Its Contexts*, ed. Charles Capper and Conrad Edick Wright (Boston: Massachusetts Historical Society, 1999), 404.
86. Samuel A. Schreiner Jr., *The Concord Quartet: Alcott, Emerson, Hawthorne, Thoreau, and the Friendship That Freed the American Mind* (Hoboken, NJ: Wiley, 2006), 194.
87. George Fredrickson, *Inner Civil War: Northern Intellectuals and the Crisis of the Union* (New York: Harper & Row, 1965), 38, 41, 49.
88. Thoreau, *Journal*, 420.
89. Emerson, *Journals and Miscellaneous Notebooks*, 332; Ralph Waldo Emerson, *The Letters of Ralph Waldo Emerson*, ed. Ralph L. Rusk, vol. 5 (New York: Columba University Press, 1939), 178.
90. Mary Chesnut, *Mary Chesnut's Civil War*, ed. C. Vann Woodward (New Haven, CT: Yale University Press, 1981), 245.
91. George Fitzhugh, *Cannibals All! Or, Slaves without Masters* (Richmond, VA: A. Morris, 1857), 281, 284, 315, University of North Carolina at Chapel Hill: Documenting the American South, http://docsouth.unc.edu/southlit/fitzhughcan/fitzcan.html.
92. "The Sword of Justice," *Daily Dispatch* (Richmond, VA), February 11, 1865, Chronicling America: Historical American Newspapers, Library of Congress, http://chroniclingamerica.loc.gov/lccn/sn84024738/1865-02-11/ed-1/seq-1/.
93. War-Time Letters from Seth Rogers, M.D. Surgeon of the First South Carolina Afterwards the Thirty-Third U.S.C.T. 1862–1863, Florida History Online, https://history.domains.unf.edu/floridahistoryonline/projects-proj-b-p-html/cir-index-htm/war-time-letters-from-seth-rogers.
94. Thomas Wentworth Higginson, *Army Life in a Black Regiment* (East Lansing: Michigan State University Press, 1960), 41.
95. Edward Waldo Emerson, *Emerson in Concord: A Memoir Written for the "Social Circle" in Concord, Massachusetts* (Boston: Houghton, Mifflin, 1889), 76, 87.
96. Wirzbicki, "Black Transcendentalism," 272.
97. Edward Waldo Emerson, *Emerson in Concord*, 77.
98. Emerson, 78.
99. Emerson, 81.
100. Emerson, *Letters of Ralph Waldo Emerson*, 253; Edward Waldo Emerson, *Emerson in Concord*, 89.
101. Leonard Neufeldt, "Emerson and the Civil War," *Journal of English and Germanic Philology* 71, no. 4 (October 1972): 512; Emerson, "Resources," in *WRWE*, 8:142.

102. Quoted in Philip Van Doren Stern, *Henry David Thoreau: Writer and Rebel* (New York: Crowell, 1972), 115.
103. Stern, *Henry David Thoreau*; George M. Fredrickson, *The Inner Civil War: Northern Intellectuals and the Crisis of the Union* (New York: Harper & Row, 1965), 73.
104. Harriet Martineau, *Harriet Martineau's Autobiography* (Boston: J. R. Osgood, 1877), 381.
105. Fuller, *Woman in the Nineteenth Century*, 324.
106. Fuller, "*New-York Daily Tribune* Columns," and "*New-York Daily Tribune* Dispatches," 370–78 and 415–72, respectively.

CHAPTER 8

1. Daniel S. Malachuk, *Two Cities: The Political Thought of American Transcendentalism* (Lawrence: University Press of Kansas, 2016), 6–28, 32–33.
2. Malachuk, *Two Cities*, 163–82.
3. Oisín Keohane, *Cosmo-Nationalism: American, French and German Philosophy* (Edinburgh: Edinburgh University Press, 2018), 41–45; Johann Gottlieb Fichte, *Addresses to the German Nation*, trans. R. F. Jones and G. H. Turnbull (Chicago: Open Court Publishing, 1922), 13.
4. Thomas Bender, *A Nation among Nations: America's Place in World History* (New York: Hill and Wang, 2006), 126.
5. Abraham Lincoln, quoted in Bender, *Nation among Nations*, 126.
6. Keohane, *Cosmo-Nationalism*, 5.
7. Georg W. F. Hegel, *The Philosophy of History* (Chicago: University of Chicago Press, 1952), 315.
8. Bender, *Nation among Nations*, 140.
9. Hegel, *Philosophy of History*, 193.
10. Henry Clay Fish, *The Valley of Achor, a Door of Hope; or, the Grand Issues of the War. A Discourse Delivered on Thanksgiving Day, Nov. 26, 1863* (New York: Sheldon, 1863), 19.
11. David Hume, "Of National Characters," in *Political Discourses by David Hume*, 2nd ed. (Edinburgh: R. Fleming, 1752), 9.
12. David Hume, "Essay V: Of the First Principles of Government," Hume Texts Online, https://davidhume.org/texts/emp/fp.
13. Hume, "Discourse XII: Idea of a Perfect Commonwealth," in Hume, *Political Discourses*, 303–4.
14. John W. Cairns, "Legal Theory in the Scottish Enlightenment," *Cambridge Companion to the Scottish Enlightenment*, 2nd ed., ed. Alexander Broadie and Craig Smith (Cambridge, UK: Cambridge University Press, 2019), 222.
15. Henry Home, Lord Kames, *Historical Law-Tracts* (Edinburgh: A. Millar, 1758), University of Michigan Library, Eighteenth Century Collections Online, Ann Arbor: Text Creation Partnership, https://quod.lib.umich.edu/e/ecco/004841432.0001.001/1:4?rgn=div1;view=fulltext.
16. Kathryn D. Temple, "William Blackstone," lecture, American Society for Eighteenth-Century Studies, Denver, Colorado, March 2019.

17. Charles Bradford Bow, "In Pursuit of 'Moral Beauty' and Intellectual Pleasures: Dugald Stewart and Edinburgh's Literary Culture, 1762–1810," in *The Scottish Enlightenment and Literary Culture*, ed. Ralph, McLean, Ronnie Young, and Kenneth Simpson (Lewisburg, PA: Bucknell University Press, 2016), 162–63.
18. Henry David Thoreau, "Slavery in Massachusetts," in Henry David Thoreau, *A Yankee in Canada with Anti-Slavery and Reform Papers* (Boston: Houghton, Mifflin, 1892), 110.
19. Sophia A. Rosenfeld, *Common Sense: A Political History* (Cambridge, MA: Harvard University Press, 2011), 149–50.
20. Thomas Reid to Lord Kames, December 3, 1772, in *Philosophical Works, with Notes and Supplementary Dissertations by Sir William Hamilton, with an Introduction by Harry M. Bracken* (Edinburg ed., 1895; repr., Hildesheim: Georg Olms Verlagsbuchhandlung, 1967), 51.
21. Thomas Reid, "Essay 4th of the Liberty of Moral Agents," MS 3061/21, Thomas Reid Papers, GB 0231 University of Aberdeen, Special Collections.
22. Thoreau, "Civil Disobedience," in Henry David Thoreau, *A Yankee in Canada with Anti-Slavery and Reform Papers* (Boston: Houghton, Mifflin, 1892), 123.
23. Wilbur Fisk, *Hard Marching Every Day: The Civil War Letters of Private Wilbur Fisk*, ed. Emil Rosenblatt and Ruth Rosenblatt (Lawrence: University Press of Kansas, 1992), 128, 68.
24. George C. Burmeister Diaries, Nov. 29, 1862, Dec. 26, 1863, MSC0906, Civil War Diaries and Letters, University of Iowa Special Collections Department, Iowa City, Iowa.
25. Fisk, *Hard Marching Every Day*, 213.
26. Roswell Lamson to Katie, September 22, 1862, in *Lamson of the Gettysburg: The Civil War Letters of Lieutenant Roswell H. Lamson, U.S. Navy*, ed. James M. McPherson and Patricia R. McPherson (New York: Oxford University Press, 1997), 69.
27. Ralph Waldo Emerson, *The Journals and Miscellaneous Notebooks of Ralph Waldo Emerson, 1835–1862, vol. 12*, ed. Linda Alladrt (Cambridge, MA: Harvard University Press, 1976), 218.
28. Roswell to Katie, Nov. 25, 1860, in *Lamson of the Gettysburg*, 8.
29. Reid Mitchell, "Soldiering, Manhood, and Coming of Age: A Northern Volunteer," in *Divided Houses: Gender and the Civil War*, ed. Catherine Clinton (New York: Oxford University Press, 1992), 46, 53.
30. Daniel Walker Howe, *Making the American Self: Jonathan Edwards to Abraham Lincoln* (New York: Oxford University Press, 1997), 92–93.
31. "Anti-Lecompton Celebration," *Kansas (Lawrence) Herald of Freedom*, September 11, 1858, Chronicling America, Library of Congress, https://chroniclingamerica.loc.gov/lccn/2013218777; "Hayti—Designs upon Her Independence," *National Era*, July 4, 1850; "The National Loan," *Chicago Tribune*, May 2, 1865.
32. Henry Wilson, *History of the Rise and Fall of the Slave Power in America, vol. 3* (Boston: J. R. Osgood, 1872), 132.
33. Immanuel Kant, "Idea for a Universal History with Cosmopolitan Intent," in *The Philosophy of Kant: Immanuel Kant's Moral and Political Writings*, ed. Carl J. Friedrich (New York: Modern Library, 1993), 132–33.
34. Johann Gottfried von Herder, *Outlines of a Philosophy of the History of Man* (New

York: Random Shack, 2016), 186. Reprint edition of translation by T. Churchill, London, 1800.
35. Carlton J. H. Hayes, "Contributions of Herder to the Doctrine of Nationalism," *American Historical Review* 32, no. 4 (1927): 720.
36. Frank E. Manuel, introduction to abridged edition, in *Reflections on the Philosophy of the History of Mankind*, by Johann Gottfried von Herder (Chicago: University of Chicago Press, 1968), xiv.
37. Herder, *Philosophy of the History of Man*, 370–71, 306.
38. Herder, 375, 385.
39. Frederick C. Beiser, *The German Historicist Tradition* (New York: Oxford University Press, 2011), 158.
40. Clare Thérèse Pellerin, "The Philosophies of History of Herder and Hegel" (master's thesis, University of Saskatchewan, 2005).
41. Johann Gottfried von Herder, *Philosophical Writings*, ed. Michael N. Forster (Cambridge, UK: Cambridge University Press, 2002).
42. Georg W. F. Hegel, *The Philosophy of History* (Chicago: University of Chicago Press, 1952), 157.
43. Hegel, *Philosophy of History*, 161.
44. Stephen Houlgate, *An Introduction to Hegel: Freedom, Truth and History*, 2nd ed. (Hoboken, NJ: Wiley-Blackwell, 2005), 10.
45. Hegel, *Philosophy of History*, 161.
46. Hegel, 160, 162.
47. Hegel, 162, 169.
48. Hegel, 176.
49. Hegel, 161.
50. Hegel, 171.
51. Georg W. F. Hegel, *Philosophy of Right* (Chicago: University of Chicago Press, 1952); Dudley Knowles, *Routledge Philosophy Guidebook to Hegel and the "Philosophy of Right"* (London: Routledge, 2002), 14.
52. Hegel, *Philosophy of History*, 199.
53. Hegel, *Philosophy of History*, 177, 166.
54. Hegel, 189.
55. David Armitage, Thomas Bender, Leslie Butler, Don H. Doyle, Susan-Mary Grant, Charles S. Maier, Jörg Nagler, Paul Quigley, and Jay Sexton, "Interchange: Nationalism and Internationalism in the Era of the Civil War," *Journal of American History* 98, no. 2 (2011): 455–89.
56. James A. Good, "A 'World-Historical Idea': The St. Louis Hegelians and the Civil War," *Journal of American Studies* 34, no. 3 (December 2000): 447–64.
57. Margaret Fuller, *Margaret Fuller, American Romantic: A Selection from her Writings and Correspondence*, ed. Perry Miller (Garden City, NY: Doubleday, 1963), 229.
58. Margaret Fuller, "*New-York Daily Tribune* Dispatches," in *The Portable Margaret Fuller*, ed. Mary Kelley (New York: Penguin Books, 1994), 412.
59. Margaret Fuller, "Woman in the Nineteenth Century," in Kelley, *Portable Margaret Fuller*, 326.
60. Ralph Waldo Emerson, "Circles," in *Works of Ralph Waldo Emerson*, 12 vols. (Boston: Houghton, Mifflin, 1903), 2:302 (hereafter cited as *WRWE*).

61. Emerson, "The Poet," in *WRWE*, 3:37.
62. Frances Winwar, *American Giant: Walt Whitman and His Times* (New York: Harper & Brothers, 1941), 188.
63. Adam Gurowski, *Diary from March 4, 1861, to November 12, 1862* (Boston: Lee and Shepard, 1862), 65.
64. Gurowski, *Diary from March 4, 1861*, 65.
65. Armitage et al., "Interchange."
66. Armitage et al., "Interchange."
67. Hegel, *Philosophy of Right*, 56.
68. Hegel, 83, 80–81.
69. Emerson, "Self-Reliance" and "Spiritual Laws," in *WRWE*, 2:88, 135, respectively.
70. Emerson, "Character," in *WRWE*, 3:91.
71. Thomas Wentworth Higginson, *Massachusetts in Mourning: A Sermon, Preached in Worcester, on Sunday June 4, 1854* (Boston: James Munroe, 1854).
72. Emerson, "Politics," in *WRWE*, 3:212.
73. Emerson, "Politics," 215–17.
74. Malachuk, *Two Cities*, 163–87.
75. Fichte, *Addresses to the German Nation*, 10.
76. Abraham Lincoln, "A House Divided," Springfield, Illinois, June 16, 1858, UVA, Miller Center, https://millercenter.org/the-presidency/presidential-speeches/june-16-1858-house-divided-speech.
77. Randall Fuller, *From Battlefields Rising: How the Civil War Transformed American Literature* (New York: Oxford University Press, 2011).
78. Elisa De Togni, "The Abolitionist's John Brown: Martyrdom through Militancy and the Onset of Civil War," American Battlefield Trust, https://www.battlefields.org/learn/articles/abolitionists-john-brown, updated December 3, 2024.
79. Malachuk, *Two Cities*, 163–87.
80. Ralph Waldo Emerson, *The Letters of Ralph Waldo Emerson*, ed. Ralph L. Rusk, vol. 5 (New York: Columba University Press, 1939), 253.
81. Emerson, "Heroism," in *WRWE*, 2:249–50.
82. Margaret Fuller, Letter to William Ellery Channing, in *The Letters of Margaret Fuller: 1839–1841*, ed. Robert N. Hudspeth (Ithaca, NY: Cornell University Press, 2018), 108.
83. Harry S. Stout, *Upon the Altar of the Nation: A Moral History of the Civil War* (New York: Viking, 2006), 114–16, 338, 347.
84. Horace Bushnell, *The Vicarious Sacrifice, Grounded in Principles of Universal Obligation* (New York: Charles Scribner, 1866), 301–2.
85. Maria Lydig Daly, *Diary of a Union Lady, 1861–1865*, ed. Harold Earl Hammond (New York: Funk & Wagnalls, 1962), 354–55.
86. John W. Darby Letters, May 18, 1864, Auburn University Libraries Special Collections and Archives, Auburn, AL.
87. William H. Ball Letters (1862–64), March 4, 1862, Auburn University Libraries Special Collections and Archives.
88. Theodore Ayrault Dodge, *On Campaign with the Army of the Potomac: The Civil War Journal of Theodore Ayrault Dodge*, ed. Stephen W. Sears (New York: Cooper Square, 2001), 7; George Washington Beidelman to his father, October 15–21, 1862, Special Collections and College Archives, Gettysburg College, PA.

89. Earl J. Hess, *The Union Soldier in Battle: Enduring the Ordeal of Combat* (Lawrence: University Press of Kansas, 1997), ix.
90. Stout, *Upon the Altar of the Nation*, 347.
91. Philip Cafaro, "Transcendental Virtue," in *The Oxford Handbook of Transcendentalism*, ed. Joel Myerson, Sandra Harbert Petrulionis, and Laura Dassow Walls (New York: Oxford University Press, 2010), 538.
92. Hegel, *Philosophy of History*, 160.
93. Hegel, *Philosophy of Right*, 35.
94. Hegel, *Philosophy of History*, 343.
95. Hegel, 344.
96. Georg W. F. Hegel, *Hegel's Philosophy of Mind*, trans. William Wallace (London: Oxford University Press, 1971), 29.
97. Hegel, *Philosophy of Mind*, 172.
98. Emerson, "History," in *WRWE*, 2:4.
99. Quoted in Earl J. Hess, *Liberty, Virtue, and Progress: Northerners and Their War for the Union* (Bronx, NY: Fordham University Press, 1997), 43.
100. Walt Whitman, "Letter to Nat Bloom and Fred Gray, March 19, 1863," in *Civil War Poetry and Prose* (Mineola, NY: Dover, 1995), 63; George M. Fredrickson, *The Inner Civil War: Northern Intellectuals and the Crisis of the Union* (New York: Harper & Row, 1965), 97.
101. Henry Ward Beecher, *Prayers from Plymouth Pulpit* (New York: Pilgrim Press, 1867), 285; Henry Ward Beecher, *Norwood; or, Village Life in New England* (New York: Charles Scribner, 1868), 499; William Henderson Journal 4, January 1–July 20, 1864, Civil War Diaries and Letters, Special Collections, University of Iowa Digital Library, https://aspace.lib.uiowa.edu/repositories/2/archival_objects/171964.
102. Fredrickson, *Inner Civil War*; Louis Menand, *The Metaphysical Club: A Story of Ideas in America* (New York: Farrar, Straus and Giroux, 2001).
103. John Hollander, ed., Notes, in *American Poetry: The Nineteenth Century*, vol. 1 (New York: Library of America, 1993), 1056.
104. Bronson Alcott, "Orphic Sayings," in *Selected Writings of the Transcendentalists*, ed. (New York: New American Library, 1966), 316.
105. Hollander, *American Poetry*, 739, 725.
106. James J. Harris to his friend Burton, August 24, 1863, Walter J. Bone Collection, Private Collections, State Archives of North Carolina.
107. Hollander, *American Poetry*, 725, 824, 780, 834.
108. Ernest Hemingway, *A Farewell to Arms* (New York: Charles Scribner's Sons, 1929), 185; Eugene B. Sledge, *With the Old Breed: At Peleliu and Okinawa* (New York: Ballantine, 1981), 146.

CHAPTER 9

1. Daniel S. Malachuk, *Two Cities: The Political Thought of American Transcendentalism* (Lawrence: University Press of Kansas, 2016), 44.
2. Godfried van Benthem van den Bergh, "Herder and the Idea of a Nation," *Human Figurations: Long-Term Perspectives on the Human Condition* 7, no. 1 (May 2018), http://hdl.handle.net/2027/spo.11217607.0007.103.

3. George Bancroft, *The History of the United States of America from the Discovery of the Continent*, ed. Russel B. Nye (Chicago: University of Chicago Press, 1966), 270, 137, 368.
4. George Bancroft, "An Oration Delivered before the Adelphi Society of Williamstown College in August, 1835: The Office of the People in Art, Government, and Religion," in *The American Intellectual Tradition: A Sourcebook*, vol. 1, *1630–1865*, 4th ed., ed. David A. Hollinger and Charles Capper (New York: Oxford University Press, 2001), 289.
5. Kurt Mueller-Vollmer, *Transatlantic Crossings and Transformations: German-American Cultural Transfer from the 18th to the End of the 19th Century* (New York: Peter Lang, 2015), 103–22.
6. Johann Gottfried von Herder, *Outlines of a Philosophy of the History of Man* (New York: Random Shack, 2016), 376, 385. Reprint edition of translation by T. Churchill, London, 1800.
7. Herder, *Philosophy of the History of Man*, 188.
8. Herder, 187.
9. Emerson, "Nature," in *Works of Ralph Waldo Emerson*, 12 vols. (Boston: Houghton, Mifflin, 1903), 3:179.
10. Emerson, "Nature," *Works of Ralph Waldo Emerson*, 12 vols. (Boston: Houghton, Mifflin, 1903), 1:10, 23.
11. Emerson, 10.
12. Henry D. Thoreau, *"A Yankee in Canada" with Anti-Slavery and Reform Papers* (Boston: Houghton, Mifflin, 1892), 111.
13. Emerson, "Nature," 1:34, 50.
14. *The Writings of Henry David Thoreau*, vol. 18, *Journal, March 2, 1859–November 30, 1859* (Boston: Houghton Mifflin, 1906), 404–7.
15. *Crime against Kansas: Speech of Hon. Charles Sumner in the Senate of the United States, 19th and 20th May, 1856* (Boston: John P. Jewett, 1856), 3–4, 14, 15, 28.
16. Margaret Fuller, *Summer on the Lakes*, in *The Portable Margaret Fuller*, ed. Mary Kelley (New York: Penguin, 1994), 85–86.
17. Henry Conrad Brokmeyer, *A Mechanic's Diary* (Washington, DC: E. C. Brokmeyer, 1910), 14.
18. Thoreau, *Yankee in Canada*, 115.
19. Olmsted, Vaux & Co., *Preliminary Report to the Commissioners for the Laying Out of a Park in Brooklyn, New York: Being a Consideration of Circumstances of Site and Other Considerations Affecting the Design of Public Pleasure Grounds* (Brooklyn: I. Van Anden's Print, 1866), 5, 7.
20. Douglas Sloan, *The Scottish Enlightenment and the American College Ideal* (New York: Teachers College Press, Columbia University, 1971), 127.
21. George Bancroft Papers, box 64, folders 6 and 7, Massachusetts Historical Society, Boston, MA.
22. Fuller, *Summer on the Lakes*, 73, 79–80.
23. Andrew Menard, *Sight Unseen: How Frémont's First Expedition Changed the American Landscape* (Lincoln: University of Nebraska Press, 2012).
24. Immanuel Kant, *"Observations on the Feeling of the Beautiful and Sublime" and Other Writings (1764)*, ed. Patrick Frierson and Paul Guyer (New York: Cambridge University Press, 2011).

25. William Gilpin, "The Cordillera of the Sierra Madre," *Kansas Herald of Freedom* (Wakarusa, KS), November 27, 1858, and Gilpin, "An Address, Delivered at Kansas City, Nov. 15, 1858, on the Gold Production of America and the Sierra San Juan," *Kansas Herald of Freedom*, January 8, 1859.
26. Daniel Ross Chandler, "Henry Ward Beecher: A Nation's Tribune," paper presented at the Gettysburg Conference on Rhetorical Transactions in the Civil War Era, Gettysburg, PA, June 24–25, 1983, ERIC database, https://eric.ed.gov/?q=Henry+ward+beecher&id=ED236713.
27. William C. Beecher and Samuel Scoville, *A Biography of Rev. Henry Ward Beecher* (New York: Charles L. Webster, 1888), 381.
28. Henry Ward Beecher, *Kansas Herald of Freedom*, September 11, 1858.
29. "The Great West, by Miss Fannie J. Barbour," *Kansas Herald of Freedom*, September 3, 1859.
30. Gilpin, "Cordillera of the Sierra Madre."
31. "The Economy of Nature," *Kanzas News* (Emporia, Kansas), September 25, 1858 (spelling of Kanzas in the original).
32. "Love of the Beautiful," *Spirit of the Age*, reprinted in *Independent* (Oskaloosa, Kansas), September 12, 1860.
33. "Twin Mound Harmonic College Circular: Articles of the Twin Mound Harmonic College Association," *Kansas Herald of Freedom*, August 21, 1858.
34. John Brown Jr., quoted in *The Life and Letters of John Brown, Liberator of Kansas, and Martyr of Virginia*, ed. Franklin B. Sanborn (Boston: Robert Brothers, 1885), 188.
35. Eric Foner, *Free Soil, Free Labor, Free Men: The Ideology of the Republican Party before the Civil War* (Oxford, UK: Oxford University Press, 1995).
36. Edwin P. Whipple, ed. *Christianity and Humanity: A Series of Sermons by Thomas Starr King* (Boston: Houghton, Mifflin, 1887), 286.
37. Winfield Scott, quoted in Charles W. Wendte, *Thomas Starr King: Patriot and Preacher* (Boston: Beacon, 1921), 223.
38. Joshua David Bellin, "Native American Rights," in *The Oxford Handbook of Transcendentalism*, ed. Joel Myerson, Sandra Harbert Petrulionis, and Laura Dassow Walls (New York: Oxford University Press, 2010), 198.
39. Quoted in Bellin, "Native American Rights," 206.
40. Molly McGarry, *Ghosts of Futures Past: Spiritualism and the Cultural Politics of Nineteenth-Century America* (Berkeley: University of California Press, 2008), 77.
41. Bellin, "Native American Rights," 199.
42. Ralph Waldo Emerson, Letter to Martin Van Buren, President of the United States, 1838, Ralph Waldo Emerson, Miscellanies, https://emersoncentral.com/texts/miscellanies/letter-to-president-van-buren.
43. Quoted in Bellin, "Native American Rights," 200.
44. Burmeister Diary 1864, January 1, 1864, March 27, 1864.
45. George Cram, *Soldiering with Sherman: Civil War Letters of George F. Cram*, ed. Jennifer Cain Bohrnstedt (DeKalb: Northern Illinois University Press, 2000), 40; Burmeister Diary 1862, September 30, 1862.
46. Andrew F. Davis Diary, 1861–62, March 2, 1862, Civil War Diaries and Letters, University of Iowa Special Collections Department, Iowa City, Iowa; Cram, *Soldiering with Sherman*, 104.
47. Wilbur Fisk, *Hard Marching Every Day: The Civil War Letters of Private Wilbur Fisk,*

1861–1865, ed. Emil Rosenblatt and Ruth Rosenblatt (Lawrence: University Press of Kansas, 1983), 8, 65–66.
48. Fisk, *Hard Marching Every Day*, 26.
49. Henry C. Work, "The Little Major," in *The Civil War Songbook*, ed. Richard Crawford (New York: Dover, 1977), 88.
50. John Greenleaf Whittier, "The Battle Autumn of 1862," in *Civil War Poetry: An Anthology*, ed. Paul Negri (Mineola, NY: Dover, 1997), 18.
51. Burmeister Diary 1863, Dec. 31, 1863.
52. Ralph Waldo Emerson, "Perpetual Forces," in *The Selected Lectures of Ralph Waldo Emerson*, eds. Joel Myerson and Ronald A. Bosco (Athens: University of Georgia Press, 2005), 293.
53. Alfred Bellard, *Gone for a Soldier: The Civil War Memoirs of Private Alfred Bellard*, ed. David Herbert Donald (Boston: Little, Brown, 1975), xii.
54. George Washington Beidelman to his father, 15–21 October 1862, Special Collections and College Archives, Gettysburg College, Gettysburg, PA.

CONCLUSION

1. Ralph Waldo Emerson, "Address at the Dedication of the Soldiers' Monument in Concord, April 19, 1867," in *Works of Ralph Waldo Emerson*, 12 vols. (Boston: Houghton, Mifflin, 1903), 11:355.
2. Louis Menand, *The Metaphysical Club: A Story of Ideas in America* (New York: Farrar, Straus and Giroux, 2001); Randall Fuller, *From Battlefields Rising: How the Civil War Transformed American Literature* (New York: Oxford University Press, 2011).
3. Joshua Lawrence Chamberlain, *The Passing of the Armies: An Account of the Final Campaign of the Army of the Potomac, Based upon Personal Reminiscences of the Fifth Army Corps* (New York: G. P. Putnam's Sons, 1915), 260, 271.
4. Horace Porter, *Campaigning with Grant* (New York: Bantam, 1991), 355.
5. Wilbur Fisk, *Hard Marching Every Day: The Civil War Letters of Private Wilbur Fisk, 1861–1865*, ed. Emil Rosenblatt and Ruth Rosenblatt (Lawrence: University Press of Kansas, 1983), 352.
6. Len Gougeon, "Politics and Economics," in *The Oxford Handbook of Transcendentalism*, ed. Joel Myerson, Sandra Harbert Petrulionis, and Laura Dassow Walls (New York: Oxford University Press, 2010), 150.
7. Alfred Bellard, *Gone for a Soldier: The Civil War Memoirs of Private Alfred Bellard*, ed. David Herbert Donald (Boston: Little, Brown, 1975), xvi; George M. Frederickson, *The Inner Civil War: Northern Intellectuals and the Crisis of the Union* (New York: Harper & Row, 1965), 172; Louis Menand, *Metaphysical Club*.
8. Menand, *Metaphysical Club*.
9. Richard Lewis Ashhurst, *Address to the Survivors' Association of the 150th Regiment, Pennsylvania Volunteers. Read at Gettysburg, Sept. 25th, 1896* (Philadelphia: Allen, Lane & Scott, 1896), 9–10.
10. Stephen Crane, *"The Little Regiment" and Other Civil War Stories* (Mineola, NY: Dover, 1997); John Hollander, ed., *American Poetry: The Nineteenth Century*, vol. 2 (New York: Library of America, 1993), 603.

11. Tony Horwitz, *Confederates in the Attic: Dispatches from the Unfinished Civil War* (New York: Vintage Departures, 1998), 126.
12. Kent Gramm, *Somebody's Darling: Essays on the Civil War* (Bloomington: Indiana University Press, 2002), 144.
13. Brian Wolfel, "How Emerson and Thoreau's Transcendentalism Could Inspire a Re-Awakening (and Consensus?) after the COVID-19 Pandemic," *Resilience*, 1 June 2020, https://www.resilience.org/stories/2020-06-01/how-emerson-and-thoreaus-transcendentalism-could-inspire-a-re-awakening-and-consensus-after-the-covid-19-pandemic/.

Index

abolition: Christian denominations and varying views of, 77–78; gender philosophy and Southern white males' views of, 85; Transcendentalist movement and importance of, overview, 3, 6, 13; Transcendentalists on bildung as universal, 132–34; and Transcendentalists on policy reform, 182–86; and Transcendentalists' support of Civil War, 186–92; Unitarian church and role in, 12–13
absolute spirit, 48, 50, 69, 71, 78, 82, 129, 149, 196, 206
academia. *See also individual names of higher education institutions*: Columbia College and early political science classes, 123; Common Sense philosophy in, 24–27, 60–61; education of females, 89–93, 97–99, 103; education of males, 81, 87–88; education reform due to Transcendentalist philosophy, 78–82, 126; elective system of, 57, 78–79; and German philosophy of character, 52–56, 57–58
active vs. passive separation of mental powers, 20, 27–28
Addresses to the German Nation (Fichte), 212
Adelphi Society, 225
Aesthetic Papers, as Transcendentalist publication, 14
aesthetics: and Germany philosophy of character, 40, 43–45; Kant on gender and aesthetics, 88–91; vs. utility, in nature, 230–31
Agassiz, Louis, 53, 172, 173, 230
Aids to Reflection (Coleridge), 55, 57, 78
Alcott, A. Bronson: Concord School of Philosophy, 244; *Conversations with Children on the Gospels*, 91; on discipline for children, 126; family of, and importance to Transcendentalists, 12; Hegel's influence on, 16; on Indigenous peoples, 235; on slavery, 184; and theories of political character of nation, 220; and Transcendentalist philosophy of character, 79–80; and women's rights, 91, 101
Alcott, Abigail, 101
Alcott, Louisa May, 12, 91, 92, 98, 126, 187, 220
Alexander the Great, 129
American Colonization Society, 178
American Notes (Dickens), 80–81
The American Quarterly, German philosophy and influence on, 56
American Slavery: A Protest against American Slavery (Unitarian church), 13
Andrew, John A., 152
Anti-Slavery Bugle, German philosophy and influence on, 57
Anti-Slavery Society, 156, 168
Appomattox, Civil War surrender ceremonies, 122, 242, 243
a priori principles, Kant on, 41, 44

289

Arnim, Bettine Brentano von, 66, 102
Aryanism, 143–44
Ashhurst, Richard, 246
atheism, 6, 25, 38. *See also* religion and religious thought
Atlantic Monthly, as Transcendentalist publication, 14

Bacon, Francis, 4, 63, 66
Bailyn, Bernard, 9
Ball, William, 216
Bancroft, George, 17, 52, 53, 57, 81, 225, 230
Barbour, Fannie J., 232
"The Base of All Metaphysics" (Whitman), 15
Beattie, James, 10, 25
Beck, Carl, 52
Beecher, Henry Ward, 12, 184, 213, 219, 232
Beidelman, George Washington, 216, 240
Beiser, Frederick, 4
Belasco, Susan, 14
Bellard, Alfred, 240
Bellin, Joshua David, 235
Bender, Thomas, 195, 196, 208, 210
Benthem van den Bergh, Godfried van, 224
Bergstraesser, Arnold, 100, 115
Berkeley, George, 34, 41
Bernasconi, Robert, 138–39
Bierce, Ambrose, 246
bildung. *See also* femininity and gender, philosophies of; German philosophy of character; masculinity and bildung in Civil War; Transcendentalist philosophies of character: bildungsroman genre of writing, 17, 93, 173; and Channing on self-culture, 59–61, 76, 80; and Christian denominations on antebellum reform, 77–78; Christ metaphor for, 179–82; Civil War letter by unidentified women as application of, 103–4; defined, 60; and educational reform, 78–82; and German philosophy of character, 17, 46–49; Goethe's views and Fuller's interpretation, 15, 83–84, 93–103, 105; race and character, Transcendentalists on bildung as universal, 132–34; self-culture concept of Channing and influence on, 59–61, 76–77, 80; Transcendentalists on universalism of, 154–56; universality of moral character as Transcendentalist ideal, 82
Black Adelphic Union society, 155
Blackstone, William, 198

Bleeding Kansas, 184–85
Blumenbach, Johann Friedrich, 142, 143, 156
"Boston Hymn" (Emerson), 187
Boston Quarterly Review, as Transcendentalist publication, 14
Bow, Charles Bradford, 10
Bowen, Francis, 26
Bridgman, Laura, 80–81
Brisbane, Addie, 83
Brisbane, Benjamin, 83
Brockhaus Enzyklopädie, 57
Brokmeyer, Henry Conrad, 1, 3, 9, 15, 208, 228–29
Brooks, Preston, 228
"Brother, When Will You Come Back?" (song), 112–13
Brown, John, Jr., 233
Brown, John, Sr.: Harper's Ferry raid, 161, 171, 185, 190, 213–14; and nation's geographic character, 228, 234, 240; and political character of nation, 193, 213–14; Transcendentalists' views on, 161, 171, 179, 181, 185–86, 189, 190
Brown, Thomas, 8, 17, 27, 35–36, 38, 62–63, 71, 72
Brown University, 60, 79
Bryant, William Cullen, 15
Buckminster, Eliza, 15
Buck-Morss, Susan, 150–51
Buehrens, John, 7
Buffon, Georges-Louis Leclerc de, 138
Burgess, John W., 210
Burmeister, George, 117–18, 200, 237, 239
Burns, Anthony, 184, 188, 212
Burr, Aaron, 25
Burschenschaften, 50
Bushnell, Horace, 12, 117, 180–81, 214–15

Cabot, James Elliot, 52, 53
Cafaro, Philip, 216
Calamus (Whitman), 70–71
Cambridge Platonists, 248
Camper, Petrus, 142
Carlyle, Thomas, 15, 20, 94, 229, 248
Carrington, Henry, 127–28
Carus, Carl Gustav, 157
Carver, Jonathan, 172–73
cause and effect: Hume on, 21, 38; Reid on, 30
Central Park (New York City), 229
Chamberlain, Joshua, 117, 122, 243
Channing, William Ellery: Fuller's biography

co-written by, 102; Herder's influence on, 17; Higginson's relationship to, 187; on self-culture, 59–61, 76, 80; Transcendentalist movement and importance of, 12; and Transcendentalists' views on race, 160, 167, 175, 178–79; "Unitarian Christianity," 14
Channing, William Henry, 155
character. *See* bildung; German philosophy of character; Transcendentalist philosophies of character
The Characteristics of the Present Age (Fichte), 55
Cherokee removal policy, 166, 168–69, 175, 183, 235, 236
Chesnut, Mary, 124, 186
Chicago Tribune, on slavery, 201–2
Child, Lydia Maria, 235
Children of Adam (Whitman), 71
Christian Examiner: German philosophy and influence on, 56; Walker as editor of, 26
Christianity: bildung and Christian denominations on antebellum reform, 77–78; bildung and Christ metaphor, 179–82; on death, 129; Hegel and Lutheranism on race, 149; Kant and Protestant perspective on race, 139; politics and spiritual principle of state, 193, 196, 198, 203–8, 215–22; Transcendentalists on missionary work, 175
"Circles" (Emerson), 209
"Civilization in Relation to the Physical Circumstances That Have Contributed Thereto" (McCune), 155
Civil War. *See also* masculinity and bildung in Civil War; political character of the nation: abolition and Transcendentalists' support of Civil War, 186–92; Appomattox surrender ceremonies, 122, 242, 243; Battle of Gettysburg, 112; bildung concept and Christian denominations on antebellum reform, 77–78; Black soldiers in, 108, 132–33, 144, 153, 187; book sales during, 120, 172; Forty-Eighters' and influence on, 51; gymnasium aspect of self-culture and masculinity, 81; letter by unidentified women as application of bildung, 103–4; and political character of the nation, 195–96, 200–202, 213–22; post–Civil War events, 242–43; soldiers' perception of nature and nation's geographic character, 237–40; study of, 248–50; and

Transcendentalists' legacy, 244–48; and Transcendentalists on sentiment and moral feeling, 35–36; and Transcendentalists on universal moral character, 35–36, 76, 82; Whitman on, 68, 70, 76
Clarke, James Freeman: Civil War masculinity and gender philosophy, 119, 122, 123; Fuller's biography co-written by, 102; German philosophy and influence on, 55; and nation's geographic character, 235; *Self-Culture: Physical, Intellectual, Moral, and Spiritual*, 244; Transcendentalist movement and importance of, 12; and Transcendentalist philosophy of character, 72; and Transcendentalist views on race, 155
class, freedom and rights tied to property ownership, 85, 236
classification system, Linnaeus on, 138
Clausewitz, Carl von, 106, 123–24, 125, 130
Clay, Henry, 77
climate, race theories about, 137, 140, 158–59, 160, 170
coeducational classes, Transcendentalists on, 80
Cogswell, Joseph, 52, 53, 81
Coleridge, Samuel Taylor, 15, 17, 20, 29, 31, 40, 55, 57, 78
Colfax, Richard, 140–41, 143
Columbia College (University), 123, 210
Commentaries (Blackstone), 198
Common Sense (Paine), 14
Common Sense school. *See* Scottish philosophy of character
Compromise of 1850, 184
Concord School of Philosophy, 244
"Confessions of a Fair Saint" (Goethe), 97, 114
Congregationalists, 13
Conversations of Goethe with Eckermann (Fuller's translation), 94
Conversations with Children on the Gospels (Peabody and B. Alcott), 91
Conway, Moncure, 12, 16, 189, 190, 232
Cook, James, 135
Corsan, William, 124–25
Cousin, Victor, 15, 17, 26
Cram, George, 117, 237
Cranch, Christopher Pearse, 235
Crane, Stephen, 246–47
credit system, in American universities, 79
Critique of Pure Reason (Kant), 41, 55

Crummell, Alexander, 134, 155
Cudworth, Ralph, 55
cultural expression of Civil War era: about nation's geographic character, 238–39; masculinity and bildung exhibited by, 111–14, 118–21; racist drawings/paintings, 143

Daly, Maria Lydig, 215
Dana, Charles Anderson, 187
Darby, John W., 215–16
Davis, Andrew F., 237
death: Civil War-era views of, 129–30, 218–22; rural cemeteries and nation's geographic character, 229–30; Whitman on, 68
Declaration of Independence, 24–25
De l'Allemagne (*Germany*, de Staël and Schlegel), 51, 52
Descartes, René, 51, 54
The Dial: Fuller's writing in, 94, 100; German philosophy and influence on, 56; Transcendentalist movement and importance of, 14
Dickens, Charles, 80–81
"didactic Enlightenment," 10
discipline and self-discipline, during Civil War era, 126–29
"Divinity School Address" (Emerson), 28, 54
Dix, Dorothea, 12, 80, 81, 124
Dodge, Theodore Ayrault, 216
"Don't send him off to war . . ." (song), 118
Douglas, Stephen, 194
Douglass, Frederick: Civil War masculinity and gender philosophy, 108; *A Narrative of the Life of Frederick Douglass*, 166–67; *New-York Daily Tribune* and autobiography of, 167; on race and character, 152; and theories of political character of nation, 193; Transcendentalist movement and importance of, 6; and Transcendentalist philosophy of character, 77; and Transcendentalists' views on race, 168, 178, 190, 191
"Dragon-Fly" (Herder), 57
Dred Scott case, 184, 198

Echoes of Harper's Ferry (book), Transcendentalists' contributions to, 185
Eddy, Mary Baker, 244
Edinburgh Review, Hamilton's essays in, 27
education, Civil War-era book sales on, 120. *See also* academia
Edwards, Jonathan, 65, 85

1848 Revolutions, 16, 195, 209
Elective Affinities (Goethe), 94
electives, in American universities, 57, 78–79
elementary school, Transcendentalists on, 80
Elements of Logick; or a Summary of the General Principles and Different Modes of Reasoning (Hedge), 25–26, 37
The Elements of Logic (Tappan), 55
The Elements of Moral Science (Wayland), 60, 61
Elements of the Philosophy of Right (Hegel), 16, 17, 55, 207
Elements on the Philosophy of the Human Mind (Stewart), 25, 26
Eliot, Charles W., 79
Emerson, Edward Waldo (son), 188–89
Emerson, Ellen Louisa Tucker (first wife), 219–20
Emerson, Lidian (second wife), 101, 183
Emerson, Ralph Waldo, 42, 242; on Brown, 185–86, 189; Civil War masculinity and gender philosophy, 113; on emotion and character, 85; German philosophy and influence on, 44, 45, 51, 54, 55; on Goethe, 93–95, 100; on materialists vs. idealists, 20, 42, 66; nature and nation's geographic character, 227–30, 232, 235, 236, 239; Scottish Common Sense and influence on, 20, 26–29, 36–39; supernatural (metaphysical) interpretation of Scottish and German philosophies, 60–69, 71, 72, 74–75, 77, 79; and theories of political character of nation, 201, 209, 211–12, 214, 218, 219–20; Transcendentalist movement and importance of, 1, 8, 12, 13, 14, 16–17; and Transcendentalists' legacy, 244, 249; on women's rights, 101–2
Emerson, Ralph Waldo, on race: and Christ metaphor for bildung, 179–82; on Civil War, 187–92; European thought on race and influence on, 158; and Fuller's views on race, 173, 175; and policy approach to abolition, 182–86; racial theory of, overview, 161–69; study of, 154–56; and Thoreau's views on race, 171, 172
Emerson, Ralph Waldo, written works: "Boston Hymn," 187; "Circles," 209; "Divinity School Address," 28, 54; "Lecture on the Times," 182; "Nature," 30–31, 172; "The Over-Soul," 29–30, 40, 42
Emerson, Waldo (son), 219–20

Emerson, William (brother), 52
Émile (Rousseau), 48, 89
Empirical Psychology (Hickok), 55
empiricism. *See* realism
Encyclopædia Americana: A Popular Dictionary of Arts, Literature, History, Politics, and Biography (Lieber), 57
Engels, Friedrich, 16
An Essay on the History of Civil Society (Ferguson), 137
Essay on the Understanding (Locke), 25
Essays on the Intellectual Powers (Reid), 25, 26
Essays on Truth (Beattie), 25
Everett, Edward, 52, 53, 124, 173, 210

Faraday, Michael, 220, 239
Faust (Goethe), 94, 96, 98–100, 105, 114–16
femininity and gender, philosophies of, 83–105; and bildung, 76–77; Civil War as philosophical framework, overview, 15, 17; Civil War letter by unidentified women as application of bildung, 103–4; coeducational classes, Transcendentalists on, 80; education of females, 89–93, 97–99, 103; Emerson on women's rights, 101–2; female education, Kant on, 89–91; female education, nineteenth century thought about, 86, 91–93; female mediums and public speaking, 73; Fuller on women's intuition, 93; Goethe's views and Fuller's interpretation, 15, 83–84, 93–103, 105; Kant on gender and aesthetics, 88–91; male and female character qualities, nineteenth century thought about, 83–85; phrenology on, 142; Scottish Common Sense on gender, culture, and societal advancement, 85–88; societal roles, Germany philosophy on, 47; and Transcendentalists' views on race, 159, 174; women's freedom and rights during Civil War era, 85, 107, 109
Ferguson, Adam, 137
Feuerbach, Ludwig, 6
Fichte, Johann Gottlieb, 8, 15, 55, 56, 123, 193, 194–95, 212
54th Massachusetts Volunteer Infantry, 133, 144, 187
Figal, Sara Eigen, 123
Finley, Robert, 183
1st South Carolina Colored Volunteers, 132–33, 153, 187
Fish, Henry Clay, 196

Fisk, Wilbur, 106, 112–13, 117, 128, 200–201, 237–38, 243–44
Fitzhugh, George, 186
Flying Pigeon (Native American woman), 174
Follen, Charles, 50, 52, 53, 81, 155
Foner, Eric, 233
Forty-Eighters, 50–51
Fourier, Charles, 186
Fox sisters, 73
Francis, Convers, 235
Franklin, Benjamin, 85
Frederickson, George, 219
Frederick the Great, 224
freedom. *See* femininity and gender, philosophies of; political character of the nation; race and character, European inheritance on; race and character in America
Free Soil Party, 184–85
Frémont, John Charles, 231
French Revolution, 10, 11, 202, 224
Fruitlands, 101, 186
Fugitive Slave Law, 184, 188
Fuller, Margaret: and abolitionist movement, 190–92; and Christ metaphor for bildung, 180–82; death of, 179; on Douglass, 167; early life of, 98; Emerson on, 102; German philosophy and influence on, 45; Great Lakes trip of, 173, 235; in Italy, 176–77; nature and nation's geographic character, 228, 230–31, 235; paranormal (spiritual) interpretation of Scottish and German philosophies, 60–62, 70–76; racial theory of, overview, 172–79; Scottish Common Sense and influence on, 27, 35–36; study of, 154–56; and theories of political character of nation, 209, 214; Transcendentalist movement and importance of, 8, 12, 16–17; on women's education, 92–93; women's rights and interpretation of Goethe's views, 15, 83–84, 93–103, 105
Fuller, Margaret, written works: *Conversations of Goethe with Eckermann* (translation), 94; *Summer on the Lakes*, 73, 172; "What Fits a Man to be a Voter? Is It to Be White Within, or White Without," 177–78; *Woman in the Nineteenth Century*, 15, 94
Fuller, Randall, 7, 213, 222, 243

Gall, Franz Joseph, 142
Gandhi, Mahatma, 214

Garrison, William Lloyd, 168, 171, 183, 185, 186, 189, 192, 234
Gemüth, Hegel on, 49–50
gender roles. *See* femininity and gender, philosophies of; masculinity and bildung in Civil War
General Principles of the Philosophy of Nature (Stallo), 16, 156–58
geographic character of nation. *See* nature
Georgia, and Cherokee removal policy, 166, 168–69, 175, 183, 235, 236
German philosophy of character, 40–58. *See also* Hegel, G. W. F.; Herder, Johann Gottfried von; race and character, European inheritance on; and American academia, 52–56, 57–58; and American publications, 56–57; and bildung concept, 17, 46–49; Bowen on, 26; Civil War as philosophical framework, overview, 6–9, 11, 15–16, 17–18; and Forty-Eighters, 50–51; German Higher Criticism, 54; Hegel on *Gemüth*, 49–50; Herder on *die Kräfte*, 46–47, 129, 146; Herder's model of nationality, 223–28, 231, 232, 236; Scottish Common Sense merged with, by Transcendentalists, 60, 75; Staël's influence in United States, 43, 45, 51–52; Transcendentalists and Hegel's influence, 47–50, 52, 53, 56, 57; Transcendentalists and Herder's influence, 45–47, 49, 51, 54, 55, 57; Transcendentalists and Kant's influence, 40–45, 47, 51–54; and Transcendentalists on deficiencies of Scottish Common Sense, 39, 40; World War I and end of, 245
Germany: Forty-Eighters and political climate in, 50–51; German literature in Civil War-era United States, 120
Gettysburg, Battle of, 112
Gilpin, William, 231, 232–33
God, interpretations of, 96, 149, 151, 179–80. *See also* Christianity; religion and religious thought; Transcendentalist philosophies of character
Goethe, Johann Wolfgang von: and American academia, 53, 54, 55; Civil War masculinity and gender philosophy, 106, 114–17, 120–30; *Conversations of Goethe with Eckermann* (Fuller's translation), 94; de Staël influenced by, 51; Fuller's interpretation of written works of, 15, 83–84, 93–103, 105; gender philosophy and ideas of resignation and reverence, 97, 99, 115–22; and Transcendentalist philosophy of character, 65, 66; and Transcendentalists' views on race, 173
Goethe, Johann Wolfgang von, written works: "Confessions of a Fair Saint," 97, 114; *Elective Affinities*, 94; *Faust*, 94, 96, 98–100, 105, 114–16; *The Sorrows of Young Werther*, 116; *Tasso*, 93; *Werther*, 96; *Wilhelm Meister*, 17, 94–95, 96–97, 99, 100, 102–3, 105, 114–16
good and evil, Whitman on, 68–69
Gramm, Kent, 76, 249
Grant, Ulysses, 230
Greeley, Horace, 186, 189, 191
Greenberg, Amy, 110–11
Greene, William, 187
Grimké sisters, 186
Gross, Robert, 7
Groundwork of the Metaphysics of Morals (Kant), 55
gunpowder invention, 217
Gura, Philip F., 6
Gurowski, Adam, 209–10
gymnasium (physical education), self-culture aspect of, 81

Haitian Revolution, 150, 151, 159
Halleck, Henry W., 123, 124
Hamilton, William, 26, 27
The Harbinger, as Transcendentalist publication, 14
Harper's Ferry raid, 161, 171, 185, 190, 213–14
Harris, James, 221
Harris, William Torrey, 15, 208
Harvard University: "Divinity School Address" (Emerson), 28, 54; electives in, 79; German philosophy of character and influence on, 52–55, 58; Scottish Common Sense philosophy at, 25; Transcendentalist movement and importance of, 13, 17
Hauffe, Frederica, 73–74
Haven, Joseph, 55
Hawthorne, Nathaniel, 120
Hayden, Lewis, 134, 184
Hedge, Frederic Henry, 17, 25, 52, 53, 57–58
Hedge, Levi, 25–26, 37
Heeren, Arnold H. L., 17, 57
Hegel, G. W. F.: Bowen on, 26; on dialectical method, 47–49, 64; German philosophy of character and influence in United States,

47–50, 53, 55–57; "master-slave dialectic" of, 150–51, 181, 182; race and character theories, 148–52, 153; race and character theories, influence on Transcendentalists, 157–58, 162–65, 169, 173, 177, 179–82; on reason vs. understanding, 31, 151; and theories of political character of nation, 193, 195, 196, 204–8, 210–11, 216–18, 219; Transcendentalist movement and importance of, overview, 6, 8, 9, 15–17; and Transcendentalist philosophy of character, 62–64, 65, 67, 68, 71; and Transcendentalists on nation's geographic character, 224, 229, 236
Hegel, G. W. F., written works: *Introduction to the Philosophy of History*, 17; *Logic*, 15, 17, 56; *The Phenomenology of Spirit*, 15, 52, 56, 115, 150; *The Philosophy of History*, 16, 56, 67, 150, 152, 206; *The Philosophy of Right*, 16, 17, 55, 207
Hemingway, Ernest, 122, 221
Henderson, William, 219
Herder, Johann Gottfried von: Civil War masculinity and gender philosophy, 106, 129, 130; Fuller's translation of, 100; German philosophy of character and influence in United States, 45–47, 49, 51, 52, 54, 55, 57, 58; on *die Kräfte*, 46–47, 129, 146; nation concept of, 223–28, 231, 232, 236; natural environment and model of nationality of, 223–28, 231, 232, 236; race and character theories, 145–48, 153; race and character theories, influence on Transcendentalists, 162, 163, 169, 176, 179; and theories of political character of nation, 195, 202–5, 206, 208, 210; Transcendentalist movement and importance of, overview, 8, 15, 17; and Transcendentalist philosophy of character, 65, 69, 71, 72, 74
Herder, Johann Gottfried von, written works: "Dragon-Fly," 57; *Philosophy of the History of Mankind*, 52; *On the Spirit of Hebrew Poetry*, 52, 57; *Zerstreute Blätter (Scattered Leaves)*, 58
Herndon, William, 12
Hess, Earl J., 113, 216
Hickok, Laurens Perseus, 55
Higginson, Thomas Wentworth: and Fuller, 98; race and character theories, 133, 153; and theories of political character of nation, 212; and Transcendentalist philosophy of character, 81; views on race, 184, 185, 187–88
high school diploma, development of, 79
History of the Rise and Fall of the Slave Power in America (Wilson), 202
History of the United States (Bancroft), 17, 57, 225
Hitchcock, Ethan Allen, 123
Hoar, Samuel, 188
Home, Henry (Lord Kames), 137
Horwitz, Tony, 248–49
Hosmer, James Kendall, 187
Howe, Daniel Walker, 29, 76, 84–85, 109, 201
Howe, Julia Ward, 12, 124
Howe, Samuel Gridley, 12, 80, 124, 185
Humboldt, Alexander, 8, 56
Humboldt, Wilhelm, 8
Humboldt's Letters to Varnhagen von Ense (A. Humboldt), 56
Hume, David: Hegel on, 47; Kant on, 41; "Of Miracles," 61; "Of National Characters," 196–97; on race and character, 136–37; rebuttal of Humean skepticism, 20–23, 26; Scottish Common Sense philosophy and rebuttal of Humean skepticism, 20–23, 26, 29, 34, 37, 38; and theories of political character of nation, 194; Transcendentalist movement and importance of, overview, 7; and Transcendentalist philosophy of character, 61, 63; *Treatise of Human Nature*, 20
Hutcheson, Francis, 32–34, 197

"I" concept, 49, 148, 218
"idea" concept, 33
idealism. *See* intuition
idealism, German. *See* German philosophy of character
Independent, and nation's geographic character, 233
Index, as Transcendentalist publication, 14
Indigenous Americans: Cherokee removal policy, 166, 168–69, 175, 183, 235, 236; race theories about, 135, 137, 141, 149; Thoreau's arrowhead interest, 169, 176; Transcendentalists on treatment of, 161, 162, 166, 168–70, 173–76, 179, 183
individualism: Civil War-era views of, 129–30; "I" concept, 49, 148, 218; and political character of nation, 207–8
Inquiry into the Human Mind (Reid), 25

An Inquiry into the Original of Our Ideas of Beauty and Virtue (Hutcheson), 32–34
Introduction to the Philosophy of History (Hegel), 17
intuition: Fuller on women's intuition, 93; and idealism (Scottish vs. German), 3–4; moral realism vs. ethical sentimentalism, 32–34, 37; perception, defined, 33; Scottish Common Sense on realism (empiricism) and, 22; Transcendentalism and role of, 37–39
Irish Catholics, prejudice against, 144
Izenberg, Gerald N., 5

Jackson, Andrew, 57
James, William, 246
Jefferson, Thomas, 85
Jesus, 12, 54, 215–16. *See also* Christianity
Johns Hopkins University, 79
Jouffroy, Theodore Simon, 15, 26

Kames, Lord (Henry Home), 137, 197–99, 200
Kansas, on slavery, 184–85
Kansas Herald of Freedom: and nation's geographic character, 231–33; on slavery, 201
Kansas-Nebraska Act of 1854, 228
Kant, Immanuel: Bowen on, 26; German philosophy of character and influence in United States, 40, 41–45, 47, 51–54; influence on Transcendentalists' views on race, 156, 163, 164, 166; and philosophy of gender and femininity, 83, 88–91, 92, 97, 105; race and character theories, 138–42, 145, 146, 148, 151; and theories of political character of nation, 194, 202–5, 208, 216; Transcendentalist movement and importance of, overview, 8, 15, 17; and Transcendentalist philosophy of character, 62, 63, 67
Kant, Immanuel, written works: *Critique of Pure Reason*, 41, 55; *Groundwork of the Metaphysics of Morals*, 55; *Observations on the Feeling of the Beautiful and Sublime*, 88–91, 231; *Remarks*, 91; *Toward Perpetual Peace*, 142; *On the Use of Teleological Principles in Philosophy*, 141
Kanzas News, and nation's geographic character, 233
Katha Upanishad, 220
Kaufmann, Peter, 16
Kaufmann, Walter, 95

Keller, Helen, 81
Kendi, Ibram, 134
Keohane, Oisín, 195
Kerner, Justinus, 73–74
Kidd, Colin, 144
kindergarten, Transcendentalists on, 80
King, Martin Luther, Jr., 214
King, Thomas Starr, 234
Kleingeld, Pauline, 141–42
Klemm, Gustav, 157
Knight, Joseph, 198
Knight v. Wedderburn (Scotland, 1778), 198, 199
knowledge, internal sources of, 40–41. *See also* Transcendentalist philosophies of character
Know-Nothing Party, 57, 144
Knox, Robert, 143–44, 158–59, 160, 161–62
Kojève, Alexandre, 151
die Kräfte, Herder on, 46–47, 129, 146
Kuehn, Manfred, 47
Kytle, Ethan J., 3, 6

Lamson, Jeremiah, 118–19
Lamson, Roswell, 128, 201
Leaves of Grass (Whitman), 70–71, 209
"Lecture on the Times" (Emerson), 182
Lectures on the Philosophy of the Human Mind (Brown), 27
Lee, Robert E., 215
"Lessons from the Sierra Nevada" (King), 234
Liberty Party, 184
Lieber, Francis: Civil War and Lieber Code, 106, 123–27; *Encyclopædia Americana: A Popular Dictionary of Arts, Literature, History, Politics, and Biography*, 57; German philosophy and influence in United States, 50, 52, 53, 57; and theories of political character of nation, 210; and Transcendentalist philosophy of character, 81
Lincoln, Abraham: assassination of, 215; German philosophy of character and influence in United States, 51, 53, 57; and nation's geographic character, 230, 234; on race, 144; and Republican Party formation, 51; and theories of political character of nation, 193, 195, 198, 202, 208, 210, 212; Transcendentalist movement and importance to Civil War, overview, 6, 12; and Transcendentalists' views on race, 156, 179, 187

Lincoln, Willie, 230
Linnaeus, Carl von, 137–38
"The Little Major" (song), 238
Little Men (L. M. Alcott), 98, 126
Little Women (L. M. Alcott), 92
Locke, John: Emerson on, 40; *Essay on the Understanding*, 25; German philosophy on views of, 42, 45, 51; Hume on, 21; and theories of political character of nation, 210; Transcendentalist movement and importance of, overview, 4; Winkler on, 32–33
Logic (Hegel), 15, 17, 56
Logick (Hedge), 25–26, 37
Long, Thomas, 153
Longfellow, Henry Wadsworth, 52, 53
Louis XVI, 224
Lowell, Charles Russell, 187, 246
Lukács, Georg, 150
Luther, Martin, 129–30

Madison, James, 25
magnetism, Fuller on, 72–75
Malachuk, Daniel, 193, 194, 213
Mann, Horace, 12, 52, 60, 79–81, 190
Manning, Chandra, 107–8
The Marble Faun (Hawthorne), 120
Marcuse, Herbert, 151
marriage, and philosophies of gender, 87, 93–94, 97, 100–101, 103
Marsh, George Perkins, 230
Marsh, James, 55, 56, 57, 78–79
Martineau, Harriet, 120, 159–60, 176
Marx, Karl, 16
masculinity and bildung in Civil War, 1–2, 106–31. *See also* femininity and gender, philosophies of; German philosophy of character; Scottish philosophy of character; Transcendentalist philosophies of character; and Clausewitz's influence on, 106, 123–25, 130; contemporary theories of, 6–7; cultural expression and emotional aspects of, 111–14, 118–21; death and individualism, 129–30; discipline and self-discipline, 126–29; education of males, 81, 87–88; gender and women's role in, 15, 17; German Idealism and influence on, 6–9, 11, 15–16, 17–18; Goethe's influence on, 106, 114–17, 120–30; and gymnasium aspect of self-culture, 81; Idealism (Scottish vs. German) and role in, 3–4; intellectual history approach to, 9; and lack of personal animosity toward enemy, 121–22, 243; and Lieber Code, 106, 123–27; male and female character qualities, nineteenth century thought about, 83–85; "muscular manhood" ideal, 81, 110; Northern vs. Southern white men's views of, 107–10, 130–31; as revolution, 1–2; Romanticism and role in, 3–6; Scottish Common Sense and influence on, 7–8, 9–11, 16–18; soldiers' dedication to cause of war, 19–20, 106–7, 117–19, 243–44; Transcendentalism and role in, 8, 11–12, 13–15; Unitarian church and role in, 12–13
Massachusetts: 54th Massachusetts Volunteer Infantry, 133, 144, 187; "Slavery in Massachusetts" (Thoreau), 189; Unitarian split from Congregationalists, 13
Massachusetts Quarterly Review, as Transcendentalist publication, 14
McCosh, James, 60–61
McCune, James, 155
McDowell, John, 151
McGarry, Molly, 176
McPherson, James, 19, 111–12
Meade, George, 128
Memorial, to the Legislature of Massachusetts (Dix), 80
Menand, Louis, 242–43, 246, 247
Mental Philosophy (Haven), 55
mental powers, active vs. passive separation of, 20, 27–28
Mesmer, Franz Anton, 72–73
Metternich, Klemens von, 50
Mexican-American War, 183–84, 240
militärische Aufklärung concept, Clausewitz on, 123–25, 130
Millar, John, 85–86
Missouri Compromise, 229
Mitchell, Reid, 107, 109, 201
Molina, Eduardo, 43
Montaigne, Michel de, 66
morality. *See also* bildung; sexuality: and Civil War soldiers' dedication to cause of war, 19–20, 106–7, 117–19; *Groundwork of the Metaphysics of Morals* (Kant), 55; Kant on gender and moral virtue, 89–91; moral action, perception as, 20, 29–35; moral realism vs. ethical sentimentalism, 32–34, 37; *Philosophy of the Active and Moral Powers of Man* (Stewart), 55; Scottish

morality (*continued*)
Common Sense, moral realism vs. ethical sentimentalism, 32–34, 37; Scottish Common Sense, perception as moral action, 20, 29–35; *Self-Culture: Physical, Intellectual, Moral, and Spiritual* (Clarke), 244; and Transcendentalists on sentiment and moral feeling, 35–36; Transcendentalists on universal moral character, 35–36, 76, 82; universality of moral character as Transcendentalist ideal, 76, 82
Mueller-Vollmer, Kurt, 56
Muir, John, 230
Mulcaire, Terry, 68

Napoleon, 11, 130, 200
A Narrative of the Life of Frederick Douglass (Douglass), 166–67
nation concept, Herder on, 223–28, 231, 232, 236
nation's geographic character. *See* nature
natural (pantheistic humanism) concepts, of Whitman, 60–62, 68–71, 74–76
nature, 223–41; and Civil War-era masculinity and bildung, 114–15; Civil War soldiers and perception of, 237–40; conservation concept, 230; Emerson, Whitman, and Fuller on, 75; and Herder's model of nationality, 223–28, 231, 232, 236; nation's geographic character and disregard for racial diversity of West, 234–35; nation's geographic character and slavery arguments, 227–34; parks and rural cemeteries, 229–30; slavery arguments and nation's geographic character, 227–34, 236–38; Transcendentalists' political philosophy on geographic landscape, 223; and Transcendentalists' view on race, 156; Transcendentalists' views as novel approach to, 240–41; utility vs. aesthetics of, 230–31
"Nature" (Emerson), 30–31, 172
Nell, William Cooper, 134, 155, 188
New American Cyclopedia (Ripley), 56
New Bedford Lyceum, 188
Newton, Isaac, 4
New-York Daily Tribune: Douglass's autobiography in, 167; and German philosophy and influence on, 56
Nichols, Ashton, 77
Noll, Mark, 136

North American Review, and German philosophy and influence on, 56
Norton, Andrews, 54, 60–61
Norton, David, 33
Norwood (Beecher), 219
Nullification Crisis, 159–60

Observations concerning the Distinction of Ranks in Society (Millar), 85–86
Observations on the Feeling of the Beautiful and Sublime (Kant), 88–91, 231
"Of Miracles" (Hume), 61
Ohio Hegelians, 16
Oken, Lorenz, 156–57, 158
Olmsted, Frederick Law, 229
"On National Characters" (Hume), 136–37
On the Spirit of Hebrew Poetry (Herder), 52, 57
"On the Spirit of the Hebrew Scriptures" (Peabody), 15
On the Use of Teleological Principles in Philosophy (Kant), 141
On War (Clausewitz), 123–24
Ossoli, Giovanni Angelo, 100
"The Over-Soul" (Emerson), 29–30, 40, 42
Owen, Robert, 186

Paine, Thomas, 14, 25, 199–200
panentheism, 179–80
paranormal (spiritual) concepts, of Fuller, 60–62, 70–76
Parker, Theodore, 6, 12, 14, 155, 184, 185, 232
parks, and nation's geographic character, 229–30
Peabody, Elizabeth, 12, 15, 45, 79–80, 91, 92, 101, 187
Peabody, Mary, 12, 92
Peabody, Sophia, 12, 92
Perkins School for the Blind, 80–81
Pestalozzi, Johann, 91
Petersen, Richard, 60–61, 66
The Phenomenology of Spirit (Hegel), 15, 52, 56, 115, 150
Phillips, Wendell, 184
The Philosophy of History (Hegel), 16, 56, 67, 150, 152, 206
The Philosophy of Right (Hegel), 16, 17, 55, 207
Philosophy of the Active and Moral Powers of Man (Stewart), 55
Philosophy of the History of Mankind (Herder), 52

phrenology, 142–43, 174–75
physical education (gymnasium), self-culture aspect of, 81
Pillsbury, Parker, 12, 57
Pinchot, Gifford, 230
Plato, 23, 42, 63, 64, 72, 75, 172, 179, 180
"Plea for Captain John Brown" (Thoreau), 185
Plotinus, 66
Plutarch, 66
Poe, Edgar Allan, 120
political character of the nation, 193–222; abolition and Transcendentalists on policy reform, 182–86; aspirationalist view, 193–94, 213; Civil War in context of, 195–96, 200–202, 213–22; early political science classes at Columbia College, 123; German Idealism on national cultures/characteristics, 196, 202–11; Know-Nothing Party, 57, 144; originalist view, 193–94; proceduralist view, 193–94; "progress" vs. "progression," 204–5, 216–18; role of nation as world actor, 193–96, 205–8, 215–18; Scottish Common Sense on national cultures/characteristics, 194–95, 196–200; spiritual principle of state, 193, 196, 198, 203–8, 215–22; Transcendentalists on, 199–201, 209–20; and Union concept, 210
polygenesis vs. monogenesis theories, 134–35, 137–39, 143, 172–73, 181
Porter, Horace, 243
Porter, Noah, 26
Poteet, Francis, 121
Powell, John Wesley, 244
Pratt, John, 127
The Present, as Transcendentalist publication, 14
Priestley, Joseph, 25
Princeton University, 10, 24–25, 53
prisoners, and Lieber Code, 123–27
"progress" vs. "progression," 204–5, 216–18
property ownership, freedom and rights tied to, 85, 236
Prose Writers of Germany (Hedge), 17, 57–58

Quaker doctrine, Whitman on, 70

race and character, European inheritance on, 132–53; biblical literalism on, 134–36, 146; German Idealism and Aryanism, 143–44; German Idealism on race, 47; German Idealism on race, Hegel, 147–53; German Idealism on race, Herder, 145–48, 153; German Idealism on race, Kant, 138–42, 145, 148, 151; monogenesis vs. polygenesis theories, 134–35, 137–39, 143, 172–73, 181; and phrenology, 142–43, 174–75; racial categorization on white Southerners, 143; racial "germs" concept, 139–40, 148; Scottish Common Sense on race, 136–38; theories about Indigenous Americans, 135, 137, 141, 149; Transcendentalists on bildung as universal, 132–34; Transcendentalist thought influenced by, 156–61; US ethnologists and European influence, 134, 152–53
race and character in America, 154–92. *See also* abolition; Civil War; Emerson, Ralph Waldo, on race; Fuller, Margaret; political character of the nation; race and character in America; Thoreau, Henry David, on race; abolition and Transcendentalists on policy reform, 182–86; abolition and Transcendentalists' support of Civil War, 186–92; bildung and Christ metaphor, 179–82; bildung as universal, 76–77; bildung commitment of Transcendentalists, 154–56; Black soldiers in Civil War, 108, 132–33, 144, 153, 187; contradiction in Transcendentalist thought, 161; Dred Scott case, 184, 198; Emerson on racial theory, 161–69; European influence on Transcendentalist thought, 156–61; freedom and rights tied to property ownership, 85; Fuller on racial theory, 172–79; gender philosophy and freedom issues of, 85; nation's geographic character and disregard for racial diversity of West, 234–35; slavery arguments and nation's geographic character, 227–34, 236–38; Thoreau on racial theory, 169–72
The Races of Men, a Fragment (Knox), 158–59, 161–62
The Radical, as Transcendentalist publication, 14
Radical Republican Party, 242
Rankin, John, 118, 218
Rational Cosmology (Hickok), 55
Rational Psychology (Hickok), 55
Rauch, Frederick A., 53
realism: Hume on Realism and Idealism classifications, 20; moral realism vs. ethical sentimentalism, 32–34, 37;

realism (*continued*)
  Romanticism as ontological realism, 3–4; Scottish Common Sense on intuition (idealism) and, 22
reason vs. understanding, 20, 28–29, 31
The Red Badge of Courage (Crane), 246–47
Reid, Thomas: on active vs. passive mental powers, 27–29; *Essays on the Intellectual Powers*, 25, 26; on imagination and knowledge, 24–25; *Inquiry into the Human Mind*, 25; on material effects and immaterial causes, 30; race and character theories, 137–38, 141, 153; on realism and intuition contained in one system, 22–23; sword analogy of, 33, 35; and theories of political character of nation, 199, 200, 201; Transcendentalist movement and importance of, overview, 8, 10, 17; and Transcendentalist philosophy of character, 62, 64, 66, 67, 69, 71; Transcendentalists influenced by, 31–37
religion and religious thought. *See also* Christianity; Transcendentalist philosophies of character; Unitarianism: biblical literalism on race and character, 134–36, 146; Civil War-era book sales on, 120; German philosophy of character and influence on, 40, 42, 43–44, 45–48, 53–54; panentheism, 179–80; and Scottish Common Sense philosophy, 22, 25, 28, 31; sin and self-improvement, Goethe on, 115–16; and stigma of atheism, 6, 25, 38; Transcendentalist beliefs about, 12
Remarks (Kant), 91
Republican Party, 51, 156, 158, 171, 184, 189, 242
Revis, Daniel, 121
Revolutionary War, women's letter to soldiers during, 104
Reynolds, David, 70–71
Richardson, Robert, 17
Richter, Jean Paul, 15, 54
Ripley, George, 12, 56, 57
Ripley, Sophia, 12
"Roaming in Thought" (Whitman), 15
Rodgers, Thomas, 19
Rogers, Seth, 132, 187–88
Romanticism: Civil War as philosophical framework, overview, 3–6; Sturm und Drang movement, 11, 51; Transcendentalist movement and importance of, overview, 1–7, 11, 15
Roosevelt, Theodore, 82, 230

Round Hill School, 81
Rousseau, Jean-Jacques, 48, 88, 89
rural cemeteries, and nation's geographic character, 229–30

Sanborn, Franklin, 155, 185, 186, 190
Sandford, Stella, 139
Sanitary Commission, 13
Saturday Club, 172, 230
Schaff, Philip, 53
Schelling, Friedrich, 8, 15, 51, 55, 63
Scherb, Emmanuel Vitalis, 17
Schiller, Friedrich, 8, 15, 37, 54
Schlegel, August, 8, 51
Schlegel, Friedrich, 8
Schleiermacher, Friedrich, 8, 55, 67
Schurz, Carl, 51, 210
Science and Health with Key to the Scriptures (Eddy), 244
Scientific American, and nation's geographic character, 233
Scott, Cora, 73
Scott, Winfield, 234
Scottish philosophy of character, 19–39. *See also* Brown, Thomas; race and character, European inheritance on; Reid, Thomas; Stewart, Dugald; active vs. passive separation of mental powers, 20, 27–28; Civil War soldiers and their dedication to cause of war, 19–20; Common Sense philosophy in American academia, eighteenth and nineteenth centuries, 24–27, 60–61; Common Sense school, overview, 7–8, 9–11, 16–18; on gender, culture, and societal advancement, 85–88; German Idealism merged with, by Transcendentalists, 60, 75; imagination and knowledge, 20, 24–25; moral realism vs. ethical sentimentalism, 32–34, 37; perception as moral action, 20, 29–35; reason vs. understanding, 20, 28–29; rebuttal of Humean skepticism, 20–23; Transcendentalists' questioning of, 39, 40; Transcendentalist thought influenced by, 20–21, 26–32, 35–39
The Seeress of Prevorst: Revelations concerning the Inward Life of Man, and the Projection of a World of Spirits into Ours, Communicated by Justinus Kerner (Kerner), 73–74
self, concept of, 22
self-culture. *See* bildung
Self-Culture: Physical, Intellectual, Moral, and Spiritual (Clarke), 244

"self-made" individual, concept of, 77
Seward, William, 187
sexuality: Goethe on, 94–95; race and theories about, 143, 147; Whitman on, 70–71
Shakespeare, William, 66, 67
Shaw, Robert Gould, 133, 144, 153, 187, 188
Shedd, William, 53
Sigel, Franz, 51
Sims, Thomas, 188
sin and self-improvement, Goethe on, 115–16
slavery. *See* abolition; race and character in America
"Slavery in Massachusetts" (Thoreau), 189
Sledge, Eugene, 127, 221
Sloan, Douglas, 25
Smith, Adam, 87
Smith, Gerritt, 185
Smith, Henry Boynton, 53
Snider, Denton, 208
Society in America (Martineau), 159–60
songs, of Civil War era, 112–13, 118
The Sorrows of Young Werther (Goethe), 116
South Carolina: 1st South Carolina Colored Volunteers, 132–33, 153, 187; and Nullification Crisis, 159–60
Specimens of Foreign Standard Literature (Ripley), 57
Speed, Joshua, 144
Spinoza, Baruch, 40, 45, 63, 123
Spirit of the Age: and nation's geographic character, 233; as Transcendentalist publication, 14
Spurzheim, Johann Gaspar, 142
St. Louis Hegelians, 9, 15–16, 79, 196, 228
Staël, Madame de, 15, 17, 43, 45, 51–52
Stallo, Johann Bernhard, 16, 17, 156–58, 159, 160
Stanton, Edwin, 123
Stearns, George Luther, 185
Stewart, Dugald: *Elements on the Philosophy of the Human Mind*, 25, 26; Emerson influenced by, 27, 40; on intuition, 38; and philosophy of gender and femininity, 86; *Philosophy of the Active and Moral Powers of Man*, 55; Reid's influence on, 24; and theories of political character of nation, 198–99; Transcendentalists influenced by, 8
Stewart, Matthew, 6, 144
"Still, in the cannon's pause, we hear" (poem), 238–39
Stirling, Dr., 67

Stone, Kate, 119, 120
Stout, Harry S., 6, 214, 216
Stowe, Harriet Beecher, 167–68, 186
Strong, George Templeton, 125
Sturm und Drang movement, 11, 51
Sullivan, Annie, 81
Summer on the Lakes (Fuller), 73, 172
Sumner, Charles: German philosophy and influence on United States, 52; and nation's geographic character, 228, 239, 240; Transcendentalist movement and importance of, overview, 12, 124; views on race, 155, 186, 188
supernatural (metaphysical) concepts, of Emerson, 60–69, 71, 72, 74–75, 77, 79
Swedenborg, Emanuel, 8, 63, 123, 129
sword analogy, 33, 35
Symonds, John Addington, 70

Tacitus, 165
Tappan, David, 25
Tappan, Henry, 55
Tasso (Goethe), 93
Taylor, Charles, 4, 5, 145
The Temple of Truth (Kaufmann), 16
theory of mind, Goethe on, 95
Thompson, C. Bradley, 9
Thoreau, Henry David: Civil War masculinity and gender philosophy, 114; death of, 189, 190; German philosophy and influence on, 55; nature and nation's geographic character, 227–28, 229, 235; "Plea for Captain John Brown," 185; Scottish Common Sense influence on, 27, 36; "Slavery in Massachusetts," 189; and theories of political character of nation, 199–200, 213–14, 220; Transcendentalist movement and importance of, overview, 8, 12, 16–17; *Walden*, 114, 170, 172, 173; vs. Whitman's influence on Transcendentalist philosophy of character, 60, 61
Thoreau, Henry David, on race: on Brown, 171, 181, 185, 214; and Christ metaphor for bildung, 179–81; and Fuller's views on race, 172, 175, 176; and policy approach to abolition, 182, 184, 185, 186; racial theory of, overview, 169–72; study of, 154–56; Transcendentalists and Civil War support, 187, 189; and Underground Railroad, 191
Thoreau, John (brother), 220
Ticknor, George, 52, 53, 124
Ticknor and Fields (publishing house), 120

Toward Perpetual Peace (Kant), 142
"To You" (Whitman), 180
transcendental "apperception," Kant on, 151
transcendental idealism, Kant on, 41–42
Transcendentalism. *See also* Civil War; Emerson, Ralph Waldo; Fuller, Margaret; nature; Thoreau, Henry David: Emerson on name of, 42; Fruitlands, 101, 186; on internal knowledge vs. external cause and effect, 40; intuition and importance to, 37–39; post-Civil War popularity of, 219; publisher of Transcendentalists, 120; support of Civil War by, 186–92, 213; time frame and legacy of, 244–48; Transcendentalists on Scottish philosophy of character, 20–21, 26–32, 35–39
Transcendentalist philosophies of character, 59–82; Civil War as philosophical framework and overview of, 8, 11–12; Civil War experience and key issues of (character, gender, race, nationhood), 18; Emerson's supernatural (metaphysical) interpretation of Scottish and German philosophies, 60–69, 71, 72, 74–75, 77, 79; Fuller's paranormal (spiritual) interpretation of Scottish and German philosophies, 60–62, 70–76; Scottish Common Sense and German Idealism merged in, 60, 75; as Scottish Common Sense and German Idealist amalgamation, 2–3; self-culture (bildung) and Christian denominations on antebellum reform, 77–78; self-culture (bildung) and educational reform, 78–82, 126; self-culture (bildung) concept of Channing, 59–61, 76, 80; self-culture (bildung) concept of Channing and influence on, 59–61, 76–77, 80; universality of moral character as ideal, 35–36, 76, 82; Whitman's natural (pantheistic humanism) interpretation of Scottish and German philosophies, 60–62, 68–71, 74–76; written works and lectures, overview, 13–15
Travels through the Interior Parts of North America (Carver), 172–73
Treatise of Human Nature (Hume), 20
Treaty of Vienna, 50, 204
truth, Emerson on, 62–68
Tryon, Warren S., 120
Twin Mound Harmonic College, 233

Una, as Transcendentalist publication, 14
Uncle Tom's Cabin (Stowe), 167–68
Underground Railroad, 188, 191
"Unitarian Christianity" (Channing), 14
Unitarianism: and bildung (self-culture) concept, 76; Transcendentalism and role in, 12–13, 14
University of Jena, 50
University of Michigan, 79
University of Vermont, 56, 57–58, 78

Van Buren, Martin, 183, 235
Very, Jones, 61
The Vicarious Sacrifice (Bushnell), 117, 180–81, 214–15

Wainwright, Charles, 128
Walden (Thoreau), 114, 170, 172, 173
Walker, James, 26, 55, 60, 61
Walt and Vult (Richter), 15
Washington University, 79
Wayland, Francis, 60, 61, 79
Webster, Daniel, 188, 193
Webster's dictionary (1828), 145
Wedderburn, John, 198
Werther (Goethe), 96
Westbrook, Robert, 104–5
The Western Messenger: Civil War masculinity and gender philosophy, 123; German philosophy and influence on, 56; as Transcendentalist publication, 14
"What Fits a Man to be a Voter? Is It to Be White Within, or White Without" (Fuller), 177–78
White, LeeAnn, 107, 109
white Northern males. *See* masculinity and bildung in Civil War
white Southern males. *See* masculinity and bildung in Civil War
Whitman, Walt: Civil War masculinity and gender philosophy, 114; German philosophy and influence on, 48; natural (pantheistic humanism) interpretation of Scottish and German philosophies, 60–62, 68–71, 74–76; and theories of political character of nation, 218–19, 220–21; Transcendentalist movement and importance of, overview, 8; views on race, 187
Whitman, Walt, written works: "The Base of All Metaphysics," 15; *Calamus*, 70–71;

Children of Adam, 71; *Leaves of Grass*, 70–71, 209; "Roaming in Thought," 15; "To You," 180
Whitney, Eli, 135
Wight, O. W., 52
Wilhelm Meister (Goethe), 17, 94–95, 96–97, 99, 100, 102–3, 105, 114–16
Willcox, Orlando B., 19
Williams, George, 121
Williamstown College, 225
Willich, August, 16
Wilson, Henry, 202
Winkler, Kenneth, 32–33
Wirzbicki, Peter, 6, 155

Witherspoon, John, 10, 24–25, 61, 230
Wolfel, Brian, 250
Woman in the Nineteenth Century (Fuller), 15, 94
Wood, Gordon, 9
World War II: military discipline and punishment, 127; pin-up culture of, 104–5

Yale University, 26, 53, 79

Zammito, John, 145
Zerstreute Blätter (*Scattered Leaves*, Herder), 58
zymosis, 67

AREN LERNER CRAIG holds a PhD in History from the University of Aberdeen. Her work has appeared in the *New England Journal of History* and *The World of Antebellum America: A Daily Life Encyclopedia*. She has also contributed short stories to *Frontier Tales* and published a historical fiction series, *Beneath Old Glory*, that involved detailed research into the daily life and culture of the Civil War era.

www.ingramcontent.com/pod-product-compliance
Lightning Source LLC
Chambersburg PA
CBHW021649230426
43668CB00008B/566